SANDWICHES

ITEM	AMOUNT	SUGGESTED SERVING TEMP.	POWER LEVEL	APPROX. TIME MINS.
Moist Filling; such as sloppy joe, barbecue, ham salad, etc. in bun ⅓ cup/serving	1 serving	110°	M. High	½-1
	2 servings	110°	M. High	1-1½
	4 servings	110°	M. High	1½-2½
Thick Meat-Cheese Filling; with firm bread	1 serving	110°	M. High	1½-2½
	2 servings	110°	M. High	2½-3½
	4 servings	110°	M. High	5-7

SOUP

ITEM	AMOUNT	SUGGESTED SERVING TEMP.	POWER LEVEL	APPROX. TIME MINS.
Water Base 1 cup/serving	1 serving	150°-170°	High	2½-3½
	2 servings	150°-170°	High	4-5½
	4 servings	150°-170°	High	7-9
	1 can 10-oz. reconstituted	150°-170°	High	5-7
Milk Base 1 cup/serving	1 serving	140°	M. High	3-4
	2 servings	140°	M. High	5-7
	4 servings	140°	M. High	10-12
	1 can 10-oz. reconstituted	140°	M. High	8-10

Tip: Use paper towel or napkin to cover sandwiches. Cover soups with wax paper or plastic wrap.

VEGETABLES

ITEM	AMOUNT	SUGGESTED SERVING TEMP.	POWER LEVEL	APPROX. TIME MINS.
Small Pieces such as peas, beans, corn, etc. ½ cup/serving	1 serving	150°-160°	High	1-1½
	2 servings	150°-160°	High	2-3
	4 servings	150°-160°	High	3-4
	1 can 16-oz.	150°-160°	High or M. High	4-4½
Large Pieces or whole such as asparagus spears, corn on the cob, etc.	1 serving		High	2-2½
	2 servings		High	3-3½
	4 servings		High	4-4½
	1 can 16-oz.		High	4-4½
Mashed ½ cup/serving	1 serving	150°-160°	High	1-2
	2 servings	150°-160°	High	2-3
	4 servings	150°-160°	High	6-7

Tip: Cover vegetables for most even heating.

SAUCES

Dessert such as chocolate, butterscotch

ITEM	AMOUNT	SUGGESTED SERVING TEMP.	POWER LEVEL	APPROX. TIME MINS.
Room Temp.	½ cup	125°	High	¼-½
	1 cup	125°	High	½-1
Ref. Temp.	½ cup	125°	High	1-1½
	1 cup	125°	High	1½-2

Meat or Main Dish

ITEM	AMOUNT	SUGGESTED SERVING TEMP.	POWER LEVEL	APPROX. TIME MINS.
Chunky type such as giblet gravy, spaghetti sauce, etc.	½ cup	150°-160°	High	2-2½
	1 cup	150°-160°	High	3½-4½
	1 can 16-oz.	150°-160°	High	5-6
Creamy Type	½ cup	140°-150°	High	1½-2
	1 cup	140°-150°	High	3-3½

Tip: Cover food to prevent spatter.

BAKERY FOODS
Room Temperature

ITEM	AMOUNT	SUGGESTED SERVING TEMP.	POWER LEVEL	APPROX. TIME MINS.
Cake, Coffee Cake, Doughnuts, Sweet Rolls, Nut or Fruit Bread	1 piece	90°	Low	½-1
	2 pieces		Low	1-1½
	4 pieces		Low	1-2
	9-in. cake or 12 rolls or doughnuts	90°	Low	2-3
Dinner Rolls, Muffins	1	90°	Medium	¼-½
	2		Medium	½-¾
	4		Medium	½-1
	6-8		Medium	1-1¾
Pie, Fruit or Nut ⅛ of 9-in. pie = 1 slice	1 slice	110°	High	¼-½
	2 slices		High	½-1
	4 slices		M. High	2-2½
	9-in. pie	110°	M. High	2½-3
Pie, Custard ⅛ of 9-in. pie = 1 slice	1 slice	110°	M. High	½-1
	2 slices		M. High	1-1½
	4 slices		M. High	2-2½
	9-in. pie	110°	M. High	2½-3

GRIDDLE FOODS
Room Temperature

Pancakes

ITEM	AMOUNT	SUGGESTED SERVING TEMP.	POWER LEVEL	APPROX. TIME MINS.
Plain, no topping	Stack of 3	120°	High	½-1
With syrup & butter	Stack of 3	120°	High	1-1½
With 2 sausage patties	Stack of 3	120°	High	1¼-1½

French Toast

ITEM	AMOUNT	SUGGESTED SERVING TEMP.	POWER LEVEL	APPROX. TIME MINS.
Plain, no topping	2 slices	120°	High	½-1
With syrup & butter	2 slices	120°	High	1-1¼

Waffles, 3"×4"

ITEM	AMOUNT	SUGGESTED SERVING TEMP.	POWER LEVEL	APPROX. TIME MINS.
Plain, no topping	2	120°	High	½-1
With syrup & butter	2	120°	High	1-1¼

BEVERAGES

ITEM	AMOUNT	SUGGESTED SERVING TEMP.	POWER LEVEL	APPROX. TIME MINS.
Coffee, Tea, Cider, other water based	1 cup	160°-170°	High	1½-2½
	2 cups		High	3½-4½
	4 cups		High	6-7
Cocoa, other milk based	1 cup	140°	M. High	2-3
	2 cups		M. High	4-5
	4 cups		M. High	7-8

Tip: Do not cover bakery foods, griddle foods (pancakes, etc.) or beverages.

PRECAUTIONS TO AVOID POSSIBLE EXPOSURE TO EXCESSIVE MICROWAVE ENERGY

1. **Do Not Attempt** to operate the oven with the door open since open-door operation can result in harmful exposure to microwave energy. It is important not to defeat or tamper with the safety interlocks.

2. **Do Not Place** any object between the oven front face and the door or allow soil or cleaner residue to accumulate on sealing surfaces.

3. **Do Not Operate** the oven if it is damaged. It is particularly important that the oven door close properly and that there is no damage to the (1) door (bent), (2) hinges and latches (broken or loosened), (3) door seals and sealing surfaces.

4. **The Oven Should** not be adjusted or repaired by anyone except properly qualified service personnel.

Printed in Japan

How to Use This Book

This book was written especially for your small size, big capacity microwave oven. With this extra-wide oven, you'll be able to accomplish many types of multiple food cooking , and the large-size window enables you to view food easily as it cooks.

Recipes and techniques in this book have been specially developed to help you make the best possible use of your microwave oven. A section has been included showing how to cook complete meals in your microwave; how to combine microwave with conventional cooking, using each to its best advantage; how to microwave whole-meal dishes, store and reheat them for fresh-cooked flavor; and how to cook large quantities of food in the microwave, saving both time and cooking energy.

To make the most effective use of this book, first read the introductory guide, which teaches you the principles and techniques of microwaving. Many will be familiar, some, new. All are clearly illustrated with photographs.

Then go on to the recipe chapters where Microlessons demonstrate how to cook specific foods. We show you what to do, what to expect, how the food should look, and how to tell when it's done. You'll soon learn that successful microwaving is not only faster, but often easier than conventional cooking.

Paula Cooper Matthews

Paula Cooper Matthews
Consumer Information Testing Laboratory

Many thanks
to home economists,
Diana Williams Hansen
Marita A. Duber
Jean. E. Kozar
Brigid Lally Bowels

Contents

Microwaving: How it Works

The microwave oven has added a new term to our cooking language. "Microwaving" means to cook, heat or defrost foods with microwave energy. Microwaving is a new type of cooking, which has its own special benefits, and produces its own food characteristics. Some microwaved foods may be different from what you expect when cooking in a conventional oven or on the range top. The difference may be in appearance, in improved flavor and juiciness, or in cooking technique.

The microwave oven is called an "oven" because it looks more like an oven than any other conventional appliance, but it can take over many of your top-of-range jobs with less time, attention and clean-up. Foods which you used to bake in a conventional oven will taste the same, but may look different. For example, a casserole will heat through quickly, but will not crust over, because the air in a microwave oven is room temperature, not hot and dry.

Like any new skill, microwaving takes a little practice. Until you are used to its speed, you may overcook. Some foods will be removed from the oven before they look done, because they finish cooking with internal heat. This book is designed to teach you what to expect, and how to achieve successful results with microwaving. You'll find learning to microwave easy and exciting.

Water Boils in a paper cup. One of the remarkable characteristics of microwave energy is that it heats the food, not the utensil. Utensils become warm when heat from food has transferred to them.

HOW MICROWAVE WORKS

Microwaves are very short, high-frequency radio waves, and your microwave oven is similar to a miniature broadcasting system. Microwaves are the same type of energy as AM, FM or CB radio, but the wave length is much shorter.

Where other types of radio waves broadcast over a distance, the microwave broadcasting system is self-contained. When the door is closed and the oven is turned on, a transmitter, called a magnetron, sends a signal to a receiver within the oven. The moment you open the door, the microwave oven stops broadcasting, just as your radio will not play if the station has "signed off". No energy will be received from the oven while the door is open.

The receiver deflects the microwave energy into the metal-lined oven cavity, where it agitates food molecules. Since microwaves cannot penetrate metal, all the energy remains inside the oven, where it turns to heat in the food.

Television is radio waves converted to a picture on the screen. Microwave energy is very short radio waves converted to heat in food.

"HEAT" PHOTOS SHOW HOW MICROWAVES COOK

A new process, called thermography, which makes images of heat, demonstrates the different ways in which foods cook. At the General Electric Major Appliance Laboratory, potatoes were heated on a range top, in a conventional oven, and in a microwave oven, then cut in half and thermographed to show how heat is distributed in each cooking method.

On the thermograph scale, blue stands for cool areas, red represents warmth and yellow indicates the hottest area. The "halo" of blue around the potatoes is thermal reflection and occurs when the potatoes are removed from heat to room temperature for photography.

RANGE TOP

Cut Potato in a skillet is placed on a range surface unit set at medium heat. Potato was sliced so that a large flat surface could be exposed.

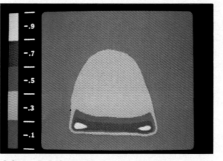

After 3 Minutes some heat from the surface unit has transferred through the pan to the cut side of the potato. On a range top, the bottom part of the food is always the hottest.

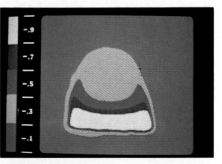

After 8 Minutes the hot yellow area has increased and heat is being conducted into the red, warm portions. The top of the potato is still cool.

CONVENTIONAL OVEN

Whole Potato is placed on the shelf of a conventional oven preheated to 400°. The air inside the oven is hot and dry.

After 7 Minutes, thin yellow areas indicate that air in the oven has heated the surface of the potato. Prolonged exposure to hot, dry air will make the outside dry and crusty.

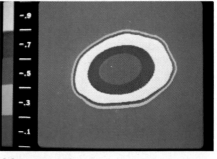

After 15 Minutes, heat is gradually spreading to the interior through conduction, although the center is still cool. It takes about 1 hour to bake a potato conventionally.

MICROWAVE

Potato is placed on oven floor with paper towel or napkin to absorb moisture, and is microwaved at High Power. Air in oven is room temperature.

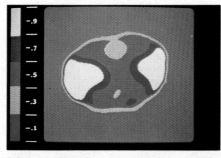

After 1 Minute, yellow areas of heat appear inside the potato, showing that microwave energy penetrates ¾ to 1¼-in. through food surfaces. Heat is conducted inward and outward.

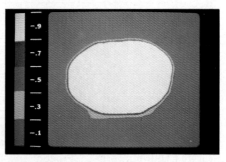

After 4 minutes, potato is heated throughout although a brief standing time is needed to cook it thoroughly.

COMPARISON OF MICROWAVE & CONVENTIONAL COOKING

Range Top. On the range top, heat from the surface unit transfers through the pan to the bottom of the food. Stirring the food while it cooks brings heated portions to the top and prevents scorching. Covering the pan holds in steam and speeds cooking. Rearranging or turning foods over helps them cook evenly. Because the bottom of the pan is hot, fried or griddled foods become crisp or crusty.

Conventional Oven. In a conventional oven, the heating units heat the air inside the oven. The oven may be preheated until the air reaches the proper cooking temperature. Heat from this hot dry air enters the food through its exterior surfaces, and gradually spreads to the interior through conduction. The process is usually slow, so by the time the center is done, the surfaces have become dry and crusty.

Microwave Oven. Microwaves penetrate ¾ to 1¼-in. through all food surfaces; top, bottom and sides. At this depth they are absorbed by moisture, sugar or fat molecules, which begin to cook. Heat is then conducted into the center and out to the surfaces. The food cooks by internal heat, not by contact with hot air or a hot pan. Because microwaves penetrate foods and cook them below the surface, cooking is faster for most foods, but the surface remains moist, not dry and crusty. Occasionally, the surface is the last place to cook.

COMPARISON OF MICROWAVE & CONVENTIONAL ENERGY CONSUMPTION

Microwaving can save energy and reduce electric bills, but savings depend on what, and how much, you cook. Many foods make efficient use of microwave energy, as shown in chart below.

The amount of food cooked affects energy consumption, too. Four baked potatoes require 61% less energy when microwaved, but about 12 potatoes bake more efficiently in a conventional oven. Greatest savings result when heating medium or small quantities of dense foods.

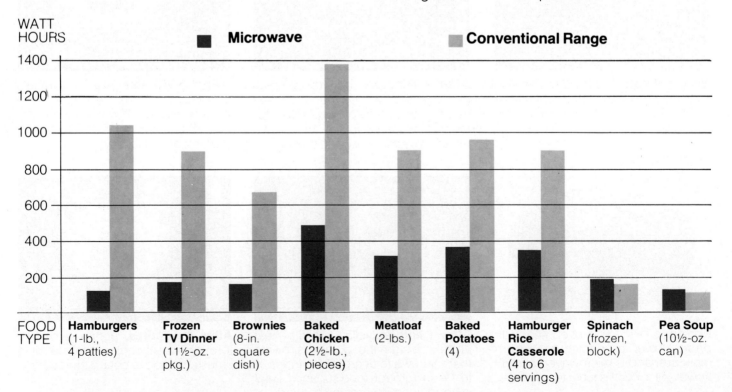

SOME FOODS MICROWAVE WITH EXCEPTIONAL QUALITY

Some foods microwave so well that you may never want to cook them any other way. Foods which demand constant stirring on the range top, such as sauces, puddings frostings and candies, need stirring at intervals in your microwave oven. Many can be measured, mixed and cooked in the same utensil for easy clean-up.

The excellent flavor and texture of microwaved fish, vegetables and fruits makes superior flavor the principle reason for cooking them by microwaves. Saving in time, while important, becomes a secondary advantage. In addition, there are some things unique to microwaving which cannot be done any other way.

Vegetables retain their fresh, crisp texture and bright color when microwaved according to chart, page 208.

Baked Potato microwaves fluffy, moist and tender. As an added benefit, you save time and energy. A potato microwaves in about 5 minutes.

Leftovers stay moist and taste freshly cooked. Roasted meats don't have a "leftover" flavor, rice reheats without overcooking.

Defrost foods rapidly. 1 pound of ground beef is ready to cook in 8 to 9 minutes. "I forgot to defrost", is never an emergency.

Melt Chocolate right in its paper wrapper. You have nothing to clean up and there is no danger of scorching or overcooking.

Eggs scramble fluffy, with greater volume. Compare 1 egg, cooked conventionally, left, with 1 microwave scrambled egg.

Reheat a meal right on the serving plate. If family members eat at different times, cook once and serve everyone a hot meal.

Fish steam tender and moist in their own natural juices, without additional water, for delicate flavor and pleasing texture.

Bacon microwaves crisp, brown and flat on paper towels. You don't have to turn it over, drain it, or scour a crusty pan.

MORE FOODS THAT MICROWAVE WITH EXCEPTIONAL QUALITY

Rich, fudgy brownies can be microwaved in 7 minutes for a quick dessert or impromptu treat.

Casseroles can be microwaved, refrigerated and reheated in the same dish. They'll taste just as fresh the second day.

Hot Appetizers and snacks microwave in seconds on a paper napkin. They're so easy you can treat your family or guests to a variety.

Omelets have greater volume and are fluffier when microwaved. No crust develops, so the surface is as tender as the interior.

Puddings and custards cook smooth and creamy with no more than an occasional stirring. Cook and serve them from one dish.

Blanch vegetables for the freezer when they are at the peak of flavor. You and your kitchen will keep cool.

Candies that used to take constant stirring and attention are simplified by microwaving. The real, old-fashioned flavor is the same.

Hot Fruit desserts take less water to cook, so juices have true fruit flavor. Fruit keeps its fresh color and texture.

Heat frozen entrees rapidly whether you buy them ready-made or freeze leftovers in individual servings.

THESE MICROWAVED FOODS SAVE TIME AND RESULTS COMPARE TO CONVENTIONAL COOKING

A Hamburger microwaves in 2 to 3 minutes, right on a paper or microwave ovenproof plate. It won't stick to the dish, so you save clean-up time.

Chicken pieces are tender, juicy and ready to serve quickly. A cut up broiler-fryer microwaves in about 20 minutes. Skin will not be crispy.

Meatloaf takes about 15 to 20 minutes to microwave. Add another 8 to 9 minutes if you must defrost the meat first.

Upside-down Cake becomes a last-minute dessert or afternoon snack when it takes only about 10 minutes.

Sirloin Tip roast will be tender and medium-rare when microwaved at Medium Power for about 11 minutes per pound.

Popcorn microwaves in 3 to 5 minutes, using a special microwave popper or bags labeled "microwave popcorn". For successful popping, make sure corn is fresh, not dried out.

SOME FOODS DO NOT MICROWAVE WELL

No single appliance does everything well, and your microwave oven is no exception. Some things should not be done, either because results are not satisfactory, or because conventional cooking is more efficient.

Large food loads, such as a 25-lb. turkey or a dozen potatoes cook more efficiently in a conventional oven.

Eggs in Shells and shelled boiled eggs can burst.

Pancakes do not crust, but they reheat well. Fully-prepared, frozen pancakes are available for microwaving.

Popcorn is too dry to attract microwave energy unless you use a special popcorn accessory or use popcorn labeled "microwave popcorn".

Canning requires prolonged high temperatures.

Deep Fat Frying can cause burns.

Bottles with narrow necks may shatter if heated.

FACTORS WHICH AFFECT SPEED AND EVENNESS OF COOKING

Several factors which influence timing and results in conventional cooking are exaggerated by microwave speed. From conventional cooking you are familiar with the idea that more food takes more time. Two cups of water take longer to boil than one. Size and shape of foods are important, too. Cut-up potatoes cook faster than whole ones, and round shapes microwave more evenly than angular ones. The delicacy of food is another factor. Lower temperature and longer cooking time keep these foods from toughening.

These differences are more apparent in microwaving since energy penetrates and turns to heat directly in the food. Knowing what affects speed and evenness of cooking will help you enjoy all the advantages of microwaving.

Delicacy. Foods with a delicate texture are best cooked at lower power settings to avoid toughening. Custard on the left was cooked at Low Power and custard on the right at High.

Piece Size. Small pieces cook faster than large ones. Pieces which are similar in size and shape cook more evenly. With large pieces of food, reduce the power setting for even cooking.

Starting Temperature. Foods taken from the refrigerator take longer to cook than foods at room temperature. Timings in our recipes are based on the temperatures at which you normally store the foods.

Density of Food. In both conventional and microwave cooking, dense foods, such as a potato, take longer to cook or heat than light, porous foods, such as a piece of cake, bread or a roll.

Quantity of Food. In both types of cooking, small amounts usually take less time than large ones. This is most apparent in microwave cooking, where time is directly related to the number of servings.

Shape of Food. In both types of cooking, thin areas cook faster than thick ones. This can be controlled in micro-waving by placing thick pieces to the outside edge with thin pieces to the center.

Height in Oven. In both types of cooking, areas which are closest to the source of heat or energy cook faster. For even microwaving, turn over or shield vulnerable foods which are higher than 3 inches.

Boiling. Microwaves exaggerate boiling in milk-based foods. A temperature probe turns off the oven before foods boil over. Use a lower power setting and watch carefully when not using a probe.

Prick Foods to Release Pressure. Steam builds up pressure in foods which are tightly covered by a skin or membrane. Prick potatoes (as you do conventionally), egg yolks and chicken livers to prevent bursting.

Round Shapes. Since microwaves penetrate foods to about 1-in. from top, bottom and sides, round shapes and rings cook more evenly. Corners receive more energy and may overcook. This may also happen when cooking conventionally.

Bury Vulnerable Foods. Foods which attract micro-wave energy, such as cheese or meat, should, when possible, be buried in sauce or other ingredients. In con-ventional stewing or pot roasting, meat not covered with liquid dries out.

Microwaving Techniques for Best Results

SOME TECHNIQUES YOU KNOW FROM CONVENTIONAL COOKING

Many of the techniques used in microwaving are the same ones you use in conventional cooking. Most of them either speed cooking or promote even heating. While the techniques may be familiar, their application may be somewhat different because of the unique way in which microwave energy cooks.

Stirring. In range-top cooking, you stir foods up from the bottom to help them heat evenly. When microwaving, you stir cooked portions from the outside to the center. Foods which require constant stirring conventionally will need only occasional stirring.

Turning Over. In range top cooking you turn over foods such as hamburgers, so both sides can directly contact hot pan. When microwaving, turning is often needed during defrosting, or when cooking foods such as hamburgers without a cover, or from frozen state.

Arranging on Oven Shelf. In conventional baking, you position foods, such as tomatoes or potatoes, so that hot air can flow around them. When microwaving, you arrange foods in a ring, so that all sides are exposed to microwave energy.

Rearranging. In conventional cooking, you reposition foods in the pan, especially when there are several layers. When microwaving, you also rearrange foods part way through the cooking period.

Standing Time. In conventional cooking, foods such as roasts or cakes are allowed to stand to finish cooking or set. Standing time is especially important in microwave cooking. Note that the microwaved cake is not placed on a cooling rack.

"HEAT" PHOTOS DEMONSTRATE NEED FOR TURNING AND ROTATING FOODS

Turning over, rotating, shielding and arranging are techniques you know from conventional cooking. However, you may not apply these techniques to some conventionally-cooked foods which need them when microwaving, due to faster cooking. The heat photos below show why these techniques are necessary. Heat photos, or thermographs, are further defined on page 5.

FOODS YOU TURN OVER

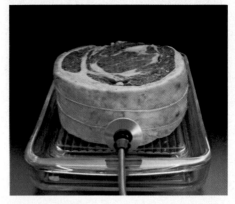

Rolled Roast cooks on a trivet in a microwave oven-proof dish. Top of roast is close to source of microwave.

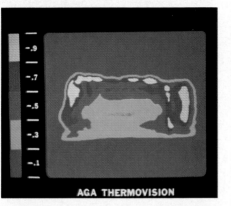

At internal temperature of 90°, heat photo shows yellow area at top is hotter than bottom of roast. Fat at sides is rapidly absorbing energy.

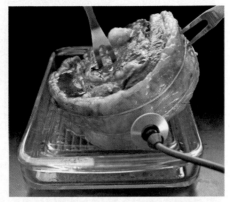

Turning the roast over exposes other side to more energy to promote even heating.

MORE FOODS YOU TURN OVER

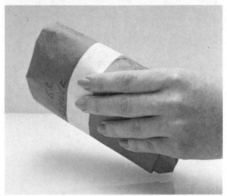

Frozen Hamburger must be turned over and outer thawed areas scraped off when defrosting.

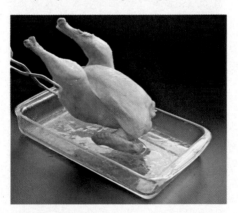

Whole Chickens can overcook in certain areas. Turn over to cook evenly.

Vegetables that are large or dense can be turned over to avoid overcooking the top surfaces.

FOODS YOU ROTATE

Meatballs, casseroles and many batter-type foods are not turned over or stirred. These foods are often high in moisture, fat or sugar which attract microwaves.

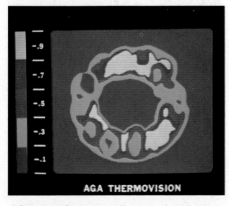

After 3 minutes yellow and red areas show meatballs are hotter in some areas than others. Uneven mixing of ingredients can exaggerate this.

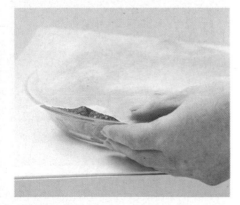

Rotate meatballs after half of cooking time for even microwaving.

FOODS YOU SHIELD

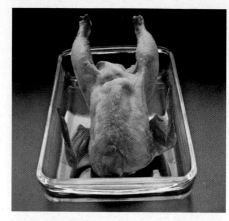

Defrosting poultry and meats which are uneven in shape and composition, often requires shielding with foil.

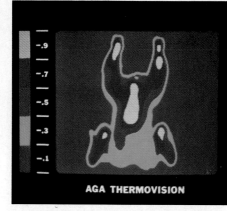

AGA THERMOVISION

After partial defrosting, heat photo shows yellow and red in warm leg and wing tip. Top of breast (closest to source of energy) is warm also.

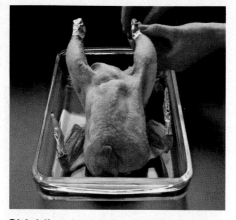

Shielding these thin areas with foil prevents overcooked, dried out edges.

OTHER FOODS YOU SHIELD

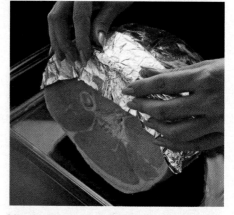

Ham edges and meaty cut area cook quickly. Shield with foil to prevent drying out.

Roast becomes warm in certain areas while defrosting. Cover these areas with foil and continue defrosting.

Fish tail and the head can be covered with foil which will prevent them from overcooking.

MORE SHIELDING TIPS

Water is a good shield against overcooking when poured on top of a frozen meatloaf, casserole, soup or stew.

Sauce shields meat to keep it from drying out during reheating. It also adds flavor.

Foods which are tolerant to microwaving, can be layered over less-tolerant foods to shield them.

SELECTING ROUND SHAPES

Square or Rectangular Shapes may overcook and dry out in the corners where more energy penetrates.

After 2 Minutes, yellow areas indicate corners continue to cook faster than some interior areas.

Round Shapes eliminate uneven heating of corners, and require less rotating during microwaving.

SELECTING RING SHAPES

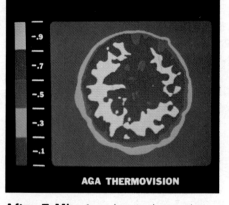

Biscuit Ring receives more energy on outside areas and cooks faster at edges.

After 7 Minutes, heat photo shows edges are completely cooked, but some center areas remain underdone.

Ring Arrangement, achieved by removing food in center, allows all areas to microwave more evenly.

MORE ROUND AND RING-SHAPED FOODS

Fluted Tube Cake Pan shape enables microwaves to penetrate food equally from all directions.

Brownies in a round shape lends visual interest to a favorite food. Round shape needs only one rotation while squares need 2 to 3.

Ring Arrangement with thicker portions to the outside is ideal for foods like chicken.

COVERING TECHNIQUES FOR RETAINING MOISTURE IN FOODS

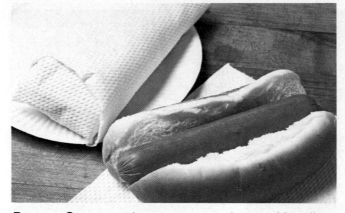

Porous Cover, such as paper towel or napkin, allows steam to escape while it promotes even heating and prevents spatters. Use to cover bacon, sandwiches and some vegetable custards.

Light Cover of wax paper holds in heat for faster cooking without steaming food. It is frequently used to cover some fruits and meats, such as chicken, hamburgers or roasts, which do not need steam to tenderize them.

Tight Cover of plastic wrap holds in steam as well as heat. Turning back one edge as a vent allows excess steam to escape, so wrap will not split during cooking. Vegetables and fish should be steamed.

Utensil Cover can be used instead of plastic wrap when you are microwaving vegetables, saucy casseroles and meats which require moisture and steam to tenderize.

Natural Cover formed by skins of some foods holds in moisture and heat. Tight-skinned foods like potatoes and apples must be pricked or slit to prevent bursting.

Freezer Bags hold moisture in foods and serve as both cooking utensil and cover. Pierce the top of the bag with a knife to vent. Package leftovers in single portions for easy-to-heat homemade frozen entrees.

HOW TO ADD MOISTURE TO FOODS

Sprinkle a little fruit juice or water over dried fruits, cover with plastic wrap and microwave ½ to 1 minute at High to moisten and plump them.

Wet Paper Towel, with excess water squeezed out, provides enough moisture to steam fish fillets and scallops. Wrap tortillas or crepes in damp towel and microwave at High ½ minute or more to soften them.

Add Water or sauce when reheating dry leftovers. A tablespoon of water or sauce is sufficient, and will not change the flavor of food or cause overcooking. Moisture creates steam for even reheating.

Soften lumpy brown sugar by placing in a microwave ovenproof container with a slice of apple. Cover or seal tightly and microwave ¼ minute or more, until moisture from the apple has softened the sugar.

HOW TO REMOVE MOISTURE FROM FOODS

Freshen Snacks, chips, pretzels, etc. by microwaving them, uncovered, for a few seconds. Let stand a minute or two to crisp. Dry a quart of bread crumbs or croutons at High 6 to 8 minutes, stirring every 2 minutes.

Paper Napkins or Towels absorb excess moisture. Dry herbs at High between two layers of towel or napkin until herbs can be crumbled. Check herbs regularly after ½ minute in the oven; small amounts can overheat and ignite. Use paper towel to absorb moisture on cake bottoms, as shown on page 264.

Combining Microwave and Conventional Cooking Benefits

Your new microwave oven combines with your conventional oven and range top to offer a convenient total cooking center. Having all these appliances in one center enables you to make the most efficient use of your time and your appliances' capabilities.

Some foods are best prepared conventionally, while many other foods are ideal for the microwave. At times you may want to prepare a dish partially by microwave and part conventionally. Microlessons in this book compare results of foods cooked by microwave and conventional appliances. Use this information to determine which cooking method will give optimum results for the foods you want to serve. Select the method that cooks foods the way they taste and look best.

Spaghetti sauce microwaves in about the same time it takes to boil spaghetti on the range top. Foods requiring large quantities of boiling water are more efficiently cooked on the range top. Use your broiler for garlic bread, if desired.

Steak broils in conventional oven, while potatoes crisp fry on the surface unit, and vegetables microwave at the same time. Fruit dessert finishes microwaving, while main course is being eaten.

Chicken and Biscuits cook quickly using two ovens. Bake crusty, golden biscuits in the conventional oven, while chicken microwaves tender and moist. You may want to crisp the chicken by heating 5 minutes, uncovered, in the conventional oven, already hot from baking the biscuits.

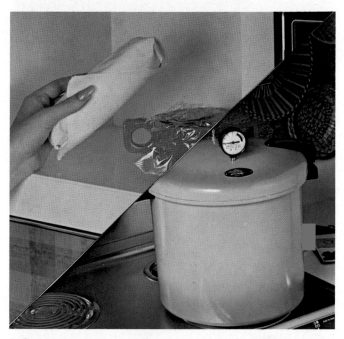

A Quick Lunch can be made in the microwave on days when the kitchen is otherwise occupied with canning jobs. Heat soup in its own serving cup and team with a hot dog or other favorite sandwich. The microwave is not recommended for canning, as noted on page 9 of this book.

Frosting Ingredients melt in the microwave, while angel food cake bakes in the conventional oven. Microwave is not recommended for foods like angel food cake, chiffon cake and popovers because they require dry heat to form their characteristic structure.

Breakfast bacon cooks in the microwave between paper towels to absorb the moisture and eliminate messy pan clean-up. Heat syrup in the microwave and prepare pancakes on the griddle.

Complete Meal Microwaving

Your microwave oven has a large cavity enabling you to cook several foods at once for a complete meal. Follow microwave techniques for even cooking such as stirring, rotating and turning. Some added procedures will ensure that all foods cook fully and can be served at once.

Foods that cook in the same amount of time singly are easy to team for complete meal microwaving. Cook them simultaneously in double the time it would take each food. For example, two foods taking 10 minutes each microwave together in 20 minutes; rotate or rearrange after half the time. Reheat several portions of leftovers at once; heat two dinners on 8-in. luncheon plates as shown on page 29.

Foods which cook at different rates should be added at different times. Add dense and large foods first. If one food cooks twice as long as another, the second food should be added when the first food is half done. Due to microwave speed, you can remove one food from the oven and let it stand to complete cooking while the second food finishes cooking. With a reduced oven load, the second food cooks more quickly, and both foods are hot at serving time.

When planning complete meals for microwaving, be sure the containers fit the oven cavity and that foods fit containers. Generally, meat or larger amounts of food should be placed on the right side of the oven when cooking complete meals. Check the variations for more complete meal ideas.

Ham, garnished with cranberry relish and apple baked with brown sugar filling. Serve with lettuce wedge and rolls.

HOW TO MICROWAVE HAM AND APPLES

Shield 5 to 6-lb. pre-cooked ham and cover with plastic wrap. **Microwave at Medium High 30 Minutes.**

Turn Over ham and add 6 pierced and cored apples, filled with brown sugar and butter.

Cover and **Microwave at Medium High 20 to 30 Minutes** more.

Variation: Substitute 4 acorn squash halves for apples. Place 5-lb. shielded ham in 9-in. pie plate in center of oven cavity; cover with plastic wrap. Arrange plastic wrapped squash halves in each corner of the oven cavity. **Microwave at Medium High 20 minutes,** turn over and rearrange squash. Turn ham over; reshield and recover. **Microwave at Medium High 20 to 30 minutes** more, removing squash after 20 minutes or when tender. Fill squash cavities with butter, brown sugar and cinnamon and let stand few minutes to melt.

HOW TO MICROWAVE BACON AND EGGS

Arrange 4 slices bacon on paper towel-lined pottery plate; place to left in oven. Scramble 4 eggs, 4 teaspoons melted butter, ¼ cup milk in 2-cup measure; place beside bacon. **Microwave at High 3 Minutes.** Rotate plate; stir eggs. **Microwave at High 3 Minutes** more, stirring eggs every minute.

Single Serving: Use 2 bacon strips. Mix 2 eggs, 2 teaspoons melted butter, 2 tablespoons milk. **Microwave at High 3 to 3½ Minutes,** rotating bacon and stirring eggs after half the time.

Variation: Hot Cereal and Cocoa
In each of 2 microwave-proof cereal bowls, mix a serving of instant hot cereal with water as pkg. directs. Place to oven rear. In 2 mugs (8-oz. each), place 2 to 4 tablespoons instant hot chocolate. Stir in water or milk as pkg. directs. **Microwave at High 4 to 6 Minutes.** No attention needed.

HOW TO MICROWAVE SOUP AND SANDWICH

Place 2 bowls soup (from 10-oz. can) in oven center. **Microwave at High 3 Minutes.** Wrap paper towel around 2 hot dogs in buns; place on either side of soup. **Microwave 2 Minutes at High.**

Single Serving: Microwave at High 2 Minutes a bowl of canned or room temperature soup. Add paper towel-wrapped sandwich and **Microwave at High 2 Minutes** more. For soup at refrigerator temperature, **Microwave at High 3 Minutes** before adding sandwich.

VARIATION: Canned Entree and Vegetables
Spoon 1 can (15-oz.) entree (like spaghetti) into 1-qt. dish; cover. Place in center of oven. Divide 10-oz. pkg. frozen peas, or other loose pack vegetable, between 2 custard cups; add 1 tablespoon water to each; cover. Place to right side of cavity. **Microwave at High 8 Minutes,** stirring entree and vegetable after 4 minutes. Add room temperature dinner roll and **Microwave at High 1 Minute** more. For food placement see picture on page 21.

Bacon and Scrambled Eggs. Serve with toast and beverage.

Hot Dog and Chicken Noodle Soup. Add beverage and an apple or banana for dessert.

Lemon Lovers Meatloaf, page 92 and Potatoes

Chicken 'N' Dressing, page 140, and Broccoli

HOW TO MICROWAVE MEATLOAF AND POTATOES

Prepare Lemon Lovers Meatloaf, page 92, in a 9-in. pie plate; cover; place in oven center. Prick 4 baking potatoes (8-oz. each); place two on each side of meatloaf. **Microwave at High 15 Minutes.** Rotate meat ½ turn; rearrange potatoes by moving to opposite corners of the oven. **Microwave at High 13 to 17 Minutes.** Check meatloaf at minimum time; remove from oven if done.

VARIATION: Barbecue Chicken and Corn on the Cob
Prepare Saucy Chicken, page 140. Place in 8-in. square dish; cover with wax paper; place to left in oven. Wrap 4 ears corn in wax paper or plastic wrap; place beside chicken. **Microwave at High 15 Minutes.** Rotate chicken; rearrange corn. **Microwave at High 13 to 17 Minutes.** Check corn at minimum time; remove from oven if done.

HOW TO MICROWAVE CHICKEN CASSEROLE DINNER

Make Chicken 'N' Dressing, page 140, in 8-in. square dish. Cover with wax paper; place to right side in oven. Place 10-oz. pkg. frozen broccoli and 2 tablespoons water in 9×5×3-in. dish; cover with plastic wrap; place beside chicken. **Microwave at High 15 Minutes.** Rotate chicken ½ turn; break up, stir broccoli. **Microwave at High 10 to 15 Minutes** more or until chicken is tender.

VARIATION: Ham Slice & Yams Hawaiian Style
Place ham slice and ¼ cup water in 8-in. square dish. Cover with vented plastic wrap; place to left in oven. Prepare Yams Hawaiian Style, page 225; spoon into 9×5×3-in. dish; place beside ham. **Microwave at High 15 Minutes.** Rotate ham; add pecans and sugar to yams. **Microwave at High 10 to 15 Minutes** more.

HOW TO MICROWAVE HAMBURGERS AND BAKED BEANS

Shape 4 patties (4-oz. each); place in 8-in. square dish. You may top with steak sauce or seasoning; cover with wax paper; place to right in oven. Pour 1 can (16-oz.) beans in 9×5×3-in. dish; stir in favorite flavorings. Cover; place beside patties. **Microwave at High 6 Minutes.** Rotate the meat dish ½ turn; stir beans. **Microwave at High 5 to 7 Minutes** more.

VARIATION:
Basic Meatballs and Potato-Cheese Hurry Up
Prepare meatballs, page 84; Potato-Cheese Hurry Up, page 222. Put meat in 9-in. pie plate; cover; place to right in oven. Prepare potatoes in 9×5×3-in. dish; place beside meat. **Microwave at High 15 Minutes;** stir potatoes and rotate meat ½ turn every 5 minutes.

HOW TO MICROWAVE FISH STEAKS AND VEGETABLES

Arrange 2 fish steaks (½-in. thick, about ¼-lb. each) in 8-in. square dish. Brush with mixture of 1 tablespoon each butter and lemon juice. Cover with plastic wrap; place on left. Pour 10-oz. pkg. frozen peas and onions and 2 tablespoons water in 9×5×3-in. dish; cover with plastic wrap; place to right of fish. **Microwave at High 4 Minutes.** Rotate fish ¼ turn; stir vegetables; recover. **Microwave at High 4 to 6 Minutes** more.

VARIATION:
Coated Fish Fillets and Tomato Pepper Quickie
Coat 1-lb. fish fillets with seasoned coating mix for fish as in recipe, page 162. Place in paper towel lined 8-in. square dish; cover with wax paper; place to left in oven. Prepare Tomato Pepper Quickie, page 224, in a 9×5×3-in. dish and cover with vented plastic wrap. **Microwave at High 15 Minutes;** rotate fish dish and stir tomatoes every 4 minutes.

Hamburgers and Baked Beans. Serve with potato chips and apple-sauce or cole slaw.

Salmon Steaks and Green Peas. Serve with crescent rolls and fruit salad.

Reheat chili in storage or serving containers.

Microwaving Whole Meal Dishes

STORING AND REHEATING

Nutritious whole meal dishes like chili, stuffed peppers, stews and casseroles can be prepared days ahead and refrigerated or frozen in individual portions. Later, needed portions can be defrosted and reheated in the microwave. Food waste is minimized, and because of the microwave oven's cooking speed, the reheated foods retain their fresh-cooked flavor and texture.

Your microwave oven allows you to cook big quantities of a dish for more than one meal. A recipe that has been doubled requires 1½ times the microwaving for the same recipe in its standard-size quantity. A recipe that is cut in half requires slightly more than half the cooking time called for with the same standard-size recipe. For tips on reheating foods, see pages 26 to 31.

Many types of containers can be used for both storage and microwave cooking. Look over dishes you already have at home, and save containers from purchased convenience foods. Ovenable paperboard dishes are convenient for storage and heating. They should be used only once, as the plastic finish washes off, and under some conditions, the dishes can catch on fire. Ovenable plastic bags, sandwich bags and plastic wraps also are useful. Sandwich bags and plastic wrap should be heavy duty if used in the microwave to heat foods. Thinner plastic materials do not withstand hot food temperatures.

Paper Hot Cups or Double-Thick Paper Bowls double as storage and heating containers. An 8-oz. serving of chili cooks at High from frozen in 5 to 7 minutes and from refrigerated temperature in 3 to 5 minutes.

Glass or Ceramic Dishes take lasagna from freezer or refrigerator to microwave for reheating. Ovenable paperboard containers also are convenient but should be used only once.

TV Dinner Trays, both aluminum and plastic varieties, can be saved and reused to store and cook homemade dinners made of small portions of leftovers. Most plastic lids on trays are not microwave-safe and should be replaced with wax paper. See page 29 for reheating instructions and TV Dinner Chart.

Plastic Wrap is ideal for odd-shaped foods like stuffed peppers. Wrap each individually to freeze. At cooking time, unwrap and place into a bowl that can double as serving container. Add 2 tablespoons of water, cover and microwave.

Bag Sealer lets you freeze and cook food in same bag. Put equal amounts in all bags so they cook in equal time. To reheat, prick or slash bag to vent; flex midway through cooking. Check convenience food charts throughout cookbook and similar size prepared product for times; 12 to 16-oz. bag takes about 8 to 12 minutes at High.

Plastics vary in their microwave suitability. Those shown here are good for warming foods to room temperature. Remove food to other containers when heating to higher temperatures. Check the utensil section for guidelines in using plastics for microwaving.

How to Freeze Foods for Microwaving

Foods cooked at home and raw foods can be frozen for later defrosting and cooking in the microwave. Certain techniques should be used in preparing the foods for freezing to assure even cooking later. Undercook pasta and rice for casseroles, as they will complete cooking when defrosted and heated. Add crumb or cheese toppings after removing from the freezer for defrosting and heating. Saucy foods work well for freezing and microwave cooking. Anything without a sauce should have moisture added (e.g., oil on chicken) to prevent drying out. If cornstarch is used as a thickener, substitute flour because cornstarch breaks down when frozen, and the resulting sauce may be too thin. Arrange foods in the best microwave shapes as identified earlier in this book.

Check pages 24 and 25 to be sure that containers are appropriate for the freezer. Some paper containers, for example, are recommended only for short term freezing. Cover the container well.

Unless your freezing container is microwave-safe, pop the food out of the container before defrosting and heating. Freeze food in individual serving containers for faster defrosting and reheating.

The pictures and chart (opposite) show favorite foods you prepare often and might want to freeze for microwave cooking. Recipes for all these foods are included in this book.

MICROLESSON: HOW TO FREEZE FOODS FOR MICROWAVING

Cut wings and drumsticks from breasts and thighs. Wash and spread separately on cookie sheet to freeze, package in freezer bags.

Basic Meatloaf, p. 91

Shape meatloaf in a ring, using a 2-quart casserole with a paper cup in the center. Freeze slices or wedges of cooked meatloaf individually.

Basic Meatballs, p. 84

Freeze stuffed peppers, mushrooms, cabbage rolls and meatballs on cookie sheet, with space between. Package in plastic bags.

Chow Mein, p. 119, Quick 'N' Easy Macaroni & Cheese, p. 196

Spread foods evenly in shallow dishes, (pie plates, 8-in. round, square or 12×8×2-inch dishes), up to 1 inch from top. Keep casseroles half full.

Round Steak Stew, p. 95

Omit potatoes from stews and soups. After defrosting and heating food, add canned or microwaved potatoes and reheat briefly, if needed.

Round Steak Stew, p. 95

Submerge pieces of meat and vegetables in broth when freezing soups and stews. Freeze pouches in dishes so they will be bowl shaped.

TIPS FOR EVEN DEFROSTING AND HEATING

Fish with Clam Chowder

Basic Meatloaf, p. 91   Round Steak Stew, p. 95

Chicken with Sauce, p. 142.

Defrost 1 lb. of fish fillets 4 minutes. Quarter, place in 8-in. dish; coat with 1 can undiluted soup; cover with plastic wrap. Defrost 10 minutes. Let stand 5 minutes. Cook 10 to 12 minutes at Medium.

Add ½ cup water, bouillon or tomato juice to top of stew or whole cooked meatloaf before defrosting and heating. Top slices or wedges of meatloaf with sauce.

Arrange food with saucy or frosty area on top to prevent drying or over-cooking. Exceptions are lasagna and one crust pot pies, which cannot be turned over. Two crust pot pies are not recommended.

HOME-FROZEN FOODS

Foods prepared from recipes in this book may be defrosted and cooked or heated, according to this chart. Start by defrosting the food; let it stand and then cook as specified. Allowing frozen foods to stand between defrosting and cooking periods helps to finish defrosting evenly. If you choose to reconstitute these frozen foods completely at High Power, you will need to check frequently and rearrange, stir or break up foods during cooking period. Directions here are for full or half recipes or for individual servings.

FOODS YOU PREPARE YOURSELF

ITEM	AMOUNT	DEFROST TIME	HOLD TIME	COOK TIME	COMMENTS
Meatballs Raw	1 recipe (12), 9-in. pie plate	5	5	4-6 High	Arrange in a circle. Cover with plastic wrap. Rotate ¼ turn after 4 min. Let stand covered 5 minutes before serving.
Meatloaf Raw	1 recipe, round, 9-in. pie plate or 8-in. round	30	15	20-25 High	Cover with plastic wrap. Rotate ¼ turn after 15 min. cooking. Let stand 10 minutes before serving.
	1 recipe, ring shape	25	20	15-20 High	
Cooked	1 recipe, round, 9-in. pie plate	30	15	23-28 M. High	Add ½ cup liquid. Cover with plastic wrap. Let stand 5 minutes before serving.
	8-oz.	8	5	4-5 M. High	
Chicken Ala King	1 recipe, (1½ qts.), 12×8×2-in.	30	none	25-30 High	Cover with plastic wrap. Stir before serving.
Chili, Spaghetti Sauce	½ recipe, (3 cups), 1-quart casserole	15	none	14-16 High	
	8-oz.	8	5	4-5 M. High	
Soup Chunky or Thin	1-qt. from plastic freezer container 2-qt. casserole	20 20	15 none	15-18 M. High 20-25 High	Cover.
	8-oz.	8	5	4-5 M. High	
Beef Stew	1 recipe, (2-qts.), 13×9×2-in.	25	15	25-30 High	Using 2 or 3-qt. casseroles, increase Defrost and Hold time by 5 minutes each. Stir before serving.
	½ recipe, (1½-qts.), 12×8×2-in.	25	15	20-25 High	
	8-oz.	8	5	4-5 M. High	
Fish Frozen, raw	1-lb. block, 8-in. square dish	10	5	10-12 M. High	Follow directions under picture above.

Break Up frozen foods before defrosting or as soon as possible during defrosting. Stir foods midway during defrosting and heating.

Defrosting and Heating Frozen Foods

Convenience foods can be purchased or made at home for fast and easy freezer to microwave meals. Certain techniques help food defrost evenly and quickly. Some convenience foods have microwave instructions on the package. In general, use an appropriate size casserole and cover with a lid on plastic wrap. In addition to the general tips given here, there are other convenience charts throughout this book which give directions for defrosting and heating specific foods.

If you wish to warm pies, coffee cakes or breads for a just-baked flavor, program the oven to Defrost, Hold and Time Cook at Low Power (3). Set a warming time equal to Defrosting time.

FROZEN CONVENEINCE FOODS CHART

AMOUNT	DEFROST TIME	HOLD TIME	COOK TIME (MED. HIGH)
8-oz.	10	5	4–5
9½–12-oz.	10	5	8–9
14–16-oz.	15	5	9–10
21-oz.	15	10	8–10
2-lb.	15	10	20–25

FROZEN BAKED GOODS CHART

ITEM	DEFROST	HOLD	TIME COOK, LOW(3)
Coffeecake			
(10- to 20-oz.)	3–4	10	3–4
Sweet rolls			
(7- to 10-oz.)	2	5	2
(11- to 16-oz.)	4	10	4
Muffins (6)	3	15	3
Pies			
Nut (20- to 22-oz.)	4	15	4
Fruit			
(8-oz.)	3½	10	3½
(22-oz.)	8	15	8
(44-oz.)	14	20	14
Pumpkin			
(6½-oz.)	3	10	3
(24-oz.)	12	20	12

TIPS FOR DEFROSTING AND HEATING

Place dry food like thick-crust pizza, egg rolls, sandwiches, coffee cakes and sweet rolls on a trivet for a more crisp or dry texture.

Stir dishes of food and flex frozen bags midway through cooking to equalize food temperature and shorten cooking time.

Turn Over individual pieces of food which are dense or thick to cook evenly throughout.

TV DINNERS

Most TV dinners come in foil trays. These trays can be used in the microwave oven if the precautions stated below are followed. The foil cover must be removed as explained below. Foods in metal trays cook only from the top; trays should be no more than ¾-in. deep. To avoid electrical sparks: "arcing", place trays at least 1 inch from oven walls. Foods in deeper trays should be removed to microwave oven-proof containers.

You can microwave TV dinners at either High or Medium High Power. Medium High results in a more evenly microwaved dinner. Both methods require rotation as below.

TV DINNER CHART

Size	Cook Time at HIGH	Alternate Cook Time at M. HIGH
8-oz. (entree-type or breakfast)	4 to 6	6 to 8
10 to 12-oz. (regular-type)*	6 to 8	8 to 12
16 to 20-oz. (hearty or man-size type)*	7 to 10	9 to 13

*See tip below about avoiding crisp or baked-type foods.

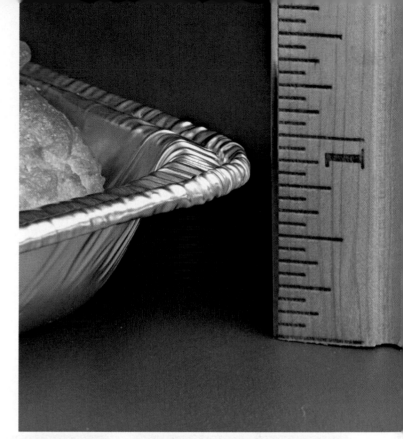

Height of TV foil tray should be ¾-in. or less.

HOW TO HEAT FROZEN FOODS IN A FOIL TRAY

Peel Off foil lid from shallow tray to allow microwaves to enter and heat the food. Return tray to box.

Place box in oven. To prevent arcing, allow 1 inch between tray and sides of oven. Microwave at High or Medium High for first half of time, see chart.

Rotate ½ turn and Microwave at High or Medium High for remaining half of time (Box may have cooking directions.)

TIPS

Cover dinner plate of food removed from foil tray with wax paper or vented plastic wrap. Follow minimum cooking times on chart, above.

Avoid French fries, doughs and foods which do not microwave well, or remove them from the tray and cook conventionally.

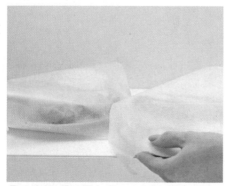

Double Up TV dinners in the microwave by removing food to 8-in. luncheon plates. Cook two at once by doubling microwave time and rearranging after half of time.

Heating

One of the big advantages of microwaving is that foods can be heated or reheated without changing their quality. Foods can be prepared in advance, when cooking may be more convenient, and reheated at serving time. Plates of food can be set aside and heated to give late comers a hot meal. Leftovers will taste freshly cooked when reheated.

Many types of fruit dishes, desserts and breads can be heated to enhance their flavor. See the appropriate sections in this book for tips on heating.

The microwave also can help you speed certain recipe steps and meal preparation. Ice cream can be softened, butter can be softened or melted and chocolate can be melted quickly in the microwave.

Consult the chart on the inside front cover for times and power levels recommended for various types and quantities of food. When heating by time, stir, turn over or rotate foods as needed.

Leftover Containers. Microwave-safe plastic, ceramic and paperboard dishes hold leftovers for reheating.

Starting Temperature. Foods taken from the refrigerator take longer than foods stored on your pantry shelf.

Quantity. One serving heats faster than several. Heat large amounts at Medium and rotate or stir after ½ of time for even heating.

Automatic Temperature Probe. Heat foods by temperature for accuracy. Moist casseroles heat well. Serve at 150° to 160°.

TIPS FOR MULTI-FOOD HEATING

Food Quantity. Begin cooking larger quantities and more dense foods first. Later add smaller quantities and less dense foods.

Food Temperature. Frozen vegetables in small amounts heat in same time as larger, more dense canned entrees at room temperature. See cooking method on page 21. Add roll during last minute of cooking time.

Multiple Single Servings. Microwave these in about 1 minute per serving if at room temperature and about 2 minutes per serving if at refrigerator temperature. Check and continue cooking if necessary.

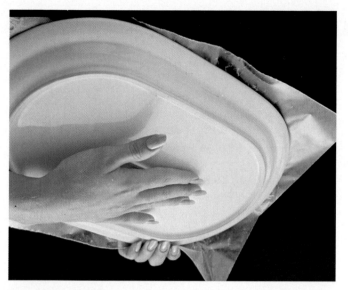

Doneness Test. The bottom of plate should be warm to touch when food is hot. If plate is cool, food may be warm but will lose heat to the plate and taste cool when served.

HEATING SINGLE PLATES OF FOOD

Arrange plates with hardest to heat foods on the outside of dish. Make a depression in dense foods like mashed potatoes, to give them a ring shape. Where possible, spread foods to keep a low, even profile.

When assembling plates from leftovers, start with foods of the same temperature; all refrigerated or all room temperature. Fast heating items can be added at the end.

Cover most foods with wax paper, tucking it under the plate before placing in microwave oven, to hold in heat and prevent spatters without steaming. When more moisture is desired, cover with plastic wrap. Be careful of steam when removing wrap.

When heating by time at High, you may want to rotate the plate after ½ the time. Heat for 3 to 5 minutes and test by feeling the bottom of the plate. See Doneness Test, left.

Arrange thick areas and dense foods to the outside of dish, with easy-to-heat foods on the inside.

Stir foods like beef stew for uniform heating and to speed cooking.

Spread saucy, moist foods, such as chow mein or creamed tuna with noodles flat for absorption of energy. Rotate layered foods.

Add Sauce to sliced meat and arrange vegetables with thick, fibrous areas to outside to speed heating. Add frozen roll for the last ½ to 1 minute, if desired.

Delicate foods which can overheat, such as macaroni and cheese or seafood, may be microwaved at Medium to keep them tender.

Cover foods with plastic wrap to keep them moist and saucy.

The Automatic Temperature Probe

The automatic temperature probe takes the guesswork out of timing. Factors which influence time cooking, such as the amount, type and starting temperature of food are automatically adjusted in temperature cooking. Foods cook to a pre-set internal temperature, then the oven signals you and turns off.

Probe placement is important for accurate results. Throughout this book you will find pictures and instructions for positioning the probe in different types of food. Here are a few general rules:

Insert probe into foods as directed in recipes, making

sure the disc does not touch food. Use the clip to keep probe in place while heating. Cover foods as directed for moisture control and speedy, even heating. Adjust recommended temperatures to your personal tastes, if desired.

Where choice of power levels is given, lower setting will heat more evenly but requires a little more time.

If food has been frozen, make sure it is completely defrosted before inserting the probe. Do not use the probe with TV dinner trays or with the Brown 'N Sear Dish.

ACCURATE COOKING

Roast Beef to rare, medium or well done at Medium High Power. Insert probe into center of meaty areas, without touching fat or bone.

Cook Meatloaves without special attention, following recipes for power levels and internal temperatures. Insert probe into center of loaf or ring.

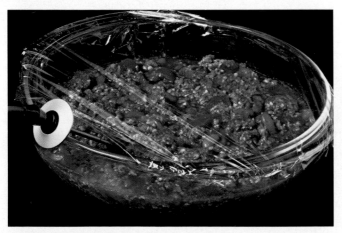

Cook Casseroles at High or Medium, to accurate internal temperature as directed in recipes. Insert probe so tip is in center of casserole.

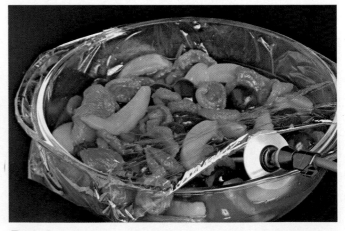

Fruit Compote cooks at High to an internal temperature of 160°. The cable can be shortened as needed by using the attachment available.

The Cook Code

Many of the recipes in this book include a two or three-digit "Cook Code." This handy code is a time-saving short-cut method for entering time and power level desired for the dish you are preparing. Cook Codes are only used for recipes which need little or no attention, and which require no change of power level during cooking. Recipes which require additional ingredients, attention or change of power level during microwaving should be cooked in the usual manner. Also, recipes with cooking time of less than one minute or more than 99 minutes do not carry Cook Codes.

The Cook Code feature is easy to use. If your microwave oven is equipped with Cook Code, use it by simply touching the Cook Code pad. The readout display will display O and "Enter Code" will flash, indicating that the oven is ready to be programmed with the numerals designating cooking time and power level desired. Now you touch the number pads which correspond to the three-digit Cook Code given in the recipe you are using. The first two digits indicate the time in whole minutes. The last digit shows the selected Power Level setting. The code for High Power is "0", meaning Power Level 10. Be sure to enter any zeros that are given in the code. For single digit minutes, there is no need for entering a "0" before, but make sure you enter double digits with "0" after the numeral, as in 20 minutes. You must enter at least two digits and no more than three for the oven to carry out the Code that you desire for your cooking. If you enter an incorrect number and need to start over,

simply touch "Clear Off" and then "Cook Code" pad and later new numerals. When you have made the correct Cook Code entry for your recipe, just touch the "Start" pad to begin cooking. The microwave oven will automatically decode your instructions. The readout display will show "Cook Time Left" and display area will count down in seconds, showing time remaining. The Power Level being used will also be displayed.

It's easy to invent Cook Codes for your own recipes. Just select one or two digits representing the length of cooking time desired, and a final digit for the Power Level required. Then program your new "Cook Code" in the same way as shown above. You can also change the codes given in a recipe in order to suit your individual taste. Cook Codes are given for the minimum time needed, to avoid overcooking which can dry out food and make it tasteless and tough. If you feel that more cooking is needed, add additional time by changing the Cook Code. You cannot add seconds to the cycle time— Cook Codes are for whole minutes only. If your recipe calls for Power Level changes or different amounts of time needed between addition of ingredients, you may set one Cook Code for the first part of the recipe, then after completion, set another Cook Code for that period of time and Power Level.

Remember that Cook Codes are for microwaving by time only. If you are microwaving by temperature, you must use the Temp Cook or Auto Roast functions.

TYPICAL TIME COOK RECIPE

TIME "COOK CODE"

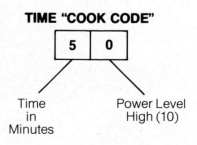

| 5 | 0 |

Time in Minutes   Power Level High (10)

Coffeecake microwaves at High 5 to 7 minutes, 5 (5 minutes), 0 (High).

Menu Planning

A special section devoted to Complete Meal Microwaving, pages 20 to 23, shows how to microwave two or more foods together. Many entrees and their accompaniments can share the microwave oven for convenient meal preparation. Finish your menu simply, with salad, crisp relishes, dinner rolls or toast, beverage and dessert.

Some sequential microwaving, however, will be needed in preparing meals in which foods are served at different temperatures or when foods need a standing time to complete cooking. The menus here illustrate these principles. Both the cake and the pie are microwaved ahead of time and cooled. The meatloaf meal has both a standing time and a second vegetable requiring last-minute microwaving.

Potatoes are very tolerant to microwaving and may be cooked with the entree in extra oven space. If the entree takes 20 minutes or less, add 4 potatoes at the start of cooking. Add to the cooking time of the entree about 15 minutes more than when cooking it alone. Rotate or rearrange potatoes and entree after ½ of total time. If an entree takes more than 20 minutes, add 4 potatoes during last ½ hour; rearrange them after 15 minutes. If necessary, continue cooking the entree during the standing time for the potatoes.

If the standing time of an entree, such as meat roast or whole poultry, is over 15 minutes, you may want to microwave the potatoes during the entree's standing time. When cooking a second vegetable, however, you can microwave potatoes with the entree, as suggested above. Cook the second vegetable during the standing time for the entree and potatoes.

Very delicate or sensitive foods like souffles should be microwaved alone for best results. This enables you to give the dish individual attention.

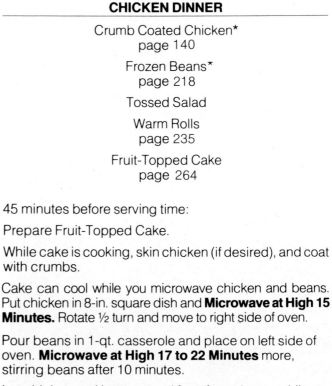

CHICKEN DINNER

Crumb Coated Chicken*
page 140

Frozen Beans*
page 218

Tossed Salad

Warm Rolls
page 235

Fruit-Topped Cake
page 264

45 minutes before serving time:

Prepare Fruit-Topped Cake.

While cake is cooking, skin chicken (if desired), and coat with crumbs.

Cake can cool while you microwave chicken and beans. Put chicken in 8-in. square dish and **Microwave at High 15 Minutes.** Rotate ½ turn and move to right side of oven.

Pour beans in 1-qt. casserole and place on left side of oven. **Microwave at High 17 to 22 Minutes** more, stirring beans after 10 minutes.

Let chicken and beans stand for a few minutes while warming rolls in the microwave and tossing salad.

* To fit both utensils in oven, use 8-in. square dish for chicken and 1-qt. casserole for green beans.

Chicken Dinner

MENU PLANNING TIPS

Meats and Main Dish Casseroles. As a general rule, start cooking the meat or main dish casserole first. Meats cooked with a sauce or other ingredients improve in flavor if allowed to stand a few minutes before serving. Many meats and main dishes require standing time to finish cooking.

Appetizers. Early in the day, get appetizers ready to microwave and refrigerate them if necessary. At serving time, microwave them and serve them hot. If you must remove another food from the oven while you heat appetizers, it will not harm the food.

Meat Roasts: Plan these foods so they may be served precisely when ready. If it stands too long, a rare or medium roast may be overdone. If you plan to microwave a vegetable or casserole after roast has finished, undercook the roast by 5 or 10 degrees to allow for extended standing time.

MEATLOAF DINNER

Lemon Lovers Meatloaf
page 92

Baked Potatoes
with Bacon Crumbles and Sour Cream
page 210

Frozen Carrots and Peas
page 209

Apple Graham Pie
page 261

Early in the day:

Make Apple Graham Pie. Refrigerate if made more than 4 hours in advance.

About 50 minutes before serving time:

Microwave bacon and crumble when cool.

Prepare meatloaf and potatoes for cooking. **Microwave at High 28 to 32 Minutes,** rotating meatloaf and rearranging potatoes after 15 minutes.

Let meatloaf and potatoes stand while microwaving carrots and peas.

Reheat pie while clearing the table.

Vegetables. We recommend a short standing time of 4 to 6 minutes for frozen vegetables and most fresh vegetables. During this time, heat rolls or microwave a beverage.

Desserts. Many desserts such as cakes, brownies or refrigerated pies may be microwaved several hours ahead of serving time. Others, such as baked apples or defrosted frozen cakes and pastries, may be prepared while dishes from the main course are being cleared from the table.

Baked Breads and Rolls. Warm breads and rolls for only a few seconds just before serving dinner.

Meatloaf Dinner

POWER LEVELS

Each power level on your microwave oven serves a definite purpose and should be used when recommended in this cookbook. Where a choice of power levels is given, the lower setting will cook and heat more evenly although it will take a little more time. Some foods may be cooked at a higher power level with additional attention such as frequent stirring, turning over or rotating. Delicate or slow simmering foods should not be attempted at higher settings.

Low Power (about 30% of the oven's full power) is recommended for delicate foods like custard, not tolerant of fast cooking, stews and other foods requiring slow simmering to tenderize and for defrosting.

Medium Power (about 50% of oven's full power) or **Medium High Power** (about 70% of oven's full power) is used for ease in heating and cooking foods requiring extra attention at High Power.

High Power (full 100% power) is used for fast cooking, and for foods which tolerate heat and speed. Many foods in this book, including fish, vegetables and sauces call for High Power.

ADAPTING OUR RECIPES

These recipes were developed for microwave ovens of 625 watts. However, house power varies around the country and during peak consumption periods, such as in early evening and hot or cold weather. To avoid overcooking, check food often and stir, turn or rotate as needed. Recipes cooked by time direct you to check for doneness after minimum cooking time, adding more time as needed. Power fluctuations do not affect cooking with the temperature probe.

If you are uncertain about your house power, or have purchased this book for use with a different microwave oven, you can determine wattage with a simple test using tap water. You'll need a 1-qt. measure, a 1 cup measure and a watch or clock with a second hand. Follow steps below.

USING OTHER MICROWAVE RECIPES

Sometimes you may want to use microwave recipes from a source other than this book. These recipes may have been tested on a different style or brand of oven than your own. Therefore, you may need to adjust power levels and times allowing the recipe to work well in your oven. Observe the food as it microwaves to see what cooking alterations are necessary, checking frequently to determine stage of doneness. Watch for uneven boiling or uneven color changes. Surface appearance of many foods will tell you if the outside is cooking more quickly than interior.

Combine 1 cup cold tap water with 8 ice cubes. Stir together for 1 minute.

Pour Off 1 cup of water without ice cubes. Temperature of water will be about 38°.

Timing Carefully, microwave water at High until many bubbles break on the surface (212°).

Calculate the amount of time required to bring tap water from cold to boil, following the steps shown in the pictures. If the time is approximately 2½ to 3 minutes, recipe times in this cookbook should be correct for you. If your timing is significantly longer, expect recipe times to be about the maximum time given or even more. Use the minimum cooking times or less time if your timing with this test is shorter than 2½ to 3 minutes.

HOW TO CONVERT CONVENTIONAL RECIPES FOR MICROWAVING

Before converting your recipe, study it in terms of micro-waving. Is it one of the many foods which microwave well? Look for cooking techniques which are similar to microwaving techniques, such as covering, steaming or cooking in sauce or liquid. If the food requires a crisp, fried crust or very dry surface, you will prefer to cook it conventionally. Some recipes may not be exactly the same when microwaved, but you will be pleased with the results.

If the food is suitable for microwaving, refer to a Micro-lesson or similar recipe for cooking techniques, power level, timing and possible changes in ingredients.

Many recipes will not need changing. Moist, rich cakes, candies and moist meatloaves are examples.

Since liquids do not evaporate when microwaved, reduce the amount in saucy casseroles. Add more thickening to sauces and gravies. Reduce some seasonings also; they will not lose intensity in short microwaving times. Salt meats and vegetables after cooking. If an ingredient takes longer to microwave than others in the same dish, substitute one which is precooked or quick-cooking, as we have done in the following example.

CONVENTIONAL SPANISH RICE

COOKING TIME: 45 to 50 min., total

Use Chuck

1 lb. ground beef . . . . .In 10-in. skillet crumble ground beef. Cook over medium high heat 10 minutes, uncovered.

Use 3 qt. casserole

Skip

Omit
Substitute
1 cup precooked rice
Reduce

1½ cups water . . . . .Add water, rice, chili powder, onion, salt, pepper and tomatoes. Stir very well. Cover and cook over medium heat 35 to 40 minutes.
¾ cup long grain rice
2 tablespoons chili powder
2 tablespoons instant minced onion
2 teaspoons salt
⅛ teaspoon pepper
1 can (1-lb. 12-oz.) tomatoes

Microwave at High 12 to 14 minutes, stirring after 6 minutes

Makes 4 to 6 servings

MICROWAVE SPANISH RICE

POWER LEVEL: High
MICROWAVE TIME: 12 to 14 min., total

1 lb. ground chuck beef . .Into 3-qt. casserole crumble beef. Add remaining ingredients and mix well, cutting tomatoes to distribute evenly. Cover. **Microwave at High 12 to 14 Minutes,** stirring after 6 minutes. If top of food appears dry during cooking, stir again, then return to oven to finish cooking.
1 cup packaged precooked rice (minute)
1 can (1-lb. 12-oz.) tomatoes
1 tablespoon instant minced onion
2 tablespoons chili powder
2 teaspoons salt
⅛ teaspoon pepper

Makes 4 to 6 servings

Microwave Utensil Guide

Special Utensils for microwaving are now available because of the increasing popularity of microwave ovens. These utensils are made of microwave ovenproof materials and satisfy some of the special needs of microwave cooks.

Many manufacturers are designing utensils which can be used both in microwave and conventional ovens. Special utensils also include many everyday items of glass, pottery, plastic and paper which were never considered cooking utensils until microwaving made it possible to use them.

Brown 'N Sear Dish (9-in. square) has a special coating on the bottom which attracts microwave energy. When preheated, it fries eggs and browns hamburgers or chicken. A cover controls moisture and spatters.

BROWN 'N SEAR COOKING CHART POWER LEVEL: **High (10)**

Preheat Brown 'N Sear Dish before each use. Use potholders and avoid touching bottom. If cooking many foods consecutively, preheat dish 1 to 1½ minutes between foods. Use the cover when cooking the foods listed on the chart below.

ITEM	AMOUNT	PREHEAT TIME/MINUTES	FIRST SIDE TIME/MINUTES	SECOND SIDE TIME/MINUTES
Steaks, Rib Eye or Delmonico (6-oz. each, ½-in. thick)	2	7 to 8	1	1½ to 2
Hamburgers, (¼-lb. each, ½-in. thick)	1 or 2	4 to 6	2 to 2½	1 to 1½
	3 or 4	6 to 8	2½ to 3	1½ to 2
Pork Chops (5-oz. each, ¾-in. thick)	1	3 to 4	2	4 to 6
	2	5 to 6	4	4 to 6
Pork Sausage Links (Uncooked, 8-oz.)	6 to 8	4 to 5½	1	2 to 2½
Ham Slice (¼ to ½-in. thick)	1	3½ to 4½	1 to 2	1 to 2
Chicken, Fried (pieces coated with seasoned flour and paprika)	3	6 to 7 (add 1 tablespoon oil after preheat)	3	3 to 4
	6	7 to 8 (add 1 tablespoon oil after preheat)	4	3 to 5
Fish Fillets (6-oz. each, ½-in. thick) (seasoned flour on outsides)	2	5 to 6 (add 1 tablespoon oil after preheat)	1½ to 2½	2 to 3
Lamb Chops (4-oz. each, ¾-in. thick)	2	5 to 6	3	3 to 4
	4	6 to 8	3 to 4	4 to 5

Casserole Dishes come in varied sizes including individual serving dishes. They go directly from freezer or refrigerator to microwave. Non-stick finishes or smooth surfaces make cleaning easier.

Trivet fits in its own dish or in microwave oven-safe dishes you already have. It holds meat out of juices to prevent stewing. Made of glass or plastic, trivets are in circular and rectangular styles. If you don't have a trivet, cook meat on a microwave ovenproof plate or saucer inverted in the baking dish.

Ovenable Paper Dishes may be purchased at supermarkets, packaged in multiples. Sometimes they are used as containers for frozen convenience foods. Do not reuse, as the coating washes off. Paperboard manufacturers say foods cook faster because no heat is lost to the dish.

Domes are even more convenient than wax paper or plastic wrap when covering foods to be cooked or reheated. They prevent spatters and retain moisture during microwaving. Circular styles cover plates, while rectangular styles are ideal for microwave roasting. Domes without venting holes on the top can double as casserole dishes.

Ring Molds (fluted and straight sided) and cupcakers are ideal for cakes, quickbread and meatloaf. All provide the ring shape preferred for microwaving as well as an attractive appearance. Some plastic dishes are available with non-stick coating.

Divided Dinner Trays of plastic or aluminum, saved from TV dinners, are convenient for reheating. Generally, plastic covers on the trays are not microwave-proof. See page 29 for heating instructions.

Utensils You Already Have may be suitable for microwaving. Oven glass casseroles, cooking dishes, measuring cups and custard cups are common household utensils. Pottery or china dinnerware which does not have gold or silver trim or glaze with a metallic sheen can be used. Most glass ceramic oven-to-table ware is labeled "suitable for microwave". If you are uncertain about a dish or container, use the dish test described below.

WHAT TO LOOK FOR WHEN BUYING UTENSILS FOR MICROWAVING

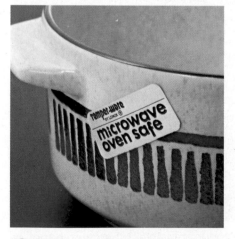

"Suitable for Microwave" or "Microwave Oven Safe" may appear on the label or sticker, or may be stated in the warranty of the utensil.

Lugs and Handles make dishes easier to use. While microwave energy does not heat the dish directly, heat from foods will transfer to the bottom and sides of it. Lugs and handles generally do not become hot.

Test Dishes. Measure 1 cup of water in a glass cup. Place in oven on or beside dish. Microwave 1 minute at High. If water becomes hot, dish is microwave safe. If dish heats, it should not be used for microwaving.

MICROWAVE UTENSIL GUIDE

Use this guide to help you evaluate and select utensils for microwaving. Some items can only be used for heating. Others are suitable for cooking. Many microwave utensils are designed both for cooking and attractive serving. Brands listed are among those recommended by their manufacturers for microwaving.

TYPE OF UTENSIL	**Paper Towels and Napkins, Wax Paper**	**Paper or Styrofoam Plates and Cups such as:** Chinet, Diamond International, Dixie, St. Regis, Sweetheart
MICROWAVE USES	Cooking Bacon. Absorbing moisture and preventing spatters. Heating and serving sandwiches or appetizers. Light covering to hold in steam.	Heating and serving foods and beverages. Styrofoam should be used for short-term heating to low temperatures and for serving.
COMMENTS	Recycled paper products can contain metal flecks which may cause arcing or ignite. Paper products containing nylon or nylon filaments should be avoided, as they may also ignite. Dye from some colored paper products may bleed onto food.	Be sure paper plates are plastic coated if heating saucy foods. Also see column on left about recycled paper and dyes. "Hot drink" cups may be used for soups and beverages. Styrofoam distorts when bacon and other high-fat foods are microwaved on it.

Glass jars, such as for baby foods, vegetables, entrees, syrups, salad dressing.

Plastic Wrap, Cooking Bags, Boil-in-bags, Storage Bags, such as: Glad Wrap, Handi-Wrap, Saran Wrap, Cooking Magic, Reynolds, Baggies, Ziploc.

Boilable Hard and Soft Plastics, such as: Rubbermaid

Avoid heating baby food in jars, especially meat and egg mixtures. Remove metal caps to warm syrup or soften salad dressing from refrigerator.	Covering to hold in steam (wrap). Cooking (cooking and boil-in-bags). Heating (storage bags).	Cooking ground beef (colander). Defrosting. Heating.
Jars which aren't heat tempered should not be used to heat food to very hot temperatures. Most vegetables and entrees are best removed to glass or plastic microwave-proof container.	Storage bags can melt at high temperatures.	May discolor from fat. May distort when used with foods with high fat content (except colander).

TYPE OF UTENSIL	**Microwave Plastics such as:** Anchor Hocking Microware, Bangor Plastics, Mister Microwave, NordicWare, Republic, Tara, Wearever Nupac.	**Oven Glass such as:** Anchor Hocking, Fire King, Glassbake, Heller, Jena, Pyrex	**Glass-Ceramic (Pyroceram), such as:** Corning Ware, Progression G. by Noritake
MICROWAVE USES	Specialized cooking (see pages 38-40 for details.)	Cooking and heating.	Cooking and heating.
COMMENTS	Never microwave these utensils without food or liquid in them.	Inexpensive and readily available in supermarkets, hardware and department stores.	Attractive for serving. Plastic storage lids, available with individual casseroles, should not be used for microwaving.

TYPE OF UTENSIL	**Specialty Glass-Ceramic and Porcelain, such as:** El Camino, F. B. Rogers, Heller, Marsh Industries, Pfaltzgraff, Shafford	**Straw and Wood**	**Boxes lined with paper or plastic, Paper or plastic packages, Styrofoam base, Shallow frozen dinner tray.**
MICROWAVE USES	Recommended for microwave oven-to-table cooking of special foods.	Short term heating (baskets and boards). Cooking (spoons, whisks, picks and skewers).	Refresh foods, defrost meat and baked goods. Cook vegetables. Heat frozen foods.
COMMENTS	Microwave ovenproof ceramics may be sold with metal holders. Ceramic part, but not holders, may be used in microwave oven.	Spoons and whisks may be left in foods while microwaving.	Do not use foil trays higher than ¾-in.

Handmade Pottery, Porcelain, Stoneware

Cooking and heating.

Avoid glazes with metallic sheen.
Use the dish test, page 40, to determine if hand-made pottery is microwavable.

Regular Dinnerware, such as:
Corelle by Corning, Dansk Generation, Denby, El Camino, Franciscan, International Stoneware, Lenox Temperware, Marsh, Mikasa, Pfaltzgraff

Heating and some cooking.

Check for "Recommended for microwave" seal, or use dish test. Avoid metal trim.

Unsuitable Dinnerware, such as: Corning Centura, Fitz and Floyd Oven-to-table Ware, Melamine, Dishes with metal trim

None

Warranty for Centura and Fitz and Floyd dishes states unsuitability for microwave.

Foil-lined Paper Bags, Boxes and Baking Trays

Avoid. Use only foil trays ¾-in. or less. Foil or metal will reflect microwaves, thus preventing even heating. Arcing can occur if foil is closer than 1-in. to oven walls.

Check for foil lining before attempting to microwave food in original packages.

Metal or part metal pots, Pans, Thermometers, Skewers and Foil Trays

Avoid. See explanation left.

Glass, pottery, pyroceram, wood or straw with metal fittings (screws, handles, clamps, etc.)

Avoid or remove metal parts.

NOTE: *Electrical sparks (arcing) can occur in a microwave oven when two pieces of metal are placed within 1 inch of each other. Metal walls, wires, utensils or foil strips can cause arcing which can pit oven walls or cause fire within the utensil or the food. To prevent arcing, avoid utensils as listed above and carefully follow the recommendations for other uses of metal foil in recipes in this book.*

Beef Stew simmers 6 to 8 hours, controlled automatically by the temperature probe.

In the Morning, prepare vegetables and combine with beef, liquid and seasonings in the casserole. Place the probe with its tip submerged in liquid.

In the Evening, serve savory, tender beef stew. Microwave a dish of brownies in 6 to 7 minutes for a popular family dessert.

Auto Roast Code 6 or Automatic Simmering & Slow Cooking

If your microwave oven is equipped with a simmer or slow cook setting, or Auto Roast Code 6, use it to prepare delicious, old-fashioned in-a-pot dishes. Most of these hearty foods are a meal in themselves made from popular, yet inexpensive, meats and vegetables.

In-a-pot meals are versatile enough to serve as a sustaining family dinner or easy-on-the-hostess party fare. Just add a crisp green salad, crusty French bread and microwave a quick dessert.

Slow cooked dishes, except for tall or chunky roasts, need no attention during microwaving. The temperature probe controls cooking automatically, keeping foods at a slow simmer to develop rich homemade flavor and fork tender texture. If desired, however, you may check or stir the food at any time while it's cooking.

Our recipes call for refrigerated meat, but you may also start with frozen meat. Adjust the cooking time according to the chart below. Fresh vegetables in large chunks may be started with frozen meat and will not overcook in the minimum time.

Recipes for crocks and slow cookers may be used for microwave simmering. Reduce cooking time by about 2 hours less than minimum time given in the slow cook recipe. Check food and continue as necessary.

AUTOMATIC SIMMERING AND SLOW COOKING CHART

Always add at least ½ cup liquid when simmering foods. Place the temperature probe IN THE LIQUID with the tip submerged. It should rest on the bottom of the utensil, about halfway between the center and side of dish.

Unlike regular microwave recipes, automatic simmer recipes can microwave one or even two hours beyond their minimum time. At minimum time, food will be very tender but firm enough to hold its shape when lifted from the pot. At this point in cooking, you may wish to stir the food or even if it is a roast, turn it over. Maximum time will produce "fall off the bone" tenderness.

For soups and stews, select a microwave-proof casserole which is roomy enough to allow all the liquid in the recipe. Where large amounts of water are called for, it is important to add all of it to prevent overcooking the meat or vegetables. Also follow the tip for chili and stew for "floating" a layer of water over the top to keep it moist.

Remember, that microwave energy comes into the oven from the top and the top surfaces of tall foods are vulnerable to overcooking. Follow the utensil directions given in recipes here, but if in doubt, arrange the food in a flat even layer in a low sided dish such as a 13x9x2 in. size. This low flat arrangement works best for most of the saucy meat casseroles in this section.

Do not use a lid on the casserole. Instead, cover with plastic wrap, folding or gathering it loosely around the probe to allow steam to escape.

ITEM	APPROXIMATE AUTOMATIC SIMMER TIME/HOURS
Beef Chuck Roast (5-lb.)	
Fresh	6 to 8
Frozen	9 to 11
Beef Stew	6 to 8
Chicken, Stewing (4 to 6-lb.)	
Fresh	11 to 12
Frozen	12 to 14
Chicken, Broiler-Fryer (2½ to 3½-lb.)	
Fresh	4 to 6
Frozen	6 to 8

ITEM	APPROXIMATE AUTOMATIC SIMMER TIME/HOURS
Chili and other Saucy Hamburger Mixtures	11 to 13
Ham or Pork Roast (5-lb.)	4 to 6
Pork and Beans	9 to 11
Punch or Cider (your favorite recipe)	4 to 6
Soup Stock	4 to 6
Split Pea Soup	13 to 15
Vegetable Soup	3 to 4

Beef

Savory stews, tender pot roasts and hearty casseroles microwave carefree with automatic simmering. To keep these meats tender and juicy, bury them beneath vegetables or cover them with liquid or sauce.

HOW TO MICROWAVE BEEF STEW WITH AUTOMATIC SIMMERING

Combine 1 can undiluted beef broth, 1½ cups liquid, ½ cup minute tapioca and 2 tablespoons brown bouquet sauce in casserole.

Bury stew meat and vegetables under liquid. Gently pour water over surface. Insert the temperature probe and cover with plastic wrap.

Vary the recipe with different meats and vegetables. Special seasonings such as curry give stews international flavor.

BASIC BEEF STEW

POWER LEVEL: Automatic Simmer
MICROWAVE TIME: 6 to 8 hr.

2 lb. beef stew meat,...	In 5 qt. casserole place
cut in 1-in. cubes	beef, potatoes, carrots,
2 large potatoes,	onions, celery, broth,
peeled, cut into	water, tapioca, brown
chunks	bouquet sauce, salt,
5 medium carrots,	pepper and garlic pow-
peeled, sliced	der. Mix together very
2 medium onions,	thoroughly. Press
sliced	chunks of meat to sub-
2 stalks celery, sliced	merge under liquid. Over
1 can (10½-oz.) beef	back of a spoon, gently
broth	pour the additional 1½
1½ cups water	cups water onto top sur-
½ cup minute tapioca	face; do not stir in. (See
2 tablespoons brown	tip next page.) Insert
bouquet sauce	temperature probe so tip
2 teaspoons salt	rests on bottom of dish,
¼ teaspoon pepper	halfway between center
¼ teaspoon garlic	and side. Cover tightly
powder	with plastic wrap, ar-
Additional 1½ cups	ranging loosely around
water	probe to vent. Attach

cable end at receptacle. **Microwave at Automatic Simmer 6 to 8 Hours.** Stir before serving.

Makes about 6 servings

VARIATIONS

Beef Curry: Prepare Beef Stew, omitting potatoes and carrots. Blend ½ cup raisins and 3 tablespoons curry powder into mixture and microwave as in recipe. Serve over rice.

Beef Goulash: Prepare Beef Stew, omitting potatoes and carrots. Stir 2 tablespoons paprika into mixture and microwave as in recipe. Just before serving, stir in 1 cup (8-oz.) sour cream. Serve over noodles.

Irish Stew: Substitute lamb for beef. Just before serving, stir in 1 pkg. (10-oz.) frozen peas. **Microwave at High 5 to 10 Minutes,** until peas are tender.

BEEF STEW WITH WINE

This French beef stew is also called Boeuf Bouguignon. Serve with buttered wide noodles.

POWER LEVEL: Automatic Simmer
MICROWAVE TIME: 6 to 8 hr.

Make Basic Beef Stew (left), except omit potatoes and celery. Add 1 can (6-oz.) tomato paste, 1 can (8-oz.) mushrooms, drained and substitute 1 cup red burgundy for 1 cup of the water.

Insert temperature probe so tip rests on bottom of dish, halfway between center and side. Cover tightly with plastic wrap, arranging loosely around probe to vent. Attach cable end at receptacle. **Microwave at Automatic Simmer 6 to 8 Hours.** Stir before serving. If desired, garnish each serving with crumbled bacon, (Microwave 4 to 6 strips bacon at High 4 to 6 minutes), and chopped parsley.

Makes 8 to 10 servings

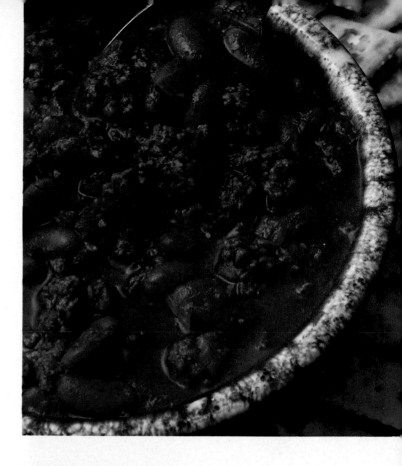

CHILI

To eliminate the first step of precooking the beans use about 3 cups canned pinto or kidney beans (2 cans, 1-lb. each)

POWER LEVEL: High (10) and Automatic Simmer
MICROWAVE TIME: 11 to 13 hr.

To Prepare Beans: In 4-qt. casserole place **½ lb. dry pinto beans** and **2 qts. water.** Soak overnight. Before finishing chili, drain beans and add **6 cups fresh water. Microwave uncovered at High 60 Minutes.** Drain.

2 lb. ground chuck beef	In 4-qt. casserole crumble beef. **Microwave at High 8 to 10 Minutes,** stirring after 4 minutes. Drain off fat.
2 cans (1-lb. each) tomatoes **1 can (6-oz.) tomato paste** **2 medium onions, coarsely chopped** **1 green pepper, coarsely chopped** **2 cloves garlic, crushed** **2 to 3 tablespoons chili powder** **½ teaspoon pepper** **½ teaspoon cumin** **2 teaspoons salt** **1 cup water** **Additional 1-2 cups water**	Add drained beans, tomatoes, tomato paste, onions, peppers, garlic, chili powder, pepper, cumin, salt and water. Stir well. Over back of spoon, gently pour additional water onto top surface (see tip below): do not stir in. Insert temperature probe so tip rests on bottom of dish, halfway between center and side.

Cover tightly with plastic wrap, arranging loosely around probe to vent. Attach cable end at receptacle. **Microwave at Automatic Simmer 10 to 12 Hours.** Stir before serving.

TIP: Before automatic simmering chili or stew, pour water over the back of a spoon to form a layer over surface to keep the top from drying out. Stir water into mixture before serving.

GERMAN MEATBALLS

POWER LEVEL: Automatic Simmer
MICROWAVE TIME: 6 to 8 hours

2 lb. ground veal, pork and beef mixture **1 medium onion, finely chopped** **2 eggs** **2 tablespoons flour** **2 tablespoons dry onion soup mix** **1 teaspoon salt** **¼ teaspoon pepper** **Boiling water** **2 bay leaves** **2 tablespoons dry onion soup mix** **1 teaspoon salt** **1 teaspoon brown bouquet sauce (optional)**	In mixing bowl mix together ground meat, onion, eggs, flour, soup mix, salt and pepper. Form into medium sized balls (up to ¼ cup per ball). Set aside. Pour 1-qt. boiling water into 3-qt. casserole. Add bay leaves, soup mix, salt and brown bouquet sauce. Carefully add meatballs. Add more boiling water if needed to cover. Insert temperature probe so tip rests in liquid on bottom of dish, halfway between center and side.

Cover tightly with plastic wrap, arranging loosely around probe to vent. Attach cable end at receptacle. **Microwave at Automatic Simmer 6 to 8 Hours.** Thicken broth (below), if desired.

To Thicken Broth: Remove meatballs from broth and keep warm. Into hot broth in dish, stir mixture of ¼ cup cornstarch and ¼ cup water. Add additional dry onion soup mix for onion gravy. **Microwave at High 4 to 6 Minutes,** stirring every 2 minutes.

Makes 16 to 18 meatballs

AUTOMATIC SIMMERING POT ROASTS

Depending on your time schedule, select a flat roast, like beef chuck or blade roast, or a chunky roast, such as rolled rump or sirloin tip. Flat roasts may be simmered for 6 to 8 hours, but chunky roasts, because they are usually tall, should be checked every 2 hours and turned over, if necessary at that time.

CHUCK ROAST

Arrange vegetables as flat as possible in dish. Vegetables which cover roast should be checked or rearranged before minimum time.

POWER LEVEL: Automatic Simmer
MICROWAVE TIME: Fresh 6 to 8 hr.—
                    Frozen 9 to 11 hr.

1 fresh or frozen beef chuck or arm roast, about 5-lb.
2 to 3 potatoes, peeled and cut in large chunks
4 to 6 carrots, scraped and cut in chunks
2 large onions, cleaned and quartered
2 cans (10½ oz.) beef consomme or beef broth

In 13x9x2-in. dish or 5-qt. casserole, place roast. Arrange vegetables around edges of dish. Pour consomme over top. Insert temperature probe so tip is in liquid on bottom of dish. Cover tightly with plastic wrap, arranging loosely around probe to vent. Attach cable end at receptacle. **Microwave at Automatic Simmer 6 to 8 Hours,** for fresh meat, or **9 to 11 Hours,** for frozen.

Makes 6 to 8 servings.

VARIATIONS: **Pot Roast with Wine:** Use above recipe except omit vegetables and consomme. Sprinkle 1 cup chopped onions over top of roast; top with mixture of 1 can (10-oz.) beef gravy and ½ cup red cooking wine.

With Other Vegetables: Fresh rutabagas, turnips, and parsnips, peeled and cut in large chunks, or 1 pkg. (32-oz.) frozen stew vegetables may be substituted for carrots and potatoes in basic recipe.

Place probe, with tip submerged in liquid, next to meat in microwave ovenproof cooking dish.

Chuck Roast

Pork & Ham

Pork and ham products are delicious when simmered slowly, but they can become dry on top and care must be taken to prepare them properly for automatic simmering. Small pieces, such as ribs, chops, bacon or sausages can be buried beneath vegetables or in liquid.

Pork roasts and hams may be simmered in 13x9x2-in. dish with 3 cups water, using probe and tight cover of plastic wrap as for chuck roasts (see picture on opposite page). Simmer time will be 4 to 6 hours, but meat must be checked and if needed turned over after half the time. Look for a thick rind when you buy hams for automatic simmering.

SMOTHERED PORK CHOPS

POWER LEVEL: High (10) and Automatic Simmer
MICROWAVE TIME: 4 to 5 Hours

6 pork rib or loin chops (¾ in. thick)
¼ cup Worcestershire sauce

Score fat on chops and brush both sides with Worcestershire sauce. Arrange in 13 x 9 x 2-in. dish so "tails" are in center. Cover with plastic wrap, turning back one corner to vent. **Microwave at High 14 Minutes, rearranging after 7 Minutes.** Drain off liquid.

2 cans (10-¾ oz. each) cream of mushroom soup
2 tablespoons water
½ teaspoon salt
¼ teaspoon pepper
1 cup chopped onion

In small mixing bowl, combine soup, water, salt and pepper. Spread evenly over chops. Top with chopped onion. Insert temperature probe so tip is in liquid on bottom of dish. Cover tightly with plastic wrap, arranging loosely around probe to vent. **Microwave at Automatic Simmer 4 to 5 Hours.** Check at minimum time.

Makes 6 servings.

VARIATIONS:
Soup: Substitute 1 can cream of celery, onion or other favorite cream soup for 1 can of the cream of mushroom soup.
Vegetables: Substitute 1 cup sliced celery for 1 cup chopped onion.
Cheese: After automatic simmering has been completed, top with 1 cup shredded cheddar cheese and **Microwave** uncovered **at High for 1 to 2 Minutes** to melt cheese.

Sausage and Tomato Stew

SAUSAGE AND TOMATO STEW

Of Polish origin, sometimes called Hunters Stew. Very hearty. Sauerkraut becomes mild over the long cooking period.

POWER LEVEL: Automatic Simmer
MICROWAVE TIME: 8 to 10 hr.

1 lb. polish sausage (kielbasa) sliced diagonally in 1-in. pieces
1 can (4-oz.) mushroom pieces, undrained
1 large apple, peeled, cored and sliced
1 can (1-lb.) sauerkraut, drained
1 medium onion, chopped
1 bay leaf
5 peppercorns
1 clove garlic, minced
1 can (1-lb.) tomatoes
2 strips microwaved bacon, crumbled

In 3-qt. casserole layer ½ of each of the following, in the order listed: sausage, mushrooms, apple, sauerkraut, onion, bay leaf, peppercorns, garlic and tomatoes. Sprinkle with all of bacon. Repeat layers. Insert temperature probe so tip rests in liquid in bottom of dish. Cover tightly with plastic wrap, arranging loosely around probe to vent. **Microwave at Automatic Simmer 8 to 10 Hours.**

Makes about 5 to 6 servings

SPARERIBS APPLES AND SAUERKRAUT

POWER LEVEL: High (10) and Automatic Simmer
MICROWAVE TIME: 4 to 6 hr.

3 to 3½ lb. lean pork spareribs, cut in serving pieces	In 13x9x2 in. dish place ribs cover. **Microwave at High 15 Minutes,** rearranging meat after 7 minutes. Drain off liquid.
1 teaspoon salt **¼ teaspoon pepper** **2 tablespoons bottled steak sauce** **2 apples, quartered, cored and sliced** **2 large onions, thinly sliced** **1 can (16-oz.) sauerkraut** **1 cup water**	Sprinkle salt and pepper over ribs. Evenly distribute steak sauce over tops. Cover with apple slices and undrained sauerkraut, then layer onions over top; add water. Insert temperature probe so tip rests in water on bottom of dish.

Cover tightly with plastic wrap, arranging loosely around probe to vent. Attach cable end at receptacle. **Microwave at Automatic Simmer 4 to 6 Hours.** If desired, sprinkle casserole with 1 teaspoon fresh or dried dill weed before serving.

Makes 3 to 4 servings

HAM AND SHRIMP CREOLE

Fresh onion and pepper, chopped, may be used; measure 1½ cups of each.

POWER LEVEL: Automatic Simmer
MICROWAVE TIME: 4 to 5 hours

2 lb. cooked ham cut in ¾″ cubes **2 cans (4½ oz.) whole shrimp, drained, reserve liquid** **2 cans (10-oz. each) condensed tomato bisque soup** **1 cup dry red wine** **1 pkg. (12-oz.) frozen chopped onion** **1 pkg. (12-oz.) frozen chopped green pepper** **1 pkg. (10-oz.) frozen chopped okra** **1 teaspoon creole seasoning or chili powder** **1 teaspoon salt** **½ teaspoon brown bouquet sauce** **¼ teaspoon pepper** **½ teaspoon hot pepper sauce (tabasco)** **Shrimp liquid plus water to total 1 cup**	In 4-qt. casserole, place the ham, shrimp, soup, wine, onion, pepper, okra, creole seasoning, salt, bouquet sauce, pepper and liquid pepper seasoning. Mix together very well. Press chunks of meat to submerge under liquid. Over back of spoon, gently pour shrimp liquid and water mixture onto top surface. Do not stir in. Insert temperature probe so tip rests on bottom of dish. Cover with plastic wrap, arranging loosely around probe to vent. Attach cable end at receptacle. **Microwave at Automatic Simmer 4 to 5 Hours.**

Stir before serving.

Makes about 6 servings

OLD-FASHIONED BAKED BEANS

POWER LEVEL: High (10) and Automatic Simmer
MICROWAVE TIME: 9 to 11 hours, total.

To Prepare Beans: In 4-qt. casserole, place **1½ lb. (3½ cups) navy (pea) beans** with enough **water** to cover, about 2 qts. Let stand at room temperature to soak several hours or overnight.

After soaking, drain water from beans and add **1 teaspoon soda, 1 teaspoon salt** and **6 cups hot water.** Cover casserole with lid or plastic wrap. **Microwave at High for 1 Hour,** stirring after 30 minutes until beans are almost tender. Drain.

1 cup brown sugar, packed **1 cup ketchup** **2 cups hot water** **½ cup chopped onion** **¼ cup prepared mustard** **¼ cup molasses** **¼ cup vinegar** **1 tablespoon salt** **6 slices bacon** **Additional ½ cup water**	In small mixing bowl stir together well the brown sugar, ketchup, water, onion, mustard, molasses, vinegar, and salt. Add and blend well into drained beans. Layer bacon on top of beans. Over back of spoon, gently pour additional water onto top surface; do not stir.

Cover tightly with plastic wrap, arranging loosely around probe to vent. Attach cable end at receptacle. **Microwave at Automatic Simmer 8 to 10 Hours.** Stir before serving.

Makes 8 to 10 servings.

BACON WITH FRESH GREEN BEANS

POWER LEVEL: High (10) and Automatic Simmer
MICROWAVE TIME: 10 to 11 hr.

9 slices bacon, cut in 1-in. pieces	In 3-qt. casserole place bacon pieces. **Microwave at High 4 to 5 Minutes,** until just partially cooked. Do not drain.
1 lb. fresh green beans washed and cut **2 onions, sliced** **2 cups water** **1 bay leaf, optional** **1 clove garlic, minced** **1 teaspoon salt** **¼ teaspoon pepper**	To bacon and fat in dish, add beans and stir. Cover with onions. In 1-qt. measure stir together water, bay leaf, garlic, salt and pepper. Add to casserole.

Insert temperature probe so tip rests in water on bottom of dish, halfway between center and side. Cover tightly with plastic wrap, arranging loosely around probe to vent. Attach cable end at receptacle. **Microwave at Automatic Simmer 10 to 11 Hours.**

Makes about 4 servings

VARIATION:

With Ham: Substitute ½ lb. ham cubes or pieces for bacon. Microwave as above.

Poultry

Slowly simmered chicken is an international favorite. It's tender, tasty and economical, too. With automatic simmering you can microwave stewing chickens or broiler-fryers, either fresh or frozen, without attention. Just put them in the pot and forget about them until dinner time.

STEWING CHICKEN

POWER LEVEL: Automatic Simmer
MICROWAVE TIME: 11 to 12 hr.

1 large onion, chopped **1 stewing chicken (4 to 6-lb.) cut up** **4 cups water** **2 tablespoons chicken bouillon granules** **1 teaspoon salt**	In 5-qt. casserole, spread out onions in even layer. Cover with chicken pieces, bony-side-up, with meatiest pieces to edges of dish. In small bowl mix water, bouillon granules and salt. Pour over chicken.

Insert temperature probe so tip rests in liquid on bottom of dish, halfway between center and edge. Cover tightly with plastic wrap, arranging loosely around probe to vent. Attach cable end at receptacle. **Microwave at Automatic Simmer 11 to 12 Hours.** Let pieces stand in broth until cool. Strip off skin and remove meat from bones. Skim fat from broth.

Makes about 1 qt. meat (about 8 servings)

CHICKEN 'N' DUMPLINGS: Prepare dough for Fluffy Dumplings (recipe with Bohemian Steak, Meat Chapter) or use favorite recipe. To broth in casserole, add the deboned and cut up chicken pieces along with a mixture of ¼ cup each cornstarch and cold water. **Microwave at High until hot and bubbly, 5 to 8 Minutes.** Drop dumplings around edges of dish. **Microwave at Medium 7 to 9 Minutes,** until dumplings appear set and dry.

CHICKEN 'N' NOODLES OR RICE: For noodle variation, prepare homemade noodles (recipe with Short Ribs, Meat Chapter) except do not dry them by microwaving; or use 1 to 1½ cups packaged egg noodles. After cooked meat has been removed, and fat skimmed off, **Microwave broth at High until boiling, 5 to 8 Minutes.** Add noodles or, for rice variation, add ¾ cup long grain rice and continue to **Microwave at High 10 to 12 Minutes** for noodles or **15 to 20 Minutes** for rice, until tender, stirring after half of time. Add deboned and cut up chicken. **Microwave at High 10 Minutes more,** until thickened, well blended and bubbly.

CHICKEN FRICASSEE

POWER LEVEL: Automatic Simmer and High (10)
MICROWAVE TIME: 11 to 12 hr.

2 medium onions, sliced **1 stewing chicken (4 to 6-lb.), cut up** **2 teaspoons salt** **1 teaspoon paprika** **1 bay leaf** **3 stalks celery, sliced** **2 carrots, pared and sliced** **1 cup chicken broth** **Water**	In 5-qt. casserole spread out onions in even layer. Cover with chicken pieces, bony-side-up with meatiest pieces to edges of dish. Sprinkle with salt, paprika and top with bay leaf. Add celery and carrots. Pour chicken broth over top. Add additional water to cover (up to 5 cups). Insert temperature probe so tip rests in broth on bottom of dish, halfway between center and side.

Cover tightly with plastic wrap, arranging loosely around probe to vent. Attach cable end at receptacle. **Microwave at Automatic Simmer 11 to 12 Hours.** Cool. Strip off skin and remove bones from chicken. Skim fat from broth and thicken (see below) just before serving.

To Thicken Broth: Stir together 1 cup flour, 1 teaspoon salt and 1 cup water well. Add chicken pieces to broth and stir in flour-water mixture. **Microwave at High 10 to 13 Minutes,** until hot and bubbly. Serve over mashed potatoes or noodles.

HOW TO STEW CHICKEN WITH AUTOMATIC SIMMER

 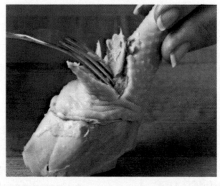 

Submerge chicken pieces in liquid and add seasoning. Place the probe with the tip in liquid halfway between the center and side of the dish.

Strip Meat from bones after microwaving. Use meat in cooked chicken recipes or return it to the casserole.

Vary chicken in broth by dropping dumplings on top or adding rice or noodles. Microwave as directed in the recipes on this page.

Simmered Chicken

SIMMERED CHICKEN

One of the simplest of ways to cook chicken, and one of the best.

POWER LEVEL: Automatic Simmer
MICROWAVE TIME: Fresh 4 to 6 hr.—
Frozen 5 to 7 hr.

1 whole chicken (2½ to 3½-lb.) Paprika 1 cup chicken broth	In 3-qt. casserole place chicken. Rub chicken with paprika. Add broth.

Insert temperature probe so tip is in liquid on bottom of dish. Cover tightly with plastic wrap, arranging loosely around probe to vent. Attach cable end at receptacle. **Microwave at Automatic Simmer 4 to 6 Hours** for fresh chicken; or **5 to 7 Hours** for frozen.

Makes 4 servings

SPANISH STYLE CHICKEN

This is a version of the famous Arroz Con Pollo.

POWER LEVEL: Automatic Simmer and High (10)
MICROWAVE TIME: 4 hr. to 6 hr.

1 chicken (2½ to 3½-lb.) cut up 1 teaspoon salt ¼ teaspoon pepper ¼ teaspoon chili powder 1 clove garlic, minced ⅛ teaspoon saffron powder 2 cups chicken broth 2 tablespoons sherry	In 3-qt. casserole, place chicken bony-side-up and meaty pieces around edges. Sprinkle with salt, pepper, chili powder, garlic and saffron. Add broth and sherry. Insert temperature probe so tip rests in liquid on bottom of dish, halfway between center and side.

Cover tightly with plastic wrap, arranging loosely around probe to vent. Attach cable end at receptacle. **Microwave at Automatic Simmer 4 to 6 Hours.**

TO FINISH: To casserole, **add 2 cups cooked rice, 1 pkg. (10-oz.) defrosted frozen peas and ½ cup sliced stuffed olives.** Cover and **Microwave at High 5 Minutes,** until vegetables are hot.

Makes 4 to 6 servings

CHICKEN IN ITALIAN SAUCE

Sometimes known as Chicken Marengo.

POWER LEVEL: Automatic Simmer and High (10)
MICROWAVE TIME: 4 to 6 hr.

1 chicken (2½ to 3½-lb.) cut up 1 pkg. (1½-oz.) spaghetti sauce mix ½ cup water or dry white wine	In 2-qt. casserole, place chicken bony-side-up and meaty pieces around edges. Stir together sauce mix and liquid; pour over top.

Insert temperature probe so tip rests in liquid on bottom of dish, halfway between center and side. Cover tightly with plastic wrap, arranging loosely around probe to vent. Attach cable end at receptacle. **Microwave at Automatic Simmer 4 to 6 Hours.**
Garnish as described below.

To Garnish: Stir **2 peeled fresh tomatoes,** cut in quarters and **¼ lb. fresh mushrooms,** cut in ½-in. slices, into chicken. **Microwave at High 5 Minutes** to heat. If desired, serve with ½ cup sliced black olives and ¼ cup snipped fresh parsley. Serve over rice.

CHICKEN IN WINE

Coq au Vin is its French name. This makes a delicious supper when served with rice and a salad.

POWER LEVEL: Automatic Simmer
MICROWAVE TIME: 4 to 6 hr.

1 medium onion, chopped (¾ cup) 1 chicken (2½ to 3½-lb.) cut up 1 tablespoon paprika 3 tablespoons minute tapioca Sauce (below)	In 3-qt. casserole, spread onion evenly. Rub paprika on chicken then arrange chicken bony-side-up with meaty pieces around edges. Sprinkle with tapioca. Pour sauce (below) over all. Insert temperature probe so tip rests in sauce on bottom of dish. Cover tightly with plastic wrap, arranging loosely around the probe to vent. Attach cable end at receptacles. **Microwave at Automatic Simmer 4 to 6 Hours.**
1 lb. large fresh mushrooms, quartered 2 tablespoons fresh snipped parsley	Add mushrooms and parsley to casserole. Cover and **Microwave at High 5 Minutes** to heat.

Makes about 4 servings.

Sauce: In small bowl stir together **1 cup white wine, ½ bay leaf, ½ teaspoon thyme, 1 teaspoon salt and ⅛ teaspoon freshly ground pepper.**

Soups & Sauces

With automatic simmering you can microwave good, old-fashioned soups, mellowed sauces and the full-bodied broth essential to many Italian, French and Chinese recipes. Freeze poultry carcasses, or roast bones with some meat on them, until you have enough for stock. If you bone meat before cooking, save these scraps, too. When making stock for soup, add extra chicken backs or beef soup bones for flavor.

Split Pea Soup

BEAN SOUP

POWER LEVEL: High (10) and Automatic Simmer
MICROWAVE TIME: 13 to 15 hr.

1 lb. navy beans **Water**	Wash and sort beans. Place in 4-qt. casserole with water to cover and soak overnight. In the morning, drain beans and add 6 cups fresh water. **Microwave uncovered at High 60 Minutes.**
1 meaty ham bone **or 2 cups diced** **cooked ham** **1 cup celery, finely** **chopped** **1 onion, finely chopped** **2 tablespoons parsley,** **finely chopped** **1 teaspoon salt** **¼ teaspoon pepper** **1 bay leaf** **3 cups water**	To beans, add ham, celery, onion, parsley, salt, pepper, bay leaf and additional 3 cups water. Insert temperature probe so tip rests in liquid on bottom of dish, halfway between center and side. Cover tightly with plastic wrap, arranging loosely around probe to vent. Attach cable end at receptacle.

Microwave at Automatic Simmer 12 to 14 Hours, until beans are very tender. Remove ham bone and bay leaf. Cut meat off bone, return meat to bean soup. Serve hot.

Makes 8 to 10 servings.

CHICKEN NOODLE SOUP

A very nice chicken soup may be made by adding about 1-qt. chicken broth to Chicken 'N' Noodles, page 51.

SPLIT PEA SOUP

For a creamy version of this chunky soup, puree in blender before returning ham to soup.

POWER LEVEL: High (10) and Automatic Simmer
MICROWAVE TIME: 13 to 15 hr.

1 lb. dried split peas	In 5-qt. casserole place peas with water to cover. Soak overnight. Drain. Add 6 cups fresh water. **Microwave uncovered at High 60 Minutes.**
1 can (1 lb.) **tomatoes, cut up** **1½ cups sliced carrots** **1 cup chopped celery** **¾ cup chopped onion** **1 clove garlic, minced** **1 teaspoon salt** **1 meaty ham bone or** **boneless ham** **chunks** **2 cups water**	Add tomatoes, carrots, celery, onion, garlic and salt. Stir well and add ham bone. Over the back of a spoon, gently pour the additional 2 cups water onto top surface; do not stir in. See tip with chili, this section. Insert temperature probe so tip is in liquid touching bottom of dish. Cover tightly with plastic wrap, arranging loosely around probe to vent.

Attach cable end at receptacle. **Microwave at Automatic Simmer 12 to 14 Hours.** Cut meat off bone and return to soup.

Makes about 12 servings.

HOW TO MAKE BASIC STOCK

Save meat and bones until you have enough. (See Basic Beef Stock.) Add water, seasonings and carrots, onions and celery tops for flavor.

Strip meat from bones after microwaving and return it to stock when making soup. Or, strain stock and freeze for broth.

Skim fat if using immediately, or refrigerate stock until fat solidifies and can be lifted off.

BASIC BEEF STOCK

Substitute 1 to 2 lb. bony chicken pieces for beef to make chicken stock.

POWER LEVEL: Automatic Simmer
MICROWAVE TIME: 4 to 6 hr.

2-3 lbs. soup bones or beef shortribs
1 teaspoon salt
1 teaspoon celery salt
1 small onion, chopped
1 cup diced carrots
½ cup diced celery
Water

In 5-qt. casserole place meaty bones, salt, celery salt, onion, carrots, celery and water to cover. Insert temperature probe so tip rests on bottom of dish, halfway between center and side. Cover tightly with plastic wrap, arranging loosely around probe to vent. Attach cable end at receptacle. **Microwave at Automatic Simmer 4 to 6 Hours.** Remove fat from surface. Remove meat from bones; chop and return to broth.

Makes about 2½ quarts stock.

Make Soup or Basic Stock
ahead and freeze in one cup containers. Defrost rapidly by microwaving when ready to use. Any main dishes which call for water will taste richer if you substitute stock.

MINESTRONE

The popular Italian vegetable soup.

POWER LEVEL: Automatic Simmer
MICROWAVE TIME: Stock 4 to 6 hr.—
                Soup 6 to 8 hr.

Basic Beef Stock (recipe left)
1 medium onion, chopped
2 carrots, diced
2 stalks celery with tops sliced
1 cup diced leaks, optional
1 can (1-lb.) tomatoes
1 pkg. (10-oz.) frozen mixed vegetables
½ cup uncooked vermicelli, broken into 2-in. pieces
1 zucchini, sliced
1 cup shredded cabbage
2 teaspoons dried basil
1 clove garlic, minced
1 tablespoon salt
1 teaspoon oregano
1 can (6-oz.) tomato paste
Water

Prepare stock in 5-qt. casserole as in recipe. Cool and return meat and marrow from bones to stock. Add onion, carrots, celery, leeks, tomatoes, mixed vegetables, vermicelli, zucchini, cabbage, basil, garlic, salt and oregano. Add tomato paste for heartier flavor. Submerge the chunks beneath broth surface, add additional water if needed to cover. Insert temperature probe so tip rests on bottom of dish, halfway between center and side. Cover lightly with plastic wrap, arranging loosely around probe to vent. Attach cable end at receptacle. **Microwave at Automatic Simmer 6 to 8 Hours.** To serve, ladle into bowls and sprinkle with Parmesan cheese. Serve with crusty bread.

Makes 8 to 10 servings

VEGETABLE BEEF SOUP

POWER LEVEL: Automatic Simmer
MICROWAVE TIME: Stock 4 to 6 hrs.—
                  Soup 3 to 4 hrs.

Basic Beef Stock .... **(recipe opposite page)**	Prepare stock in 5-qt. casserole as in recipe. Cool and return meat and marrow from bones to stock.
2 cups diced, peeled .... **potatoes** **1 can (1-lb.) whole kernel corn, undrained** **1 can (1-lb.) tomatoes, cut up** **2 diced, peeled turnips** **1 can (6-oz.) tomato paste** **4 beef bouillon cubes** **½ teaspoon marjoram** **½ teaspoon salt** **¼ teaspoon pepper**	Add potatoes, corn, tomatoes, turnips, tomato paste, bouillon, marjoram, salt and pepper. Stir. With back of spoon press meat and vegetable chunks to submerge under water. Insert temperature probe so tip rests in liquid on bottom of dish, halfway between center and side. Cover tightly with plastic wrap, arranging loosely around probe to vent. Attach cable end at receptacle. **Microwave at Automatic Simmer 3 to 4 Hours.**

Makes 8 to 10 servings

Vegetable Soup

SPAGHETTI SAUCE

If desired, you can omit sauteeing the onion in butter by lengthening simmering time 2 hours.

POWER LEVEL: High (10) and Automatic Simmer
MICROWAVE TIME: 3 to 4 hr.

2 cups chopped onion ...... **2 tablespoons butter**	In 3-qt. casserole, place onion and butter. **Microwave at High 4 to 5 Minutes,** until onion is slightly cooked.
2 cans (1-lb. 14-oz.) .... **tomatoes, cut up** **2 cans (6-oz.) tomato paste** **½ cup snipped parsley** **¼ cup brown sugar** **2 teaspoons salt** **1 tablespoon dried oregano, crushed** **½ teaspoon dried thyme, crushed** **2 bay leaves**	Add tomatoes, tomato paste, parsley, brown sugar, salt, oregano, thyme, and bay leaves. Mix together well. Insert temperature probe so tip is in liquid on bottom of dish. Cover tightly with plastic wrap, arranging loosely around probe to vent. Attach cable end at receptacle. **Microwave at Automatic Simmer 3 to 4 Hours.**

Makes 2 to 3 quarts

TIP: Freeze in ice cube trays. When frozen hard, remove to plastic bags. Only amounts needed can be easily thawed and/or heated.

MARINARA SAUCE

This sauce starts with convenience ingredients and results 3 to 4 hours later, in a rich homemade taste. Serve with meatballs, spaghetti or chicken.

POWER LEVEL: Automatic Simmer
MICROWAVE TIME: 3 to 4 hr.

1 jar (2-lb) spaghetti .... **sauce** **1 can (28-oz.) tomatoes, cut up** **1 can (16-oz.) stewed tomatoes, cut up** **1 can (10½-oz.) tomato puree** **1 cup onion, chopped** **½ cup red cooking wine** **1 tablespoon sugar** **2 teaspoons garlic powder** **1 teaspoon thyme**	In 4-qt. casserole mix together spaghetti sauce, tomatoes, stewed tomatoes, tomato puree, onion, wine, sugar, garlic powder and thyme. Insert temperature probe so tip rests on bottom of dish, halfway between center and side. Cover tightly with plastic wrap, arranging loosely around probe to vent. Attach cable end at receptacle. **Microwave at Automatic Simmer 3 to 4 Hours.**

Makes 2 to 3 quarts.

Temperature Holding

Scrambled Eggs remain tender and flavorful for late risers. Eggs pictured above were microwaved ¾ minute per egg, then covered with plastic wrap and held with temperature hold setting at 150° on Low (3) Power for 30 minutes.

If your oven has a temperature hold setting, use it to keep foods at serving temperature while you're preparing other foods, setting the table or while waiting for latecomers. Microwaved foods are characteristically moist and tender. Temperature hold is designed to keep many vegetables, casseroles, and even scrambled eggs hot and ready to serve even after they are finished microwaving. Roasts, ham and poultry, too, may be kept table ready with this feature. You can even warm up leftovers.

The temperature hold cycle can be used as the last step in automatic time cooking or temperature cooking. When cooking, remember the temperature probe must be placed in the food for the oven to work at the temperature hold setting. For temperature cooking and holding, you can choose one finished temperature and power level for the cooking cycle and, if you want, another temperature and power level for the temperature hold cycle. Temperature hold does not turn off automatically so you can control the holding time.

Holding Times of two hours or less are recommended for best eating results and, in some foods, to prevent spoilage which can occur in milk and egg mixtures. The exceptions are simmer cooking and cultured food recipes, such as yogurt. The temperature probe must always be used.

Holding Temperatures for most foods must be 150° or above, to prevent spoilage. This Mexican Chicken Casserole has been held 1½ hours at 155° at Medium power.

Solid Meat Roasts, because they are uncut and interior areas have never been exposed to air or bacteria, may be held at temperatures below 150°. This excludes rolled and tied roasts. See section on temperature holding meats, on the following pages.

MICROLESSON

Practically any food suitable for temperature controlled cooking can be temperature held in your microwave oven. The temperature hold setting requires the temperature probe. As with any form of temperature cooking, correct placement of probe is important in assuring good results. Because microwaved foods tend to stay moist and fresh tasting, temperature holding is a good way to keep foods hot and appealing prior to serving them.

Tender Vegetables stay fresh and colorful. These frozen green beans and fresh carrots were held for 30 minutes at Medium (5) power level. In most cases, vegetables should be covered with plastic wrap during cooking and holding for best results.

Lasagna, Moist Casseroles and Soups develop richer flavor when held at 150° to 160° at Medium (5) power. Use the temperature hold feature, to reheat these main dish meals straight from the refrigerator. Saucy and liquid foods should be stirred occasionally when reheating.

Hot Beverages and Party Punches can be held at a serving temperature of 150° to 160°. Children's drinks are more suitable at 130°. Alcoholic punches retain their alcohol content if temperature does not exceed 165°.

MICROLESSON: HOW TO AUTOMATIC SIMMER OR SLOW COOK RECIPES WITH TEMP HOLD

Recipes in the automatic simmer section on preceeding pages were especially developed for long, slow cooking. If you do not have the automatic simmer feature, you can manually set Temp Hold at 180° and Medium (5) power to achieve the same flavor and tenderness, using those recipes.

To speed up the simmering process, use the method pictured to the right. You can cut the time in half for most simmer-cooking recipes with no risk of toughening because with the temperature probe you do not exceed the recommended temperature.

Food cooked by the method at right may not be as flavorful or tender as with slower cooking. Stirring and attention are necessary, but time will be shorter.

HOW TO SPEED UP AUTOMATIC SIMMER RECIPES

STEP 1:
Temperature cook the simmer recipe at High (10) power until it reaches 185° (approximately one hour). While at High power, stir or rearrange food about every 15 minutes.

STEP 2:
Temperature hold at 185° and Medium High (7) power level for half of the time stated in the recipe. Stir or rearrange occasionally.

A strip of foil around the top of a large beef roast helps promote cooking from top to bottom.

Temperature Holding Meats

Medium and well-done meats may be microwaved and temperature held for serving, following the instructions below. As in conventional cooking, rare roasts should not be held after cooking or before eating. Because degree of doneness for rare is more critical than for other meats, temperature hold should not be used.

When microwaving beef roasts as large as 5 lbs., much heat is stored in the exterior of the meat where microwaves have penetrated. This heat further cooks the meat during the holding period by spreading to the interior of the roast.

For example, a 5 lb. standing rib roast such as the one pictured at left may be temperature cooked to 115° at Low (3) and then temperature held at 120°, Warm (1) for 2 hours. Stored heat will continue to cook the roast until the inside temperature has risen to 140° or 145°. This rise in heat registers on the oven's temperature display. Although the internal temperature before holding this roast was for very rare, stored heat cooked it to medium during the holding period.

If you plan to temperature hold your beef roast after microwaving, allow for the extra cooking by stored heat. Undercook the roast about 20° to 25°, then temperature hold at desired serving temperature.

TIP: *If you have already microwaved your beef roast before deciding to temperature hold it, remove from oven and let it stand uncovered for 10-15 minutes before temperature holding. This releases some of the stored heat.*

Whole Chicken or Turkey Breast may be microwaved as recommended in this cookbook, then temperature hold it at 170°, Medium (5) power, until serving, or temperature hold medium size turkeys which you have conventionally roasted.

Pork Loin or Rib Roasts should be microwaved at Medium (5) power to 170°, following the directions given in this cookbook. Temperature hold 170° and Low (3) power.

Basic Meat Loaf is cooked at High (10) power to 165° (5° less than recommended in the recipe in this cookbook). Temperature hold at 150°, Medium (5) power. Hold ham loaves and other ground meat loaves at 150°.

MICROLESSON: TEMPERATURE HOLDING OTHER FOODS

Time, as well as temperature and power level, has an effect on the quality of temperature held foods. Delicate foods or bright colored vegetables, such as green peas, may be held only a limited amount of time before showing signs of over-cooking. Using lower power levels extends this time somewhat, but change of texture and loss of color and freshness will occur if they are held for extended periods of time.

Compare peas held for different time periods at 150° and Medium (5) power level. The peas held for 30 minutes are still tender and fresh appearing. Peas held for one hour show some signs of overcooking. Peas held for 1½ hours look brown and shriveled.

Appetizers such as Sweet Tart Franks and Meatballs Hawaiian (recipes in this cookbook) may be kept hot at 150° and Low (3) power level to replenish party trays. When holding two similar type dishes together at one temperature, place temperature probe in center of the larger dish.

Desserts such as compotes and bakery pies taste appealing when warm. Use Medium power. Hold fruit desserts at 150° and fruit or nut pies at 110° to 120°. Hold chocolate sauce at 125°.

Deli Foods or foods you have barbe-qued, baked or grilled, may be held with temperature hold. Refer to heating guide inside front cover for suggested serving temperatures.

Homemade Yogurt

HOMEMADE YOGURT

Start the first batch with 2 tablespoons commercial yogurt, then save out yogurt from each homemade batch as a starter for the next one. Serve with fruit or other topping.

POWER LEVEL: High and Medium High
MICROWAVE TIME: See Recipe

In 1½ qt. casserole place **1 cup water, 1 cup milk** and **1 cup non-fat dry milk.** Stir until well blended. Insert temperature probe so tip rests on center bottom of casserole. **Set Temp., Set 180°. Microwave at High.** Remove from oven and let stand uncovered on counter until mixture has cooled to 110°, about 1 hour.

To cooled mixture, add **2 tablespoons plain all-natural yogurt** and blend well. Insert temperature probe and cover with plastic wrap. **Microwave at Medium High. Set Temp Hold. Set 110°. Temp Hold for 4 hours.** Refrigerate and serve as desired.

Appetizers & Hot Snacks

Microwaving makes exciting hot appetizers and snacks as easy to serve as the more ordinary cold ones. A minute or two after your guests arrive, you can offer them hot and tempting nibbles to stimulate appetites and conversation. Since all the preparation is done ahead, you can serve an unusual variety without last minute fuss.

Many fully prepared packaged and frozen appetizers today have microwave cooking directions on the package. Use the directions provided and check the following pages for additional convenience appetizer ideas.

1. Bacon Poles, page 67
2. Seaside Cheese Dip, page 65
3. Curried Pineapple and Piggies, page 66
4. Cheese Crock, page 65

MICROLESSON:

Appetizers and snacks are among the easiest food to microwave. On these pages you'll find the basic principles of microwaving which assure success, some possibilities unique to microwave, and helpful ideas for using your microwave oven to make entertaining easier and more varied.

For best results follow these techniques and recipe directions carefully. Apply the principles for successful microwaving, as described earlier in this book, when preparing appetizers and hot snacks.

Arrange pieces, such as meatball, mushrooms or canapes in a circle for even heating. To serve, place a bowl of sauce or another snack, such as pretzels, in center.

The Temperature Probe turns the oven off when dips such as Chili Con Queso, page 64 reach correct serving temperature. Stir dip well before serving.

Dry Mixtures, such as Party Mix, page 67, must be stirred, as in conventional cooking, but they cook much faster in the microwave oven.

Wooden or Plastic Picks, even those with frills, may be used in the microwave oven. Use bamboo skewers instead of metal, when making kabobs.

Cover foods according to the amount of moisture needed. Paper towels absorb it, waxed paper holds in a little, plastic wrap and lids seal it in.

Soften Cream Cheese for spreads or dips by removing foil wrap and microwaving at **Medium** 1 to 1½ Minutes.

Dry Croutons, page 67, for snacks, using leftover bread, herbs and butter. Also great for salads and soups.

Sloppy Joe Filling, canned or deli, spooned on buttered bun, makes an easy snack in ½ Minute at High.

Warm Cheese from refrigerator ½ to 1 Minute at Medium High which makes it easier to slice.

Use Paper Plates for heating and serving. Let guests microwave their own hors d'oeuvres.

Shell Nuts easily. Microwave 2 cups pecan or Brazil nuts in 1 cup water 4 to 5 Minutes at High.

Soften Tortillas and crepes in their package or by wrapping them in a damp towel and warming at High ½ to 1 Minute.

Refresh Salty Snacks, by microwaving a few seconds at High. Let stand to crisp.

For Fast Canapes, spread ham salad or cheese spread on crackers. Microwave at High a few seconds.

SOUR CREAM DIPS WITH VARIATIONS

POWER LEVEL: Low (3)   TEMP: 90°
APPROX. MICROWAVE TIME: 4 to 5 min.

1. Use **1 cup (8-oz.) dairy sour cream** as a basis for the following variations. In 1-qt. casserole or microwave ovenproof bowl, stir sour cream together with ingredients of one of the variations. Insert temperature probe so tip is in center of dip. Cover with plastic wrap, arranging loosely around probe to vent.

2. Attach cable end at receptacle. **Microwave at Low. Set Temp, Set 90°.** Stir before serving.

NOTE: Due to the delicate nature of sour cream, it is best microwaved at **Low.**

VARIATIONS:

ONION DIP

1 packet (½ of 2⅞-oz. box) onion soup mix
1 teaspoon lemon juice
1 tablespoon sherry wine (optional)
Makes about 1 cup

ZIPPY DIP

2 tablespoons chili sauce
1 tablespoon minced green pepper
Makes about 1 cup

DEVILED HAM DIP

1 can (4½-oz.) deviled ham
2 tablespoons chopped green olives
2 teaspoons instant minced onion
⅛ teaspoon pepper
Makes about 1½ cups

PUB DIP

POWER LEVEL: Medium (5)   TEMP: 120°
APPROX. MICROWAVE TIME: 4 to 5 min.
Cook Code: 45

2 jars (5-oz. each) . . . . . . **sharp Old English cheese spread, softened**	In 1½-qt. casserole stir together cheeses, beer, Worchestershire sauce and pepper sauce. Insert temperature probe so tip is in center of dip. Attach cable end at receptacle. **Microwave at Medium. Set Temp, Set 120°.**
1 pkg. (8-oz.) cream cheese, softened	
⅓ cup beer	
1 teaspoon Worcestershire sauce	
5 to 6 drops hot pepper sauce (optional)	
4 strips bacon, ... **microwaved crisp and crumbled**	When oven signals, stir in crumbled bacon. Serve with pretzels, crackers or other crisp dippers.

Makes about 1½ cups

CREAM CHEESE DIPS WITH VARIATIONS

POWER LEVEL: Medium (5)   TEMP: 120°
APPROX. MICROWAVE TIME: 4 to 7 min.
Cook Code: 45

1. Use **1 pkg. (8-oz.) cream cheese** as a basis for the following variations. In 1-qt. casserole place cream cheese. **Microwave at Medium 1 to 2 Minutes,** to soften. Stir in ingredients of one of the variations. Insert temperature probe so tip is in center of dip. Cover with plastic wrap, arranging loosely around probe to vent.

2. Attach cable end at receptacle. **Microwave at Medium. Set Temp, Set 120°.** Stir before serving.

VARIATIONS:

SHRIMP DIP

1 can (7-oz.) broken shrimp, drained
2 teaspoons ketchup
1 teaspoon instant minced onion
1 teaspoon prepared mustard
1 teaspoon Worcestershire sauce
¼ teaspoon garlic salt
Makes about 2 cups

HOT CRAB DIP

1 can (6 to 8-oz.) crab meat, drained and flaked
2 tablespoons milk
1 tablespoon instant minced onion
1 tablespoon lemon juice
1 tablespoon sherry wine (optional)
1½ teaspoons grated lemon rind
1 teaspoon cream-style horseradish
Makes about 2 cups

CHILI CON QUESO DIP

Served fondue style, and accompanied by a salad, Chili Con Queso makes a nice informal luncheon. Dip is very thick and should be served with sturdy dippers such as large tortilla chips.

POWER LEVEL: Medium High (7)   TEMP: 140°
APPROX. MICROWAVE TIME: 8 to 11 min.
Cook Code: 87

1 lb. block pasteurized . . . . . **processed cheese, diced in 1½-in. pieces**	In 1½-qt. casserole stir together diced cheese and chili.
1 can (1-lb.) chili with beans	

Insert temperature probe so tip is in center of dip. Attach cable end at receptacle. **Microwave at Medium High. Set Temp, Set 140°.**
When oven signals, stir well. Let stand a few minutes before serving. Serve with tortilla chips.

Makes about 3 cups

SEASIDE CHEESE DIP

POWER LEVEL: Medium (5)   TEMP: 120°
APPROX. MICROWAVE TIME: 4 to 6 min.
Cook Code: 45

1 can (6½-oz.) minced or chopped clams	Drain clams, saving ¼ cup juice. In 1½-qt. casserole place drained clams, with reserved juice, along with sharp cheese spread, cream cheese, Worcestershire sauce, pepper and onion. Stir together well.
2 jars (5-oz. each) sharp Old English cheese spread, softened	
1 pkg. (8-oz.) cream cheese, softened	
1 tablespoon Worcestershire sauce	
½ medium green pepper, chopped (about ⅓ cup)	
2 green onions, chopped (about 2 tablespoons)	

Attach cable end at receptacle. **Microwave at Medium. Set Temp, Set 120°.**
When oven signals, stir before serving. Excellent with fresh raw vegetables such as celery, cucumbers, radishes and cauliflowerets.

Makes about 2 cups

CHEESE CROCK

Cheese Crock may be used immediately; however, aging truly improves the flavor, and makes an excellent gift.

POWER LEVEL: Medium (5)   **Cook Code:** 35
MICROWAVE TIME: 3 to 5 min., total

4 cups (1-lb.) shredded sharp cheddar cheese	In large glass mixing bowl place cheeses. **Microwave at Medium 3 to 5 Minutes** until soft, stirring after 2 minutes. Stir in brandy, oil, salt and mustard. Beat well until thoroughly blended. Mixture will be soft and creamy. Pack into a container with a tight-fitting lid or cover well. Refrigerate 1 week to age before using. Spread on crackers or cocktail rye rounds.
1 pkg. (3-oz.) cream cheese	
2 to 3 tablespoons brandy	
1 to 2 tablespoons olive oil	
1 teaspoon garlic salt	
1 teaspoon dry mustard	

Makes about 3 cups

Soft Smokey Cheese Ball

SOFT SMOKEY CHEESE BALL

This cheese ball is soft and easily spreadable on crackers. For a more smokey flavor, add a few drops liquid smoke or smoke-flavored salt to taste.

POWER LEVEL: High (10)
MICROWAVE TIME: 2 to 2¼ min., total

1 roll-shaped pkg. (6-oz.) smokey cheese spread	Unwrap cheeses. In 1½-qt. casserole place smokey cheese. **Microwave at High 1 Minute.** Add cream cheese. **Microwave at High 1 to 1¼ Minutes** more, until cheeses can be mixed together. Add Worcestershire sauce and blend mixture well. Stir in shredded cheese. Mixture should remain gold-flecked.
2 pkgs. (3-oz. each) cream cheese	
1 teaspoon Worcestershire sauce	
1 cup (4-oz.) shredded sharp cheddar cheese	
½ cup chopped fresh parsley	Chill cheese mixture about 15 to 30 minutes in freezer or about 1 hour in refrigerator, until it can be formed into a ball with the hands. Roll cheese ball in parsley, then pecans. Chill to set. Serve with crackers.
½ cup chopped pecans	

Makes 1 (14-oz.) cheese ball

CHEESE PASTRY SNACKS

POWER LEVEL: High (10)   **Cook Code:** 30
MICROWAVE TIME: 2¾ to 3¼ min., per plate

1 cup (4-oz.) shredded cheddar cheese **¾ cup unsifted all-purpose flour** **¾ cup coarsely crushed crisp rice cereal** **½ cup chopped walnuts** **½ teaspoon garlic salt** **⅓ cup butter, softened** **6 strips crisp cooked bacon, crumbled** **2 tablespoons cold water**	In large mixing bowl mix together cheese, flour, cereal, walnuts, garlic salt, butter, bacon and water with a fork until a dough forms. Drop 7 level tablespoonfuls in a circle onto each of 3 lightly buttered plates suitable for microwave. (Butter plates only around edges, where dough will be placed.)
Paprika	Sprinkle with paprika. Microwave one plate at a time.

Microwave at High 2¾ to 3¼ Minutes, rotating dish ¼ turn after 1½ minutes. Dough will be slightly puffed when done and will crisp on drying. Remove immediately from plate. Serve hot or cold. Repeat with remaining mixture.

Makes 21 snacks

ALMOND FILLED CHEESE BALLS

POWER LEVEL: High (10)   **Cook Code:** 10
MICROWAVE TIME: ¾ to 1¼ min., per plate

2 tablespoons soft butter **1 cup (4-oz.) shredded sharp cheese** **½ cup unsifted all-purpose flour** **Dash cayenne pepper** **½ teaspoon celery seed**	In small mixing bowl, mix together butter and cheese until smooth. Add flour, pepper and celery seed, blending well, kneading dough with hands if necessary to form a ball.
1 pkg. (3-oz.) hickory smoked, barbecue or cheese flavored almonds	Measure dough by level teaspoonfuls and shape smoothly around each almond to form a ball.

Place 9 balls in a circle on each of 4 paper plates. **Microwave at High ¾ to 1¼ Minutes,** rotating dish ¼ turn after ½ minute. Dough will be slightly puffy and dry when cooked. Remove from dish and cool a few minutes before serving. Repeat, cooking all cheese balls.

Makes about 3 dozen cheese balls

Arrange cheese balls in a ring around the outside of the dish so heat can penetrate evenly.

CURRIED PINEAPPLE AND PIGGIES

A Brown 'N Sear dish recipe. Serve with toothpicks.

POWER LEVEL: High (10)
MICROWAVE TIME: 6½ min., total

1 pkg. (8-oz.) brown 'n' serve sausages, cut crosswise in halves **1 can (13-oz.) pineapple chunks, drained** **Curry powder** **Seasoned salt**	Preheat Brown 'N Sear Dish by placing in microwave oven, uncovered. **Microwave at High 4 Minutes.** Add sausages and cover. **Microwave at High 1 Minute.** Turn sausages over. Add pineapple and sprinkle with curry powder and seasoning salt. Cover. **Microwave at High 1½ Minutes** more, until hot.

Makes 8 to 12 appetizer servings

CRAB-SWISS CRISPS

POWER LEVEL: Medium High (7)
MICROWAVE TIME: ¾ to 1 min., per plate

1 can (7½-oz.) crab, drained and flaked **1½ tablespoons sliced green onion** **1¼ cup shredded Swiss cheese** **½ cup mayonnaise** **1 teaspoon lemon juice** **¼ teaspoon curry powder** **36 crisp round crackers**	Combine crab, onion, cheese, mayonnaise, lemon juice and curry powder. Shortly before serving, place level teaspoonful on each cracker round. Place appetizers in circle on paper plates or other plates suitable for microwave oven. Cook about 12 at a time. **Microwave at Medium High ¾ to 1 Minute,** rotating dish ¼ turn after ½ minute, until hot.

Makes 36 appetizers

MEXICAN CORN CHIP SNACKS

A version of the popular Nachos.

POWER LEVEL: High (10)
MICROWAVE TIME: ¼ to ½ min., per plate

Large corn chips (plain or taco flavored) **Jalapeno bean dip or refried beans** **Hot pepper cheese**	Mound about 1 teaspoon bean dip or refried bean mixture on each tortilla corn chip. Top with ⅛-in. thick slice of cheese, to cover bean dip. Place 8 to 12 pieces in circle on paper plate or small pottery plate, leaving center space open. **Microwave at High ¼ to ½ Minute,** until cheese is melted.

BACON POLES

POWER LEVEL: High (10)
MICROWAVE TIME: See Recipe
Cook Code for 20 sticks: 90—for 7 sticks: 30

10 strips bacon . . . . **20 long, thin garlic bread sticks or sesame bread sticks**	.With scissors, cut bacon strips in half lengthwise, making 2 long, thin strips from each slice. Wrap one strip in a spiral "barber pole fashion" around each bread stick.

TO MICROWAVE ENTIRE RECIPE: Place 2 paper towels in bottom of 13×9×2-in. dish. Distribute wrapped bread sticks so they don't touch each other. Cover with paper towel. **Microwave at High 9 to 12 Minutes,** rotating dish ½ turn after 5 minutes, until bacon is cooked.

TO MICROWAVE 7: On each of 3 microwave-safe pottery or china plates, place 2 thicknesses of paper towels. Arrange wrapped bread sticks on top. Cover with paper towel. **Microwave each plate at High 2½ to 4 Minutes,** until bacon is cooked.

Total recipe makes 20

CROUTONS ITALIANO

POWER LEVEL: High (10)
MICROWAVE TIME: 10 to 12 min., total

1½ qts. bread cubes . . . . . **(6 cups)**	.In 12×8×2-in. dish place cubes. **Microwave at High 6 Minutes,** stirring every 2 minutes, until cubes begin to dry.
2 tablespoons Italian herb seasoning **½ teaspoon garlic salt** **½ cup (¼-lb.) melted butter**	.Sprinkle herb seasoning and garlic salt evenly over bread cubes. Drizzle with butter, tossing to coat cubes.

Microwave at High 4 to 6 Minutes, stirring every minute, until crisp and dry.

Makes 1½ quarts

PARTY MIX

POWER LEVEL: High (10)
MICROWAVE TIME: 6 to 7 min., total

6 tablespoons butter . . . . **4 teaspoons Worcestershire sauce** **1 teaspoon seasoned salt**	.In 13×9×2-in. dish place butter, Worcestershire sauce and salt. **Microwave at High 1 Minute,** or until butter is melted. Stir well.
2 cups corn chex . . . . . . **2 cups wheat chex** **2 cups rice chex** **2 cups thin stick pretzels** **1½ cups (12-oz.) mixed nuts**	.Add cereals, pretzels and nuts, mixing thoroughly to coat. **Microwave at High 5 to 6 Minutes,** stirring after 3 minutes, until evenly toasted.

Makes about 2½ quarts

Sugar Glazed Walnuts & Toasted Butter Pecans

SUGAR GLAZED WALNUTS

POWER LEVEL: High (10)
MICROWAVE TIME: 6 to 8 min., total

½ cup (¼-lb.) butter	.In 1½-qt. casserole place butter. **Microwave at High 1 Minute,** or until melted.
1 cup brown sugar (packed) **1 teaspoon cinnamon**	.Stir in brown sugar and cinnamon. **Microwave at High 2 Minutes.** Mix well to combine butter and sugar.
1 lb. walnut halves or large pieces (about 4 cups)	.Add nuts and mix to coat. **Microwave at High 3 to 5 Minutes.** Spread out onto wax paper and cool slightly. Serve warm or cold.

Makes 1 pound

TOASTED BUTTER PECANS

POWER LEVEL: High (10) **Cook Code:** 50
MICROWAVE TIME: 5 to 6 min., total

1 lb. pecan halves . . . . **(about 4 cups)** **1 tablespoon seasoned salt** **¼ cup butter**	.In 1½-qt. casserole place pecan halves. Sprinkle with seasoned salt. Cut butter into 4 pieces and arrange evenly over top.

Microwave at High 5 to 6 Minutes. Mix to evenly distribute butter. Serve warm or cold.

Makes 1 pound

Tacos

TACOS

POWER LEVEL: High (10)
MICROWAVE TIME: 11 to 13 min., total

1 lb. ground chuck
    beef
½ cup chopped onion
½ cup chopped green
    pepper
1 clove garlic, minced
	In 2-qt. casserole break up ground beef in very small chunks. Add onion, green pepper and garlic. Cover. **Microwave at High 6 to 7 Minutes,** stirring every 2 minutes. Drain well.

1 can (8-oz.) tomato
    sauce
1 teaspoon
    Worcestershire
    sauce
⅛ to ¼ teaspoon
    cayenne pepper
½ teaspoon chili powder
½ teaspoon salt
	Add tomato sauce, Worcestershire sauce, pepper, chili powder and salt. Cover. **Microwave at High 5 to 6 Minutes,** stirring after 3 minutes.

Use meat to fill prebaked, packaged taco shells, filling about half full. Finish tacos by topping with 2 or more of the following: shredded lettuce, shredded cheese, chopped tomatoes and chopped onions. Add hot sauce if desired.

Makes 12 tacos

EASY TACOS

POWER LEVEL: High (10)
MICROWAVE TIME: 9 to 11 min., total

1 lb. ground chuck
    beef
1 can (8-oz.) tomato
    sauce
1 pkg. (1⅛ to 1¼-oz.)
    taco seasoning mix
	In 2-qt. casserole crumble beef. **Microwave at High 6 Minutes,** stirring after 3 minutes. Drain well. Mix in tomato sauce and taco seasoning mix. **Microwave 3 to 5 Minutes.** Stir well and serve as above.

CURRIED BEEF BALLS

For convenience, make meatballs ahead of time and refrigerate on cooking dish or paper plate. Microwaving time may be slightly longer.

POWER LEVEL: High (10)
MICROWAVE TIME: See Recipe
Cook Code for 24 balls: 40—for 12 balls:20

½ cup buttery flavored
    cracker crumbs or
    slightly crushed
    herb seasoned
    stuffing mix
⅓ cup evaporated milk
¼ teaspoon salt
1½ to 2 teaspoons curry
    powder
1 lb. ground chuck
    beef
	In large mixing bowl thoroughly combine crumbs, milk, salt and curry powder. Add beef and blend well. Shape meat mixture into 48 (1-in.) balls.

TO MICROWAVE ENTIRE RECIPE: In 8-in. square dish place about 24 balls. Cover with wax paper. **Microwave at High 4 to 5 Minutes,** rotating dish ¼ turn after 2 minutes. Repeat with other half of beef balls.

TO MICROWAVE A DOZEN BEEF BALLS IN CIRCLE ON PAPER PLATE: Cover plate with wax paper. **Microwave at High 2 to 3 Minutes,** rotating dish ¼ turn after 1 minute.

Makes 4 dozen hors d'oeuvres

EASY MEXICAN MEATBALLS

1 lb. ground chuck
    beef
1 egg
½ pkg. (1⅛ to 1¼-oz.,
    about 2 table-
    spoons) taco
    seasoning mix
	In large mixing bowl, thoroughly combine beef, egg and seasoning mix. Shape into 36 (1-in.) balls. Cook as directed above.

Makes 3 dozen hors d'oeuvres

APPETIZER FRANKS

If desired, 2 cans (4-oz. each) Vienna sausages, drained and halved, may be substituted for frankfurters.

POWER LEVEL: High (10)   **Cook Code:** 20
MICROWAVE TIME: 2 to 3 min., per plate

3 frankfurters
¼ cup apricot preserves
    or apple jelly
1 tablespoon prepared
    mustard
	Cut frankfurters into eighths and arrange in circle on plastic coated paper plate. Mix together preserves and mustard and spread over pieces. Stick each piece with wooden pick. **Microwave at High 2 to 3 Minutes,** until hot.

Chili Franks: Substitute chili sauce for preserves and mustard.

Makes 24 hors d'oeuvres

Curried Beef Balls can be microwaved quick and easy in 4 minutes.

BACON-WRAPPED CHICKEN LIVERS

This is often known by its Polynesian name of Rumaki.

POWER LEVEL: High (10)
MICROWAVE TIME: 6½ to 7½ min., per plate

1 lb. thinly sliced bacon	**Microwave at High 1 Minute,** in the package until slices easily separate. Divide bacon slices between 4 paper towel lined microwave-safe pottery or china plates. Cover with paper towel. Microwave one plate at a time. **Microwave at High 2½ Minutes.** Cut each partially cooked slice in half.
1 can (8-oz.) water chestnuts	Drain and cut each chestnut in half.
½ lb. chicken livers (about 20)	Rinse and drain livers. in half.

To assemble, sprinkle bacon strips lightly with ground cloves and brown sugar. Place one piece of chicken liver and one piece of water chestnut at the end of each bacon strip. Roll up, securing with a toothpick. Arrange 10 in a circle on each of 4 paper towel lined (1 sheet) microwave-safe pottery or china plates. Cover with paper towel. Recipe may be refrigerated at this point if desired. Microwave one plate at a time. **Microwave at High 3 to 4 Minutes,** rotating dish ¼ turn after 1½ minutes. When microwaving from refrigerator temperature, increase time for each plate ½ to 1 minute.

Makes 40 hors d'oeuvres

SWEET-TART FRANKS FOR A CROWD

Sauce is great with many types of meat.

POWER LEVEL: High (10)
MICROWAVE TIME: 7 to 10 min., total

In 3-qt. casserole, stir together 2 lbs. frankfurters, cut in 1-in. pieces, and Sweet-Tart Sauce, below. **Microwave at High 6 to 8 Minutes,** stirring every 2 minutes, until franks are hot. Serve immediately or transfer to chafing dish, if desired.

Makes about 80 hors d'oeuvres.

Sweet-Tart Sauce
Stir together in small bowl 1 jar (10-oz.) currant jelly and 1 jar (6-oz.) prepared mustard. **Microwave at High 1 to 2 Minutes** until mixture can be stirred smooth.

Wrap bacon around liver and water chestnut and secure with a toothpick. Arrange in a ring for cooking.

ESCARGOTS MICROWAVE

POWER LEVEL: High (10)
MICROWAVE TIME: 1½ to 2½ min., per plate

½ cup (¼-lb.) butter **1 teaspoon garlic powder** **½ teaspoon minced parsley flakes**	In 1-pt. glass measure, place butter, garlic and parsley. **Microwave at High 1 Minute,** or until melted. Stir well.
1 can (4-oz.) medium size escargot (about 24 snails) with shells	Drain and rinse snails. Pour small amount of butter sauce into each shell, add snail then a little more sauce.

Snail should be placed into shell loosely, not plugging hole, because steam will cause it to pop out in heating. Place 6 snails on each of 4 plates. Microwave one plate at a time. **Microwave at High 1 to 1½ Minutes,** until hot.

Makes about 24

NOTE: If snails come without shells place 6 snails each in 4 small sauce dishes with ¼ of sauce. Or, use the special glass or pottery snail dishes which have 6 small compartments. Half fill each compartment with sauce, then add snails.

SHRIMP IN SPECIAL GARLIC BUTTER

POWER LEVEL: High (10)   TEMP: 170°
APPROX. MICROWAVE TIME: 4 to 6 min.
Cook Code: 40

1 lb. raw, shelled deveined shrimp	In 2-qt. casserole place shrimp.
½ cup (¼-lb.) butter **2 tablespoons sauterne wine** **2 teaspoons freeze dried or frozen chives** **⅛ teaspoon instant minced garlic or 1 clove fresh garlic, crushed** **1 to 2 drops liquid pepper seasoning (tabasco)**	Stir together butter, wine, chives, garlic and pepper seasoning. Pour over shrimp and stir to coat. (Butter mixture will solidify because of temperature of shrimp.) Insert temperature probe so tip rests on center bottom of dish. Cover with plastic wrap, arranged loosely around probe. Attach cable end at receptacle. **Microwave at High. Set Temp, Set 170°.**

When oven signals, stir shrimp before serving with cocktail picks.

Makes about 1 pound

NOTE: If desired, shrimp can be cooked in individual 10-oz. paper bowls. Fill bowls ½ full and microwave with probe. Approximate time is 1 to 2 minutes per bowl.

STUFFED MUSHROOMS

Choose large or medium-sized firm, fresh mushrooms. When fresh, mushrooms are pale grey or white and the gills (the accordian-like vents on the underside of the cap) should be tightly closed and firmly attached.

POWER LEVEL: See Recipe   **Cook Code: 30**
MICROWAVE TIME: 3½ to 4½ min., per plate

1. For each of the following stuffings, use **12 large, fresh mushrooms,** 2-in. in diameter.

2. Wash mushrooms well, removing stems. Dry.

3. Prepare one of the following stuffing recipes. Divide evenly among caps and mound slightly. Arrange caps in a circle on plate suitable for microwave oven.

4. **Microwave at High 3½ to 4½ Minutes,** rotating plate ¼ turn after 2 minutes. If mushroom size is not uniform, smaller caps may cook in a shorter time.

NOTE: Mushroom stems may be finely chopped (about ⅔ cup) and added to stuffing, except Spinach Stuffing, if desired.

MUSHROOM STUFFINGS: Cook Code: 40
HAM OR BACON-ONION STUFFING

Stems from mushrooms, finely chopped **½ cup finely chopped onion**	In 1½-qt. casserole place chopped stems and onion. Cover. **Microwave at High 4 Minutes,** stirring after 2 minutes.
1 pkg. (3-oz.) cream cheese **¼ cup fine dry bread crumbs** **½ cup chopped, cooked ham or bacon (8 slices)**	To hot mixture above, add cream cheese, mashing and mixing well. Stir in crumbs and ham or bacon.

Stuffs 12 large mushrooms

CLAM STUFFING
Cook Code: 20

1 pkg. (3-oz.) cream cheese, softened
1 can (7-oz.) minced clams, drained
1 tablespoon minced parsley
½ teaspoon garlic powder
.....In small bowl mix together cream cheese, clams, parsley and garlic powder.

¼ cup crushed french fried onions
.....Sprinkle onion pieces over top.

NOTE: If mushroom stems are used, in 1-qt. casserole place chopped stems, ⅓ cup finely chopped onion and 2 tablespoons butter. **Microwave at High 2 Minutes,** stirring after 1 minute. Add remaining ingredients.

Stuffs 12 large mushrooms

CRUNCHY STUFFING
Cook Code: 30

2 tablespoons butter
⅓ cup finely chopped or grated onion
½ cup finely chopped walnuts
1 tablespoon chili sauce
1 teaspoon lemon juice
⅛ teaspoon salt
.....In 1-qt. casserole place butter and onions. **Microwave at High 3 Minutes,** until onion is limp. Add walnuts, chili sauce, lemon juice and salt.

NOTE: If mushroom stems are used, add chopped stems to butter and onions. Microwave following recipe directions.

Stuffs 12 large mushrooms

SAVORY BREAD CRUMB STUFFING
Cook Code: 30

¼ cup finely chopped onion
¼ cup finely chopped green pepper
¼ cup finely chopped celery
3 tablespoons butter
.....In 1-qt. casserole place onions, green pepper, celery and butter. **Microwave at High 3 Minutes,** until slightly cooked.

1 pkg. (3-oz.) cream cheese, softened
1 cup fine, soft bread crumbs (3 slices)
1 teaspoon lemon juice
½ teaspoon salt
⅛ teaspoon pepper
.....Add cream cheese, crumbs, lemon juice, salt and pepper. Mix together well.

NOTE: If mushroom stems are used, add chopped stems to butter and onions. Microwave following recipe directions.

Stuffs 12 large mushrooms

SPINACH STUFFING
Cook Code: 15

1 pkg. (12-oz.) frozen spinach souffle
.....Remove from foil container. With sharp knife cut in half. Return half to freezer; place other half in 1-qt. casserole. **Microwave at Medium 1 to 1½ Minutes,** until partially defrosted. Mash with fork.

½ cup softened bread crumbs (about 1 slice)
1 teaspoon lemon juice
½ teaspoon instant minced onions
¼ teaspoon salt
.....Mix in crumbs, lemon juice, onion and salt.

Stuffs 12 large mushrooms

SWEET 'N' SOUR HAM CUBES

POWER LEVEL: High (10)   TEMP: 160°
APPROX. MICROWAVE TIME: 10 to 13 min.
Cook Code: 100

1 lb. ham cut into ½-in. cubes (60 to 70) **1 can (20-oz.) pineapple chunks, drained** **1 large green pepper, cut into ½-in. squares or 2 stalks celery, diagonally sliced ½-in. thick** **1 jar (10-oz.) sweet and sour sauce**	In 2-qt. casserole stir together ham, pineapple, green pepper or celery and sweet and sour sauce, mixing well.

Insert temperature probe so tip rests on center bottom of dish. Cover with plastic wrap, arranging loosely around probe to vent. Attach cable end at receptacle. **Microwave at High. Set Temp, Set 160°.**

When oven signals stir mixture before serving. Serve with cocktail picks.

Makes about 12 appetizer servings

KABOB VARIATION: Use 28 thin bamboo skewers, about 5-in. long. Before adding sauce, thread 3 pieces of ham and 4 other pieces onto each skewer, beginning and ending with ham. Place 6 on a plastic coated paper plate. Spoon sauce over kabobs to coat. Cover with wax paper. **Microwave at High 3½ to 4½ Minutes,** rotating dish ½ turn after 2 minutes, until hot. Repeat with remaining kabobs.

BEEF TERIYAKI BITES

POWER LEVEL: High (10)
MICROWAVE TIME: 1½ to 2 min., each plate

1 lb. beef tenderloin or sirloin	Cut tenderloin into ¼-in. slices, then into 1-in. squares to make about 90 pieces.
¼ cup sherry wine **¼ cup honey** **¼ cup soy sauce** **30 thin bamboo skewers, 5-in. long**	In a deep bowl stir together sherry, honey and soy sauce. Add meat and stir to coat all pieces with teriyaki mixture. Cover with plastic wrap and marinate at least 1 hour or overnight stirring once or twice so all meat is marinated.

On each skewer thread 3 pieces of meat, skewering each piece twice, in opposite corners, so it looks as though there are 3 diamond shapes on each skewer. Place 6 skewers on a plate suitable for microwave oven. **Microwave at High 1½ to 2 Minutes,** rotating dish ½ turn after ¾ minute until beef is just cooked. Repeat with rest of skewers.

Makes about 30 skewers

Beef Teriyaki Bites & Sweet 'N' Sour Ham Cubes

Pizza-On-A-Plate is quick and tasty but may be slightly irregular in shape since it starts with triangles of dough.

PIZZA-ON-A-PLATE

Pizza may be microwaved in rectangular shape on microwave proof trivet.

POWER LEVEL: Medium High (7)
MICROWAVE TIME: 10 to 14 min., per plate

1 can (8-oz.) . . . .
refrigerated crescent roll dough
2 teaspoons cooking oil

On each of two 12-in. pieces of wax paper, press ½ of dough to form a 9-in. circle. Press perforations together to seal. Brush each lightly with cooking oil. Place wax paper on microwave oven-proof plates. Microwave one pizza at a time. **Microwave at Medium High 4 Minutes.** Holding wax paper, flip dough over onto plate and carefully peel off wax paper. **Microwave at Medium High 3 to 5 Minutes** more, rotating ¼ turn after 2 minutes, until set and crisp. There will be some brown spots.

1 can (8-oz.) tomato . . . . . .
sauce
1 pkg. (4-oz.) pepperoni
1 cup (4-oz.) shredded mozzarella cheese

Divide tomato sauce evenly between crusts, spreading to edges. Top each with half of pepperoni and sprinkle with half of cheese.

Microwave at Medium High 3 to 5 Minutes, rotating plate ¼ turn after 2 minutes. Remove immediately to cooling rack for crisper crust.

Makes 2 (9-in.) pizzas

REHEATING PIZZA

POWER LEVEL: High (10)
MICROWAVE TIME: See Recipe

Pizza, with the exception of Pizza-On-A-Plate, is best *reheated,* in the microwave oven *after* it has been cooked conventionally. A frozen, uncooked pizza, if microwaved, will not have a crisp crust and the center tends to be soggy as there is no hot air to dry out the crust or topping.

1. To reheat a 10" cooked pizza, cut into 8 wedges. Place each wedge on a paper towel or paper plate. Microwave one wedge at a time. **Microwave at High** according to chart below.

	MINUTES PER WEDGE
Room Temperature	¼ to ½
Refrigerated	½ to ¾
Frozen	¾ to 1

2. Time may vary due to the size of pizza and amount of topping. Pizza topped with pepperoni and cheese was used to determine times above.

TIPS: If more than 1 pizza wedge is heated at one time, use amount of time given for *each* wedge, rotating dish ½ turn after half of total time. Place points to center of plate, as they are usually the first to melt.

For more even heating, use a lower power setting and increase time slightly.

For crisper bottom crust, place on cooling rack immediately after heating so crust can dry out.

MICROLESSON: APPETIZER CONVENIENCE FOODS

Many frozen appetizers can be microwaved rapidly at High Power. Pastry, however, will not be as crisp as when baked conventionally for a longer time.

Frozen Egg or Pizza Rolls: For 1 pkg. of 15 rolls (6½-oz.), place on a trivet. **Microwave at High 3 to 4 Minutes,** turning rolls over and rotating trivet ½ turn after 2 minutes. Let stand about 5 minutes to crisp before serving. Rolls will not be as crisp as when cooked conventionally.

Meat Chunks: Cut 6-oz. precooked canned, packaged luncheon meat, or leftover roast into bite-size pieces. Place in microwave-proof bowl. Add ½ cup chili sauce, cocktail sauce or Sweet-Tart Sauce (page 69), if desired. Cover with wax paper. **Microwave at High 1 to 1½ Minutes.**

Pizza Pieces: Cut ¼ of 10-in. pre-cooked pizza into bite-size pieces; place on trivet. For color, top with chopped fresh green pepper, olive slices, pimento or fresh grated cheese. **Microwave at High 1 Minute.** Observe while cooking, adding time or rotating if necessary.

Microwave Popcorn: Follow directions provided with your microwave popcorn popper. Cooking time for ½ cup is about 3 to 5 minutes. If you don't have a microwave popper, use only popcorn labeled "microwave popcorn". Time will be 4 to 6 minutes.

HOW TO MICROWAVE SPREADS ON CRACKERS

Spread 1 teaspoon canned meat or deli spread on each of 12 crackers. The type of filling used determines power setting.

Arrange crackers in a circle on a microwave-proof plate. A paper plate can double as a serving piece.

Microwave at High for most meat spreads and **Medium** for delicate mayonnaise and cheese-based spreads. **Microwave 15 seconds,** check for doneness. Remove if done or rotate and cook 15 seconds more.

Soups & Sandwiches

Hot soups or sandwiches are popular choices for a be-tween meal break, lunch, or, together as a hearty sup-per. Microwaving makes both fast and easy-to-clean-up. Soups can be heated right in the serving dish or cup. Most sandwiches are heated in a paper napkin or towel, so if you serve them casually, there's no clean-up at all!

Some sandwiches are such meal-time staples that we have featured them in other sections. See:

Frankfurters, page 130; Melted Cheese, page 186; Ham-burgers, page 86; Sloppy Joes, page 81 and 63; Bacon-Lettuce-Tomato, use your microwave oven to cook the bacon, page 126.

Frozen prepared sandwiches can be microwaved by re-moving from foil packages and wrapping in paper towel. For each sandwich, **Microwave at High 1 to 1½ Min-utes.** Let stand about 5 minutes to continue heating through.

See page 21 for heating soup and sandwich together. We have provided directions for microwaving 1 or 2 soup-and-sandwich meals at once.

French Onion Soup, page 76

MICROLESSON: HEATING SOUPS BY MICROWAVE

Water-Based Soups can be heated at **High.** A can of condensed soup, diluted with water in a 1-qt. glass mea-sure or a 1½-qt. casserole takes 5 to 7 minutes. One cup (⅔ to ¾ full) takes 2½ to 3½ minutes; or use temperature probe. **Set Temp, Set 150° to 170°.**

Cream Soups should be heated at **Medium High** because milk boils over rapidly so times will be slightly longer. For care-free heating, use the temperature probe. **Set Temp, Set 140°.**

Make Ahead or Save leftover soup and freeze in individual 8-oz. con-tainers. See pages 24 and 27 for reheating tips. Up to 4 cups reheat well together. Rearrange containers halfway through cooking by moving to opposite corners of oven.

FRENCH ONION SOUP

POWER LEVEL: High (10)
MICROWAVE TIME: 18¾ to 21 min.

3 medium onions, ... **sliced thinly** **3 tablespoons butter**	.In 3-qt. casserole, place onions and butter. Cover. **Microwave at High 10 Minutes,** stirring after 5 minutes.
2 cans (10-oz. each) . . . . **beef broth** **1½ cups water** **1 teaspoon salt** **⅛ teaspoon pepper**	.Add broth, water, salt and pepper. Cover and **Microwave at High 8 to 10 Minutes.**
6 slices toasted . . . . **French bread** **1½ cups shredded** **Swiss cheese**	. Spoon soup into 6 individual bowls and top each serving with 1 slice toasted bread. Divide cheese evenly among servings (¼ cup per serving). **Microwave** up to 3 bowls at a time, allowing **¾ to 1 Minute** per serving.

Makes 6 servings

CORN CHOWDER SOUP

POWER LEVEL: High (10)   **Cook Code:** 170
MICROWAVE TIME: 17 to 19 min., total

1 can (10¾-oz.) cream . . . **of potato soup** **2 cans (1-lb. each)** **cream-style corn** **1 can (13-oz.)** **evaporated milk** **1½ cups milk** **¼ cup finely chopped** **green pepper** **(optional)** **1 tablespoon instant** **minced onion** **1 teaspoon salt** **¼ teaspoon pepper**	.In 3-qt. casserole combine soup, corn, milks, green pepper, onion, salt and pepper. Cover. **Microwave at High 17 to 19 Minutes,** stirring after 10 minutes, until hot.
Fresh frozen or . . . . . . **freeze dried chives**	.Add chives and serve.

Makes 8 one-cup servings

INTERNATIONAL SANDWICH

POWER LEVEL: High (10)   **Cook Code:** 20
MICROWAVE TIME: 2 to 3 min., total

1 thick (1-in.) slice . . . . . . **French bread** **Butter** **1 slice bologna** **1 slice salami** **½ cup sauerkraut*** **½ cup grated mozzarella** **cheese**	.Spread the bread with butter. Cut bologna and salami in halves. Alternate the half-slices over bread, then top with sauerkraut. Sprinkle cheese over top.

Place sandwich on paper or china plate. **Microwave at High 2 to 3 Minutes,** rotating sandwich ½ turn after 1 minute.

Makes 1 sandwich

*8-oz. can sauerkraut, drained, makes 2 sandwiches, 1-lb. to 1-lb. 4-oz. can makes 5 to 6 sandwiches.

NOTE: To heat 4 sandwiches, place on plate or platter and heat 6 to 7 minutes, rotating plate ½ turn after 3 minutes.

HOT HOAGIE SANDWICH

POWER LEVEL: Medium High (7)   TEMP: 110°
APPROX. MICROWAVE TIME: 5 to 7 min.
Cook Code: 57

½ loaf unsliced Italian . . . . **or French bread (10** **to 12-in. in length)** **Mayonnaise** **Mustard** **½ lb. meat**** **3 to 4 oz. sliced** **cheese****	.Cut bread lengthwise to make two long, thin layers. Spread both cut sides evenly with mayonnaise and mustard, spreading completely to edges. Cover both sides with meat slices, then cover bottom of loaf with cheese.

Place meat covered top half of bread over bottom half. This arrangement results in cheese in center of sandwich with meat on either side. Place on board or platter with piece of paper towel over sandwich and tucked under edges. Insert temperature probe about ⅓ the length of bread loaf so tip is "sandwiched" into center of filling. Attach cable end at receptacle. **Microwave at Medium High. Set Temp, Set 110°.** Let stand a few minutes before slicing.

Makes 3 to 4 servings

**Meat Fillings: Choose thin sliced hard salami, pastrami, pepperoni, corned beef, boiled ham, or a combination of these.

***Cheese Fillings: Choose sharp or milk cheddar, brick, Monterey Jack, Swiss, or a combination of these.

Hot Hoagie Sandwich

TIPS FOR MICROWAVING HOT SANDWICHES

Layer filling with cheese in the center. Cheese attracts microwaves and by hiding it in the middle of the sandwich you promote rapid heating and avoid overcooking the cheese.

Wrap the sandwich in a paper towel or napkin, to absorb moisture from the bread. For an attractive presentation, microwave the sandwich on a wooden board. (Wood is not affected by short heating times.)

Meats

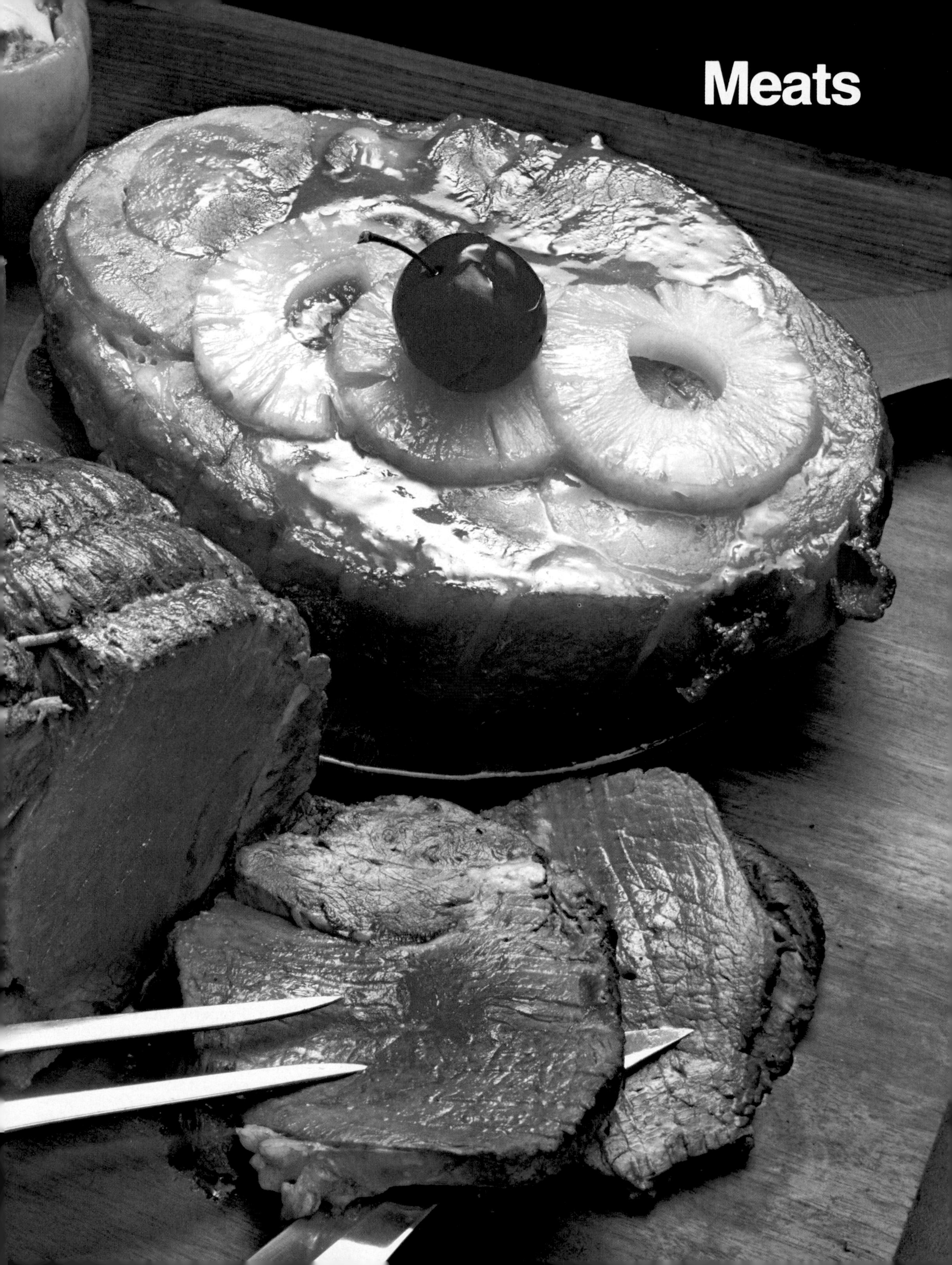

Microwaved meats cook tender and juicy in ⅓ to ½ the time it takes to cook them conventionally. Meat cooking techniques and power settings are determined by the type of microwave oven. Therefore, follow the meat cooking directions in this book for best results.

Some meat recipes in this book cook by time and power settings, while others recommend use of the automatic temperature probe. With the probe, you simply set the dial for the finished temperature, and a signal tells you when the meat is cooked.

Since meat continues to cook on standing, we recommend that you carve rare meats immediately. For well done meats, especially poultry, roast pork and meatloaf, the standing time is especially important, since it is actually part of the cooking process. The meat finishes cooking while it stands.

Each recipe section starts with small pieces and progresses to large, from simple recipes to the more complex, from hearty everyday food to party fare. Each cut of meat has its own instructions for defrosting and microwaving, located where they will be most available and useful to you while cooking, plus special tips which will help you microwave all of them.

When microwaving meat, take the same care you would as when roasting conventionally. While dish handles may not be hot, the meat and bubbling juices will be. Also, less juice evaporates when microwaving, so the volume of juice in the dish may be greater than when oven roasting.

GROUND BEEF DEFROSTING CHART
POWER LEVEL: **Defrost**

AMOUNT	FIRST SIDE	SECOND SIDE	SCRAPE OFF, BREAK UP AND FINISH
1 pound	3 minutes	3 minutes	2 to 3 minutes
2 pounds	6 minutes	6 minutes	5 to 6 minutes
5 pounds	12 minutes	12 minutes	12 to 14 minutes*

*Second scraping may be needed after minimum time.

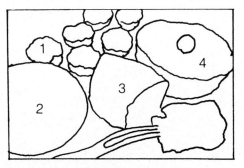

1. Favorite Stuffed Peppers, page 83
2. Barbecued Franks, page 131
3. Sirloin Tip, page 106
4. Ham Slice, page 120

HOW TO DEFROST GROUND BEEF

Ground Beef is packaged in a variety of shapes. Defrosting procedure is the same, but some shapes take more time and attention. Flat, circular packages, 1 to 1½-inches thick, are easiest to defrost. Tubes should be rotated frequently, and broken up as soon as possible. The ends defrost rapidly and may cook before center is defrosted.

Place Package wrapped in plastic or paper in oven set at **Defrost.** Microwave first side. Turn package over. Microwave second side. With a fork, scrape softened meat onto wax paper and set aside. Scraping off defrosted meat is a very important step. Break remaining block into small pieces and return to oven. Continue defrosting, turning pieces over often.

When Properly Defrosted, crumbled beef should be cool, soft and glossy. Meat is red and fat still white. (Fat which turns transparent is beginning to cook.) It looks much like fresh ground beef, but feels colder. Some moisture may be apparent. It will make patties that hold together during cooking.

Ground Beef Crumbled

Crumbled ground beef is the basic ingredient for a variety of popular main dishes, which take a minimum of time and attention when microwaved. Many can be mixed, cooked and served in the same casserole.

Our recipes were written for 1-step ease, but if you wish to lower calories, you may cook ground beef until it loses its pink color, then drain off fat. Add a little more water to the recipe if it seems dry.

To cook and drain fat from ground beef in one easy step, try our simple colander method. (Plastic colanders are widely available in the housewares section of department, hardware stores or supermarkets.)

Place crumbled ground beef in plastic colander, set over a casserole or bowl. For one pound of meat **Microwave at High 5 to 6 Minutes,** until meat loses its pink color, stirring after ½ the time. Discard fat and place meat in the cooking dish.

Sloppy Joes

HOW TO DEFROST & COOK FROZEN GROUND BEEF IN 1-STEP

Unwrap 1 pound of frozen ground beef and place it in the same cooking utensil called for in the recipe you plan to follow. **Microwave at High 10 to 12 Minutes,** breaking up and stirring meat with a fork every 5 minutes. Some areas will still be pink. Let meat stand 1 to 2 minutes until the pink color disappears.

SLOPPY JOES

POWER LEVEL: High (10)
MICROWAVE TIME: 11 to 12 min., total

1½ lb. ground chuck beef	In 1½-qt. casserole crumble beef. Add onion, celery and green pepper. Cover. **Microwave at High 6 Minutes;** stirring after 3 minutes. Drain meat well.
⅔ cup finely chopped onion	
½ cup diced celery	
¼ cup diced green pepper	
½ cup ketchup	To cooked meat mixture, add ketchup, Worcestershire sauce, salt and pepper. Cover. **Microwave at High 5 to 6 Minutes,** stirring after 3 minutes, until hot. To serve, spoon onto buns or crusty French rolls.
1 tablespoon Worcestershire sauce	
½ teaspoon salt	
⅛ teaspoon pepper	

Makes 6 to 8 sandwiches

Sloppy Joes With Cheese: Add 1 cup (4-oz.) shredded cheddar cheese to meat mixture along with ketchup.

Sloppy Joes With Beans: Add 1 can (16-oz.) pork and beans to meat mixture along with ketchup.

CABBAGE ROLLS ITALIAN STYLE

Prepare for two meals at once by doubling the recipe and freezing half. Follow directions earlier in this book for defrosting and reheating.

POWER LEVEL: High (10)
MICROWAVE TIME: 21 to 25 min., total

8 large cabbage leaves **(from outer layers of cabbage)** **½ cup water**	.In 3-qt. casserole place cored cabbage and water. Cover, **Microwave at High 7 to 9 Minutes,** until pliable.
1 lb. ground chuck beef **1 egg** **1 cup packaged precooked (minute) rice** **3 tablespoons chopped onion** **1 teaspoon salt**	.Meanwhile, mix ground beef, egg, rice, onion, salt. Shape rolls as picture directs. Return to 3-qt. casserole, placing rolls seam side down.
2 cans (8-oz. each) **tomato sauce** **1 tablespoon sugar** **1 teaspoon oregano**	.Blend sauce, sugar and oregano. Pour over rolls. Cover.

Microwave at High 14 to 16 Minutes, rotating ¼ turn and basting after 9 minutes. Let stand 5 minutes.

Makes 8 cabbage rolls

CABBAGE ROLL VARIATION:

SWEET-SOUR CABBAGE ROLLS

Filling: Mix 2 tablespoons water, ¼ cup minced onion, ½ lb. ground chuck beef, 1 tablespoon catsup, 1 egg, 2 tablespoons packaged precooked (minute) rice, ½ teaspoon salt, ⅛ teaspoon pepper, ¼ cup gingersnap crumbs. Roll up.

Sauce: Blend 1 can (8-oz.) stewed tomatoes, 2 tablespoons raisins, 2 tablespoons cider vinegar, 2 tablespoons brown sugar, 2 tablespoons dark corn syrup. Pour on; microwave.

Sprinkle with ¼ cup gingersnap crumbs before serving.

Shape meat mixture into 8 rolls, about 3-in. long. Place roll on base of leaf over heavy vein. Fold sides over meat; roll up. Secure with pick, if needed.

CHILI

Microwaved with the temperature probe, it requires no stirring during cooking. Beef is softer prepared this way. For more distinct texture, precook ground beef before combining with other ingredients and microwave to 160°, about 20 minutes. Stir well before serving.

POWER LEVEL: High (10)   TEMP: 190°
APPROX. MICROWAVE TIME: 50 to 55 min.
Cook Code: 500

1½ lb. ground chuck **beef**	.In 2½ to 3-qt. casserole crumble beef.
1 can (28-oz.) **tomatoes,** **undrained** **1 can (6-oz.) tomato** **paste** **2 cans (1-lb. each)** **kidney beans,** **undrained** **1 medium green** **pepper, finely** **chopped** **1 tablespoon instant** **minced onion** **1 to 2 tablespoons** **chili powder** **2 teaspoons salt**	.Mix in tomatoes, tomato paste, beans, green pepper, onion, chili powder and salt. Insert temperature probe so tip rests on center bottom of dish. Cover tightly with plastic wrap, arranging loosely around probe to vent. Attach cable end at receptacle. **Microwave at High. Set Temp, Set 190°.** When oven signals, stir and let chili stand about 10 minutes to blend flavors before serving.

Makes 6 to 8 servings

BEEFBURGER STROGANOFF

POWER LEVEL: High (10)   **Cook Code:** 130
MICROWAVE TIME: 13 to 15 min., total

1 lb. ground chuck beef **½ cup finely chopped** **onion** **1 garlic clove, minced** **1 can (8-oz.)** **mushrooms,** **undrained** **1 can (10½-oz.)** **condensed cream of** **mushroom soup** **3 tablespoons** **all-purpose flour** **1 teaspoon salt** **¼ teaspoon pepper**	.In 2-qt. casserole crumble beef. Add onion, garlic, mushrooms, soup, flour, salt and pepper. Mix thoroughly. Cover. **Microwave at High 13 to 15 Minutes,** until hot.
1 cup (8-oz.) **dairy sour cream** **½ teaspoon bottled** **brown bouquet** **sauce**	.Stir casserole thoroughly, then stir in sour cream and bouquet sauce. Serve over cooked rice or chow mein noodles.

Makes 6 servings

FAVORITE STUFFED PEPPERS

For crisper pepper and brighter color, remove cooked peppers from dish immediately. Separate them and let stand uncovered. Sprinkle top with grated rather than sliced cheese to assure melting.

POWER LEVEL: High (10)   **Cook Code:** 240
MICROWAVE TIME: 24 to 28 min., total

6 medium green peppers . . . . Cut off tops of green peppers; remove seeds and membrane.

1½ lb. ground chuck beef
1 cup cooked long grain rice
1 small onion, chopped (about ½ cup)
1½ teaspoons salt
¼ teaspoon pepper
1 clove garlic, minced . . . . . Mix beef with rice, onion, salt, pepper and garlic. Fill peppers with meat mixture. Arrange snugly around edge of 3-qt. casserole.

1 can (10¾-oz.) condensed tomato soup
½ cup water . . . . Mix together soup and water; pour over and around peppers. Cover. **Microwave at High 24 to 28 Minutes,** rotating dish ½ turn after 12 minutes.

6 slices (1-oz. each) sharp cheese (optional) . . . . . Remove peppers and let stand, covered, 5 to 10 minutes before serving. If desired, cheese slices may be placed over tops of peppers to melt before casserole stands. Recover.

Makes 6 servings

BEEF AND CORN CASSEROLE

POWER LEVEL: High (10)
MICROWAVE TIME: 14 to 16 min., total

1 lb. ground chuck beef
¼ cup chopped onion
¼ cup chopped green pepper . . In 2-qt. casserole, crumble beef. Add onion and green pepper. **Microwave at High 6 Minutes,** stirring after 3 minutes. Drain meat well.

1 can (16-oz.) tomatoes
1 can (12-oz.) whole kernel corn, drained
1 can (8-oz.) tomato sauce
½ cup sliced stuffed olives
1 to 2 teaspoons chili powder . . Drain tomatoes, reserving ¼ cup juice. Dice tomatoes and add to meat mixture with reserved tomato juice, corn, tomato sauce, olives and chili powder. Cover. **Microwave at High 6 to 8 Minutes,** until hot.

1 cup coarsely crushed corn chips
½ cup shredded cheddar cheese . . Remove cover, stir and sprinkle corn chips and cheese over top. **Microwave at High 2 Minutes,** uncovered, until cheese melts.

Makes 4 to 6 servings

MICROLESSON: GROUND BEEF CASSEROLES

Arrange individual portions in a ring so heat will penetrate evenly and cook all servings in the same time.

Stir halfway through cooking to distribute heat. Stir again when cooking is completed, especially when adding cheese or crumb topping just before you serve.

Rotate or Rearrange casserole-type foods like cabbage rolls and stuffed peppers which cannot be stirred.

Basic Meatballs

Ground Beef Meatballs

Meatballs microwave exceptionally well, and turn brown after a short standing time, so they need no special browning.

Arrange meatballs in a ring around the edge of a 9 or 10-in. pie plate. Small meatballs form a double row. After half the cooking time, rotate the dish ¼ turn. Using these well-tested favorite recipes as models, it will be easy to adapt your own special recipes for microwaving.

BASIC MEATBALLS

POWER LEVEL: High (10) **Cook Code:** 60
MICROWAVE TIME: 6 to 8 min., total

1 lb. ground chuck beef **1 egg** **½ cup fine bread crumbs** **1 teaspoon salt** **¼ teaspoon paprika** **⅛ teaspoon pepper**	Mix together beef, egg, crumbs, salt, paprika and pepper. Shape into 12 balls and arrange in a circle in 9 or 10-in. pie plate. Cover with wax paper. **Microwave at High 6 to 8 Minutes,** rotating dish ¼ turn after 3 minutes, until done. If desired, serve with Italian Sauce, page 194.

Makes 12 meatballs

VARIATIONS:
Add one of the following flavor combinations:
1 tablespoon Worcestershire sauce and ¼ cup chopped onion
1 tablespoon steak sauce and 1 clove crushed garlic (or ½ teaspoon garlic powder)
1 tablespoon chili sauce and ¼ cup finely chopped green pepper
1 tablespoon ketchup and 1 teaspoon prepared mustard
2 tablespoons red wine and 1 teaspoon oregano

SWEDISH MEATBALLS

POWER LEVEL: High (10)
MICROWAVE TIME: 12 to 16 min., total

1 lb. ground chuck beef **1 cup soft bread crumbs** **¼ cup milk** **1 egg** **1 pkg. (½ of 2¾-oz. box) onion soup mix** **¼ teaspoon salt** **¼ teaspoon nutmeg**	Mix together beef, crumbs, milk, egg, soup mix, salt and nutmeg. Shape meat mixture into 20 balls. Arrange in circle in 9 or 10-in. pie plate. Cover with wax paper. **Microwave at High 7 to 9 Minutes,** rotating dish ¼ turn after 4 minutes. Remove meatballs from dish and keep warm, reserving meat drippings.
1 tablespoon unsifted all-purpose flour **½ cup milk** **1 tablespoon brown bouquet sauce** **½ cup (4-oz.) dairy sour cream**	To ¼ cup drippings in dish, add flour, stirring until smooth. Gradually stir in milk and brown bouquet sauce. **Microwave at High 4 to 5 Minutes,** stirring every minute, until thickened. Add sour cream. Stir well. Return meatballs to dish, mixing to coat evenly. **Microwave at High 1 to 2 Minutes,** until hot. Serve over noodles or rice.

Makes 20 meatballs

PORCUPINE MEATBALLS

Fast cooking rice is used in this recipe because the short cooking time does not allow regular rice to soften.

POWER LEVEL: High (10)
MICROWAVE TIME: 10 to 14 min., total

1 lb. ground chuck . . . . . . .Mix together beef, rice, ½
beef   can of soup (about ½ cup),
1 cup packaged   egg, water and onion salt.
precooked (minute)   Shape into 12 balls and ar-
rice   range in a circle in 9 or
1 can (10-oz.)   10-in. pie plate. Cover with
condensed tomato   wax paper. **Microwave at**
soup (divided)   **High 8 to 10 Minutes,** rotat-
1 egg   ing dish ¼ turn every 3
¼ cup water   minutes.
1 teaspoon onion salt

Spoon topping (below) over meatballs. **Microwave at High 2 to 4 Minutes** to heat. If desired, mound center of meatball ring with rice before serving.

TOPPING: Into remaining ½ can undiluted tomato soup, stir 2 tablespoons ketchup and 1 teaspoon prepared mustard.

Makes 4 to 6 servings

Porcupine Meatballs

MEATBALLS HAWAIIAN

These meatballs microwave very quickly because of the moist pineapple filling.

POWER LEVEL: High (10)
MICROWAVE TIME: 9 to 11 min., total

1 can (1-lb. 4-oz.) . . . . .Drain pineapple well, re-
pineapple chunks   serving syrup.

1 lb. ground chuck . . . . . .Mix together beef, egg,
beef   bread crumbs, onion, salt,
1 egg   cloves, allspice and syrup.
2 slices fresh bread,   Mold small amount of mix-
crumbled   ture around 24 pineapple
1 tablespoon instant   chunks. Place meatballs
minced onion   in two rows around edge
1 teaspoon salt   of 10-in. pie plate. Cover
⅛ teaspoon ground   with wax paper. **Micro-**
cloves   **wave at High 6 Minutes,**
⅛ teaspoon allspice   rotating dish ¼ turn after
2 tablespoons reserved   3 minutes. Pour off meat
pineapple syrup   juices.

⅓ cup reserved . . . . .Stir together syrup, ketch-
pineapple syrup   up and brown sugar. Pour
½ cup ketchup   over drained meatballs.
⅓ cup brown sugar   **Microwave at High 3 to 5**
(packed)   **Minutes** longer, rotating
                                               dish ¼ turn after 2 minutes,
                                               until done. Serve with rice
                                               or noodles, or serve with
                                               toothpicks as an appetizer.

Makes 24 meatballs

COLORFUL RING OF MEATBALLS

POWER LEVEL: High (10)
MICROWAVE TIME: 12 to 14 min., total

1 lb. ground chuck . . . . . . .Mix together beef, egg,
beef   crumbs, salt, paprika and
1 egg   pepper. Shape into 12
½ cup fine bread   balls and arrange in a cir-
crumbs   cle in 9 or 10-in. pie plate.
1 teaspoon salt   Cover with wax paper. **Mi-**
¼ teaspoon paprika   **crowave at High 5 Min-**
⅛ teaspoon pepper   **utes.**

1 medium onion . . . . .While meatballs are cook-
1 medium lemon   ing, peel onion and lemon.
1 medium green pepper   Slice onion, lemon and
1 cup (8-oz.) dairy   pepper ¼-in. thick. Mix to-
sour cream   gether sour cream, chili
½ cup chili sauce   sauce and brown sugar.
2 tablespoons brown   Rotate dish ¼ turn. Distri-
sugar (packed)   bute onion rings and lem-
                                               on and pepper slices over
                                               meatballs. Pour sour cream
                                               mixture evenly over slices.

Microwave at High 7 to 9 Minutes, uncovered. Serve with buttered noodles, if desired.

Makes 4 to 5 servings

Ground Beef Hamburger Patties

Hamburgers are America's all-time favorite for lunch or supper. (Some people even like them for breakfast.) With microwaving, hamburgers defrost and cook so quickly and successfully that, if you keep a supply in the freezer, you can serve hamburgers at a moment's notice. You

MICROLESSON: HOW TO MICROWAVE HAMBURGER PATTIES

Fresh Patties should be covered with wax paper for juicy hamburgers; rotate after ½ of time. For hamburgers with drier surface, microwave uncovered (on a trivet, if desired) throughout cooking but turn patties over after ½ of time. Use High Power for both cooking methods.

Frozen Patties should be microwaved at High, covering with wax paper as well as turning over after part of total time. A chart on page 88 gives cooking times for fresh and frozen patties.

MICROLESSON:

Illustrated below are several ways additional browning can be achieved. Browning agents should be added before cooking.

Plain hamburger immediately after microwaving   Barbecue Sauce   Teriyaki Sauce

may microwave hamburgers in the Brown 'N Sear dish, but they will be equally delicious when cooked on a paper or pottery plate suitable for microwaving; and you'll save even more cooking and clean-up time.

Let Patties Stand a few minutes after microwaving. On removal from the oven, hamburgers will look grey, but they will turn brown after standing.

Serve on buttered buns with your favorite condiments. Notice the change in appearance after standing time. This hamburger was cooked without a browning agent.

Onion Soup Mix   Brown Bouquet Sauce With Butter   Brown 'N Sear Dish

TIPS FOR MICROWAVING GROUND BEEF PATTIES

Thickness and type of ground beef determine cooking time. The time chart is for medium-lean ground chuck. Fattier hamburgers might take less time, very lean ones more.

A Paper Plate lined with a double thickness of paper towel gives you no-clean-up convenience. Cover patties with a single paper towel to control spatter and retain moisture.

For Lower Calorie hamburgers, place patties on a trivet set over a plate or dish. Cover with wax paper and rotate dish ½ turn after half the cooking time. Fat drains into dish.

GROUND BEEF PATTY COOKING CHART

Timings are based on medium-lean ground chuck shaped into 6, 4 or 2 patties per pound and microwaved to well done. Use paper, pottery or glass plate.

Preheat Brown 'N Sear dish when using this cooking method. Follow the timings given on the chart below, but turn fresh hamburgers over after ⅔ cooking time. For frozen hamburgers, turn as directed on the chart. Use the Brown 'N Sear dish cover to prevent spatters, but preheat dish uncovered.

Extended Hamburgers. Hamburgers may be extended with soy protein, following directions on the package.

You may also use oatmeal, crushed corn flakes or crackers, according to your favorite recipe. Extended hamburgers microwave in ½ to 1 minute less time per patty, and give greater volume per pound of meat. The following recipe uses bread as an extender.

Meatloaf Burgers. Mix together 1 pound ground chuck, 1½ cups cubed bread (2 slices), 1 egg and ½ teaspoon salt. Shape into size and thickness of patties preferred. Microwave ½ to 1 minute less time per patty than for regular hamburgers.

POWER LEVEL: **High (10)**

PATTY SIZE	NO. OF PATTIES	FRESH TIME/MINUTES	FROZEN TIME/MINUTES		PREHEAT BROWNING DISH TIME/MINUTES
6 per pound	1	1 to 1½	3		4
(about ½" thick)	2	2 to 2½	5 to 5½	Turn over after ½ of time	4
	3	3 to 3½	6 to 6½		6
	4	4 to 4½	7 to 7½		6
Arrange in circle on dish; rotate dish ½ turn after ½ time.	5	5 to 6	8 to 8½	Turn over every ⅓ of time	
	6	6 to 7	9½ to 10½		
4 per pound	1	2 to 3	4 to 5	Turn over after ½ of time	4
(about ¾" thick)	2	3 to 4	5 to 6		6
	3	4½ to 5½	8 to 9	Turn over every ⅓ of time	6
	4	5½ to 6½	11 to 12		8
2 per pound	1	3 to 4	6 to 8	Turn over every ⅓ of time	6
(about ¾" thick)	2	6 to 7	13 to 15		

SALISBURY STEAKS

If you prefer creamy gravy, substitute milk for water.

POWER LEVEL: High (10)
MICROWAVE TIME: 10 to 13 min., total

1 lb. ground chuck beef . . .Combine beef, onion, salt
½ small onion, chopped and pepper. Shape into 2
1 teaspoon seasoned large oval patties in 8-in.
   salt square dish. Cover with
⅛ teaspoon pepper wax paper. **Microwave at High 7 to 9 Minutes,** rotating dish ¼ turn after 4 minutes. Remove patties from dish and keep warm.

3 tablespoons flour . . . . .Mix flour and water to
½ cup water make a smooth paste. Add
½ teaspoon brown quickly to hot drippings,
   bouquet sauce stirring until smooth. Add
1 can (2-oz.) mushroom brown bouquet sauce and
   stems and pieces, mushrooms, stirring well.
   undrained **Microwave at High 2 Minutes,** stirring after 1 minute, until gravy thickens. Place patties in gravy, spooning some over the top. **Microwave at High 1 to 2 Minutes,** until hot.

Makes 2 generous servings

Stuffed Hamburgers

STUFFED HAMBURGERS

POWER LEVEL: High (10)   **Cook Code:** 70
MICROWAVE TIME: 7 to 9 min., total

1 lb. ground chuck beef . . .Shape beef into 8 thin pat-
   Salt ties. Sprinkle with salt and
   Pepper pepper. Place selected fill-
   Filling (below) ing over 4 patties and top with other 4 patties. Seal fillings inside by pinching firmly around edges. Arrange 4 stuffed patties in 8-in. square dish. Cover with wax paper. **Microwave at High 7 to 9 Minutes,** rotating dish ½ turn after 4 minutes. Serve on buttered buns.

Makes 4 patties

HAMBURGER PATTY STEW

When arranging this casserole, be sure that the top layer of beef patties is well covered with vegetables or it will overcook. Be sure to set Medium High Power.

POWER LEVEL: Medium High (7) **Cook Code:** 257
MICROWAVE TIME: 25 to 28 min., total

2 medium potatoes . . . . Peel vegetables and slice
2 medium carrots into ¼-in. slices.
2 medium onions

1 lb. ground chuck . . . . . Form beef into 12 small
   beef flat patties. In 2-qt. casse-
1½ teaspoons salt role layer half of beef pat-
⅛ teaspoon pepper ties then half of vege-
¼ cup water tables, sprinkling layers
   Paprika with salt and pepper. Repeat. Add water. Press down into casserole. Sprinkle with paprika. Cover. **Microwave at Medium High 25 to 28 Minutes,** rotating dish ¼ turn after 12 minutes. Let stand 5 minutes before serving.

Makes 4 servings.

FILLINGS:
Ham 'N' Cheese: Use a thin ham slice and 1 thin cheese slice per patty.
Cordon Bleu: Use ¼-in. thick slices Canadian bacon and 1 tablespoon crumbled bleu cheese per patty.
Hot Dog Burgers: Use ½ of a hot dog sliced lengthwise, 1 tablespoon ketchup and scant teaspoon prepared mustard per patty.

Cover and Rotate Hamburger Patty Stew ¼ turn after half of microwave time.

Ground Beef Meatloaf

In the microwave oven, meatloaf cooks in 15 to 20 minutes, instead of the hour, or hour and a half you expect conventionally. Microwaved meatloaves are round and flat. We do not recommend square shapes because the corners absorb too much energy and will be overcooked by the time the center is done.

A conventionally baked meatloaf occasionally has areas on the top which are overbrown. When microwaved, these areas may appear on the bottom edges of the loaf. Because microwave energy is attracted to sweet mixtures toppings which contain sugar, syrup or preserves can increase overbrowning if they come in contact with the bottom edges. When applied before microwaving, they should be brushed only on the top.

Plain meatloaf looks grey. It needs a topping, sauce or

browning agent for attractive color. For this picture, we brushed the left side of the meatloaf with a browning sauce, leaving the right side plain. Ketchup, chili or barbecue sauces make easy toppings. For delicious flavor variety, try one of our homemade toppings.

Basic Meatloaf

HOW TO MICROWAVE PIE-SHAPED MEATLOAF

Use 1 to 2 pounds ground beef. If you are adapting a recipe, choose a moist mixture. Spread the mixture directly in a pie plate, not on a trivet. The top should be very flat and about even with the top of the dish.

Brush the top with a browning agent or sauce. If you are not using a probe, cover dish tightly with plastic wrap, turning back about 2-in. at edge to vent. After cooking, let loaf stand 5 to 10 minutes to complete cooking and make it easier to slice.

Insert temperature probe as horizontally as possible, so that tip is in the center of the loaf. Make sure disc does not touch the food. Cover tightly with plastic wrap, arranging loosely around probe to vent.

BASIC MEATLOAF

Add ¼ teaspoon herbs or dry mustard to vary flavor.

POWER LEVEL: High (10)   TEMP: 170°
APPROX. MICROWAVE TIME: 15 to 20 min.
Cook Code: 150

1½ lbs. ground chuck . . . . .
  beef
¾ cup chopped onion
½ cup fine dry bread
  crumbs
1 egg
2 tablespoons ketchup
1 cup milk
1 teaspoon salt
¼ teaspoon pepper
⅛ teaspoon paprika
	Mix together beef, onion, crumbs, egg, ketchup, milk and seasonings. Mold into a rounded, flat loaf in 9-in. pie plate.

2 tablespoons . . . . **ketchup**	Spread ketchup evenly over top of loaf.

Insert temperature probe and cover as shown in picture on preceding page. Attach cable end at receptacle. **Microwave at High. Set Temp, Set 170°.**

When oven signals, remove meatloaf and let stand about 10 minutes to firm before serving. Serve in wedges.

Makes 6 servings

SOUPER MEATLOAF

POWER LEVEL: Medium High (7)   TEMP: 170°
APPROX. MICROWAVE TIME: 20 to 25 min.
Cook Code: 207

2 lbs. ground chuck . . . . .
  beef
½ cup fine dry bread
  crumbs
⅓ cup chopped onion
1 egg, slightly beaten
1 can (10½-oz.)
  condensed cream of
  mushroom soup,
  (divided)
2 tablespoons beef
  bouillon granules
	Mix together beef, crumbs, onion, egg, ½ of soup and bouillon. Shape into flat loaf in 10-in. pie plate. Insert temperature probe as shown in picture at left. Attach cable end at receptacle. **Microwave at Medium High. Set Temp, Set 170°.** When oven signals, let stand 10 minutes before serving. Serve with Topping (below).

Topping: Mix remaining soup with 1 teaspoon beef bouillon granules and ⅓ cup water. **Microwave at High 2 to 3 Minutes,** stirring every minute, until hot.

For best results, this loaf must be cooked in the 10-in. pie plate at Medium Power.

CHEESE STUFFED MEATLOAF

This meatloaf tastes like a cheeseburger and will be popular with your family.

POWER LEVEL: High (10)   TEMP: 170°
APPROX. MICROWAVE TIME: 20 to 25 min.
Cook Code: 200

1½ lbs. ground chuck . . . . .
  beef
3 slices fresh bread,
  cubed
1 cup milk
2 teaspoons salt
½ teaspoon pepper
	Make meatloaf mixture: In large mixing bowl, mix together beef, bread, milk, salt and pepper.

½ cup chopped . . . .
  onion
¼ cup chopped green
  pepper
¼ cup chopped celery
2 tablespoons lemon
  juice
1 egg, slightly beaten
1 cup (4-oz.) shredded
  cheddar cheese
3 slices fresh bread,
  finely crumbled
	Make cheese stuffing: In 1½-qt. casserole place onion, pepper, celery and lemon juice. **Microwave at High 3 Minutes,** until lightly sauteed. Add egg to hot vegetables and stir to blend well. Stir in cheese and fine bread crumbs.

To assemble meatloaf: Pat half of meat mixture in bottom of 10-in. pie plate. Mold filling evenly over meat leaving about 1-in. uncovered at edges. Spread remaining meat mixture over filling. (Meat mixture is soft and spreads easily.) Seal around edges. Brush assembled meatloaf with 1 tablespoon Worcestershire sauce.

Insert temperature probe so tip is in center of stuffing. Cover tightly with plastic wrap, arranging loosely around probe to vent. Attach cable end at receptacle. **Microwave at High. Set Temp, Set 170°.**

When oven signals, remove meatloaf and let stand about 10 minutes to firm before serving. Serve in wedges.

Makes 4 to 6 servings

Loaf-Shaped Meatloaf, 1½-lbs., can be microwaved at Medium High (7) to 170°, about 25–30 minutes.

SAUERBRATEN BEEF RING

POWER LEVEL: High (10)   **Cook Code:** 240
MICROWAVE TIME: 24 to 28 min., total

1¼ cups finely crushed . . . .Reserve ½ cup ginger-
gingersnap cookies snap crumbs for meatloaf.
2 cups beef broth In 1-qt. glass measure, mix
½ cup brown sugar together remaining ¾ cup
(packed) crumbs, broth, brown sug-
¼ cup raisins ar, raisins and lemon juice.
¼ cup lemon juice **Microwave at High 8 to 10**
Minutes, stirring every 3
minutes, until thickened.
Set aside.

2 lbs. ground chuck . . . . .In 2-qt. casserole mix to-
beef gether reserved crumbs,
1 cup soft bread beef, bread crumbs, on-
crumbs (1½ slices) ion, lemon juice, water, salt
½ cup chopped onion and pepper. Invert 6-oz.
¼ cup lemon juice custard cup in center of
¼ cup water same 2-qt. casserole. Di-
1 teaspoon salt vide meat into 12 equal
¼ teaspoon pepper parts. Shape into ovals
and arrange as shown be-
low around custard cup.
Pour 1 cup sauce over
meat. Cover.

Microwave at High 16 to 18 Minutes, rotating dish ¼
turn after 8 minutes. Let stand 10 minutes. Invert serving
plate over casserole. Carefully but quickly invert beef
ring onto serving plate. (*Caution;* Custard cup in center
of ring will be filled with hot meat liquid. Keep casserole
over serving plate until meat and custard cup slip onto
plate.) Remove custard cup full of liquid. Serve beef ring
with remaining sauce, heated before serving, if necessary.

Makes 6 to 9 servings

LEMON LOVERS' MEATLOAF

POWER LEVEL: High (10)   TEMP: 170°
APPROX. MICROWAVE TIME: 15 to 20 min.
Cook Code: 150

¾ cup ketchup . . . . .In small bowl mix together
¼ cup brown sugar ketchup, brown sugar, dry
(packed) mustard, allspice and
¾ teaspoon dry cloves. Set aside.
mustard
¼ teaspoon allspice
Dash ground cloves

1½ lb. ground chuck . . . . .Mix together beef, bread
beef cubes, egg, lemon juice,
3 slices day-old bread, onion and salt. Mold into
cubed rounded flat loaf in 9-in. pie
1 egg, slightly beaten plate.
⅓ cup lemon juice
¼ cup chopped onion
2 teaspoons seasoned
salt

6 very thin lemon . . . . . .Spread half the reserved
slices sauce over loaf and ar-
range lemon slices on top.

Insert temperature probe so tip is in center of loaf. Cover
tightly with plastic wrap, arranging loosely around probe
to vent. Attach cable end at receptacle. **Microwave at
High. Set Temp, Set 170°.**

When oven signals, remove loaf and let stand 5 minutes
to firm. Spread remaining sauce over loaf before serving.

Makes 6 servings

Mini Meatloaves: Shape meat mixture into 6 individual
loaves and arrange in 8-in. square dish. Cover with wax
paper. **Microwave at High 4 Minutes.** Evenly divide half
of sauce over loaves. Top each loaf with a lemon slice.
Recover with wax paper. Rotate dish ¼ turn. **Microwave
at High 11 to 13 Minutes,** until done. Heat and spoon
remaining sauce over loaves before serving.

MICROLESSON: HOW TO MAKE A SAUERBRATEN BEEF RING

Pack oval-shaped meatballs around an inverted
6-oz. custard cup center-
ed in casserole.

Cover casserole with
serving plate after microwaving and standing for
10 minutes.

Invert casserole over
plate. When meat and cup
slip onto plate, remove
the casserole.

Lift out custard cup with
tongs. Cup will be filled
with hot meat liquid.

Beef Convenience Foods

Canned convenience foods, or foods frozen in metal trays, should be removed from their containers to suitable microwave plates or casseroles. Small boil-in-bag pouches (about 5 to 10-oz.) can be placed directly in the oven. Slit or pierce the top of the pouch before microwaving and open carefully after heating to avoid burns from steam. Large boil-in-bags may be placed in a serving dish. When contents are partially defrosted, open the bag, slide food into the dish and stir before continuing to microwave.

TIPS FOR MICROWAVING BEEF CONVENIENCE FOODS

Stirring. Part way through the heating period, stir food from the outside to the center of the dish. Foods which cannot be stirred, such as meatloaf, lasagna or salisbury steak, should be rotated, rearranged or turned over.

Covering. To shorten cooking time and prevent spatters, use a covered casserole. When heating foods on a serving plate, or in a dish without a cover, use wax paper or plastic wrap to cover the food. Prick or slash the plastic wrap and remove carefully when stirring.

Probe. Before inserting temperature probe, make certain that frozen foods are completely defrosted. Heat fully cooked foods to 150° to 160°. For proper probe placement, and temperature of uncooked foods, follow instructions given with similar home-cooked recipes.

CONVENIENCE GROUND BEEF COOKING CHART

Main Dishes such as: barbecue beef, chili, hash, meatballs, patties or pieces with gravy, stew, meatloaf, salisbury steak, stuffed cabbage rolls and stuffed peppers can be microwaved following directions below.

Dry Casserole Mixes. Always use hottest tap water and 3-qt. casserole for dishes containing pasta or rice. Stir once or twice during cooking. Let them stand uncovered, 5 minutes after cooking.

POWER LEVEL: **High (10)**

CANNED AMOUNT	TIME MIN.	COOK CODE	COMMENTS
Up to 16-oz.	3—5	30	Stir after ½ of time or use temperature probe set for 150°.
Over 16-oz.	5—8	50	
FROZEN AMOUNT			
8 to 16-oz.	5—11	50	Stir, redistribute or rotate after ½ of time. Use temperature probe only if completely defrosted.
16 to 32-oz.	11—22	110	

TYPE	TIME MIN.	COOK CODE	COMMENTS
Add Hamburger	18—22	180	Microwave crumbled ground beef 5 minutes, stirring after 3 minutes. Drain before adding remaining ingredients. Stir once or twice during cooking.
Add Cooked Beef	18—22	180	If milk is used for part of liquid add 2 to 3 minutes cooking time.
One-pot Main Dish (freeze-dried beef)	11—13	110	Add crumb topping just before serving.

NOTE: For TV Dinners including ground beef, see page 29.

Beef Strips & Chunks

Less tender beef, such as round or chuck, microwaves best when cut in small pieces and simmered gently at Low or sometimes Medium power setting. The temperature probe is not appropriate for small pieces of less tender meat. Recipes which call for Low power setting will not be as tender if cooked at Medium. Slower cooking allows the meat to simmer in its sauce until it is fork tender. When defrosting strips or chunks, place them in the cooking dish, separate and spread them out as soon as possible. Any juices which appear during defrosting can be added to the liquid in the recipe.

HOW TO DEFROST STRIPS & CHUNKS

1. Place plastic or paper wrapped package in oven. **Microwave at Defrost** ½ the minimum total time.

2. Turn package over and defrost second ½ of time.

3. Separate pieces with a table knife; let stand to complete defrosting, or microwave 1 to 2 minutes more.

POWER LEVEL: **Defrost**

---

4 to 8 Minutes Per Pound

Add cut-up vegetables to partially microwaved round steak cubes (recipe on page 95). **Microwave at Low 15 to 20 Minutes.** Add other ingredients and **Microwave at High 5 to 10 Minutes.**

MICROLESSON: MICROWAVING BEEF STRIPS & CHUNKS

A Tight Cover not only speeds cooking but holds in steam which helps tenderize meat. If your casserole does not have a tight cover, seal the top with plastic wrap, turning back about 2-in. at one edge to vent.

Low Power Setting cooks meat gently in liquid and steam until it becomes fork tender. Microwave time will be slightly shorter than conventional cooking. Some recipes may call for Medium power.

Stirring distributes heat evenly. Stir often when microwaving chunks of meat and vegetables in a sauce. When stirring, remove the cover carefully to avoid scalding hot steam.

SHORT RIBS AND HOMEMADE NOODLES

POWER LEVEL: High (10) and Low (3)
MICROWAVE TIME: 1 hr. 40 min. to 1hr. 52 min., total

2 lb. short ribs, cut into 2 or 3 rib pieces **1 small onion, sliced** **1 stalk celery with leaves, cut in half** **2 teaspoons salt** **3 cups water**	. . . .In 3-qt. casserole place short ribs, onion, celery, salt and water. Cover. **Microwave at High 20 Minutes.** Stir. Cover. **Microwave at Low 70 to 80 Minutes,** stirring after 30 minutes, until tender.
Homemade Noodles or 1½ cups (½ of 6-oz. pkg.) narrow egg noodles	. . . .Remove ribs and keep warm. Add dry noodles to broth. Cover. **Microwave at High 10 to 12 Minutes,** until tender.

Makes 2 to 3 servings

HOMEMADE NOODLES

Beat together 1 egg, 2 tablespoons milk and ½ teaspoon salt. Add 1 cup unsifted all-purpose flour and mix to make a stiff dough. Roll out very thin on floured surface; let stand 20 minutes. Roll up loosely; slice ¼-in. wide. Spread loosely in 13×9×2-in. dish. **Microwave at Low 10 to 12 Minutes,** stirring every 4 minutes, until noodles are dry.

Makes 3 cups cooked noodles

ROUND STEAK STEW

POWER LEVEL: High (10), Medium (5) and Low (3)
MICROWAVE TIME: 2 hr. 8 min. to 2 hr.19 min., total

2 beef bouillon cubes **2 cups water**	. . . . In 3-qt. casserole place bouillon cubes and water. **Cover. Microwave at High 3 to 4 Minutes.** Stir.
2 lbs. round steak, cubed **1 teaspoon bottled brown bouquet sauce**	. . . . . Add round steak and brown bouquet sauce to bouillon. **Cover. Microwave at Low 1 Hour and 45 Minutes,** stirring every 20 minutes.
2 large potatoes, cut up **1 cup sliced carrots** **½ cup sliced celery** **1 tablespoon diced onion**	. . . . Add potatoes, carrots, celery and onion to stew. **Microwave at Medium 15 to 20 Minutes.**
¼ cup cold water **2 tablespoons cornstarch** **1½ teaspoons salt** **¼ teaspoon pepper** **1 pkg. (10-oz.) frozen peas, defrosted**	. . . . In small bowl stir together water and cornstarch. Slowly add to hot mixture, stirring well. Add salt, pepper and peas, stirring well. **Cover. Microwave at High 5 to 10 Minutes,** until vegetables are tender.

Makes 6 to 8 servings

CUBE STEAK STEW

POWER LEVEL: Medium (5) and High (10)
MICROWAVE TIME: 79 to 90 min., total

4 cube steaks, cut in ½-in. strips **1 large onion, thinly sliced** **1 teaspoon bottled brown bouquet sauce** **1½ teaspoons salt** **¼ teaspoon pepper** **1 can (16-oz.) tomatoes** **1 can (8-oz.) tomato sauce**	. . . . In 3-qt. casserole combine meat, onion, brown bouquet sauce, salt, pepper, tomatoes and tomato sauce. Stir well. Cover. **Microwave at Medium 60 to 65 Minutes,** stirring after 15 minutes.
4 medium potatoes, peeled and cut in 1-in. cubes	. . . .Add potatoes to stew, stirring well. Cover. **Microwave at High 15 to 20 Minutes,** until potatoes are tender.
1 pkg. (10-oz.) frozen peas, defrosted **½ medium green pepper, cut in strips**	. . . .Add peas and pepper to stew. Cover. **Microwave at High 4 to 5 Minutes,** until peas are tender but pepper is still crisp. Stir well before serving.

Makes about 6 servings

STEWED BEEF WITH VEGETABLES

POWER LEVEL: Medium (5) and High (10)
MICROWAVE TIME: 1 hr. 20 min. to 1 hr. 30 min., total

2 lbs. beef stew meat, cut into 1-in. cubes **2 cups water** **2 cans (6-oz. each) tomato paste** **1 pkg. dry onion soup mix (half of 2¾-oz. box)** **¼ teaspoon garlic powder** **¼ teaspoon pepper**	. . . . In 3-qt. casserole combine meat, water, tomato paste, onion soup mix, garlic powder and pepper. Stir well. Cover. **Microwave at Medium 60 Minutes,** stirring every 20 minutes.
2 medium potatoes, cut into 1-in. cubes **2 medium carrots, sliced**	. . . . . Add potatoes and carrots to stew. **Microwave at Medium 15 to 20 Minutes** more, until meat is tender.
1 can (12-oz.) yellow kernel corn	. . . . Add corn, stirring well. **Microwave at High 5 to 10 Minutes,** until vegetables are tender. Stir well before serving.

Makes 8 to 10 servings

Beef Steaks
Less Tender Cuts

Less tender steaks, such as round, flank or cubed should be microwaved in liquid at Low or Medium. Steam produced by the liquid softens the meat during its longer, slower cooking at the lower power setting. Low Power is preferred for most recipes; if Medium Power is used, meat will not be as tender.

In some of our recipes, we recommend the traditional technique of pounding meat, or having it processed through the butcher's tenderizing machine, before cooking.

Frequently, less tender steaks are cooked with a slightly acid liquid, such as tomato juice or wine, which helps tenderize them. Marinating both tenderizes and imparts a delicious flavor to steaks. Try one of the marinades on page 98, and use some of the marinade as the cooking liquid.

HOW TO DEFROST STEAKS

POWER LEVEL: **Defrost**

4 to 8 Minutes Per Pound

1. Place plastic or paper wrapped package in oven. **Microwave at Defrost** ½ the minimum total time.

2. Turn package over and defrost second ½ of time.

3. Separate pieces with a rubber spatula and let stand to complete defrosting, or **Microwave 1 or 2 Minutes** more.

Swiss Steak

Separate steaks as soon as possible and let stand until ice is no longer apparent. If meat is to be cut into strips, do this while it is still partially frozen. It will slice neatly and easily. Any juices which appear during defrosting can be added to the liquid in the recipe.

Rearrange steak pieces after partial microwaving as recipe directs. Re-moisten tops and outside surfaces to prevent drying and overcooking.

SWISS STEAK

POWER LEVEL: Medium (5)   **Cook Code:** 605
MICROWAVE TIME: 60 to 70 min., total

1½ lb. round steak, ... **½-in. thick,** **tenderized or** **pounded with meat** **mallet** **¼ cup flour** **1½ teaspoons salt** **⅛ teaspoon pepper** **1 medium onion,** **sliced thin** **1 can (1-lb.) tomatoes**	Cut meat in 6 pieces, then coat with mixture of flour, salt and pepper. Place in 3-qt. casserole. Cover with onion. Break up tomatoes with fork and pour over top. Cover. **Microwave at Medium 60 to 70 Minutes,** rearranging meat after 30 minutes, until tender.

Makes 6 servings

Easy Swiss Steak: Substitute 1 can (10½-oz.) condensed tomato soup or cream of mushroom soup, 1 cup water and 2 teaspoons beef bouillon granules for flour, salt, pepper, onion and tomato. Microwave as directed in above recipe.

BOHEMIAN STEAK

POWER LEVEL: Medium (5) and Medium High (7)
MICROWAVE TIME: 73 to 84 min., total

2 lb. round steak, ... **½-in. thick,** **tenderized or** **pounded with meat** **mallet** **2 cups thinly sliced** **onion**	Cut round steak into 8 to 10 serving size pieces. In 3-qt. casserole layer meat and onion.
½ cup water . . . . **1 can (12-oz.) beer** **1 can (10-oz.) beef** **gravy** **1 tablespoon sugar** **2 teaspoons salt** **½ teaspoon minced** **garlic** **¼ teaspoon pepper**	Measure water into 1-qt. measure. Add beer, gravy, sugar, salt, garlic and pepper and mix well. Pour over meat and onions. Cover. **Microwave at Medium 70 to 80 Minutes,** rearranging meat after 40 minutes.
¼ cup cold water . . . . **2 tablespoons unsifted** **all-purpose flour**	Stir together water and flour. Gradually add to stew, mixing well. **Microwave at Medium 3 to 4 Minutes,** uncovered, until thickened. Stir well. Top with Fluffy Dumplings (below).

Makes 4 to 6 servings

Fluffy Dumplings: In small bowl mix together 2 cups buttermilk biscuit mix, ⅔ cup milk and 1 tablespoon parsley flakes just until moistened. Drop by tablespoonfuls around edges of hot stew. Cover. **Microwave at Medium High 5 to 6 Minutes,** rotating dish ¼ turn after 3 minutes, until done.

POLYNESIAN SWISS STEAK

Be sure meat is covered with sauce throughout cooking time to prevent overbrowning.

POWER LEVEL: Medium (5)   **Cook Code:** 655
MICROWAVE TIME: 65 to 75 min., total

2 lb. round steak, ½-in. . . . **thick, tenderized or** **pounded with meat** **mallet**	Trim fat from meat and cut into serving pieces.
1 can (8-oz.) crushed . . . . **pineapple, undrained** **2 cans (8-oz.) tomato** **sauce** **1 pkg. (½ of 2¾-oz. box)** **dry onion soup mix** **1 tablespoon prepared** **mustard**	In small bowl or 1-qt. measure, mix together undrained pineapple, tomato sauce, soup mix and mustard. In 3-qt. casserole, alternately layer meat and sauce. Cover. **Microwave at Medium 65 to 75 Minutes,** rearranging meat every 20 minutes, until tender.

Makes 4 to 6 servings

PEPPER STEAK

POWER LEVEL: Medium High (7), Medium (5) and High (10)
MICROWAVE TIME: 35 to 40 min., total

4 cube steaks (6-oz. . . . . . **each)** **⅓ cup steak sauce**	In 12x8x2-in. dish place cube steaks, overlapping if necessary. Brush with steak sauce. Cover with wax paper. **Microwave at Medium High 9 Minutes,** rotating dish ½ turn after 5 minutes.
1 can (10-oz.) beef . . . . **consomme** **1 teaspoon seasoned** **salt**	Transfer steaks to 2-qt. casserole. Add consomme and seasoned salt. Cover. **Microwave at Medium 18 to 20 Minutes,** rearranging steaks after 10 minutes.
¼ cup cold water . . . . **2 tablespoons** **cornstarch** **1 medium green pepper,** **cut into strips** **2 medium firm** **tomatoes, cut into** **chunks**	Remove steaks from sauce and keep warm. Mix together water and cornstarch. Add to sauce. Cover. **Microwave at High 3 to 4 Minutes,** until thickened. Stir well. Return meat to sauce and add green pepper and tomatoes. **Microwave at Medium 5 to 7 Minutes,** until hot. Let stand a few minutes before serving. Vegetables will be crisp-tender.

Makes 4 servings

Spicy Steak Strips

SPICY STEAK STRIPS

This is a variation of Greek Beef Stew, called Stifado. A good dinner dish to serve with rice, salad and hard rolls.

POWER LEVEL: High (10) and Low (3)
MICROWAVE TIME: 75½ to 85½ min., total

3 tablespoons butter	In 3-qt. casserole place butter. **Microwave at High ½ Minute,** until melted. Sprinkle meat with salt and pepper. Stir into melted butter until each piece is coated. Sprinkle onions over meat.
2 lb. round steak, ½-in. thick, cut in strips	
½ teaspoon salt	
⅛ teaspoon pepper	
1 cup chopped onion	
2 cans (6-oz. each) tomato paste	In small bowl mix together tomato paste, wine, vinegar, brown sugar, garlic, bay leaves, cinnamon, cloves, cumin and raisins. Pour over meat and onions. Cover. **Microwave at Low 75 to 85 Minutes,** stirring after 35 minutes, until tender. Let stand 10 to 15 minutes before serving.
1 cup red wine	
¼ cup vinegar	
2 tablespoons brown sugar (packed)	
2 cloves garlic, minced	
2 bay leaves	
2 small sticks cinnamon	
1 teaspoon whole cloves	
½ teaspoon cumin	
¼ cup raisins	

Makes about 6 servings

MARINATING LESS TENDER STEAKS

Marinade tenderizes less tender steaks for conventional and microwave cooking. It also adds distinctive flavor. To save time, you can substitute oil and vinegar type bottled salad dressing for prepared marinade. Large, less tender roasts may be marinated, too. Microwave as on page 104.

TOMATO MARINADE

1 can (8-oz.) tomato sauce	In cooking container or 1-qt. glass measure mix together tomato sauce, brown bouquet sauce, onion, basil, sugar and garlic powder. Use as suggested.
1 teaspoon bottled brown bouquet sauce	
1 cup chopped onion	
1 teaspoon basil	
1 teaspoon sugar	
1 teaspoon garlic powder	

Makes 1½ cups

TERIYAKI MARINADE

½ cup soy sauce	In cooking container or 1-qt. glass measure mix together soy sauce, brown sugar, garlic, ginger, monosodium glutamate and pepper. Use as suggested.
½ cup brown sugar (packed)	
1 clove garlic, minced	
2 teaspoons ground ginger	
1 teaspoon monosodium glutamate (Accent)	
½ teaspoon pepper	

Makes ¾ cup

LEMON OR VINEGAR MARINADE

½ cup lemon juice or white vinegar	In cooking container or 1-qt. glass measure mix together lemon juice, oil, parsley, bay leaves, garlic, onion, sugar, nutmeg, liquid pepper. Use as suggested.
½ cup oil	
1 sprig parsley or 1 tablespoon chopped parsley	
2 bay leaves	
1 garlic clove, crushed	
2 slices onion	
1 tablespoon sugar Pinch of nutmeg	
2 drops liquid pepper seasoning (tabasco)	

Makes 1 cup

WINE MARINADE

⅔ cup sherry	In cooking container or 1-qt. glass measure mix together wine, oil, onion, garlic, pepper and thyme. Use as suggested.
⅓ cup cooking oil	
1 medium onion, finely chopped	
1 clove garlic, minced	
½ teaspoon pepper	
¼ teaspoon dried thyme	

Makes 1 cup

MICROLESSON: MARINATING & MICROWAVING LESS TENDER STEAKS

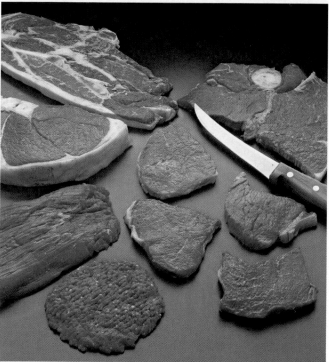

Select 2 to 3 lb. round steak, chuck steak, flank steak and cube steak for marinating. The smaller the cut of meat, the more marinade flavor it will absorb because more surface is exposed.

Marinate in glass dish covered with plastic, turning steaks over once. Refrigerate 4 to 24 hours in marinade, turning meat over after half the time.

Turn Over steaks just before microwaving and, if desired, drain off some of marinade. Recover with plastic wrap to microwave.

Microwave at Medium 25 to 30 Minutes per Pound, turning steaks over, rearranging and recovering after half the cooking time.

Beef Steaks Tender Cuts

Steaks microwaved in the Brown 'N Sear are juicy and tender. Your microwave oven can also be useful when cooking steaks conventionally. See tips below.

HOW TO DEFROST STEAKS

POWER LEVEL: **Defrost**

4 to 8 Minutes Per Pound

1. Place plastic or paper wrapped package in oven. **Microwave at Defrost** ½ the minimum total time.
2. Turn package over and defrost second ½ of time.
3. Separate pieces with a table knife; let stand to complete defrosting, or **Microwave 1 to 2 Minutes** more.

Broil extra 1-in. steaks or hamburgers while preparing a batch for dinner in the conventional broiler; undercook the extras slightly. Cool, wrap and freeze for later reheating in the microwave. Directions at right have been developed especially for this use.

Sear extra 1-in. steaks or hamburgers while charcoal grill is hot, but undercook them slightly. Cool, wrap and freeze as suggested above. You'll have charcoal flavor without re-lighting the grill.

HOW TO REHEAT FROZEN PRE-COOKED STEAKS

Always undercook steaks slightly. This two-step process produces steak which is not dry or overdone.

1. Unwrap steak and place on microwave ovenproof serving plate. Cover with wax paper. **Microwave at Defrost,** allowing 4 to 8 minutes for each 1-lb. steak. Turn steak over after ½ the cooking time. Let stand a few minutes before reheating.
2. While steak is still covered with wax paper, reheat it by **Microwaving at Medium (5),** using the following times for each 1-lb. steak:

DONENESS	TIME MINUTES	COMMENTS
Rare	5 to 7	Turn steak over after ½
Medium	6 to 8	the time. Let stand a few
Well	7 to 9	minutes before serving.

MICROWAVING STEAKS IN BROWN 'N SEAR DISH

Times are given for ¾ to 1-in. thick steaks cooked to medium (pink center). To test for doneness, cut with knife tip from edge toward center of steak. Area closest to bone is last to cook. Ground beef patties up to 1-in. thick may also be microwaved this way. **Preheat empty and uncovered browning utensil 8 minutes.**

POWER LEVEL: **High** (10)

TYPE	NO. OF STEAKS	1st SIDE MINUTES	2nd SIDE MINUTES
Cube Steak or Minute Steak (4-oz. each)	1 or 2	1	1 to 1½
Rib Eye or Strip	1 or 2	2	2 to 2½
T-Bone	1	3	2 to 3
Filet Mignon	1, 2 or 4	2	2 to 2½

TIP: For browner color, butter both sides of steak before cooking, using 1 tablespoon of butter per steak. Drain juices after cooking the first side of steak.

MICROLESSON: BROWN 'N SEAR STEAKS

Fit foods to the dish before cooking. Wipe the dish clean after fitting food; traces of fat and meat will scorch.

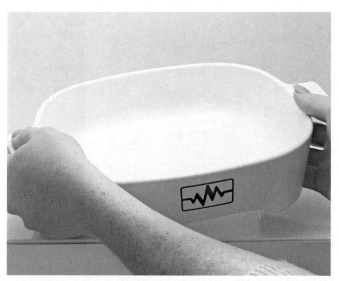

Preheat Uncovered Dish 8 Minutes or until the bottom turns yellow. For subsequent batches, preheat time will be half the original time.

Remove juices with a spoon after browning the first side of steaks.

Turn Over steaks and continue cooking according to time chart on this page.

Roast Defrosting

HOW TO DEFROST ROASTS
POWER LEVEL: **Defrost**

10 to 12 Minutes Per Pound

HOW TO DEFROST THIN ROASTS

MICROLESSON

Defrosting is one of the major benefits of the microwave oven, but it is not miraculous. Roasts up to 6 pounds can be defrosted successfully, but need attention during defrosting or they will start to cook. Follow directions carefully for handling of these expensive cuts of meat.

The procedure demonstrated here applies to lamb and veal roasts as well as beef. Warm areas after defrosting indicate that the meat has started to cook and should be roasted immediately. If you are defrosting a roast for later cooking, be especially careful. We recommend that you defrost for ¾ the time and allow the roast to finish defrosting in the refrigerator.

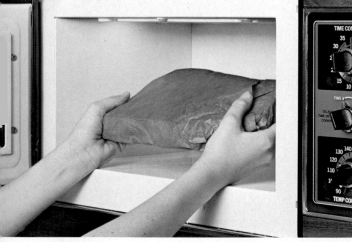

Place unopened plastic or paper wrapped roast in oven. **Defrost** for ¼ the total time.

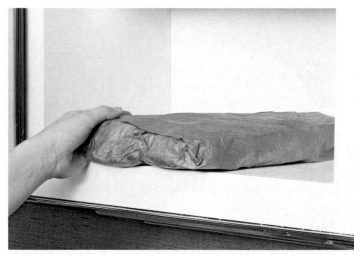

Rotate roast ½ turn. **Defrost** for second ¼ of time.

HOW TO DEFROST CHUNKY ROASTS

Unwrap roast. Place in dish and cover with tucked wax paper. **Defrost** for ¼ the total time.

Feel for warm spots; shield with foil. Turn roast over. **Defrost** for ¼ of time. Let stand 15 minutes.

Shape of Meat as well as size influences defrosting time.

Flat roasts such as brisket, chuck or sirloin defrost more rapidly than rib roasts.

Thick roasts may defrost unevenly, so turning and rotating are very important. Allow some standing time to be sure interior is completely defrosted.

Irregular roasts need shielding on thin areas. Check carefully for warm spots.

Unwrap and turn roast over into dish. Shield warm spots. **Defrost** for third ¼ of time.

Rotate dish ½ turn. Shield warm spots. **Defrost** last ¼ of time. Let stand 15 to 30 minutes until defrosted.

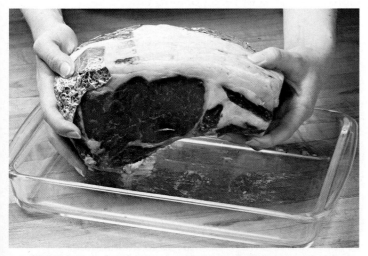

Shield warm spots; turn roast over. **Defrost** for ¼ of time. Shield and turn again. **Defrost** for last ¼ of time.

Let roast stand 30 minutes to complete defrosting. Juices begin to appear. Meat should look moist with glistening fat and should feel cool.

Beef Roasts Less Tender Cuts

In microwaving, as in conventional cooking, less tender cuts of beef call for some liquid, tight covering, and Low Power setting to make them juicy and tender. Use sirloin tip, rump, arm or blade chuck for pot roasts, and brisket or corned beef for simmered beef.

If you want vegetables with your meat, use either of two methods. One is to cook vegetables separately, either before the roast or during standing time. Add them to the meat and heat briefly. Or you may add vegetables to the meat halfway through the cooking period and microwave until meat and vegetables are fork tender.

MICROLESSON

HOW TO MICROWAVE A CHUCK ROAST OR A RUMP ROAST

Place 3 to 5 lb. rump or chuck roast in a roasting dish. If desired, brush all sides with a mixture of one teaspoon brown bouquet sauce and one tablespoon water. Or marinate several hours, see page 98.

Pour in ½ cup water or wine or, if roast has been marinated, use ½ cup marinade. Cover tightly with plastic wrap turning back corner to vent. **Microwave at Medium 19 to 23 Minutes Per Pound.** Microwave for ½ of total cooking time.

HOW TO MICROWAVE SIMMERED BEEF

Combine brisket or corned beef, weighing 3 to 3½ pounds, with 4 cups water, onion, garlic, bay leaf and peppercorns in a casserole.

Cover and **Microwave at High 15 to 25 Minutes.**

Turn Over roast end to end after ½ cooking time so that the bottom meat surface is on the top and the meat on the left side of the oven is on the right side.

Arrange vegetables around roast, if desired. If meat is more than 3-in. higher than liquid, shield top with foil, during final cooking period. Cover and microwave final ½ of cooking time or until meat is tender. Thinner roasts cook faster than thick ones.

Turn meat over and recover. **Microwave at Medium 1 to 1½ Hours,** turning meat over every 30 minutes, until tender. Let stand, covered, 10 to 15 minutes.

Carve roast diagonally across the grain in thin slices for attractive, tender meat.

HOW TO MICROWAVE LESS TENDER BEEF ROASTS

When microwaving less tender beef roasts, the meat quality determines whether you will want to microwave to medium-rare or medium doneness or whether the meat should be cooked well done and tenderized like a pot roast. Select top quality meat if you plan to microwave to medium-rare or medium. Information on this page applies to rolled and tied beef sirloin tip and rump roasts weighing 3 to 5 lbs. and no more than 4-in. in height.

Brush the roast with 1 teaspoon brown bouquet sauce mixed with 1 tablespoon water. Place in cooking dish; add ½ cup red wine or water; insert temperature probe, if desired; cover and cook following directions on this page. On removal from the oven, the roast will appear moist but the surface will dry and darken attractively after standing. Cut diagonal slices for maximum tenderness.

A Dome holds moisture inside the dish for no mess during cooking. Plastic wrap also can be used to cover.

To Microwave by Temperature, insert temperature probe in center of roast. Cover tightly with plastic wrap, arranging loosely around probe to vent or cover with microwave-safe dome. **Microwave at Medium. Set Temp, Set 90°.** When oven signals, turn roast over and continue microwaving to **130 to 135°** for medium-rare or medium- doneness and to **200°** for well done, tenderized meat.

To Microwave by Time, cover tightly with plastic wrap or with microwave-safe dome. For medium-rare to medium, estimate **11 to 16 min. per lb. at Medium,** (shortest time for medium-rare). Microwave ⅔ of time, turn over, shield with foil. Recover, finish cooking. For well done, estimate **19 to 24 min. per lb. at Medium.** Microwave ½ of time, turn over, shield with foil, (add raw vegetables, if desired). Recover and finish cooking.

FLAVORING TIPS FOR LESS TENDER ROASTS

Brush high quality sirloin tip roast with bottled teriyaki sauce or liquid smoke. Shake or rub seasoned pepper (lemon, garlic, herb or onion) on all surfaces. Follow directions for cooking medium-done roast.

Brush rolled rump roast with Worcestershire sauce and then rub with seasoned salt. Cover all except cut ends with bacon strips side by side; secure with picks. Microwave well done.

SIMMERED CORNED BEEF

POWER LEVEL: High (10) and Medium (5)
MICROWAVE TIME: 1 hr. 25 min. to 1 hr. 35 min., total

3 to 3½ lb. corned beef . . . .
    brisket
4 cups water
1 medium onion, thinly
    sliced
2 cloves garlic, minced
2 bay leaves
	In 3-qt. casserole place brisket with water. Slice onion over brisket and add garlic and bay leaves. Cover. **Microwave at High 25 Minutes.** Turn brisket over. Recover.

Microwave at Medium 60 to 70 Minutes, turning brisket over after 30 minutes. Let stand, covered, 15 minutes before serving. To serve: diagonally slice corned beef very thin for sandwiches or for serving with boiled vegetables.

Makes 6 to 8 servings

NEW ENGLAND BOILED DINNER

POWER LEVEL: High (10)
MICROWAVE TIME: 1 hr. 50 min. to 2 hrs. 5 min., total

1 recipe Simmered . . . . . . **Corned Beef (above)**	Microwave corned beef as described above. Remove meat from broth and keep warm.

2 large potatoes, cut up
4 medium carrots, cut
    lengthwise
1 medium head cabbage
    cut in 6 wedges
	Add potatoes and carrots to broth. Arrange cabbage in a pinwheel on top. Cover.

Microwave at High 25 to 30 Minutes, rearranging after 15 minutes, until vegetables are tender. Discard bay leaves. Serve with thinly sliced corned beef.

Makes 6 servings

BEEF BRISKET

POWER LEVEL: High (10) and Medium (5)
MICROWAVE TIME: 1 hr. 35 min. to 1 hr. 45 min., total

3 lb. beef brisket . . . .
4 cups water
1 tablespoon salt
¼ teaspoon
    peppercorns
1 medium onion, thinly
    sliced
	In 3-qt. casserole or 13x9x2-in. dish place brisket, water, salt and peppercorns. Place onion slices on top of brisket. Cover. **Microwave at High 15 Minutes.** Turn brisket over. Recover.

Microwave at Medium 80 to 90 Minutes, until tender, turning brisket over every 30 minutes. For maximum juiciness, let brisket stand in juices 10 minutes before serving.

Makes 6 to 8 servings.

New England Boiled Dinner

SPICY BEEF BRISKET

POWER LEVEL: High (10) and Medium (5)
MICROWAVE TIME: 1 hr. 45 min. to 2 hr., total

1 cup ketchup . . . .
2 medium onions,
    chopped
⅓ cup brown sugar
    (packed)
¼ cup vinegar
2 teaspoons basil or
    bouquet garnish
1 teaspoon garlic salt
½ teaspoon thyme
½ teaspoon salt
¼ teaspoon pepper
3 lb. beef brisket
	In small bowl mix together ketchup, onion, brown sugar, vinegar, basil, garlic salt, thyme, salt and pepper. Pour half of sauce over brisket in 12×8×2-in. dish. Cover with plastic wrap turning back one corner to vent. **Microwave at High 15 Minutes.** Turn brisket over. Recover.

Microwave at Medium 30 Minutes. Turn brisket over and pour other half of sauce over meat. Recover. **Microwave at Medium 60 to 75 Minutes,** turning brisket over and basting with sauce every 20 minutes, until meat is tender. Let stand 10 minutes, then carve into very thin slices and serve with sauce.

Makes 6 to 8 servings

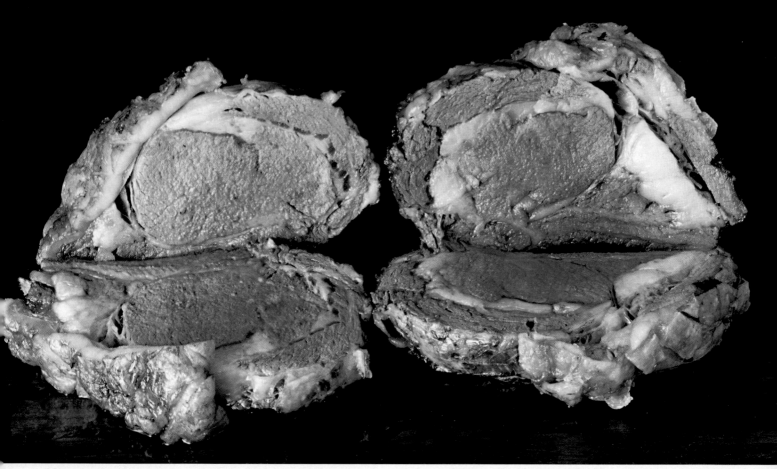

Microwave Roasted Beef. This standing rib roast was microwave roasted to an internal temperature of 130°. It has the same color internally as conventionally roasted beef, although the temperature is lower. Roast was brushed with browning agent before microwaving.

Conventionally Roasted Beef. This standing rib roast was roasted conventionally to an internal temperature of 140°. Both roasts stood about 15 minutes before carving.

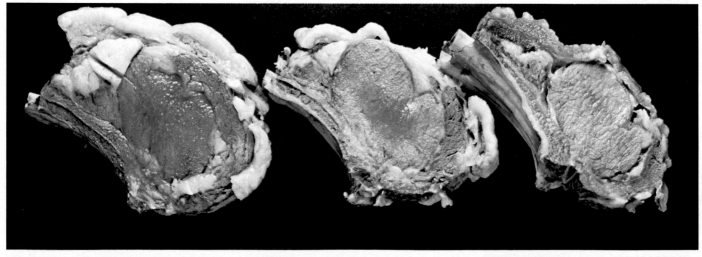

Rare. Meat microwaved to an internal temperature of 120° is red in the center, with running juices. Since microwaving is so fast, the exterior will not be browned. If you desire a brown color, brush the meat with a browning agent before roasting.

Medium. Meat microwaved to an internal temperature of 130° is rosy in the center, with pink juices. Some browning occurs on the outside. If you prefer a browner exterior, brush the meat with a browning agent before roasting.

Well Done. Meat microwaved to an internal temperature of 155° is brown in the center, with clear juices. The time needed to cook beef well done is enough to brown the exterior, so no browning agent is needed.

Beef Roasts
Tender Cuts

Tender cuts of beef, such as rolled or standing rib, or tenderloin are ideal for microwave roasting. They cook tender and juicy in a short time.

Since these roasts are expensive, and generally reserved for special occasions, you'll want to follow directions carefully. Before you purchase roasts, select meat carefully; standards for grading beef have changed recently, which may affect grain and resulting tenderness. Pay special attention to internal temperatures so you don't overcook! Since meat continues to cook while standing, rare to medium roasts are microwaved to lower internal temperature than conventional roasts. After 10 minutes standing, both reach about the same doneness.

Small, compact and evenly shaped roasts cook best. Just as in conventional cooking a roast which is thinner on one end will be done first in that area. Long, thin roasts cook faster than short, thick ones. Large roasts of 5 to 6 pounds are done uniformly because they are turned over during roasting time.

If family or guests differ in preference between rare and well-done, roast the meat to the minimum doneness. Carve it, and return some slices to the microwave oven. It takes just a short time to bring a slice from rare to well-done, and all will have meat to suit their tastes.

HOW TO MICROWAVE TENDER BEEF ROASTS

Tie standing rib roasts across the meat to secure fat. Fold the thin end of a half tenderloin under and tie the roast to maintain an even, compact shape. Tie rib eye firmly.

Brush half tenderloin or rib eye roast with equal parts brown bouquet sauce and melted butter if desired.

Place roast on a trivet in a 12×8×2 or 13×9×2-in. cooking dish. DO NOT SALT. Cover with wax paper.

MICROLESSON: HOW TO MICROWAVE TENDER ROASTS

Tie roast with string to retain shape for better appearance and more even microwaving; remove string after cooking. Outer fatty layer expands, and the roast's shape may change unless tied.

Insert temperature probe in center of roast. Cook on a trivet, like those described on page 39, placing trivet in a dish deep enough to hold drained-off meat juices. See photos below for tips on inserting the probe and positioning roast on the trivet.

HOW TO INSERT THE TEMPERATURE PROBE

Measure the distance to the center of the roast by laying the temperature probe on top of the meat. If the roast is uneven in shape or contains fat or bone, select an angle which will bring the tip of the probe to the center of the thickest meaty area without touching fat or bone.

Mark with your thumb and forefinger where the edge of the meat comes on the probe. Insert the probe up to the point marked off with your finger.

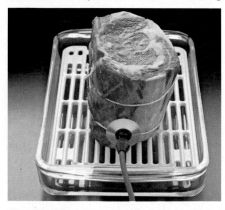

Rib Eye. Insert probe through side of roast so that tip is in the center of meat.

Half Tenderloin. Insert probe into cut end so tip is in center of roast.

Rolled Rib. Insert probe into the rolled side so that tip is in the center.

NOTE: Pictures are taken without wax paper cover to best show positioning of temperature probe.

MICROWAVING BEEF BY TIME

Estimate the cooking time for the type, size and desired doneness of your roast. (See chart at right.) Cook for the minimum time suggested on the chart, turning roast over after about ⅔ the cooking time. You may need to reset the timer to complete the minimum cycle for larger or well done roasts.

After the minimum time, remove the roast from the oven and test the temperature with a meat thermometer, following the directions for probe placement given with

your type of roast. Remember that microwave roasted meats are cooked to a lower temperature than conventionally roasted meats. If the roast has not reached the desired doneness, remove the thermometer and return the meat to the oven for a few more minutes of cooking time. *Do not use meat thermometer in the microwave oven unless it is specially designed or recommended for use in the microwave oven.*

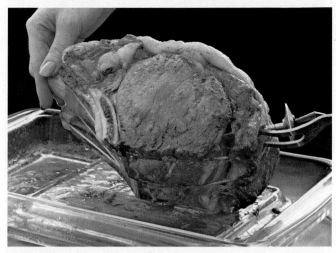

Cover roast loosely with wax paper. The covering prevents spattering and shortens cooking time slightly. No liquid is added; instead the internal juices heat and cook the meat. **Microwave at Medium High. Set Temp, Set 90°** to cook first side of roast.

Turn Over roast carefully when oven signals. Since the roast cooks from top to bottom, turning the meat helps distribute heat evenly. Recover and continue cooking to the temperature which will yield desired doneness. See chart below.

TENDER BEEF ROAST COOKING CHART

The estimated microwaving times are based on meat at refrigerated temperature. Rolled or Standing Rib roasts up to 5 pounds microwave well; select rib eye roasts of 2 to 4 pounds. If meat has been frozen, be sure to defrost thoroughly before roasting, especially if you are using the temperature probe. Carve rare roasts immediately or after standing 5 minutes. Let medium and well done roasts stand about 5 to 15 minutes before carving.

ROAST	POWER LEVEL	INTERNAL TEMP. FIRST SIDE	INTERNAL TEMP. WHEN DONE	ESTIMATED MINUTES PER POUND
Standing Rib (4 to 5 lb.)				
Rare	Medium High (7)	90°	120° to 125°	8 to 10
Medium	Medium High (7)	90°	130° to 140°	10 to 12
Well Done	Medium High (7)	90°	155° to 165°	12 to 14
Rolled Rib (3 to 5 lb.)				
Rare	Medium High (7)	90°	120° to 125°	8 to 10
Medium	Medium High (7)	90°	130° to 140°	10 to 12
Well Done	Medium High (7)	90°	155° to 165°	12 to 14
Rolled Tied Rib Eye (2 to 4 lb.)				
Rare	Medium High (7)	90°	120° to 125°	8 to 10
Medium	Medium High (7)	90°	130° to 140°	10 to 12
Well Done	Medium High (7)	90°	155° to 165°	12 to 14
Half Tenderloin (1 to 2 lb.)				
Rare	Medium High (7)	90°	120° to 125°	7 to 8
Medium	Medium High (7)	90°	130° to 140°	8 to 10
Well Done	Medium High (7)	90°	155° to 165°	10 to 12

Ham & Pork Ground

Lower power settings are ideal for ground ham, which tends to become dry and crusty at high settings due to the meat curing process. The addition of some ground pork or beef not only makes ham go farther, but adds enough moisture so that it remains tender and juicy.

Patties containing ground ham do not require use of the Brown 'N Sear Dish or a browning agent because ham has a naturally attractive pink color; however, a light brushing of brown bouquet sauce may be used.

When making ham loaf, refer to the pages in this book on preparing ground beef meatloaf. Use the same techniques for even cooking such as covering, shaping and shielding. To cook ham loaf by temperature, follow the directions given below for inserting the probe, covering and turning meat.

CLASSIC HAM LOAF

POWER LEVEL: High (10)   TEMP: 170°
APPROX. MICROWAVE TIME: 11 to 14 min.
Cook Code: 110

1 lb. ground cooked ham	Mix ground ham and pork thoroughly with crumbs, water, onion, and pepper. Mold into flat loaf in 9-in. pie plate.
½ lb. ground fresh pork	
½ cup soft bread crumbs	
½ cup water	
2 tablespoons instant minced onion	
¼ teaspoon pepper	

Insert temperature probe so tip is in center of food. Cover tightly with plastic wrap, arranging loosely around probe to vent. Attach cable end at receptacle. **Microwave at High. Set Temp, Set 170°.**

When oven signals, remove loaf from oven and let stand 5 minutes before serving.

Makes 6 servings

NOTES:

1. If a fast simple glaze is desired, spoon pineapple or apricot preserves over cooked ham loaf a few minutes before serving.

2. For best cooking results, do not exceed recommended weight of meat.

Shape ham loaf in a flat circle. Insert the temperature probe so the tip is in the center of the loaf. Cover tightly with plastic wrap, arranging loosely around probe to vent. Microwave to an internal temperature of 170°.

SWEET 'N' SOUR PORKIES

POWER LEVEL: High (10)   **Cook Code:** 140
MICROWAVE TIME: 14 to 16 min., total

1 lb. ground cooked ham	In large mixing bowl mix together ham, pork, crumbs, water, egg, celery, green pepper, onion, mustard and pepper. Shape mixture into 4 individual patties and place in 8-in. square dish.
½ lb. ground fresh pork	
½ cup soft bread crumbs	
½ cup water	
1 egg	
¼ cup minced celery	
2 tablespoons minced green pepper	
2 tablespoons instant minced onion	
½ teaspoon dry mustard	
¼ teaspoon pepper	
8 to 12 whole cloves	Score tops of patties and place 2 or 3 whole cloves in top of each.
⅓ cup brown sugar (packed)	Stir together sugar, mustard and vinegar. Pour evenly over patties.
1 tablespoon prepared mustard	
1 tablespoon vinegar	

Cover dish with wax paper. **Microwave at High 14 to 16 Minutes,** rotating dish ¼ turn after 8 minutes.

Makes 4 generous servings

TRIPLE MEATLOAF

POWER LEVEL: Medium (5) and High (10) TEMP: 170°
APPROX. MICROWAVE TIME: 22 to 25 min.

¾ lb. ground cooked ham	In large bowl place ham, beef, pork, eggs, crumbs, pepper and cloves. Mix together very well. In 9-in. pie plate form mixture into flat rounded loaf. Insert temperature probe so tip is in center of loaf. Cover tightly with plastic wrap, arranging loosely around probe to vent.
½ lb. ground chuck beef	
¼ lb. ground fresh pork	
2 eggs beaten	
½ cup graham cracker crumbs	
¼ cup diced red or green pepper	
½ teaspoon ground cloves	

Attach cable end at receptacle. **Microwave at Medium. Set Temp, Set 170°.** When oven signals, remove loaf and microwave Topping (below), spread over loaf. Let stand 10 minutes before slicing.

Makes 4 to 6 servings

Raisin Topping: In small bowl stir together ½ cup brown sugar (packed), ½ teaspoon dry mustard, 1 tablespoon vinegar, ¼ cup raisins. **Microwave at High 3 to 5 Minutes.**

Sweet 'N' Sour Porkies

HOLIDAY HAM LOAF

POWER LEVEL: Medium (5) and High (10) TEMP: 170°
APPROX. MICROWAVE TIME: 25 to 30 min.

¾ lb. ground cooked ham	In large bowl mix together ham, pork, crumbs, egg, onions and milk. In 9-in. pie plate form mixture into flat rounded loaf. Insert temperature probe so tip is in center of loaf. Cover tightly with plastic wrap, arranging loosely around probe to vent.
¾ lb. ground fresh pork	
¾ cup fine bread crumbs	
1 egg beaten	
¼ cup chopped onion	
½ cup milk	

Attach cable end at receptacle, **Microwave at Medium. Set Temp, Set 170°.** When oven signals, remove loaf; microwave Topping (below); spread over loaf. Let stand 10 minutes for topping to set, to allow loaf to firm before slicing.

Makes 4 to 6 servings

Spicy Topping: In small bowl stir together 2 tablespoons butter, ¼ cup brown sugar (packed), 1 teaspoon allspice. **Microwave at High 3 to 5 Minutes,** until dissolved.

Pork Spareribs

Everyone agrees that the barbecued sparerib is one of America's greatest inventions. No one agrees on how it should be cooked. One side advocates the moist, fork tender rib which falls off the bone and melts in the mouth. Another side is devoted to the dry, chewy rib, and considers eating ribs with anything but the fingers a sacrilege. Ever since our first Microwave Cookbook, in 1962, we've provided recipes for both types, because the staff couldn't agree on which rib was the real rib.

Whichever rib you fancy, the microwave oven cooks it fast and flavorful. The fork tender rib takes a little longer, because you add moisture which absorbs some power, and you cook part of the time at a lower power setting. Either way, turn or rearrange ribs half way through the cooking time. Both styles may be served as a main dish or as an appetizer.

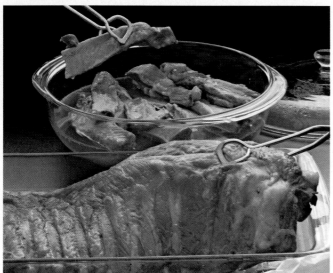

Whole Rack of Spareribs should be turned over for even cooking. Rib pieces can be rearranged.

HOW TO DEFROST SPARERIBS
POWER LEVEL: **Defrost**

4 to 8 Minutes Per Pound

1. Place plastic or paper wrapped package in oven. **Microwave at Defrost** ½ the minimum total time.

2. Turn package over and **Defrost** second ½ of time.

3. Separate the pieces with a rubber spatula and let stand to complete defrosting, or **Microwave 1 to 2 Minutes** more.

NOTE: For a rack of ribs, let stand 15 minutes to completely defrost largest end.

Chewy Style Spareribs   Fork Tender Spareribs

CHEWY STYLE SPARERIBS

POWER LEVEL: High (10)
MICROWAVE TIME: 30 to 35 min., total

3 lb. rack of spareribs . . . . .In 13×9×2-in. dish place spareribs, bone side up. Cover with wax paper. **Microwave at High 15 Minutes,** turning over after 10 minutes. Drain off liquid.

1 medium onion, very . . . . .Distribute onion and lemon
thinly sliced slices over ribs, pour
1 lemon, very thinly sauce over top. Cover. **Mi-**
sliced **crowave at High 15 to 20**
1 cup barbecue sauce, **Minutes,** rotating dish ½
bottled, or recipe turn after 10 minutes, until
page 194 no pink remains in meat. Spoon sauce over ribs before serving.

Makes about 4 servings

TO COOK RIBS IN PIECES: Cut into 2 or 3-rib pieces and microwave in 3-qt. covered casserole.

FORK TENDER SPARERIBS

POWER LEVEL: Medium (5)
MICROWAVE TIME: 1 hr. 30 min. to 1 hr. 45 min., total

3 lb. rack of spareribs
2 cups hot tap water
1 medium onion, very
  thinly sliced
1 lemon, very thinly
  sliced
	In 13 x 9 x 2-in. dish place spareribs, bone side up. Add water. Cover tightly with vented plastic wrap. **Microwave at Medium 80 to 90 Minutes,** rotating dish ½ turn every 20 minutes, until fork tender. Turn ribs over, distribute onion and lemon over top after 40 minutes.

1 cup barbecue sauce,
  bottled, or recipe
  page 194
	Drain liquid from ribs and pour sauce over top.

Microwave at Medium 10 to 15 Minutes, loosely covered with plastic wrap, until sauce has dried on top.

Makes about 4 servings

Smokey Pineapple Ribs; Cut ribs in pieces. Add 2 cups of hot tap water. **Microwave at Medium 40 Minutes.** Drain off water and turn ribs over. Top with Sauce (below). **Microwave at Medium 35 to 45 Minutes,** rearranging after 20 minutes, until tender.

Smokey Pineapple Sauce: In small bowl stir together 1 can (8½-oz.) crushed pineapple, 1 can (8-oz.) tomato sauce, ⅓ cup vinegar, 1 teaspoon garlic salt, 1 teaspoon chili powder, 2 tablespoons light molasses, 1 tablespoon prepared mustard, and 1 tablespoon liquid smoke.

SWEET-SOUR SPARERIBS

POWER LEVEL: Medium (5) and High (10)
MICROWAVE TIME: 1 hr. 25 min. to 1 hr. 39 min., total

3 lb. spareribs, cut in **serving pieces** **1 large onion, chopped** **2 cups hot tap water**	In 3-qt. casserole place ribs. Add onion and water. Cover. **Microwave at Medium 75 to 85 Minutes,** rearranging every 20 minutes. Drain meat.
¾ cup cider vinegar **¾ cup sugar** **½ cup sherry wine** **1 tablespoon soy sauce** **2 teaspoons ground** **ginger**	In small bowl stir together vinegar, sugar, wine, soy sauce and ginger. Add to drained cooked ribs. **Microwave at High 5 to 7 Minutes,** until hot.

3 tablespoons
  cornstarch
2 tablespoons cold
  water
	In small bowl stir cornstarch into cold water. Add to hot saucy ribs, mixing well. **Microwave at High 5 to 7 Minutes,** stirring after 3 minutes, until thickened.

Makes about 4 entree servings, or
8 appetizer servings

TERIYAKI RIBLETS

Ribs may be marinated in sauce several hours or overnight before cooking, if desired.

POWER LEVEL: Medium (5) and High (10)
MICROWAVE TIME: 73 to 84 min., total

3 lb. spareribs	Have butcher cut rack of spareribs in half crosswise. Cut ribs into 3-in. pieces and place in 3-qt. casserole.

¼ cup soy sauce
½ cup sliced onion
2 tablespoons brown
  sugar (packed)
1 clove garlic, minced
1 teaspoon ground
  ginger
1 teaspoon salt
2 tablespoons sherry
  wine
3 cups apricot nectar
  or orange juice
	In mixing bowl stir together soy sauce, onion, brown sugar, garlic, ginger, salt, sherry and nectar. Pour over ribs. Cover. **Microwave at Medium 70 to 80 Minutes,** rearranging every 20 minutes. Remove ribs to platter and keep warm. Skim fat from top of liquid remaining in dish.

1½ tablespoons **cornstarch** **2 tablespoons water**	In small bowl, stir together cornstarch and water. Blend into liquid in dish. **Microwave at High 3 to 4 Minutes,** stirring every minute until sauce is clear and thickened. Serve sauce over ribs.

Makes about 8 appetizer servings, or
4 entree servings

Sweet-Sour Spareribs

Pork Chops & Steaks

Just as in conventional cooking, texture of pork chops depends upon the cooking method used. Fried chops are chewy; steamed chops are more soft. Some people prefer to brown chops in a skillet on the range top, then finish them by microwaving.

HOW TO DEFROST CHOPS & STEAKS

POWER LEVEL: **Defrost**

---

4 to 8 Minutes Per Pound

1. Place plastic or paper wrapped package in oven. **Microwave at Defrost** ½ the minimum time.

2. Turn package over and defrost second ½ of time.

3. Separate the pieces with a rubber spatula and let stand to complete defrosting, or **Microwave 1 to 2 Minutes** more.

MICROWAVING CHOPS OR STEAKS

1. Select steaks or chops about ¾-in. thick. Cut steaks into pieces about 3 x 4-in. Arrange in suitable dish.

2. On each chop or steak, spread 2 tablespoons of Topping. (See suggestions below.)

3. Cover tightly with plastic wrap, vent 2-in. at one side. **Microwave at Medium,** rotating dish ½ turn after ½ of time.

4. Add salt and pepper after microwaving, as desired.

POWER LEVEL: **Medium (5)**

NO.	UTENSIL	TIME MIN.	COOK CODE	COMMENTS
2	Microwave oven-proof dinner plate or 9-in. pie plate	14 to 18	145	Rotate ½ turn after 8 minutes.
3	8-in. square	19 to 24	195	Rotate ¼ turn after 10 minutes.
4	8-in. square	26 to 32	265	Rotate ¼ turn after 15 minutes.
6	12×8×2-in.	35 to 45	355	Rotate ½ turn after 20 minutes.

TOPPINGS

1. Equal parts Worcestershire or steak sauce and water.

2. Barbecue sauce (bottled or see recipe, page 194).

3. Teriyaki sauce.

4. Marinade from page 98. Marinate chops several hours, if desired, then cook in marinade.

5. Brush meat with diluted brown bouquet sauce or soy sauce. Add 2 tablespoons water or red wine per chop.

Microwaved pork chops or steaks need to be browned or cooked in a colorful sauce. From the top: Conventional, Plain Microwaved, Steak Sauce and Water Topping, Brown 'N Sear Dish.

GOLDEN BREADED PORK CUTLETS

Pounding the cutlets thin tenderizes them and allows for fast cooking at High.

POWER LEVEL: High (10)   **Cook Code:** 120
MICROWAVE TIME: 12 to 14 min.

6 lean pork rib chops (8-oz. each)	Remove bone from each chop leaving a single solid piece of meat. Pound each chop with wooden mallet or foil-covered brick until meat is ½-in. thick.
1¼ cups buttery cracker crumbs (about 45 crackers) **¾ teaspoon salt** **2 eggs, beaten** **¼ cup butter, melted**	Combine crumbs and salt. Dip flattened cutlets into crumbs to coat, then in mixture of eggs and melted butter. Coat again with crumbs.

Place coated cutlets in 12×8×2-in. dish. Cover with wax paper. **Microwave at High 12 to 14 Minutes,** rotating dish ½ turn after 6 minutes. Let stand 5 to 10 minutes before serving. If desired, garnish with chutney.

Makes 6 servings

VARIATION: To crumb mixture add 1 tablespoon curry powder. Or, use a flavored snack cracker, such as onion or cheese cracker, to make crumbs for breading.

GOLDEN BREADED PORK CHOPS

Prepare above recipe, except use 1-in. pork chops with bone in and 13 x 9 x 2-in. dish, if necessary. **Microwave at Low 55 to 65 Minutes,** rotating dish ½ turn after 30 minutes. **Cook Code:** 553

MICROWAVING PORK CHOPS IN BROWN 'N SEAR DISH

Preheat empty dish at High. Add chops; cover and cook first side. Turn chops and recover dish. Cook second side.

POWER LEVEL: **High (10)**

NO. OF CHOPS	PREHEAT MINUTES	1st SIDE MINUTES	2nd SIDE MINUTES
1	3	2	4 to 6
2	4	4	4 to 6
3	4	4, then pour off juice	5 to 6

Golden Breaded Pork Cutlets

CHILI PORK CHOPS

POWER LEVEL: Medium (5)   **Cook Code:** 355
MICROWAVE TIME: 35 to 45 min., total

4 pork chops, 1-in. thick **4 onion slices, ¼ to ½-in. thick** **4 green pepper rings, ¼ to ½-in. thick** **1 bottle (12-oz.) chili sauce (1½ cups)**	Score fat on chops and arrange in 3-qt. casserole so "tails" are in center. Place onion and green pepper slices on top of chops. Pour chili sauce over top. Cover. **Microwave at Medium 35 to 45 Minutes,** rotating dish ½ turn after 20 minutes.

Makes 4 servings

PORK CHOPS WITH SAUERKRAUT AND BEER

When possible, assemble this dish ahead of time and allow to marinate several hours to blend flavor and tenderize meat.

POWER LEVEL: Medium (5)   **Cook Code:** 355
MICROWAVE TIME: 35 to 40 min., total

4 pork chops, 1-in thick **½ cup chopped onion** **1 can (16-oz.) sauerkraut, drained** **1 teaspoon caraway seed (optional)** **1 can (12-oz.) beer**	In 8-in. square dish arrange chops with thickest meaty areas to edge and "tails" to center. Sprinkle evenly with onion. Spread sauerkraut over top. Sprinkle with caraway. Pour beer around chops.

Cover dish tightly with plastic wrap, turning back one corner to vent. **Microwave at Medium 35 to 40 Minutes,** rotating dish ¼ turn after 18 minutes, until chops are tender.

Makes 4 servings

Cornbread Stuffed 'N' Tender Pork Chops

STUFFED 'N' TENDER PORK CHOPS

Because chops are split, each layer of meat is thinner and Medium Power may be used.

POWER LEVEL: Medium (5)   **Cook Code:** 355
MICROWAVE TIME: 35 to 40 min., total

1. Select **4 (1-in. thick) pork chops** with pocket cut in each.

2. Fill pocket with Apple stuffing or Cornbread Stuffing (below), dividing all of stuffing among chops. Arrange chops in 12x8x2-in. dish, with thickest meaty areas to edge and "tails" in center. Brush half of glaze (below) over top of chops. Cover with wax paper.

3. **Microwave at Medium 35 to 40 Minutes,** rotating dish ½ turn after 15 minutes, until tender. Let stand 5 minutes. Brush with remaining glaze before serving.

Makes 4 servings

APPLE STUFFING WITH SWEET GLAZE

2 cups chopped, ...	In mixing bowl combine
unpeeled apples	apples, raisins, egg, but-
¼ cup raisins	ter, cinnamon, salt and
1 egg, beaten	pepper. Divide evenly be-
2 tablespoons butter,	tween chops.
melted	
½ teaspoon cinnamon	
½ teaspoon salt	
⅛ teaspoon pepper	

Sweet Glaze: Mix together ⅓ cup currant jelly and 2 tablespoons orange juice.

Makes about 1½ cups

CORNBREAD STUFFING WITH SAVORY GLAZE

2 cups crumbled	In mixing bowl toss togeth-
cornbread	er cornbread, onion, green
¼ cup chopped onion	pepper, butter, egg, pi-
¼ cup chopped green	miento, salt and pepper.
pepper	Divide evenly between
¼ cup butter, melted	chops.
1 egg, beaten	
1 tablespoon chopped	
pimiento	
½ teaspoon salt	
⅛ teaspoon pepper	

Savory Glaze: Mix together ½ cup ketchup, 2 tablespoons brown sugar, 2 teaspoons prepared mustard and ¼ teaspoon chili powder.

Makes about 1½ cups

PORK CHOPS ROSADO

This dish is very saucy, so plan rice or noodles to serve under chops and sauce.

POWER LEVEL: Medium (5)   **Cook Code:** 405
MICROWAVE TIME: 40 to 50 min., total

4 center cut loin pork	In 12×8×2-in. dish ar-
chops, 1-in. thick	range pork chops with
1 large onion, cut in	thickest meaty areas to
¼-in. slices	edge and "tails" in center.
1 medium lemon or lime,	Place onion and lemon
cut in ⅛-in. slices	slices over top of chops.
1 cup ketchup	Combine ketchup and
1 cup (8-oz.) dairy sour	sour cream. Pour over top.
cream	Cover dish with plastic
	wrap, turning back one
	corner to vent.

Microwave at Medium 40 to 50 Minutes, rotating dish ½ turn after 20 minutes, until pork chops are tender. Let stand, covered about 5 minutes before serving.

Makes 4 servings

SWEET AND SOUR PORK

POWER LEVEL: Medium (5) and Medium High (7)
MICROWAVE TIME: 45 to 50 min., total

1½ lbs. fresh pork, cut into 1-in. cubes **1½ tablespoons instant minced onion** **1 tablespoon soy sauce** **1 teaspoon brown bouquet sauce** **1 can (8¾-oz.) pineapple chunks**	In 2-qt. casserole place pork, onion, soy sauce and bouquet sauce. Reserving juice, drain pineapple. Set aside. Add reserved juice to meat, stirring well. Cover. **Microwave at Medium 30 Minutes,** stirring after 15 minutes.
1 cup water **¼ cup cider vinegar** **¼ cup brown sugar (packed)** **3 tablespoons cornstarch** **½ teaspoon salt** **1 can (5-oz.) water chestnuts, drained and sliced** **1 medium green pepper, sliced in ½-in. strips**	In small bowl stir together water, vinegar, brown sugar, cornstarch and salt. Add to meat along with pineapple and water chestnuts. Cover. **Microwave at Medium High 15 to 20 Minutes,** stirring and adding green pepper after 8 minutes, until thickened and clear.
1 medium firm tomato, cut into chunks	Fold in tomato chunks and let stand, covered, 10 minutes before serving. Serve over rice or crisp noodles.

Makes 6 servings

Sweet and Sour Pork

GOLDEN PORK CASSEROLE

POWER LEVEL: High (10) **Cook Code:** 80
MICROWAVE TIME: 8 to 10 min., total

4 to 6 slices (½-in. thick) cooked pork roast (¾ to 1-lb.) **1 can (17-oz.) yams, drained and cut in 1-in. slices** **1 cup coarsely shredded, unpeeled apple** **½ cup grated sharp cheddar cheese** **3 tablespoons brown sugar (packed)** **1 tablespoon lemon juice** **2 tablespoons butter**	In 2-qt. casserole layer pork, yams, apple and cheese. Sprinkle with brown sugar and lemon juice. Dot with butter. Cover. **Microwave at High 8 to 10 Minutes,** rotating dish ½ turn after 4 minutes, until hot throughout.

Makes 4 to 6 servings

CHOW MEIN

POWER LEVEL: High (10) **Cook Code:** 200
MICROWAVE TIME: 20 to 22 min., total

⅓ cup soy sauce **3 tablespoons cornstarch** **2 cans (5-oz. each) water chestnuts, sliced and undrained** **1 can (1-lb.) bean sprouts, undrained** **1 can (7-oz.) mushroom stems and pieces, undrained** **2 cups diced cooked pork or other meat** **2 cups ½-in. diagonal sliced celery** **1 cup thinly sliced onion**	In 3-qt. casserole stir together soy sauce and cornstarch. Stir in water chestnuts, bean sprouts and mushrooms, then meat, celery and onion. **Microwave at High 20 to 22 Minutes,** stirring well after 10 minutes, until hot and thickened. Stir thoroughly and serve over cooked rice or chow mein noodles.

Makes 4 to 6 servings

Ham Slices, Steaks & Pieces

Slices, steaks and pieces of ready-to-eat ham are pre-cooked, so they need only be reheated. Because the high sugar content attracts microwaves, cooking times are short, and ham can overcook easily. Browning is not necessary, since ham has a naturally attractive color. Due to the salt, ham can become dry if moisture is not sealed in. For example, when microwaving a ham slice, 1 to 2-in. thick, add some liquid to keep it juicy and cover the dish with wax paper or plastic wrap.

Baked Ham Slice. Use a slice of fully cooked ham, 1 to 2-in. thick. Slash the fatty edges to prevent curling. Place ham in a baking dish large enough to hold it comfortably. Add a small amount of liquid. Cover.

Fried Ham. Thin slices and steaks of fully-cooked ham may be fried with the Brown 'N Sear Dish. Preheat the dish 3½ to 4 minutes. Cook ¼ to ½-in. thick slices 1 minute per side.

FRUITED HAM SLICE

POWER LEVEL: High (10)
MICROWAVE TIME: 18 to 27 min., total

1 slice fully cooked ham, 1 to 2-in. thick
1 can (11-oz.) mandarin orange segments
1 can (8¼-oz.) crushed pineapple

Score or remove fat from ham. Depending on size of slice, place in 8-in. square or 12×8×2-in. dish. Drain fruit, reserving juice. Arrange fruit attractively over ham slice. Cover with wax paper. **Microwave at High 10 to 15 Minutes.**

Juice from fruits
2 tablespoons brown sugar (packed)
1 tablespoon cornstarch
¼ teaspoon ground cloves

Combine juice, sugar, cornstarch and cloves. Pour carefully over ham slice to avoid disturbing the arranged fruit. Rotate dish ½ turn. Cover. **Microwave at High 8 to 12 Minutes,** until hot. Spoon juice over fruit and serve.

Makes 4 to 6 servings

PINEAPPLE HAM AND YAMS

POWER LEVEL: High (10)
MICROWAVE TIME: 5¼ to 7½ min., total

1 tablespoon butter
1 can (8-oz.) yams or sweet potatoes, drained
2 tablespoons brown sugar (packed)
4 slices (about 4-oz.) packaged, thinly sliced cooked ham*

In 1-qt. casserole place butter. **Microwave at High ¼ to ½ Minute,** to melt. Add drained yams and mash well. Stir in brown sugar. Divide mixture equally over one end of each ham slice. Roll up into firm rolls.

1 can (8-oz.) sliced pineapple (4 slices)

Drain pineapple, reserving juice. Place pineapple slices in 8-in. square dish. Cover each with ham roll, seam side down.

¼ cup coarsely chopped pecans
¼ cup light brown sugar (packed)
¼ cup syrup reserved from pineapple

Combine pecans, sugar and pineapple syrup. Spoon over ham rolls. Cover with wax paper.

Microwave at High 5 to 7 Minutes, rotating dish ¼ turn after 4 minutes.

Makes 4 servings

*Or use thinly sliced leftover ham, about 6-in. long by 3-in. wide.

HAM-AGETTI CASSEROLE

POWER LEVEL: High (10)
MICROWAVE TIME: 23 to 27 min., total

4 strips bacon . . . . With scissors, snip bacon into 1-in. pieces into 2-qt. casserole. **Microwave at High 4 to 5 Minutes.** Remove approximately half the fat.

2 cups cooked ham, cut, into ½-in. strips
1 can (1-lb. 14-oz.) tomatoes
1 cup spaghetti, broken into 1-in. pieces
½ cup chopped onion
¼ cup chopped green pepper
½ teaspoon salt
⅛ teaspoon pepper
. . . . . Add ham, tomatoes, spaghetti, onion, green pepper, salt and pepper. Stir well. Cover. **Microwave at High 18 to 20 Minutes,** until spaghetti is tender, stirring after 9 minutes.

½ cup shredded cheddar cheese . . . . Sprinkle with cheese. **Microwave at High 1 to 2 Minutes,** uncovered, until cheese is melted.

Makes 6 servings

CREAMED HAM

If ham is salty, omit salt when preparing White Sauce.

POWER LEVEL: High (10) and Medium (5)
MICROWAVE TIME: 16 to 19 min., total

2 cups (double recipe) White Sauce, page 175
2 cups diced cooked ham
2 hard-poached eggs, diced (below)
1 can (2-oz.) sliced mushrooms, drained
1 tablespoon chopped green pepper
1 tablespoon chopped pimiento
¼ teaspoon dry mustard
. . . . In 2-qt. casserole, mix together white sauce, ham, eggs, mushrooms, green pepper, pimiento and mustard. Cover. **Microwave at High 8 to 10 Minutes,** stirring after 4 minutes, until hot. Serve as desired, over cornbread, rice or noodles.

Makes 4 to 6 servings

Hard-poached Eggs: In 1-qt. casserole, place 2 cups water. **Microwave at High 5 to 6 Minutes,** until boiling. Break eggs onto plate, puncture membrane. Gently slip eggs into water. Cover. **Microwave at Medium 3 Minutes.** Let eggs stand in water 5 minutes before removing to dice.

Brown 'N Sear Dish Ham and Eggs

SWEET AND SOUR HAM

POWER LEVEL: High (10) **Cook Code:** 120
MICROWAVE TIME: 12 to 14 min., total

1 can (1-lb. 4-oz.) pineapple chunks
1 can (10½-oz.) condensed beef broth
3 tablespoons cornstarch
. . . . Reserving juice, drain pineapple. Set chunks aside. In 3-qt. casserole combine ⅓ cup pineapple juice, broth and cornstarch.

2 cups cooked ham, cut into 1-in. cubes
1 green pepper, cut into strips
1 small onion, thinly sliced
¾ teaspoon dry mustard
2 tablespoons brown sugar (packed)
3 tablespoons vinegar
. . . . . Add ham, pineapple, green pepper, onion, mustard, brown sugar and vinegar. Cover. **Microwave at High 12 to 14 Minutes,** stirring every 5 minutes. Serve over rice or crisp noodles.

Makes 4 servings

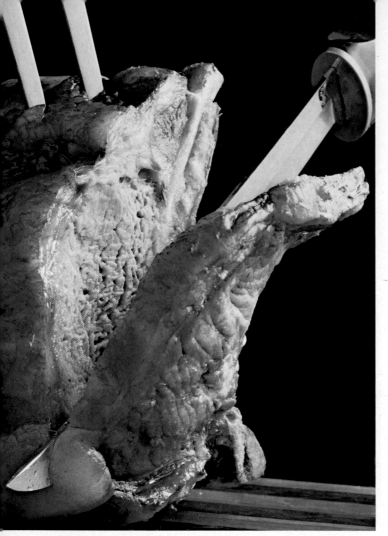
Microwaved Pork Roast

Pork Roasts

Pork is leaner than it used to be, giving you more meat and less fat. Roasted conventionally or microwaved, this leaner meat has a firm texture. We recommend using a small amount of water and covering with plastic wrap to keep roast pork tender and juicy. Start the roast bone side up and turn it over after ½ the time. When using the temperature probe, set it for 120°. When oven signals, turn roast over and reset for 170°.

Microwaved pork roasts develop browning; especially when the fat coating is thin. If the roast has a heavy coating of fat, you may want to add brown bouquet sauce.

Microwave pork roast to 170° to cook it thoroughly and maintain juiciness. Be sure to allow the entire standing time, which allows meat to complete cooking and makes it more tender.

HOW TO DEFROST PORK ROAST

POWER LEVEL: **Defrost**
10 to 12 Minutes Per Pound

1. If roast is wrapped in paper or plastic, place the unopened package in the oven and defrost for half the time. (Foil wrapping must be removed before defrosting.)

2. Unwrap roast and feel it for warm areas. Shield any warm spots with small pieces of foil. Turn roast over, place it in a roasting dish and return it to the oven.

3. Defrost for second half of time and let the roast stand for 15 to 30 minutes. For step-by-step pictures of roast defrosting, see page 102.

GLAZES FOR PORK ROASTS
The following glazes may be spooned or poured over pork roasts just before serving.

CHERRY ALMOND GLAZE

POWER LEVEL: High (10)
MICROWAVE TIME: 8 to 12 min., total

1 teaspoon butter . . . . . . .In 8 or 9-in. pie plate place
¼ cup slivered almonds butter and almonds. **Microwave at High 3 to 5 Minutes,** stirring every 2 minutes, until toasted. Set aside.

1 jar (12-oz.) cherry . . . . .In 1½-qt. casserole stir to-
preserves gether preserves, corn
2 tablespoons white syrup, vinegar, salt, cinna-
corn syrup mon, nutmeg and cloves.
¼ cup red wine vinegar Cover. **Microwave at High**
¼ teaspoon salt **5 to 7 Minutes,** stirring
¼ teaspoon cinnamon very well after 4 minutes.
¼ teaspoon nutmeg Mixture should be well
¼ teaspoon ground blended. Stir in toasted al-
cloves monds just before glazing.

Makes about 1¾ cups

WINEBERRY GLAZE

POWER LEVEL: High (10) **Cook Code: 50**
MICROWAVE TIME: 5 to 7 min., total

1 can (8-oz.) whole . . . . . .In 1-qt. casserole mix to-
cranberry sauce gether cranberry sauce,
½ cup vermouth vermouth, cornstarch and
1 tablespoon steak sauce. **Microwave**
cornstarch **at High 5 to 7 Minutes,**
1 tablespoon steak stirring after 3 minutes, un-
sauce til thickened and clear.

Makes about 1½ cups

MICROWAVING PORK ROAST BY TIME

POWER LEVEL: **Medium (5)**
9 to 11 Minutes Per Pound

Do not salt roast. Place roast bone side up in a 13x9x2-in. dish. Add ½ cup water to the dish. Cover with plastic wrap, turning back one corner to vent.

Estimate the minimum total roasting time. If your oven has a 35 minute timer you will have to reset it to complete the cooking cycle. **Microwave at Medium** for half of time; turn roast over and microwave second half of time. After the minimum time, test the internal temperature of the roast with a meat thermometer, following instructions given for probe placement. Allow 2 minutes for thermometer to register. If roast has not reached 170°, remove the thermometer and return roast to the oven for a few more minutes. When cooking is completed remove and let stand 20 minutes.

Do not place conventional metal meat thermometer in microwave oven; remove from roast if meat needs additional microwaving.

MICROLESSON: HOW TO MICROWAVE PORK ROAST BY TEMPERATURE

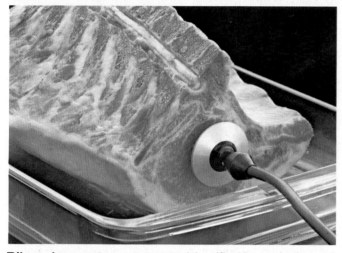

Rib end or center cut roasts. Identified by arch shaped bones on the edge of the roast and clearly defined large muscle. Insert the temperature probe slightly below center of the largest muscle, so tip is in the center of the roast. Microwave bone side up to 120° before turning over to finish.

Loin end roast. Identified by circular bone at one end of the roast and rack of bones at the bottom. Insert temperature probe into end where the round bone is located, placing it ¾ to 1-in. above the bottom of the roast on the meatiest side of the round bone. Follow bone structure, angling if necessary, so that tip of probe is in the center of the roast. Do not allow tip of probe to touch bone. Microwave bone side up to 120° before turning over to finish.

Add water to roasting dish and cover with microwave-safe plastic dome or plastic wrap. Arrange plastic wrap loosely around temperature probe to vent. **Microwave at Medium. Set Temperature for 120°.**

Turn Over roast when oven signals; recover. **Microwave at Medium and Set Temperature for 170°.** When oven signals, remove roast and let stand 20 minutes.

Ham Roasts

Most hams are now precooked and need to be heated only to 115°. Take care not to overcook, which makes them dry and tough. Canned or compressed hams are very dense and must be microwaved by time. This is because they must be turned over at a temperature lower than 90°, the lowest temperature which the probe

records. Hams with a natural shape (shank or butt end hams) may be microwaved either by time or temperature. Again most all are precooked, but a few can be purchased raw and must be cooked before eating. Directions for raw hams are covered on page 125. Purchase hams no higher than six inches for microwaving.

HOW TO MICROWAVE PRECOOKED HAM

POWER LEVEL: **Medium (5)**
12 to 14 Minutes Per Pound

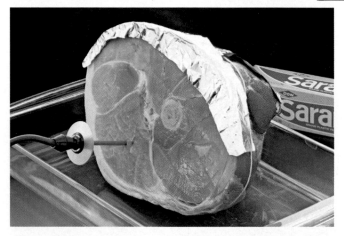

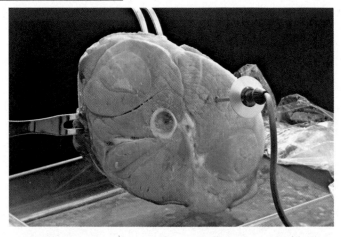

Tie string around ham to hold shape. Shield cut edge with foil (also shank bone if protruding). Place fat side up in 13×9×2-in. dish. Add ¼ cup water. Insert probe in center of lowest large muscle. Cover with plastic wrap, arranging loosely around probe to vent. **Microwave at Medium. Set Temp, Set 90°.** If microwaving by time, microwave ⅔ of total time.

Remove foil strips, turn ham over and reshield only around top cut edges. Recover. **Set Temp, Set 115°.** If microwaving by time, microwave second side remaining ⅓ of total time. Let stand 5 to 10 minutes before carving.

HOW TO MICROWAVE CANNED HAM

POWER LEVEL: **Medium (5)**
10 to 12 Minutes Per Pound

Shield ham (which has been tied) around top cut edges with 2-inch strip of foil. Place on trivet in 12×8×2-in. dish. Add ¼ cup water, and cover with vented plastic wrap. **Microwave at Medium** for first ½ of total time.

Remove foil. Turn ham over and reshield around top cut edges. Recover and vent. **Microwave at Medium** for second ½ of total time. Let stand 5 to 10 minutes before carving the ham.

Microwaved Precooked Ham with Currant Jelly Glaze

HOW TO MICROWAVE A RAW HAM

POWER LEVEL: **Medium (5)**   **Temp. 160°**
12 to 15 Minutes Per Pound

Prepare ham for microwaving the same way as described under the picture of precooked shanks or butt hams on page 124. **Microwave** raw hams at **Medium. Set Temp, Set 120°.** If microwaving by time microwave first side ⅔ of total cooking time. Remove foil and turn ham over. Reshield and recover. To microwave second side, **Set Temp, Set 160°.** If microwaving by time, microwave second side remaining ⅓ of total time. Let stand 5 to 10 minutes before carving.

Do not use meat thermometer in the microwave oven unless it is specially designed or recommended for use in the microwave oven.

To Test Time-Cooked Hams With Conventional Meat Thermometer. Insert thermometer into ham, following directions for probe placement. Allow 2 minutes for thermometer to register. If specified temperature has not been reached, remove the thermometer and return to the oven for a few more minutes. After cooking remove ham and let stand 5 to 10 minutes before carving.

KENTUCKY BOURBON SAUCE FOR HAM

POWER LEVEL: High (10)   **Cook Code:** 40
MICROWAVE TIME: 4 to 5 min., total

1 jar (10-oz.) currant	.In 1-qt. casserole place
jelly	jelly. **Microwave at High 4**
¼ cup butter	**to 5 Minutes,** stirring after
½ teaspoon dry mustard	2 minutes, until hot and
2 teaspoons prepared	melted. Add butter, mus-
mustard	tards, and bourbon, stir
¼ cup Kentucky	ring well.
bourbon	

Makes 6 to 8 servings

GLAZES

For an attractive finish, brush cooked ham with ½ cup jelly or preserves, such as pineapple, apricot or cherry; or, use bottled ham glaze. Also try Raisin Sauce, page 193 or Horseradish Sauce, page 191.

Currant Jelly Glaze: In small bowl stir together 1 jar (10-oz.) currant jelly, 1 tablespoon prepared mustard and 1 tablespoon brown sugar. Brush over microwaved ham. Let stand few minutes to set.

Browning continues as bacon stands. Left, crisp-cooked bacon as it should look when removed from oven. Right, crisp-cooked bacon after standing 5 minutes. Brown spots on paper towel are due to sugar in the bacon. A high sugar content may also cause bacon to stick to the towel slightly.

Bacon

Microwaving is a superior way to cook bacon. It is spatter-free. There is less curling and shrinkage than with conventional frying, and if you cook it on paper towels, there is no messy pan to wash.

When cooked crisp, bacon will be evenly cooked and flat. Just as in conventional cooking, under-crisp bacon may be randomly cooked with some spots fatty while others are crisp. Bacon varies in quality, depending upon the amount of sugar and salt used in curing and thickness of slices. Cook less time for extra-sweet bacon and more for thick slices.

HOW TO DEFROST BACON

POWER LEVEL: **Defrost**

4 to 6 Minutes Per Pound

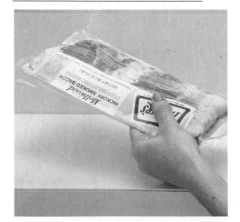

Defrost bacon by placing unopened package in oven. **Microwave at Defrost** for ½ of time. Turn package over and continue defrosting just until strips can be separated with a rubber spatula.

HOW TO MICROWAVE BACON

POWER LEVEL: **High (10)**

¾ to 1 Minute Per Slice

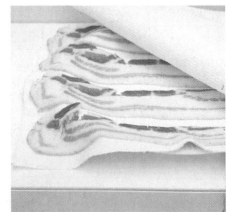

Place two layers of paper towels on pottery plate without metal trim. (Do not use paper plate; it may overheat.) Arrange bacon on towels and cover with another towel to prevent spatters. Place in oven with strips running from side to side. **Microwave at High ¾ to 1 minute** per slice.

Layer bacon when microwaving more than 6 slices. Place 5 slices of bacon on 2 layers of paper towels in a 13×9×2-in. dish. Cover with a paper towel. Add second layer of bacon. Cover and add more layers as desired. **Microwave 4 Minutes** for each layer of bacon and rotate dish ½ turn after ½ the time. A pound of bacon takes about 15 minutes.

Bacon Burgers

BACON BURGERS

POWER LEVEL: High (10)
MICROWAVE TIME: 11 to 14 min., total

8 strips bacon . . . . On microwave ovenproof plate place double thickness of paper towel. Layer bacon (4 strips per layer) and separate layers by single paper towel. Cover. **Microwave at High 3 to 4 Minutes,** just until partially cooked.

1 lb. ground chuck beef
1 teaspoon salt
⅛ teaspoon pepper . .Meanwhile, divide ground beef into 8 equal parts; shape into thin patties. Sprinkle patties with salt and pepper.

4 thin slices onion . . . . . .Place one onion and one
4 thin slices tomato tomato slice over each of 4 patties; cover with remaining 4 patties and press together edges to seal well.

Wrap 2 partially-cooked bacon slices around to encircle the edges of each hamburger patty. Fasten with toothpicks. Place patties in 8-in. square dish. Cover with wax paper. **Microwave at High 8 to 10 Minutes,** rotating dish ½ turn after 4 minutes. Serve on buttered hamburger buns if desired.

Makes 4 servings

BACON 'N' CHEESE BURGERS: Top each cooked patty with a slice of processed cheese (pimiento cheese is flavorful). **Microwave at High ½ to 1 Minute,** until cheese is melted.

HAWAIIAN BURGERS: Place four drained pineapple slices in dish. Cover with assembled patties and microwave as stated, allowing 1 to 2 additional minutes. Top with cheese (above), if desired.

To Save bacon drippings for use in frying cornbread, or microwave recipes such as wilted lettuce, cabbage or German potato salad, cook bacon on a trivet in a cooking dish. Bacon may also be cooked in a casserole or roasting dish directly in its own fat. As with conventional cooking, remove bacon to paper towel to drain and pour off drippings.

Canadian Bacon

Like most ham, Canadian bacon is precooked and needs only heating to be ready to eat. Whether cooked conventionally or by microwave, Canadian bacon will be dry if it is allowed to cook until brown.

MICROWAVING WHOLE PIECE OF CANADIAN BACON

POWER LEVEL: Medium High (7) **Cook Code:** 247
MICROWAVE TIME: 24 to 26 min., total

2 to 3-lb. piece . . . . .Remove casing from ba-
   Canadian bacon   con and arrange in 12×8×
¼ cup water   2-in. dish. Add water.

Cover tightly with plastic wrap, turning back one corner to vent. **Microwave at Medium High 24 to 26 Minutes,** turning over after 12 minutes. Let bacon stand 10 minutes before serving.

MICROWAVING SLICES OF CANADIAN BACON

Place slices in single layer on dinner plate. Cover with wax paper. Timing below is for thin slices, about ¼-in. thick, such as used for Eggs Benedict, sandwiches or as a breakfast meat.

POWER LEVEL: **High (10)**

SLICES	TIME MIN.	COOK CODE	COMMENTS
2	1—1½	10	No rotation necessary.
4	2—2½	20	Rotate ½ turn after 1 minute.
6 to 8	3—4	30	Rotate ¼ turn after 2 minutes.

Whole Canadian Bacon

Sliced Canadian Bacon

Breakfast Sausage

Breakfast sausage comes in many forms. Each defrosts and cooks differently, but all will be tender, juicy and fully cooked in a very short time. Due to quick cooking, breakfast sausage doesn't brown and, since it is rarely served with a sauce, it will be more attractive if it is brushed with a browning agent before cooking. Use equal parts of brown bouquet sauce and water. If you cook sausage frequently, keep this mixture on hand in a small covered container.

BROWN 'N SEAR SAUSAGE CHART
POWER LEVEL: **High (10)**

Preheat dish 4½ to 5½ minutes.

ITEM	1st SIDE TIME MINUTES	2nd SIDE TIME MINUTES
Pork Sausage, 4 slices ½-in. thick	1 covered	1½ to 2 covered
Pork Sausage Links, 6 to 8 links, uncooked, 8-oz.	1 covered	2 to 2½ covered
Brown 'n Serve, 10 links 8-oz. pkg.	1 covered	1½ to 2 covered

Compare link and patty sausage cooked with and without a browning agent. Both are juicy and flavorful, but sausages cooked with a browning agent have more appetite appeal.

SAUSAGE DEFROSTING & MICROWAVING CHART

The following chart gives specific directions for different types and forms of sausage. Whatever type you are microwaving, a few basic rules are common to all.

Defrost sausage in package, removing any metal closures. When defrosted, sausage should still be cold.

When cooking, select a utensil which is appropriate in size for the amount of sausage you wish to cook: a saucer for 1 or 2 links, a glass pie plate for an 8-oz. package, a roasting dish for a full pound of slices. Add browning agent, if desired, before cooking. Always cover the dish with wax paper to prevent spatters.

DEFROSTING POWER LEVEL: **Defrost**			**MICROWAVING** POWER LEVEL: **High (10)**		
ITEM	TIME MINUTES	COMMENTS	ITEM	TIME MINUTES	COMMENTS
Bulk (1-lb. tray)	7 to 9	Defrost like ground beef, page 80.	**4 Patties** (½-lb.)	4 to 5	Rotate dish ½ turn after 2 minutes.
			8 Patties (1-lb.)	7½ to 8	Rotate dish ¼ turn after 4 minutes.
Bulk (1-lb. roll)	4 to 6	Turn over after 1½ minutes.	**4 Patties** (½-lb.)	4 to 5	Rotate dish ½ turn after 2 minutes.
			8 Patties (1-lb.)	7½ to 8	Rotate dish ¼ turn after 4 minutes.
Preformed Patties (12-oz. pkg.)	2 to 3	Turn over after 1 minute.	**4 Patties Raw**	2½ to 3½	Rotate dish ½ turn after 1½ minutes.
			8 Patties Raw	4 to 5	Rotate dish ½ turn after 2 minutes.
Preformed Patties Brown 'n Serve (12-oz. pkg.)	2 to 3	Turn over after 1 minute.	**4 Patties Brown 'n Serve**	1 to 1½	No turns.
			8 Patties Brown 'n Serve	2¼ to 2½	Rotate dish ½ turn after 1½ minutes.
Link Sausage Raw (1-lb.)	3 to 4	Turn over after 1½ minutes.	**4 Links**	2 to 3	No turns.
			7 to 8 Links	4 to 5	Rotate dish ½ turn after 2 minutes.
Link Sausage Brown 'n Serve (8-oz.)	3 to 4	Turn over after 1½ minutes.	**4 Links**	1	No turns.
			6 Links	1½ to 2	Rotate dish ½ turn after 1 minute.
			10 Links	2 to 2½	Rotate dish ½ turn after 1 minute.

Add sauces and condiments, such as ketchup, mustard or relish after heating. Saucy spots absorb microwave energy and may toughen the bun.

Franks

Frankfurters are precooked so they only need heating. They react quickly to microwave energy and many beginners overheat them because they can't believe franks will be ready in such a short time.

When cooking franks in a main dish casserole, bury them under moist ingredients, such as beans or sauerkraut. If meat is on the bottom, the casserole won't need stirring.

Defrosting. For 1-lb. of franks, place unopened package in oven. **Microwave at Defrost 3 to 4 Minutes,** just until franks can be separated. For ½-lb., cut time in half.

Microwaving. Franks vary in size. Larger ones, as well as smaller sausages, such as Polish or bratwurst, will take longer. For foot-long hot dogs add ¼ to ½ minute more time, and rotate them once or twice, because they tend to get overdone on the ends.

FRANKS MICROWAVING CHART

When microwaving on microwave ovenproof plate, cover with wax paper. When microwaving in bun, wrap in paper towel. Watch carefully. If ends appear dry, it means they are overdone.

POWER LEVEL: **High (10)**

NO. OF FRANKS	TIME MIN.	COOK CODE	COMMENTS
2	1—2	10	Do not microwave more than 4 franks in buns at once.
4	3—4	30	Use casserole, add ½ cup water; rearrange after 2 minutes.
6 to 8	4—6	40	
10 (1-lb. pkg.)	7—9	70	Add ¾ cup water; rearrange after 4 minutes.

HOW TO MICROWAVE FRANKS

Franks are prone to pop or explode. You can remedy this by pricking them with a fork, but diagonal slashes are especially attractive.

To Microwave franks on a paper or pottery plate, cover them with wax paper. Use a casserole and additional water to heat 6 franks or more.

To Heat franks right in the buns, place a napkin or paper towel under the bun to absorb moisture. A bun placed directly on a plate or the oven floor gets steamy underneath. To heat more than four, do them in successive batches.

CASEROLE OF BEANS AND SAUSAGES

POWER LEVEL: High (10) TEMP: 160°
APPROX. MICROWAVE TIME: 20 min.
Cook Code: 200

1 lb. Polish sausage, diagonally sliced in 1-in. pieces **1 pkg. (8-oz.) brown and serve sausages**	In 2-qt. casserole place both kinds of sausages.
1 can (16-oz.) kidney beans, drained **1 can (15-oz.) Northern beans, drained** **1 can (15-oz.) pinto beans, drained**	Layer beans evenly over sausage.
1 can (8-oz.) tomato sauce **⅓ cup red cooking wine** **2 tablespoons brown sugar (packed)** **1 tablespoon prepared mustard** **1 teaspoon salt** **¼ teaspoon garlic powder** **⅛ teaspoon pepper**	In one of the empty cans or small bowl mix together remaining ingredients. Pour over sausages and beans. Insert temperature probe so tip rests on center bottom of dish. Cover tightly with plastic wrap, arrange loosely around probe to vent. Attach cable end at receptacle. **Microwave at High. Set Temp, Set 160°.**

When oven signals, stir casserole well and let stand, covered, 10 minutes before serving to thicken sauce.

Makes 6 to 8 servings

Shield sausages from excessive microwave energy by covering with beans. This allows both food types to cook evenly.

TAVERN FRANKS

For fuller flavor, prick franks and marinate in beer 3 to 4 hours or overnight before cooking.

POWER LEVEL: High (10) **Cook Code:** 70
MICROWAVE TIME: 7 to 9 min., total

1 lb. franks (8 to 10) **1 small onion, thinly sliced** **1 can (12-oz.) beer (1½ cups)**	In 2-qt. casserole place franks. Separate onion into rings and distribute over franks. Pour beer over all. Cover.

Microwave at High 7 to 9 Minutes, redistributing franks so bottom ones are on top after 4 minutes.

Makes 4 to 5 servings

SAUSAGE AND SAUERKRAUT

POWER LEVEL: High (10) **Cook Code:** 100
MICROWAVE TIME: 10 to 12 min., total

1 lb. franks (8 to 10) scored, or 1-lb. Polish sausage (Kielbasa) cut in ½-in. pieces **1 can (1-lb.) sauerkraut, rinsed and drained** **2 tablespoons instant minced onion** **1 teaspoon beef bouillon granules**	In 2-qt. casserole place meat. Cover with sauerkraut mixed with onions and bouillon. Cover. **Microwave at High 10 to 12 Minutes,** rotating dish ¼ turn after 5 minutes, until hot.

Makes 4 to 6 servings

BARBECUED FRANKS

POWER LEVEL: High (10) **Cook Code:** 90
MICROWAVE TIME: 9 to 12 min., total

¾ cup ketchup **1 tablespoon Worcestershire sauce** **¼ to ½ teaspoon chili powder** **1 tablespoon sugar** **½ teaspoon salt** **Dash liquid pepper seasoning (tabasco)** **½ cup water**	In 2-qt. casserole mix together ketchup, Worcestershire sauce, chili powder, sugar, salt, liquid pepper seasoning and water.
1 lb. franks (8 to 10), scored	Place in sauce, pushing pieces below surface to prevent overcooking. Cover.

Microwave at High 9 to 12 Minutes, rearranging franks every 4 minutes. Serve on buns, if desired, with generous amount of sauce over each.

Makes 8 to 10 servings

WIENER BEAN POT

POWER LEVEL: High (10) **Cook Code:** 110
MICROWAVE TIME: 11 to 13 min., total

2 cans (1-lb. each) pork and beans **⅓ cup chopped onion** **¼ cup ketchup** **¼ cup water** **2 tablespoons brown sugar (packed)** **1 tablespoon prepared mustard** **1 lb. wieners (8 to 10) cut in thirds**	In 2-qt. casserole stir together beans, onion, ketchup, water, brown sugar and mustard. Add wieners, pushing pieces below surface of beans to prevent overcooking. Cover. **Microwave at High 11 to 13 Minutes,** stirring after 6 minutes, until hot.

Makes 6 to 8 servings

Lamb & Veal

Lamb is naturally juicy and can be prepared in a variety of ways. In addition to the recipes given here, we suggest that you try some of our pork recipes with lamb or use one of the beef marinades, page 98.

Veal is dry because it has no fat marbling. Whether cooked conventionally or microwaved, chops and cutlets should be sliced thinly or pounded to tenderize them. Chunks and pieces of veal which need long slow cooking may be substituted in several of the stew and other main dish recipes.

HOW TO DEFROST CHOPS AND CUTLETS

POWER LEVEL: **Defrost**

4 to 8 Minutes Per Pound

1. Place plastic or paper wrapped package in oven. Microwave at Defrost ½ the minimum total time.

2. Turn package over and defrost second ½ of time.

3. Separate pieces with a table knife and let stand to complete defrosting, or microwave 1 to 2 minutes more.

HOW TO DEFROST ROASTS

POWER LEVEL: **Defrost**

10 to 12 Minutes Per Pound

1. If roast is wrapped in paper or plastic, place the unopened package in microwave oven. (Foil wrapping must be removed before microwaving.)

2. Defrost ¼ of total time. Rotate dish ½ turn and defrost for second ¼ of total time.

3. Turn roast over. Defrost for third ¼ of total time. Rotate dish ¼ turn and finish defrosting last ¼ of total time.

4. Let stand 30 minutes before microwaving or conventional cooking.

NOTE: Feel roast for warm areas after each microwaving period. Cover these areas with foil (warmth indicates they have begun to cook).

HOW TO MICROWAVE LAMB ROASTS

POWER LEVEL: **Medium (5)**

10 to 12 Minutes Per Pound for Medium
14 to 17 Minutes Per Pound for Well Done

If desired, brush roast with diluted brown bouquet sauce. Place roast fat side down in 13×9×2-in. dish. Cover with plastic wrap, turning back one corner to vent.

Determine total cooking time, using minutes per pound, above. Cook for ½ of total time; turn roast over and recover with plastic wrap. Cook fat side up for last ½ of time. Check internal doneness by placing conventional meat thermometer through side of roast into center of thickest muscle; it should read 130° for medium and 180° for well done. If not, return to the microwave oven a few minutes, then check again. Let stand 10 minutes before carving.

HOW TO MICROWAVE VEAL ROASTS

Microwaving works especially well on rolled and tied veal shoulder and other veal roasts.

POWER LEVEL: **Medium (5)**

8 to 10 Minutes Per Pound

If desired, brush roast with diluted brown bouquet sauce. Place roast fat side down in 12×8×2-in. dish. Cover with plastic wrap, turning back one corner to vent.

Determine total cooking time, using minutes per pound, above. Cook for half of total time; turn roast over and recover with plastic wrap. Check internal doneness by placing conventional meat thermometer horizontally through cut side into center of roast; it should read 155°. If not, return to microwave oven a few minutes, then check again. Let stand 15 minutes before carving.

MANDARIN LAMB CHOPS

POWER LEVEL: Medium High (7)
MICROWAVE TIME: 24 to 27 min., total

4 loin lamb chops, 1 to .... In 8-in. square dish arrange
1½-in. thick (1½ to chops so thickest meaty
2-lb.) areas are to edges. Cover
with wax paper. **Microwave
at Medium High 12 Min-
utes,** rotating dish ¼ turn
after 6 minutes. Drain off fat
and turn chops over.

1 can (11-oz.) mandarin ... Arrange orange segments
oranges, reserve over top. Mix ⅓ cup orange
syrup syrup with sugar, chutney
¼ cup sugar and lemon juice. Spoon over
½ cup chopped chutney chops. Recover with wax
2 tablespoons lemon paper. **Microwave at Me-
juice** **dium High 10 to 12 Min-
utes,** rotating dish ¼ turn after 5 minutes, until tender.
Remove chops to serving
platter.

1 tablespoon .... Mix cornstarch with syrup.
cornstarch Stir into juices in dish. **Mi-
2 tablespoons** **crowave at Medium High 2
mandarin orange** **to 3 Minutes,** stirring once,
syrup until thick. Spoon over
chops.   Makes 4 servings

VEAL PARMIGIANA

For a meatier entree, substitute veal cutlets for chops.

POWER LEVEL: Medium High (7)
MICROWAVE TIME: 24 to 28 min., total

6 small veal loin chops, ... Coat chops with beaten egg,
¾-in. thick then with mixture of crumbs,
1 egg, beaten salt, pepper and cheese. In
1 cup buttery cracker 12x8x2-in. dish arrange
crumbs chops so thickest meaty
1 teaspoon salt areas are close to edges and
¼ teaspoon pepper "tails" are in center. Cover
½ cup grated Parmesan with wax paper. **Microwave
cheese** **at Medium High 12 Min-
utes,** rotating dish ½ turn
after 6 minutes.

1 cup (4-oz.) shredded .... Turn chops over. Distribute
Mozzarella or pizza cheese over chops, then
cheese mixture of tomato sauce and
2 cans (8-oz. each) oregano. Top with Parme-
tomato sauce san. Cover. **Microwave at
1 teaspoon crushed** **Medium High 12 to 16 Min-
oregano** **utes** more, rotating dish ½
¼ cup grated Parmesan turn after 7 minutes, until
cheese tender. Let stand, covered,
10 minutes before serving.

Makes 6 servings

MICROWAVING LAMB CHOPS IN BROWN 'N SEAR DISH

Preheat empty dish uncovered at High. Add chops,
cover, and cook first side. Turn chops over, recover dish,
cook second side.

POWER LEVEL: **High (10)**

NO. OF CHOPS	PREHEAT MINUTES	1st SIDE MINUTES	2nd SIDE MINUTES
2	5 to 6	3	3 to 4
4	6 to 8	3 to 4	4 to 5

BROWN VEAL ROLL UPS

POWER LEVEL: High (10)
MICROWAVE TIME: 15½ to 17½ min., total

4 boneless veal cutlets ... Pound cutlets thin, using a
(4-oz. each) wooden mallet or foil cov-
1 can (4½-oz.) deviled ered brick. Mix ham with
ham minced onion and spread
1 tablespoon instant over cutlets, just to edge.
minced onion

1 pkg. (3-oz.) cream ..... Slice cream cheese into 12
cheese narrow strips. Place 3
strips on each cutlet. Roll
up firmly. Fasten each roll
with a toothpick.

2 tablespoons butter .... Place butter in small glass
½ cup fine dry bread bowl. **Microwave at High
crumbs** **½ Minute,** until melted. Dip
veal rolls in butter, then
coat with crumbs. Arrange
in 10×6×2-in. dish.

¾ cup water .... In 1-pt. glass measure,
1 pkg. (1½-oz.) dry combine water, gravy mix
mushroom gravy and sherry. **Microwave at
mix** **High 2 Minutes,** stirring
¼ cup cooking sherry or after 1 minute. Pour over
water veal rolls.

Cover with plastic wrap turning back one corner to vent.
Microwave at High 13 to 15 Minutes, rotating dish ½
turn every 5 minutes, until meat is tender and filling is set.

Makes 4 veal rolls

Roll cutlets, spread with ham and onion mixture, around
cream cheese strips. Fasten each roll with a toothpick.

Poultry

Chicken is one of America's most popular foods and microwaving chicken is one of the best uses of your microwave oven. Chicken microwaves well at High Power and stays juicy and tender. However, juiciness prevents browning because chicken crisps and browns only when the skin dries out enough to change color.

Standing time is important, because it allows the interior to finish cooking without toughening the delicate breast meat. Directions and recipes for microwaving Cornish hen and duck provide additional variety for this poultry section.

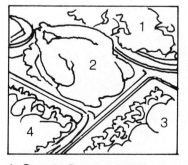

1. Crumb-Coated Chicken, page 140
2. Barbecued Stuffed Chicken, page 145
3. Saucy Turkey and Broccoli, page 154
4. Cornish Hen Halves, page 148

Chicken Defrosting

Chicken is frozen in many forms, whole or cut-up into halves, quarters or one-of-a-kind pieces, such as breasts or drum sticks. These timings are for one whole or cut-up broiler-fryer, weighing 2½ to 3½ pounds. Several cut-up chickens or a roasting chicken will take longer. Follow directions for turkey when defrosting a large roasting chicken.

HOW TO DEFROST A CUT-UP CHICKEN

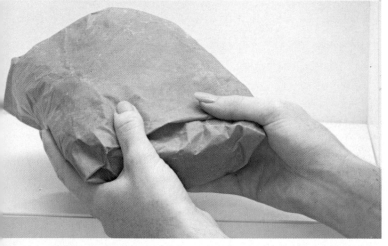

Place wrapped chicken, packaged in paper or plastic, directly on the oven shelf. If chicken is wrapped in foil, unwrap it and place it in a baking dish. **Microwave at Defrost** for ½ the time.

Unwrap chicken pieces and turn the block over into a baking dish. **Defrost** for second ½ of time, or until pieces can be separated.

HOW TO DEFROST A WHOLE CHICKEN

Whole chickens are usually frozen in a plastic bag. Remove twist tie, place package on the oven shelf and **Microwave at Defrost** ½ the time. Unwrap chicken and turn it over into cooking dish.

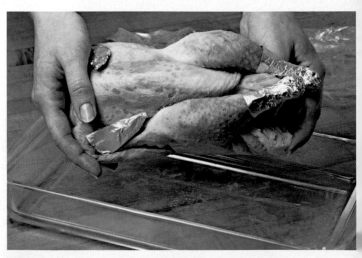

Shield wing tips, tail, ends of legs and any other areas which feel warm or have begun to change color. **Defrost** for second ½ of time.

With frozen packages of one-of-a-kind pieces, you will need to use your judgement. Bony pieces, such as wings, will take less time than meaty pieces, such as thighs.

The defrosting steps also apply to other poultry, such as ducks or cornish game hens. Two cornish hens take about the same amount of time as one chicken.

DEFROST CHART

POWER LEVEL: **Defrost**

ITEM	TIME/MINUTES
Broiler-fryer, cut up (2½ to 3½-lb.)	16 to 20
Broiler-fryer, whole (2½ to 3½-lb.)	18 to 22

Separate chicken pieces and let them stand until defrosted, or if faster defrosting is desired, arrange them in the cooking dish, meaty parts to the outside, and **Microwave 1 to 2 Minutes** more.

Defrosted chicken will be soft to the touch, very moist and cold, but not frosty. There may be a very small amount of running juice.

Giblets can be loosened but not removed. The chicken will have a glistening surface, and should be soft and cool to the touch.

Run Cold Water inside chicken until giblets can be freed. Interior will be cold but not icy.

Chicken Pieces

Chicken is naturally an excellent food for microwaving and illustrates all the advantages of microwave cooking. It is tender, flavorful and juicy. It microwaves rapidly, and takes little attention during cooking. Don't overcook chicken; it really will be done in the very short cooking periods given in the chart. Because they cook so quickly, chicken pieces do not get brown and crisp. Unless chicken is cooked in a sauce, it will be more attractive if brushed with a browning agent, coated with crumbs, or cooked in a Brown 'N Sear Dish. Plain microwaved chicken is perfect for salads and casseroles.

If you are concerned about calories or cholesterol, skin chicken before cooking, since most of the fat is located directly below the skin. If cooked in a sauce, the flavor will be absorbed by the chicken instead of the skin. Skinned chicken pieces may also be brushed with a browning agent or coated with crumbs, but cannot be cooked in the Brown 'N Sear Dish.

To prepare fried chicken in a Brown 'N Sear Dish, refer to the chart on page 38.

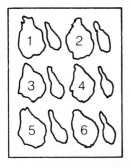

1. Plain microwaved chicken
2. Prepared coating mix
3. Brushed with melted butter, sprinkled with paprika
4. Well seasoned flour in Brown 'N Sear Dish
5. Crushed barbecue potato chips
6. Equal parts brown bouqet sauce and water

HOW TO MICROWAVE PIECES

Use utensils suitable for microwave oven. For a few pieces, use a paper plate or dinner plate. For larger amounts use a suitable size utility dish, such as an 8-in. square, 12×8×2-in., or 13×9×2-in. dish.

Brush chicken pieces with browning agent or sauce before cooking, if desired. Arrange meatiest area toward outside edge of dish.

Cover with wax paper. Microwave according to times given in chart, rotating dish ½ turn where noted. Times given below are for legs, thighs and breasts.

Let stand, covered, about 5 minutes before serving.

POWER LEVEL: **High (10)**

AMOUNT	TIME MIN.	COOK CODE	½ TURN
1 piece	2—4	20	No
2 pieces	4—6	40	After 2 minutes
3 pieces	5—7	50	After 3 minutes
4 pieces	6½—10	70	After 4 minutes
5 pieces	7½—12	80	After 4 minutes
6 pieces	8—14	80	After 5 minutes
1 chicken, 2½ to 3½-lbs., cut up	18—22	180	After 10 minutes

TIPS FOR SUCCESSFUL MICROWAVING

Arrange chicken in baking dish so that the meatiest portions are to the outside of the dish. Brush with browning agent, if desired, or add sauce.

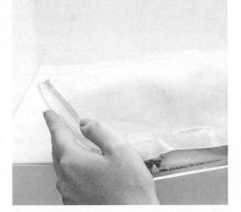

Cover plain and saucy chicken with wax paper during microwaving. Rotate dish ½ turn as recommended in the chart above when microwaving 2 or more pieces.

Test for doneness. Chicken should be fork tender, with no pinkness next to the bone. For chicken baked in sauce, remove paper after cooking and let stand 5 minutes to glaze and blend flavors.

CRUMB-COATED CHICKEN

This has the same appearance and taste as oven fried.

POWER LEVEL: High (10)   **Cook Code:** 180
MICROWAVE TIME: 18 to 22 min., total

2 eggs . . . . .In small bowl beat together
⅓ cup melted butter   eggs, butter and salt.
1 teaspoon salt

1½ cups buttery cracker   In shallow dish place
crumbs (about 50)   crumbs. Coat chicken with
1 chicken, 2½ to   crumbs, then egg mixture
3½-lb., cut up, skin   and crumbs again. In 12×
removed   8×2-in. dish arrange chick-
en with meatiest pieces to
outside edges of dish. Cover with wax paper. **Microwave at High 18 to 22 Minutes,** rotating dish ½ turn
after 10 minutes, until done.
Let stand 5 minutes before
serving.

Makes about 4 servings

EASY SAUCY CHICKEN may be made by pouring 1 cup barbecue sauce, tomato or bottled teriyaki sauce or 1 can (about 10-oz.) condensed soup or chicken gravy over 1 cut-up chicken in 12×8×2-in. dish. Cover with wax paper. **Microwave at High 18 to 22 minutes,** rotating dish ½ turn after 10 minutes. Barbecue sauce version is shown above. **Cook Code:** 180

CHICKEN 'N' DRESSING

For richer flavor, use ¼ cup melted butter for part of chicken broth.

POWER LEVEL: High (10)   **Cook Code:** 180
MICROWAVE TIME: 18 to 22 min., total

1 pkg. (8-oz.) herb . . . . . . .In 12×8×2-in. dish toss to-
seasoned stuffing   gether stuffing mix, celery,
mix   onion, pimiento, egg and
½ cup chopped celery   broth.
¼ cup minced onion
**2 tablespoons
chopped pimiento**
1 egg
**1¾ to 2 cups chicken
broth**

1 chicken, 2½ to . . . . .Dip chicken pieces into
3½-lb., cut up   melted butter, place on top
¼ cup butter, melted   of dressing with meaty
Paprika   pieces to the outside
edges of dish. Sprinkle
with paprika. Cover with
wax paper.

Microwave at High 18 to 22 Minutes, rotating dish ½ turn after 10 minutes. Let stand about 5 minutes before serving.

Makes about 4 servings

SAVORY ONION CHICKEN

Other toppings to substitute for the dry onion soup mix are ½ cup crumbs from cheese crackers or snack crackers; mixture of ¼ cup Parmesan cheese and corn flake crumbs or ¾ cup crushed potatoe chips.

POWER LEVEL: High (10)   **Cook Code:** 180
MICROWAVE TIME: 18 to 22 min., total

1 chicken, 2½ to . . . . .Dip chicken in butter. Coat
3½-lb., cut up   with dry soup mix and ar-
⅓ cup butter, melted   range in 12×8×2-in. dish,
1 pkg. (½ of 2¾-oz. box)   skin side up, with thick
dry onion soup mix   meaty pieces to the outside edges of dish. Cover
with wax paper. **Micro-
wave at High 18 to 22
Minutes,** rotating dish ½
turn after 10 minutes, until
meat is tender. Let stand 5
minutes before serving.

Makes about 4 servings

NOT THE SAME OLD CHICKEN

This golden glazed chicken is named for the comments it elicits. It really does taste special.

POWER LEVEL: High (10)   **Cook Code:** 180
MICROWAVE TIME: 18 to 22 min., total

1 chicken, 2½ to 3½-lb., cut up	In 12×8×2-in. dish arrange chicken with thickest, meaty pieces to outside edges of dish.
¼ cup mayonnaise **1 pkg. (½ of 2¾-oz. box) dry onion soup mix** **½ cup bottled Russian dressing** **1 cup apricot-pineapple preserves**	In small bowl stir together mayonnaise, onion soup mix, dressing and preserves. Spread over chicken, coating each piece. Cover with wax paper.

Microwave at High 18 to 22 Minutes, rotating dish ½ turn after 10 minutes. Allow to stand 5 to 10 minutes before serving, so chicken absorbs flavor of sauce. Serve with rice, if desired.

Makes about 4 servings

ITALIAN CHICKEN

Tastes like pizza and chicken together. Our microwave oven owners have liked this for years.

POWER LEVEL: High (10)
MICROWAVE TIME: 22 to 26 min., total

1 chicken, 2½ to 3½-lb., cut up, skin removed	In lightly greased 12×8×2-in. dish arrange chicken with meatiest pieces to the outside edges of dish.
1 can (10-oz.) condensed tomato soup **1 can (6-oz.) tomato paste** **¼ teaspoon onion salt** **¼ teaspoon garlic salt** **¼ teaspoon oregano** **1 can (4-oz.) mushroom pieces, drained**	In mixing bowl stir together tomato soup, tomato paste, onion salt, garlic salt, oregano and mushrooms. Generously spoon sauce over chicken. Cover with wax paper. **Microwave at High 20 to 22 Minutes,** rotating dish ½ turn after 10 minutes.
2 cups (8-oz.) shredded Mozzarella cheese **¼ cup grated Parmesan cheese**	Sprinkle cheese over chicken. **Microwave at High 2 to 4 Minutes,** until cheese is melted. Let stand about 5 minutes before serving.

Makes about 4 servings

ORIENTAL CHICKEN

An interesting brown raisin wine sauce gives this dish a sweet but savory flavor.

POWER LEVEL: High (10)   **Cook Code:** 110
MICROWAVE TIME: 11 to 13 min., total

2 chicken breasts split, skinned and boned	Pierce chicken breasts with cooking fork. Arrange in 3-qt. casserole.
1 tablespoon cornstarch **2 tablespoons brown sugar (packed)** **¼ teaspoon oregano** **1 clove garlic, crushed** **2 tablespoons cooking oil** **¼ cup soy sauce** **¾ cup rose wine** **⅓ cup seedless raisins**	In small bowl combine cornstarch, brown sugar, oregano, garlic, oil, soy sauce, wine and raisins. Pour over chicken. Cover. **Microwave at High 11 to 13 Minutes,** rotating dish ½ turn after 6 minutes. Serve with rice if desired.

Makes 4 servings

FIESTA CHICKEN KIEV

This recipe won $5,000 in a recipe contest exclusively for microwave cooking. Serve Kiev with taco sauce, garnish with lettuce, tomatoes and ripe olives.

POWER LEVEL: High (10)   **Cook Code:** 100
MICROWAVE TIME: 10 to 12 min., total

4 whole chicken breasts, split, skinned and boned	Pound each raw chicken piece with mallet or foil covered brick to flatten.
3 tablespoons butter **3 tablespoons old English-style sharp cheese spread** **2 teaspoons instant minced onion** **1 teaspoon salt** **1 teaspoon monosodium glutamate (accent)** **2 tablespoons chopped green chilies**	In small bowl beat together butter and cheese spread until well blended. Mix in onion, salt, monosodium glutamate and chilies. Place a portion of mixture at one end of each chicken piece, dividing evenly. Roll up each piece, tucking in ends to completely enclose filling. Fasten rolls with toothpicks.
¼ cup butter, melted **1 cup crushed cheddar cheese crackers** **1½ tablespoons taco seasoning mix**	Dip each roll in melted butter to cover, then coat with mixture of crackers and taco seasoning mix. Arrange rolls in 12×8×2-in. dish. Cover with wax paper. **Microwave at High 10 to 12 Minutes,** rotating dish ½ turn after 5 minutes, until done. Let stand about 5 minutes before serving.

Makes 8 servings

HOW TO MICROWAVE A STEWING CHICKEN

Combine in 4-qt. casserole 1 cut up stewing chicken (4 to 5-lb.), 5 cups hot tap water, 1 onion, 1 carrot and 1 celery stalk, all coarsely cut up. Add 4 peppercorns, 2 cloves and cover.

Microwave at High 15 Minutes. Rearrange chicken, bringing bottom pieces to the top. Cover. **Microwave at Medium 2 to 2¼ Hours,** rearranging chicken every 30 minutes.

Test for doneness. Chicken should be fork tender. For maximum tenderness, let chicken cool in its broth. Meat will then be easily removed from the bones. To stew a broiler-fryer, microwave 1 to 1½ hours.

CHICKEN A LA KING

The old favorite, creamed chicken, dressed up with colorful pimiento, green pepper and flavorful mushrooms. Serve over toast or in a pastry shell.

POWER LEVEL: High (10) and Medium High (7)
MICROWAVE TIME: 16 to 21 min., total

⅓ cup butter	In 2-qt. casserole place butter. **Microwave at High 1 Minute,** until melted. Blend in flour. Gradually stir in half & half and broth; mix well. **Microwave at High 8 to 10 Minutes,** stirring with whisk after 4 minutes, until thickened and smooth. Stir well again.
½ cup unsifted all-purpose flour	
2 cups dairy half & half	
1 cup chicken broth	
2 cups cubed, cooked chicken	Mix in chicken, pimiento, mushrooms, green pepper, salt and pepper. Cover. **Microwave at Medium High 7 to 10 Minutes,** stirring after 5 minutes, until hot. Let stand 5 to 10 minutes before serving, to blend flavors.
1 jar (4-oz.) sliced pimiento	
1 can (4-oz.) sliced mushrooms, undrained	
½ cup diced green pepper	
1 teaspoon salt	
¼ teaspoon pepper	

Makes 4 servings

MEXICAN CHICKEN CASSEROLE

POWER LEVEL: High (10)   TEMP: 155°
APPROX. MICROWAVE TIME: 14 to 16 min.
Cook Code: 140

1 can (10½-oz.) condensed cream of chicken soup	In small mixing bowl place soup, chilies, onion and water. Stir until well blended.
2 tablespoons green chilies, diced	
¼ teaspoon instant minced onion	
½ cup water	
2 large, firm, ripe tomatoes	Slice tomatoes in ½-in. slices.
1 pkg. (6-oz.) corn chips	In 2-qt. casserole layer ½ of corn chips. Top with 1 cup chicken, then ½ of tomato slices. Pour ½ of soup mixture over chicken; sprinkle with ¾ of cheese, reserving rest for topping after cooking. Repeat layers.
2 cups diced, cooked chicken, or 2 cans (5-oz. each) boned chicken, diced	
1 cup (4-oz.) shredded cheddar cheese	

Insert temperature probe so tip is in center of casserole. Attach cable end at receptacle. **Microwave at High. Set Temp., Set 155°.** When oven signals, sprinkle with reserved cheese and let stand 5 minutes before serving.

Makes 6 to 8 servings

CHICKEN AND DUMPLINGS

POWER LEVEL: Medium High (7)
MICROWAVE TIME: 30 to 46 min., total

1 chicken, 2½ to 3½-lb., cut up **2 cups hot tap water** **½ cup chopped onion** **½ cup chopped celery** **4 medium carrots, sliced** **2 teaspoons salt** **½ teaspoon pepper**	In 3-qt. casserole place chicken, water, onion, celery, carrots, salt and pepper. Cover. **Microwave at Medium High 15 Minutes,** rearranging chicken pieces after 8 minutes.
¼ cup cornstarch **½ cup cold water**	In small bowl stir together cornstarch and water. Stir into chicken mixture, blending well. Cover. **Microwave at Medium High 15 to 25 Minutes,** until chicken is tender. Spoon dumplings (below) around edge of dish. **Microwave at Medium High 5 to 6 Minutes,** uncovered, rotating dish ¼ turn after 3 minutes, until puffed and no longer doughy.

Makes 4 servings

Dumplings: In mixing bowl stir together 1½ cups unsifted all-purpose flour, 1 tablespoon dried parsley flakes, 2 teaspoons baking powder and ½ teaspoon salt. Add ⅔ cup milk, 1 beaten egg and 2 tablespoons cooking oil. Stir with table fork only until flour is moistened.

CHICKEN ENCHILADA CASSEROLE

POWER LEVEL: High (10)   **Cook Code:** 110
MICROWAVE TIME: 11 to 13 min., total

2½ cups diced, cooked chicken **1 can (13-oz.) evaporated milk** **1 can (10-oz.) condensed cream of chicken soup** **1 pkg. (1¼-oz.) taco seasoning mix** **1 medium onion, chopped** **½ cup chopped celery** **1 can (4-oz.) chopped green chilies, drained** **6 corn tortillas, torn into 1-in. pieces** **¾ cup diced cheddar or longhorn cheese**	.In 2-qt. casserole combine chicken, evaporated milk, soup, taco mix, onion, celery, chilies, tortillas and cheese. **Microwave at High 11 to 13 Minutes,** stirring after 5 minutes, until hot.

Makes 4 to 6 servings

BRUNSWICK STEW

If a more highly seasoned stew is desired add about 1 teaspoon Worcestershire sauce and 3 to 5 drops hot pepper (tabasco) sauce.

POWER LEVEL: Medium High (7) and High (10)
MICROWAVE TIME: 40 to 58 min., total

1 chicken, 2½ to 3½-lb., cut up **2 cups water**	In 3-qt. casserole place chicken pieces and water. Cover. **Microwave at Medium High 20 to 30 Minutes,** rearranging chicken pieces every 10 minutes, until tender. Remove meat from bones discarding skin. Cut meat into pieces and return to broth in casserole.
2 cups diced raw potatoes (2 medium) **½ cup sliced onion (1 small)** **2 teaspoons salt** **¼ teaspoon pepper**	Add potatoes, onion, salt and pepper to casserole. **Microwave at Medium High 15 to 18 Minutes,** stirring after 8 minutes.
½ cup unsifted all-purpose flour **1 can (12-oz.) whole kernel corn, undrained** **1 pkg. (10-oz.) frozen baby lima beans, defrosted** **1 can (16-oz.) tomatoes, drained**	Into small bowl drain liquid from corn and stir in flour, mixing well. Blend into hot mixture. Add corn, lima beans and tomatoes. **Microwave at High 5 to 10 Minutes,** stirring after 4 minutes, until vegetables are hot and sauce is thickened. Let stand 5 to 10 minutes before serving, to blend flavors.

Makes about 8 servings

NOTE: For stronger tomato flavor, use juice from tomatoes for part of water in which chicken is cooked.

Stirring casseroles during cooking distributes heat evenly. Rotate those which cannot be stirred. Individual casseroles can be rotated and rearranged by moving diagonally to opposite corners of the oven.

Whole Chicken

MICROLESSON

When microwaving a whole chicken, be sure to select a young, plump tender bird. The skin sould be smooth and have a pale, creamy color tinged with pink. If you are in doubt, choose a broiler-fryer. Avoid chickens with thick, bumpy skin and large amounts of bright yellow fat.

HOW TO MICROWAVE A WHOLE CHICKEN

POWER LEVEL: **Medium High (7)**

9 to 10 Minutes Per Pound

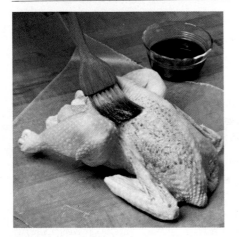

Brush chicken with a mixture of 1 tablespoon brown bouquet sauce and 1 tablespoon melted butter.

Place breast side down in cooking dish. Cover with wax paper.

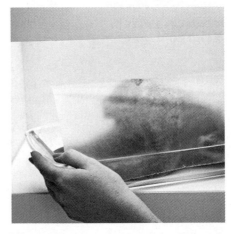

Microwave ½ of total time. Trivet is optional, but may be used if dry lower surface is desired.

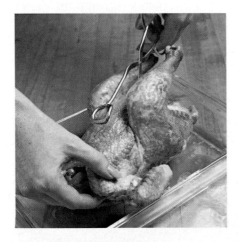

Turn chicken breast side up after first ½ of microwave time.

Shield wings and legs to prevent over-cooking; recover. Microwave last ½ time. Let stand 5 to 10 minutes.

Test for doneness by cutting skin between inner thigh and breast. Meat should show no trace of pink, and juices should run clear.

BARBECUED STUFFED CHICKEN

The loose covering of wax paper allows steam to escape away from the surface of the bird. As the skin cooks, the barbecue sauce coating dries to form a beautiful showy glaze.

This stuffing makes delicious use of stale bread. Or, for Southern style, try the cornbread variation. Stuffings made form top of range stuffing mix or dried herb seasoned stuffing mix may also be used.

POWER LEVEL: Medium High (7) **Cook Code:** 307
MICROWAVE TIME: 30 to 35 min., total

4 cups day-old ½-in. bread cubes or crumbled cornbread **¼ cup minced onion** **½ cup minced celery** **1 teaspoon salt** **1 teaspoon poultry seasoning** **¼ teaspoon pepper** **⅓ cup melted butter** **⅔ cup chicken broth**	In large bowl toss together bread, onion, celery, salt, poultry seasoning, pepper, butter and chicken broth to make stuffing.
1 whole broiler-fryer, about 3-lb. **Bottled barbecue sauce**	Fill body and neck cavities of chicken with stuffing. Tie wings flat to body with string around chicken; tie legs together. Brush all areas with barbecue sauce.

On trivet in 12x8x2-in. dish place chicken with breast side down. Cover with wax paper. **Microwave at Medium High 30 to 35 Minutes,** turning chicken breast side up and brushing with barbecue sauce after 15 minutes. Chicken is done when no trace of pink shows in meat when cut is made between inner thigh and breast. Let chicken stand 10 minutes before serving.

Makes 2 to 4 servings

TIP: Serve plain microwaved whole chicken with Cranberry Sauce, page 154, chutney, pepper relish or Apple Cider Sauce (below).

APPLE CIDER SAUCE

Good with chicken or ham.

POWER LEVEL: High (10)   **Cook Code:** 50
MICROWAVE TIME: 5 to 7 min., total

2 cups apple cider **⅓ cup cornstarch** **½ cup seedless raisins** **1 tablespoon lemon juice**	In 1-qt. measuring cup measure cider. Stir in cornstarch until thoroughly mixed. Add raisins and lemon juice. **Microwave at High 5 to 7 Minutes,** stirring every 1½ minutes, until clear and thickened.

Makes about 2¼ cups

Chicken Teriyaki

CHICKEN TERIYAKI

POWER LEVEL: Medium High (7) and High (10)
MICROWAVE TIME: 27 to 33 min., total

¼ cup soy sauce **⅓ cup honey** **⅓ cup sherry**	In 12×8×2-in. dish, mix soy sauce, honey and sherry.
1 whole broiler-fryer, about 3-lb.	Add chicken turning over and coating with sauce.

Turn chicken on its side. Cover with plastic wrap. Marinate in refrigerator 1 to 2 hours, turning chicken over after ½ of time. To microwave, place bird breast side down in dish. **Microwave at Medium High 25 to 30 Minutes,** turning breast side up after 15 minutes. Let chicken stand 10 minutes before serving. Prepare Teriyaki Sauce (below) and finish chicken as described in sauce recipe.

Makes about 4 servings.

Teriyaki Sauce: In 1-pt. glass measuring cup stir together 1 tablespoon water and 2 tablespoons cornstarch. Pour juices from cooking dish into cup. **Microwave at High 2 to 3 Minutes,** until thick and clear, stirring after 1 minute. Pour sauce over chicken just before serving.
Cook Code: 20

Chicken Liver Pate

SAUTEED CHICKEN LIVERS

POWER LEVEL: High (10)
MICROWAVE TIME: 8 to 10 min., total

1 tablespoon butter . . . . . **½ lb. chicken livers**	.Preheat Brown 'N Sear Dish (uncovered). **Microwave at High 3 to 4 Minutes.** Add butter, then livers. **Microwave at High 5 to 6 Minutes,** turning over after 3 minutes, until crisp and tender.

Makes 2 servings

Prick giblets with a fork before microwaving. As when cooking conventionally, giblets tend to pop, but the effect is more noticeable when they are microwaved.

Chicken Livers & Giblets

Chicken livers may be sauteed in the Brown 'N Sear Dish, or microwaved in liquid at Low before they are used in other dishes.

Poultry Giblet Gravy may be located on page 190.

CHICKEN LIVER PATE

Finely chopped pieces of onion add nice texture to this creamy spread. Garnish with sieved hard-poached egg, ripe olives and additional chopped onion. Serve with crackers and, if desired, butter to spread over crackers before adding the pate.

POWER LEVEL: Medium (5)   **Cook Code:** 185
MICROWAVE TIME: 18 to 22 min., total

1 lb. chicken livers . . . . . . **1 cup water**	In 2-qt. casserole place livers. Prick each liver with fork. Add water. Cover. **Microwave at Medium 18 to 22 Minutes,** stirring after 10 minutes, until tender. Drain livers, place in container of electric blender. Whir until evenly blended.
⅓ cup soft butter . . . . **1 tablespoon finely chopped onion** **1 tablespoon lemon juice** **1 tablespoon brandy** **½ teaspoon salt** **½ teaspoon dry mustard** **¼ teaspoon thyme** **3 to 4 drops liquid pepper seasoning**	In small mixing bowl stir together butter, onion, lemon juice, brandy, salt, mustard, thyme and pepper seasoning, to blend. Mix in livers well. Pack into well greased 1½ to 2 cup mold. Chill thoroughly, then turn out onto serving plate. Garnish and serve with crackers.

Makes about 1½ cups

Poultry Convenience Foods

Canned convenience foods, or foods frozen in metal trays, should be removed from their containers to suitable microwave plates or casseroles. Small boil-in-bag pouches (about 5 to 10-oz.) can be placed directly in the oven. Slit or pierce the top of the pouch before microwaving and open carefully after heating to avoid burns from steam. Large boil-in-bags may be placed in a serving dish. When contents are partially defrosted, open the bag, slide food into the dish and stir before continuing to microwave.

POULTRY CONVENIENCE FOODS CHART

Chicken Gravy and Main Dishes such as barbecue chicken, chicken a la king, chicken and dumplings, creamed chicken, croquettes, escalloped chicken with noodles, fried chicken, pieces or slices in gravy, stew and turkey tetrazzini may be microwaved according to charts on this page.

POWER LEVEL: **High (10)**

CANNED AMOUNT	TIME MIN.	COOK CODE	COMMENTS
7½ to 10½-oz.	2—4	20	Cover. Stir after 2 minutes and before serving, or use temperature probe set for 150°.
14 to 24-oz.	4—6	40	Cover. Stir after 2 minutes and before serving, or use temperature probe set for 150°.

Leftover Chicken is ideal for TV dinners you prepare at home. See page 29 for reheating directions.

POWER LEVEL: **High (10)**

CANNED AMOUNT	TIME MIN.	COOK CODE	COMMENTS
5 to 6½-oz. pouch	3—4	30	Slit pouch before microwaving.
12-oz.	7—9	70	Cover. Stir after 4 minutes.
16 to 17-oz.	11—14	110	Cover. Stir or turn over after 8 minutes.
Chicken Croquettes (12-oz. pkg.)	4—6	40	Pierce sauce pouch with fork. Place with food on plate. Cover with wax paper. Rotate dish ½ turn after 2 minutes.
Fried Chicken 2 pieces	2—4	20	Follow procedure below. Some brands of frozen fried chicken are not fully cooked. If label does not state "fully cooked", check for doneness.
Fried Chicken 1 lb., 6 pieces	6—7	60	
Fried Chicken 2 lb., 10 pieces	8—10	80	

HOW TO MICROWAVE FROZEN FRIED CHICKEN

Arrange chicken pieces in a single layer on a microwave ovenproof platter or cooking dish with meatiest parts to the outside.

Cover with wax paper. Microwave at High for ½ the heating time shown on chart above.

Rotate platter ½ turn. Microwave for second ½ of time. If package label does not state "fully cooked", check for doneness by cutting through meat to bone. Pinkness indicates more cooking is needed.

Stuffed Cornish Hens

Cornish Hens

Delicate Cornish Hens need some extra attention during defrosting or they may start to cook. We recommend defrosting in 3 steps rather than 2.

Cornish Hens are naturally tender, especially when microwaved. Because they cook so quickly, the unevenness of browning is particularly noticeable.

Plain microwaved Cornish Hen in background contrasts with a hen brushed with teriyaki sauce before microwaving. Teriyaki sauce gives a more golden color than brown bouquet sauce.

HOW TO DEFROST CORNISH HENS

POWER LEVEL: **Defrost**

9 to 12 Minutes Per Pound

1. Place unopened packages in oven. (Metal closure need not be removed.) Microwave at Defrost for ⅓ the total defrosting time.

2. Turn packages over. Microwave for ⅓ the time.

3. Unwrap and shield ends of legs with foil. Microwave for last ⅓ of time. If giblets do not move freely, run cold water into cavities.

MICROWAVING CORNISH HENS, Halved

POWER LEVEL: **High (10)**

9 to 10 Minutes Per Pound

1. Brush halves with browning sauce. Place in cooking dish, skin side up. Cover with wax paper. Microwave at High for ½ the cooking time.

2. Rotate dish ½ turn. Microwave for second ½ of time. Hen is done if juices run clear when inner thigh is pierced with a fork.

MICROWAVING CORNISH HENS, Whole

POWER LEVEL: **High (10)**

6 to 8 Minutes Per Pound

1. Stuff hens*, if desired. Brush with browning sauce. Place breast side down in suitable cooking dish. Cover with wax paper. Microwave for ½ the cooking time.

2. Turn breast side up. Microwave for second ½ of time. Let stand 10 minutes. Hen is done when leg moves freely and juices run clear when inner thigh is pierced with a fork.

*Rice is an excellent stuffing for Cornish Hens. For each hen, use about ½ cup cooked rice (white and/or wild), well-buttered and seasoned.

CORNISH HENS FAR EAST STYLE

POWER LEVEL: High (10)
MICROWAVE TIME: 18 to 20 min., total

2 cornish hens, about 1-lb. each, defrosted	Split hens in halves, using kitchen shears or a sharp knife. Place in 12×8×2-in. dish, skin side down.
¼ cup soy sauce **¼ cup sherry wine** **¼ cup pineapple juice** **1 clove garlic, crushed or ⅛ teaspoon garlic powder** **½ teaspoon curry powder** **¼ teaspoon dry mustard**	In small bowl mix together soy sauce, sherry, pineapple juice, garlic, curry powder and mustard. Stir to blend well and pour over meat in dish. Refrigerate 4 to 6 hours, or overnight.

To cook, turn skin side up and baste with marinade. Cover dish with wax paper. **Microwave at High 8 Minutes.** Brush with marinade and rotate dish ½ turn. Recover. **Microwave at High 10 to 12 Minutes** more, until meat is tender. Serve immediately.

Makes 2 to 4 servings

Duckling

Duckling with Colorful Marmalade Sauce

Like other poultry, duckling microwaves juicy and tender in a very short time. Since duckling is so fatty, browning sauce is not brushed on before the first half of cooking because it will not adhere to the skin. After the duckling has rendered some of its fat, you may brush it with browning sauce or, if you prefer, after microwaving broil it under a conventional broiler to crisp and brown the thick skin. This rich meat is traditionally served with a fruit sauce or glaze.

HOW TO DEFROST DUCKLING

POWER LEVEL: **Defrost**

4 to 6 Minutes Per Pound

1. Place plastic wrapped duckling in oven. (Metal closure need not be removed.) Microwave at Defrost for ½ the time.

2. Unwrap duckling and turn over into cooking dish. Shield wings, tail, ends of legs and any other warm areas with foil. Defrost for second ½ of time.

3. Run cold water into cavity until giblets can be removed. For step-by-step photographs, see *How To Defrost A Whole Chicken,* page 136.

MICROWAVING DUCKLING

POWER LEVEL: **High (10)**

7 to 8 Minutes Per Pound

1. Shield wings, tail and ends of legs with foil. Place duckling breast side down on trivet in a 12×8×2-in. dish. Microwave at High for ½ the cooking time.

2. Remove foil and turn breast side up. With a kitchen fork, prick skin of breast and legs to release fat. Baste duckling with drippings, then drain fat from dish. Brush with browning or barbecue sauce, if desired.

3. Microwave for second ½ of time. Duckling is done when the last drops of juice drained from the cavity run clear, without a trace of pink.

Prick skin of breast and legs with a kitchen fork after first ½ of cooking time. Brush with diluted brown bouquet sauce, if desired. For a crisp skin, omit sauce and, after microwaving, broil under a conventional broiler until crisp and brown.

Turkey Defrosting

HOW TO DEFROST WHOLE TURKEY

POWER LEVEL: **Defrost**

10 to 12 Minutes Per Pound

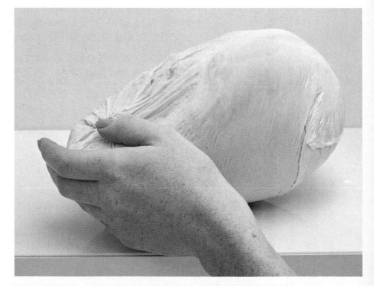

Place unwrapped turkey, breast side down, in oven. It is not necessary to remove the metal closure because of the great mass of food. **Microwave at Defrost** for ¼ the time. Let stand 10 minutes. Rotate turkey ½ turn, so legs point to opposite side of the oven. **Microwave** for ¼ the time. Let stand 10 minutes.

Unwrap turkey and place it in a cooking dish. Shield legs, wing tips and any warm or brown areas, with foil. Secure with wooden picks.

HOW TO DEFROST TURKEY PARTS

POWER LEVEL: **Defrost**

10 to 12 Minutes Per Pound

Unwrap turkey parts if in foil. Place parts in a dish and cover with wax paper. Parts in all plastic or paper packaging can be placed in microwave without unwrapping.

Microwave skin side down at **Defrost.** Rotate dish or package ½ turn after ¼ time and continue microwaving at **Defrost** for ¼ the time.

MICROLESSON

Shape as well as size influences defrosting. A broad breasted, meaty turkey takes longer to defrost than a streamlined one of the same weight. The breast may also need more shielding because it is higher in the oven and closer to the source of microwave energy.

These directions are for defrosting turkeys weighing up to 10 pounds. If you wish to start defrosting a turkey the day before you plan to roast it, defrost for ¾ the time, then place turkey in refrigerator overnight to complete defrosting.

Due to their size and shape, whole turkeys may not be cooked in your microwave oven. See page 152 for information on microwaving turkey parts.

Turn breast side up and defrost for ¼ of time. Let stand 10 minutes. Check breast for warm spots and shield if necessary. Rotate turkey ½ turn, so legs point to opposite side of the oven. **Microwave** for final ¼ of time. Let stand 15 to 20 minutes to complete defrosting.

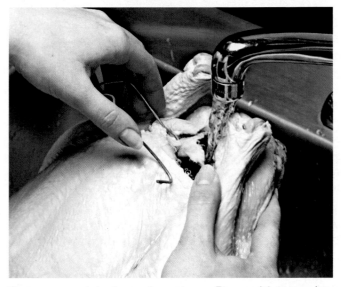

Remove metal clamp from legs. Run cold water into breast and neck cavities until giblets and neck can be removed. Turkey should feel soft and cool with a glistening surface. Interior should be cold and slightly icy.

Turn parts over. Those parts microwaved in paper or plastic packaging should now be unwrapped, placed in a dish and turned over. Check for warm spots and shield, if necessary. Cover with wax paper.

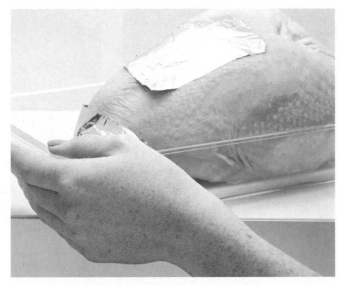

Microwave at Defrost for ¼ the time. Rotate dish ½ turn and **Microwave at Defrost** for final ¼ of time. Run cold water over parts until softened and pliable. When defrosted, the surface will be cool and glistening. The interior should be cold and slightly icy.

Turkey Parts

MICROLESSON

Although they defrost well, whole turkeys, due to their size and shape, may not be cooked in your microwave oven.

Turkey breasts and parts such as halves, quarters, and legs microwave well. When microwaving turkey breast, a covering of plastic wrap is used, but cover halves, quarters and parts such as legs with wax paper.

For even cooking of this type of poultry, microwave for half of total time, turn it over and finish microwaving.

Do not use a trivet when microwaving turkey parts. A trivet raises turkey closer to top of oven, where microwave energy is released. Overcooking on top can result.

Turkey parts will develop some browning during microwaving, but you may wish to use bottled brown bouquet sauce (diluted as described in picture below) for more even brown appearance.

Check for doneness at minimum time, you may have to reset your timer. Be sure to allow the 10 to 20 minutes standing time before serving.

HOW TO MICROWAVE TURKEY PARTS CHART

POWER LEVEL: **Medium High (7)**

ITEM	MINUTES PER LB.	COMMENTS
Frozen Packaged Turkey Roasts (1 to 4-lb.)*	18 to 20	Add ½ cup water. Can be microwaved from frozen without defrosting. Cover with plastic wrap. Turn over after ½ of time.
Turkey Legs Turkey Quarters Turkey Halves	11 to 13	Must be defrosted before microwaving to cook evenly. (See page 150.) Cover with wax paper. Turn over after ½ of time. Brush again with sauce.
Whole Turkey Breast	9 to 11	Place skin-side down in dish. Add ½ cup water. Cover with plastic wrap turning back one corner to vent. Microwave ½ of time. Turn over, shield (see picture below), recover, and microwave second ½ of time to an internal temperature of 170°.

*NOTE: When a gravy pouch is included it adds to the total package weight but should not be included in calculating total microwave time for turkey roast. For example, a two pound package frozen turkey roast may contain 6-oz. gravy pouch. Subtract weight of gravy from total package weight.

HOW TO MICROWAVE TURKEY BREAST

Brush with a mixture of 2 tablespoons brown bouquet sauce and 2 tablespoons water or melted butter. When using butter, dry skin before brushing to make sauce cling.

Place turkey breast skin side down in baking dish. Add ½ cup water to dish. Cover with plastic wrap, turning back one corner to vent. **Microwave at Medium High** for ½ total estimated time in chart on this page.

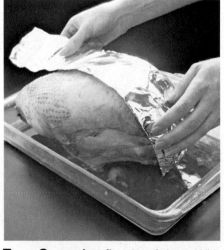

Turn Over after first ½ of time. With 3-in. foil strip, shield center as shown. Recover, continue microwaving to minimum time or until thermometer in thickest area reads 170°. Let stand 10 to 20 minutes before serving.

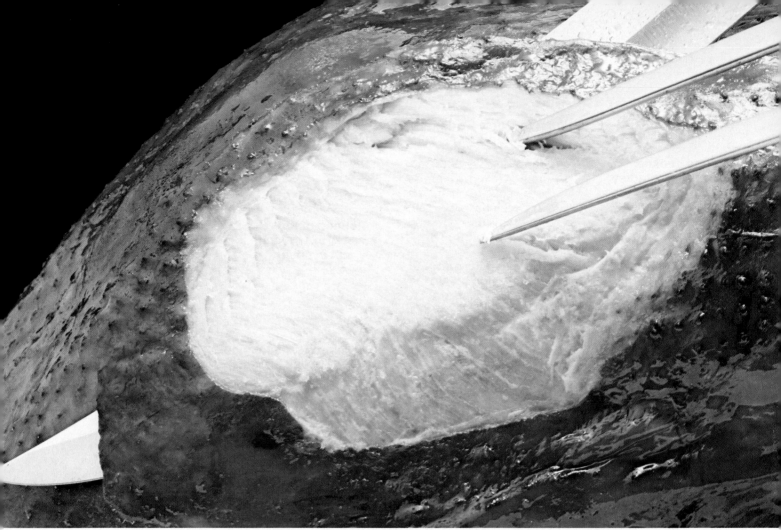

Microwaved Turkey Breast

HOW TO MICROWAVE LEGS, HALVES AND QUARTERS

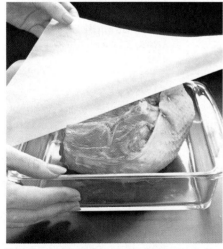

Place turkey skin side down in baking dish and brush with sauce for more browning. Cover with wax paper. **Microwave** at **Medium High** for ½ total estimated time in chart.

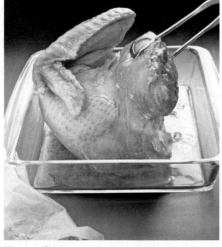

Turn Over and brush again with sauce. Continue microwaving, covered, at **Medium High** for ½ of time. Test doneness by cutting next to bone. No pink areas should be observed. Let stand 10 to 20 minutes before serving.

PREPARED TURKEY ROASTS

Microwave without defrosting. Add ½ cup water and cover with plastic wrap. **Microwave at Medium High** ½ time in chart. Turn over and continue microwaving at **Medium High.** Let stand 10 to 20 minutes and slice.

SAVORY TURKEY SQUARES

POWER LEVEL: Medium High (7) **Cook Code:** 267
MICROWAVE TIME: 26 to 30 min., total

3 cups cooked, chopped turkey **2 cups day-old bread cubes** **½ cup minced celery** **¼ cup minced onion** **2 tablespoons chopped pimiento** **1 tablespoon lemon juice** **½ teaspoon salt** **¼ teaspoon pepper** **⅔ cup milk** **½ cup chicken broth** **3 eggs, slightly beaten**	In large mixing bowl mix together turkey, bread cubes, celery, onion, pimiento, lemon juice, salt, pepper, milk, broth and eggs. Pour into 8-in. square dish. Cover with wax paper. **Microwave at Medium High 26 to 30 Minutes,** rotating dish ¼ turn every 10 minutes, until set. Let stand 5 to 10 minutes before serving.

Makes 6 to 8 servings

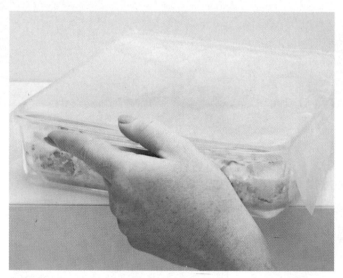

Rotate dish ¼ turn every 10 minutes during cooking.

CRANBERRY SAUCE

This sauce is so compatible with turkey, it has become a traditional accompaniment.

POWER LEVEL: High (10)   **Cook Code:** 180
MICROWAVE TIME: 18 to 20 min., total

2 cups sugar **½ cup water** **1 lb. fresh or frozen cranberries**	In **3**-qt. casserole stir together sugar, water and cranberries. Cover **Microwave at High 18 to 20 Minutes,** stirring every 6 minutes. Serve warm or cold.

Makes 3 to 4 cups

SAUCY TURKEY AND BROCCOLI

Called Turkey Divan when made with the traditional Mornay Sauce. This makes a very nice luncheon or supper dish. A salad of tomato slices is a colorful accompaniment.

POWER LEVEL: High (10)   **Cook Code:** 60
MICROWAVE TIME: 6 to 8 min., total

1 bunch (about 1¼-lb.) broccoli, cut in spears	Microwave broccoli according to directions, page 208. Drain. In 12×8×2-in. dish or microwave ovenproof platter arrange attractively.
8 large slices cooked turkey **1 recipe Mornay Sauce, or Cheese Sauce, both page 191**	Layer turkey slices over broccoli. Cover with sauce. **Microwave at High 6 to 8 Minutes,** rotating dish ½ turn after 5 minutes, until hot.

Makes 4 servings

TURKEY TETRAZZINI

POWER LEVEL: High (10)
MICROWAVE TIME: 24 to 28 min., total

1 pkg. (7-oz.) spaghetti	Cook spaghetti (see chart, page 197), except **Microwave 9 Minutes.** Drain. Place in greased 12×8×2-in. dish.
¼ cup butter **1 can (4-oz.) sliced mushrooms, drained** **1 small onion, chopped** **1½ teaspoons lemon juice**	In 2-qt. casserole place butter, mushrooms, onion and lemon juice. **Microwave at High 2 to 3 Minutes,** stirring after 1 minute.
⅓ cup unsifted all-purpose flour **1 teaspoon salt** **½ teaspoon paprika** **⅛ teaspoon ground nutmeg** **2 cups turkey or chicken broth**	Stir in flour, salt, paprika and nutmeg, until smooth. **Microwave at High 1 Minute.** Stir well. Gradually stir in broth. **Microwave at High 5 to 6 Minutes,** stirring after 3 minutes, until thickened.
½ cup dairy half & half **2½ cups cooked, cubed turkey** **½ cup Parmesan cheese** **Paprika**	Mix in half & half and turkey. Pour over spaghetti. Sprinkle with cheese and paprika. **Microwave at High 7 to 9 Minutes,** rotating dish ½ turn after 4 minutes, until hot.

Makes 4 to 6 servings

HOT TURKEY AND CHEESE SANDWICHES

These are known in the South as "Hot Browns", created at a once-famous hotel in Louisville.

POWER LEVEL: High (10) and Medium High (7)
MICROWAVE TIME: 9½ to 12 min., total

4 strips bacon	On paper plate lined with double thickness paper towels, arrange bacon. Cover with single thickness paper towel. **Microwave at High 2½ to 3 Minutes,** until partially cooked.
4 slices toast **8 to 12 large slices turkey breast** **4 slices tomato (¼-in. thick)** **1 recipe Cheese Sauce, page 191** **¼ cup Parmesan cheese**	In 2 (7 to 9-in.) oval au gratin dishes, divide toast, arranging to cover bottoms of dishes. Place 4 to 6 large slices turkey in each dish and top each with 2 tomato slices. Divide cheese sauce over sandwiches. Sprinkle tops of sandwiches with Parmesan cheese. Arrange 2 slices partially-cooked bacon over each sandwich.

Place dishes side by side in microwave oven. Cover with wax paper. **Microwave at Medium High 7 to 9 Minutes,** rearranging dishes after 4 minutes, until hot.

Makes 2 sandwiches

TURKEY GOULASH

POWER LEVEL: High (10)
MICROWAVE TIME: 11 to 14 min., total

¼ cup butter **2 large onions, thinly sliced** **1 clove garlic, minced**	In 2-qt. casserole place butter, onions and garlic. **Microwave at High 5 to 6 Minutes,** stirring after 3 minutes, until onion is limp.
3 cups cooked, cubed turkey **1½ cups turkey or chicken broth** **1 can (8-oz.) tomato sauce** **2 tablespoons paprika** **1½ teaspoons salt** **¼ teaspoon pepper**	Add turkey, broth, tomato sauce, paprika, salt and pepper. Cover. **Microwave at High 6 to 8 Minutes,** stirring after 3 minutes, until hot.
1 cup (8-oz.) dairy sour cream	Stir sour cream into hot mixture just before serving. Serve over rice or noodles.

Makes 6 servings

Hot Turkey and Cheese Sandwiches

TURKEY CONVENIENCE FOODS

Foods frozen in metal trays should be removed to suitable microwave plates or casseroles. Small boil-in-bag pouches (5 to 10-oz.) can be placed directly in the oven. Slit or pierce the top of the pouch before microwaving and open carefully after heating. Large boil-in-bags may be placed in a serving dish. When contents are partially defrosted, open the bag, slide the food into the dish and stir before continuing to microwave.

TURKEY CONVENIENCE CHART

POWER LEVEL: **High (10)**

ITEM	TIME MIN.	COOK CODE	COMMENTS
Gravy & Sliced Turkey, Frozen (5-oz. pkg.)	3—4	30	Make 1-in. slit in top of pouch with sharp knife.
Turkey Tetrazzini, Frozen (12-oz. pkg.)	7—9	70	Place food in 1-qt. casserole. Cover. Stir after 6 minutes.

Make turkey dinners for the freezer, using leftover TV trays. See page 25 for reheating directions.

Fish & Seafood

Fish and seafood are naturally tender and require minimal cooking to preserve their delicate flavor and texture. The speed and moisture retention of microwaving are decided advantages in cooking them.

Overcooking dries and toughens fish. We recommend that many seafoods, especially the meatier types, be cooked until the outer areas appear opaque but the centers are still slightly translucent. These areas will finish cooking as the seafood stands, while the outer areas remain tender.

1. Lobster Thermidor, page 176
2. Stuffed Whole Fish, page 166
3. Microwaved Shrimp in the Shell, page 170
4. Fillets in Lemon Butter, page 163

DEFROSTING FISH

Fish defrosts rapidly. It is naturally delicate and tender, so care should be taken not to toughen it by over-defrosting. Remove fish from the microwave oven while it is still slightly icy.

MICROLESSON: HOW TO DEFROST FILLETS AND STEAKS

DEFROSTING CHART
POWER LEVEL: **Defrost**

ITEM	1st SIDE TIME MINUTES	2nd SIDE TIME MINUTES
Fillets, 1-lb.	4	4 to 6
Steaks, 1–6-Oz.	2	1
Steaks, 2–6-oz.	2½	2½ to 3

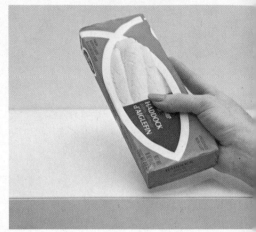

Shape of package, as well as its weight, influences defrosting time. Thick fillets or bulky packages take longer than flat packages of the same weight.

Place unopened paper or plastic package directly onto the oven floor. Fillets frozen at home in a bag of water should be placed in a dish to avoid leakage.

MICROLESSON: HOW TO DEFROST WHOLE FISH

DEFROSTING CHART
POWER LEVEL: **Defrost**

ITEM	1st SIDE TIME MINUTES	2nd SIDE TIME MINUTES
1–8 to 10-oz. Fish	2	2 to 4
2–8 to 10-oz. Fish	4	6 to 8
1–3 to 4-lb. Fish	8	11 to 13

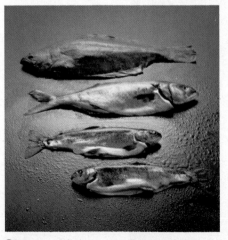

Shape of fish, as well as weight, determines defrosting time. A short, thick fish may take longer to defrost than a long, thin one of the same weight.

Arrange fish in a cooking dish large enough to hold them easily. Microwave at Defrost for first part of time.

If you or a family member like to fish, freeze your catch for fresh-tasting fish all year 'round. Seal fillets or steaks in a plastic bag with a small amount of water and freeze. Clean whole fish, then dip them in water and freeze on a baking dish. The icy coating will protect the fish from freezer burn.

When defrosting home frozen fish, use a cooking dish to collect water as it melts.

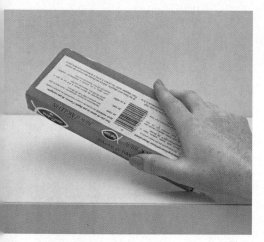

Turn package over so that the side which was closest to the left of the oven is brought to the right.

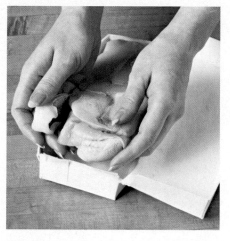

Check after minimum defrosting time. Corners should not feel warm, although outer pieces may have started to loosen.

Hold fillets under cold running water until they can be separated.

Turn fish over. Microwave for second part of minimum time.

Test the fish. It should feel cold and pliable and may still be slightly icy in the cavity.

Rinse cavity with cold running water to complete defrosting.

Fish Fillets & Steaks

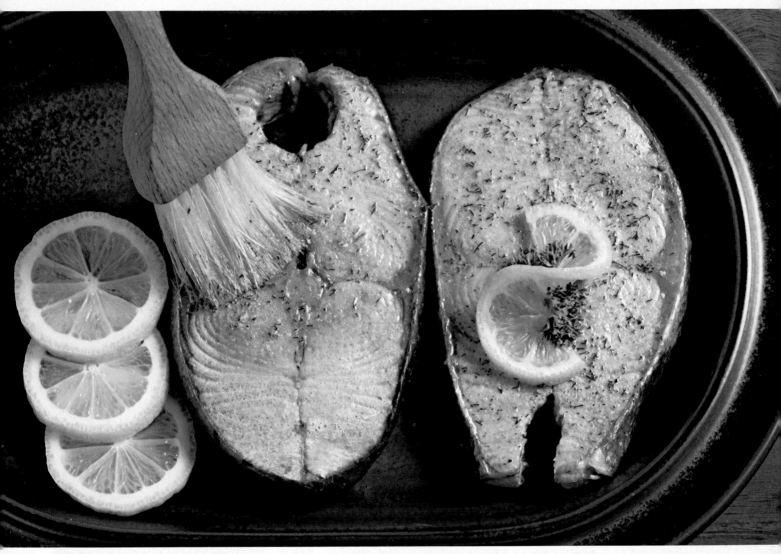

Salmon Steaks

MICROLESSON

Fillets and steaks may be microwaved in several ways to produce a variety of dishes. Microwave them in a sauce for rich flavor. Steam or poach them for a delicate, but simple dish. Smother partially cooked fillet in crumbs and cream for scalloped fish. Whether cooked conventionally or microwaved, juices of salmon or halibut steaks coagulate on the surface of the fish. To eliminate this, before microwaving, line the dish with a paper towel to absorb the excess juices, then turn over to serve. Flounder, which is extremely moist, should be microwaved on a trivet.

Fish is done when meat flakes easily with a fork. Center should still be slightly translucent.

HOW TO MICROWAVE FILLETS IN SAUCE

Arrange fillets in a cooking dish, thickest parts to outside of dish.

Pour sauce on fillets. Cover with wax paper. Microwave for ½ of time.

Rotate dish ½ turn and microwave until fish flakes easily.

HOW TO MICROWAVE STEAMED FISH

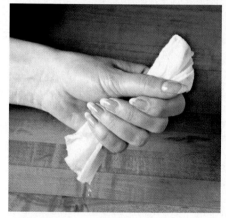

Dampen a paper towel with water. No additional moisture is needed. Arrange fish in dish with meatiest parts to the outside.

Cover with dampened towel. Microwave for ½ of time. Rotate dish ½ turn and finish steaming, or remove towel and scallop fish if desired.

Scallop fish by spreading crumbs over fillets and pouring in cream. Return to oven and microwave second ½ of time.

HOW TO MICROWAVE FISH STEAKS

Brush steaks with lemon-butter mixture. (If desired, line dish with paper towel before placing fish in it.)

Cover tightly with plastic wrap, turning back one corner to vent. Microwave for ⅓ the time.

Turn steaks over and recover, or, if paper towel was not used, rotate dish and complete cooking.

Defrosted flounder fillets and other moist fish microwave best on a trivet. Use a seasoned coating mix for color and flavor.

SCALLOPED FISH OR SCALLOPS

POWER LEVEL: High (10)
MICROWAVE TIME: 7 to 9 min., total

1 lb. white fish fillets (flounder or sole) or scallops	On microwave ovenproof platter or 9-in. pie plate place fish fillets or scallops with thickest, meaty areas to outside of dish. Cover with paper towel which has been completely dampened, with most of water squeezed out. **Microwave at High 4 Minutes.**
½ cup (¼-lb.) butter **1 cup soft bread crumbs** **1 cup saltine cracker crumbs**	Remove platter from oven and let stand covered with paper towel while preparing buttered crumbs. In 1-qt. glass measure place butter. **Microwave at High 1 Minute,** or until melted. Add bread and cracker crumbs. Mix with fork.
1 teaspoon salt **⅛ teaspoon freshly ground pepper** **⅓ cup milk or cream**	Uncover fish and sprinkle evenly with salt and pepper, then crumbs. Pour milk evenly over top. **Microwave at High 2 to 4 Minutes** until fish flakes easily with fork or scallops are tender but not overcooked.

Makes 4 servings

NOTE: Leftover scalloped seafood may be used as a good omelet filling.

Complimentary sauces for fish and seafood include Dill Butter or Herbed Butter, page 193; Hollandaise Sauce, page 192; or, use microwave oven to make Clarified Butter, page 163.

FROZEN FISH FILLETS WITH SEASONED COATING MIX

Very moist result. Cook these on a microwave trivet for drier, firmer fish.

POWER LEVEL: High (10)   **Cook Code: 60**
MICROWAVE TIME: 6 to 8 min., total

1 lb. fish fillets, defrosted **1 pkg. (2-oz.) seasoned coating mix for fish**	Separate fish fillets and coat with seasoned coating mix. Arrange in 12×8× 2-in. dish with thickest meaty areas to outside edges of dish. Cover with wax paper.

Microwave at High 6 to 8 Minutes, rotating dish ½ turn after 4 minutes, until fish flakes with fork.

Makes about 4 servings

FILLETS IN CREAMY WINE SAUCE

A dinner party dish. This French wine and cream sauce is sometimes called Bercy Sauce.

POWER LEVEL: High (10)
MICROWAVE TIME: 11½ to 14½ min., total

1 tablespoon butter **2 tablespoons minced green onions** **1 lb. sole or flounder fillets, defrosted and cut into serving pieces** **1½ cups sliced fresh mushrooms** **¾ cup dry white wine, such as Sauterne**	In 12×8×2-in. dish place butter. **Microwave at High ½ Minute,** until melted. Spread butter over bottom of dish and sprinkle with onions. Arrange fillets over onions and cover with mushrooms. Pour wine over top. **Microwave at High 7 to 9 Minutes,** rotating dish ½ turn every 3 minutes, or until fish flakes with a fork. Remove fish to microwave ovenproof platter and cover to keep warm while cooking sauce.
2 tablespoons unsifted all-purpose flour **¼ cup heavy cream** **1 teaspoon salt** **⅛ teaspoon pepper**	In 1-qt. casserole combine flour, cream, salt and pepper, until smooth. Carefully drain hot liquid from fish into cream mixture and stir well. **Microwave at High 2 to 3 Minutes,** stirring sauce every minute.
½ teaspoon lemon juice **¾ cup shredded Swiss cheese**	Stir lemon juice into sauce. Pour sauce over fish and sprinkle cheese on top. **Microwave at High 2 Minutes** more, until cheese has melted. Garnish with parsley sprigs.

Makes about 4 servings

Fish Creole

FILLETS IN LEMON BUTTER

POWER LEVEL: High (10)
MICROWAVE TIME: 10 to 13 min., total

1 lb. firm fish fillets such as sole or haddock	.In 12×8×2-in. dish, arrange fillets with thickest, meaty areas to outside edges of dish. Sprinkle with salt and pepper.
½ to 1 teaspoon salt	
⅛ teaspoon pepper	
½ cup (¼-lb.) butter	.In 1-qt. casserole place butter. **Microwave at High 1 to 2 Minutes,** until melted. Blend in parsley and lemon juice and pour over fish. Top with crumbs, then sprinkle on paprika.
½ cup chopped fresh parsley	
1 tablespoon lemon juice	
½ cup buttery cracker crumbs	
½ teaspoon paprika	

Microwave at High 9 to 11 Minutes, rotating dish ½ turn after 5 minutes, until fish flakes easily with a fork.

Makes 4 servings

CLARIFIED BUTTER: In 1-pt. measuring cup place ½ cup (¼-lb.) butter. **Microwave at High 2 Minutes,** until boiling. The clear layer which floats to top is clarified butter and may be poured off into a serving container.
Cook Code: 20

FISH CREOLE (A Low Calorie Recipe)

POWER LEVEL: High (10)   **Cook Code:** 80
MICROWAVE TIME: 8 to 10 min., total

1 lb. sole or haddock fillets, defrosted	.Rinse fish and pat dry with paper towels. In 12×8×2-in. dish arrange fish with thickest pieces to outside edges of dish.
1 can (8-oz.) tomato sauce	.In 1-qt. glass measure stir together tomato sauce, mushrooms, green pepper, celery, water, minced onion and bouillon. Pour evenly over fish. Cover tightly with plastic wrap, turning back one corner to vent. **Microwave at High 8 to 10 Minutes,** rotating dish ½ turn after 4 minutes, until fish flakes easily with fork. Let stand about 5 minutes before serving, to blend flavors.
1 can (2-oz.) sliced mushrooms, drained	
½ green pepper, diced	
1 stalk celery, diagonally sliced	
3 tablespoons water	
1½ tablespoons instant minced onion	
1 teaspoon chicken bouillon granules	

Makes about 4 servings

SALMON STEAKS

See page 161 for basic directions on microwaving fish steaks.

POWER LEVEL: High (10)   **Cook Code: 80**
MICROWAVE TIME: 8 to 9 min., total

4 (½-in. thick) salmon steaks (1-lb.) **2 tablespoons melted butter** **2 tablespoons lemon juice** **½ teaspoon dill weed**	.In paper towel lined 12× 8×2-in. dish place steaks. Mix together butter and lemon juice, then brush over steaks. Sprinkle with dill if desired. Cover dish with wax paper or vented plastic wrap.

Microwave at High 8 to 9 Minutes, rotating dish ½ turn after 4 minutes. When done, fish will flake easily with fork. Turn fish over onto serving plate. (Paper towel absorbs juices for best appearance of fish.) Garnish top of steaks with sprinkling of paprika or parsley and additional melted butter, if desired.

Makes 4 servings

FOR 2 SALMON STEAKS: Use half of all ingredients and place fish in 8-in. square dish. Cover with wax paper. **Microwave at High 4 to 5 Minutes,** no turns necessary. **Cook Code: 40**

Salmon With Cucumber Sauce: Cook 4 salmon steaks as directed above, but omit dill weed. Cook to minimum time, then spread over the tops a mixture of: ½ cup dairy sour cream, ⅓ to ½ cup shredded or chopped cucumber (¼ medium cucumber), 1 teaspoon chopped parsley, ½ teaspoon chopped chives, 1 teaspoon lemon juice and ¼ teaspoon salt. **Microwave at High 1 to 2 Minutes** more before serving. **Cook Code: 10**

ROUND SALMON LOAF

Round shape is best for fish loaves, just as it is for meat loaves.

POWER LEVEL: High (10)   **Cook Code: 90**
MICROWAVE TIME: 9 to 11 min., total

1 egg **1 cup milk** **¼ cup melted butter** **3 slices soft bread, cubed** **½ teaspoon salt** **2 cans (1-lb. each) red salmon, boned and skin removed**	.In large mixing bowl beat egg slightly and mix with milk, butter, bread cubes, salt and salmon, blending well. Pack firmly in greased 9-in. pie plate. Cover with wax paper. **Microwave at High 9 to 11 Minutes,** rotating dish ½ turn after 5 minutes. Let stand 10 minutes before slicing. Serve with Dill Butter, page 193, if desired.

Makes 6 to 8 servings

COLORFUL CREAMED TUNA

POWER LEVEL: High (10)
MICROWAVE TIME: 11 to 15 min., total

2 tablespoons butter **¼ cup chopped onion** **¼ cup chopped green pepper**	.In 2-qt. casserole place butter, onion and green pepper. **Microwave at High 2 to 3 Minutes,** stirring every minute.
1 can (2-oz.) mushrooms **1 can (10-oz.) cream of celery soup** **1 can (6½-oz.) tuna, drained** **½ teaspoon salt** **⅛ teaspoon pepper**	.Reserving 2 tablespoons juice, drain mushrooms. Add mushrooms and reserved juice to casserole along with soup, tuna, salt and pepper. Cover. **Microwave at High 7 to 9 Minutes,** stirring after 4 minutes.
2 tomatoes, cut in wedges	.Add tomatoes. Cover. **Microwave at High 2 to 3 Minutes** more, until hot. Serve over rice.

Makes 3 to 4 servings

HOT TUNA SALAD

A good dish for entertaining. Can be made ahead of time and reheated before serving. Shrimp or crab meat might also be used in place of tuna. Try this in a hot patty shell for a treat.

POWER LEVEL: Medium High (7)
MICROWAVE TIME: 10 to 13 min., total

2 cans (7-oz. each) tuna, drained **2 cups chopped celery** **2 cups croutons, divided** **1 cup mayonnaise** **½ cup whole almonds or cashews** **1 tablespoon finely chopped onion** **1 tablespoon lemon juice** **½ teaspoon salt**	In 2-qt. casserole mix together tuna, celery, 1 cup croutons, mayonnaise, almonds, onion, lemon juice and salt. Cover. **Microwave at Medium High 9 to 11 Minutes,** stirring after 5 minutes, until hot.
½ cup shredded cheddar or Swiss cheese	Sprinkle with cheese and remaining 1 cup croutons. **Microwave at Medium High 1 to 2 Minutes,** until cheese melts.

Makes 6 servings

TUNA NOODLE CASSEROLE

POWER LEVEL: High (10)
MICROWAVE TIME: 16 to 21 min., total

1 pkg. (8-oz.) fine egg noodles	.Microwave noodles (see chart, page 197), except cook 10 minutes.
3 tablespoons butter **1 clove garlic, minced** **½ cup finely chopped green onions** **½ teaspoon salt** **⅛ teaspoon pepper**	.In 3-qt. casserole place butter, garlic, onion, salt and pepper. **Microwave at High 2 to 3 Minutes,** stirring after 1 minute, until onion is softened.
¼ cup unsifted all-purpose flour **1½ cups milk**	.Stir in flour until smooth. Gradually stir in milk. **Microwave at High 4 to 6 Minutes,** stirring every 2 minutes, until smooth and thickened.
2 cans (7-oz. each) tuna, drained	.Gently stir tuna and noodles into sauce. Cover. **Microwave at High 10 to 12 Minutes,** stirring after 6 minutes until hot.
⅓ cup cracker crumbs **2 tablespoons minced parsley** **2 tablespoons melted butter**	.In small bowl, mix together crumbs, parsley and butter. Sprinkle over casserole before serving.

Makes 6 to 8 servings

SCALLOPED TUNA AND CHIPS

POWER LEVEL: High (10)   **Cook Code: 150**
MICROWAVE TIME: 15 to 17 min., total

1 can (10½-oz.) condensed cream of celery soup **1 can (7 to 8-oz.) mushrooms, stems and pieces** **1 teaspoon instant minced onion** **1 tablespoon chopped parsley** **1 cup milk** **1 tablespoon lemon juice**	.Mix soup, undrained mushrooms, onion, parsley, milk and lemon juice.
1 pkg. (5-oz.) potato chips, crushed (3 cups) **2 cans (7-oz. each) tuna, drained and flaked**	.In 2-qt. greased casserole layer 1 cup crushed chips, ½ of tuna, ½ of soup mixture. Repeat layers and top with potato chips. **Microwave at High 15 to 17 Minutes,** rotating dish ½ turn after 8 minutes, until bubbly.

Makes 6 servings

Tuna Wedges

TUNA WEDGES

A tuna loaf, microwaved in a round shape. Garnish with tomato slices and sprinkle with grated cheese if desired.

POWER LEVEL: High (10)
MICROWAVE TIME: 10 to 12 min., total

2 eggs **1½ cups cooked rice** **6 green onions, finely chopped** **2 cans (7-oz.) solid pack tuna**	.In large mixing bowl beat eggs with fork. Add rice, onions and undrained tuna. Mix well.
½ cup (¼-lb.) butter **¼ teaspoon thyme** **1 cup fine dry bread crumbs**	.In small glass bowl place butter. **Microwave at High 1 Minute,** until melted. Add to tuna along with thyme and crumbs. Mix well.

Spread mixture evenly in lightly greased 9-in. pie plate. Cover with wax paper. **Microwave at High 9 to 11 Minutes,** rotating dish ½ turn after 5 minutes. Serve in wedges.

Makes about 6 servings

Whole Fish

Whole fish makes a dramatic presentation. Microwaving is a superior way of preparing them. With a tight cover fish steam in their own natural moisture and are delicate and juicy.

For a baked appearance, brush with browning sauce and butter. For poached color, use lemon-butter sauce.

Although the head is not eaten, it should be shielded with foil to maintain its appearance for serving. The eye, which turns white during cooking, can be covered with an olive slice.

HOW TO MICROWAVE A WHOLE FISH BY TEMPERATURE (Striped Bass, Snapper, etc. 2½ to 4 pounds)

Brush entire fish with a mixture of 1 tablespoon bottled bouquet sauce and 1 tablespoon water, then with melted butter, or brush with lemon-butter sauce. Add stuffing, such as Vegetable Stuffing (below, right), if desired.

Insert temperature probe and place the fish in a baking dish with the probe on the side of the fish closest to the dish. Shield the head and thin tail area with foil.

Cover the dish tightly with plastic wrap, arranging loosely around probe to vent. Attach cable end at receptacle. **Microwave at High. Set Temp, Set 170°.**

HOW TO INSERT THE TEMPERATURE PROBE

Insert Probe from just above the gill into the meatiest area, parallel to the backbone. Probe should be on the side of the fish closest to the dish.

STUFFED RED SNAPPER

POWER LEVEL: High (10)   **Cook Code:** 90
MICROWAVE TIME: 9 to 11 min., total

1 red snapper (1½ to . . . . . .Place fish on microwave-
   2½-lb.), cleaned and   type platter or in 12×8×2-
   gutted   in. dish. Stuff cavity with
   Vegetable Stuffing   Vegetable Stuffing. Brush
   (right)   all areas with mixture of
2 tablespoons bottled   brown bouquet sauce and
   brown bouquet   butter.
   sauce
¼ cup butter, melted

Cover head and thin tail end with strips of aluminum foil. Cover platter or dish with plastic wrap, turning back one corner to vent. **Microwave at High 9 to 11 Minutes,** until fish flakes easily with fork. While letting stand 5 minutes, brush again with butter, if desired. Place cross-cut slice of pimiento-stuffed olive in eye cavity.

Makes about 2 servings

HOW TO MICROWAVE A WHOLE FISH BY TIME

Brush fish with sauce as directed in the recipe.

Shield the head and thin tail area with foil.

Cover tightly with plastic wrap, turning back one corner to vent.

Rainbow Trout

VEGETABLE STUFFING

½ cup (¼-lb.) butter, ...In mixing bowl place but-
 melted ....ter, onion, carrots, mush-
½ cup finely chopped ...rooms, parsley, bread
 onion ....crumbs, egg, lemon juice,
½ cup finely grated .....salt and pepper. Toss to
 carrots ....mix well. Pack lightly into
½ cup chopped raw .....fish.
 mushrooms
¼ cup finely minced
 parsley
½ cup fine dry bread
 crumbs
1 egg, beaten
1 tablespoon lemon
 juice
1 teaspoon salt
⅛ teaspoon pepper

Makes about 2 cups

RAINBOW TROUT

POWER LEVEL: High (10)
MICROWAVE TIME: See Recipe

Trout (8 to 10-oz. . . . . .In 12×8×2-in. dish ar-
 each) ....range 1 to 2 trout which
 ....have been cleaned and
 ....gutted.

For each fish: . . . . .Brush fish with mixture of
1 tablespoon lemon ....lemon juice and butter.
 juice
2 tablespoons butter,
 melted

Cover head and thin tail areas with strips of aluminum
foil. Cover cooking dish with plastic wrap, turning back
one corner to vent. **Microwave at High** according to
times below. When done, fish flakes easily with fork. Let
stand 5 minutes and serve with rest of lemon butter.

NO. OF TROUT	TIME/MINUTES	COOK CODE
1	5 to 6	50
2	8 to 9	80

Place cross-cut slice of pimiento-stuffed olive in eye
cavity.

Defrosting Shellfish

Small pieces of loose-packed shellfish, such as shrimp, scallops or crab fingers, are easiest to defrost, since they can be spread out in a single layer and absorb microwave energy evenly. Check at minimum time because they defrost rapidly.

MICROLESSON

POWER LEVEL: **Defrost**

HOW TO DEFROST SMALL LOOSE PIECES OF SHELLFISH

TYPE	TIME MINUTES
Crab Fingers (1-lb.)	7 to 8
Scallops (1-lb.)	7 to 8
Shrimp (1-lb.)	7 to 8

HOW TO DEFROST SHELLFISH FROZEN IN BLOCKS

TYPE	TIME MINUTES
Crab Meat (6-oz. pkg.)	4 to 5
Crab Meat (2 6-oz. pkgs.)	6 to 7
Crab Meat (1-lb. can)	13 to 15
Oysters (12-oz. can)	8 to 10
Oysters (3 12-oz. cans)	18 to 20
Scallops (1-lb. pkg.)	8 to 10

Blocks of shellfish, such as crab meat and scallops, frozen in paper packages, can be defrosted in the package. Turn over after ½ of time. Oysters and crab meat frozen in cans must be removed to a casserole. Break up these dense blocks as soon as possible.

HOW TO DEFROST LARGE SHELLFISH

TYPE	TIME MINUTES
Crab Legs (8 to 10-oz.) 1 to 2	5 to 7
Crab Legs (8 to 10-oz.) 3 to 4	10 to 12
Lobster Tails (6 to 9-oz.) 1 to 2	5 to 7
Lobster Tails (6 to 9-oz.) 3 to 4	10 to 12
Lobster Tails (12 to 16-oz.) 1 to 2	8 to 10
Whole Lobster or Crab (1½-lb.)	14 to 16 (approx. 10 min. per pound)

Large pieces such as lobster, lobster tails, whole crab or large crab legs should be turned over after ½ of time. If thinner areas feel warm, shield them with foil. Remove large shellfish from the oven while still slightly icy and allow them to stand a few minutes.

Spread shellfish loosely in a baking dish so they are in a single layer. **Microwave at Defrost** for half the time.

Rearrange pieces and **Defrost** for second half of time.

Test after minimum defrosting time. Shellfish should feel cool and soft, and still be translucent.

Place block in a casserole. Cover. **Microwave at Defrost** for ½ the time.

Turn block over and break it up with a fork. Center may still be firm. **Microwave** for second half of time, breaking off pieces as they loosen.

Pieces should be loose and still feel icy. Let stand to complete defrosting.

Arrange shellfish in a baking dish with the light underside up. Paper towels hold tails upright. **Microwave at Defrost** for half the time.

Turn over, so that the back or darker side is up. **Defrost** for second half of the time.

Defrosted shellfish should be flexible and transparent and feel cool.

Small Shellfish

MICROLESSON

Steaming is the classic method for cooking shellfish. In the microwave oven, most shellfish steam without water in a dish covered tightly with plastic wrap. For scallops, a dampened paper towel provides sufficient steam. Clams steam in their shells. We recommend cooking unpeeled raw shrimp in water with a bay leaf and vinegar to reduce cooking odors.

SMALL SHELLFISH CHART
POWER LEVEL: **High (10)**

TYPE	TIME MIN.	COOK CODE
Clams (3 to 5-oz.) 6	3—5	30
Scallops (1-lb.)	5—7	50
Shrimp, peeled (1-lb.)	5	50
Shrimp, unpeeled (1 to 2-lb.) with 2½ cups water, 1 bay leaf, 1 tablespoon vinegar, in 2-qt. casserole.	6—10	60

Cook scallops, clams and peeled shrimp as shown below.

HOW TO MICROWAVE SHRIMP

Arrange cleaned, peeled and deveined shrimp in a ring. Cover tightly with plastic wrap, turning back 2-in. to vent. **Microwave at High 5 Minutes.**

Cook 1 to 2-lbs. unpeeled, raw shrimp in a casserole dish with 2½ cups water, 1 bay leaf, 1 tablespoon vinegar. **Microwave at High 6 to 10 Minutes.**

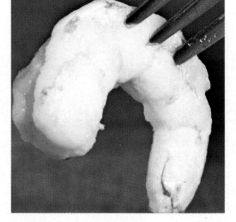

Check appearance of shrimp for doneness. It will turn from translucent to opaque.

TIPS ON MICROWAVING CLAMS AND SCALLOPS

Place 6 clams (3 to 5-oz.) in ring with hinged side out. **Microwave at High 3 to 5 Minutes,** rotating dish ½ turn after ½ time.

Remove clams from oven as soon as the shells open partially. Tightly closed shells contain bad clams and should be discarded.

Steam scallops using a damp paper towel. Arrange 1-lb. scallops in a single layer and **Microwave at High 5 to 7 Minutes.** Rotate dish ½ turn after ½ the time.

SHRIMP GUMBO

For spicy flavor, tie 1 or 2 teaspoons crab boil (found in condiment section of supermarket) in a cheesecloth bag and add along with shrimp. For bright color accent, save out about ¼ of green pepper to stir into finished gumbo.

POWER LEVEL: High (10) and Medium High (7)
MICROWAVE TIME: 28 to 30 min., total

1 medium onion, sliced (about ½ cup) ¼ cup butter (use bacon fat, if desired)	In 3-qt. casserole place onion and butter. **Microwave at High 3 Minutes,** stirring after 2 minutes, until onion is limp.
2 tablespoons cornstarch 1 cup water 2 cans (16-oz. each) stewed tomatoes 1 cup diced green pepper (2 medium) 2 cloves garlic, crushed 2 teaspoons salt 1 teaspoon ground nutmeg ¼ teaspoon pepper 1 pound raw shrimp, shelled, deveined 2 pkgs. (10-oz. each) frozen okra, defrosted, cut into 1-in. pieces	In small bowl stir together cornstarch and water. Add to onion along with tomatoes, green pepper, garlic, salt, nutmeg, pepper, shrimp and okra. Stir well. Cover. **Microwave at High 15 Minutes.** Stir. Cover. **Microwave at Medium High 10 to 12 Minutes,** until shrimp is cooked and mixture is hot.

Makes 6 to 8 servings

CREAMY SHRIMP AND RICE

POWER LEVEL: High (10)
MICROWAVE TIME: 31 to 33 min., total

1½ cups uncooked long grain rice 3½ cups water	In 3-qt. casserole place rice and water. Cover. **Microwave at High 10 Minutes.** Stir and recover. **Microwave at High 10 Minutes** more.
½ cup chopped onion ½ cup chopped green pepper 2 cups (16-oz.) dairy sour cream 1 cup milk ½ teaspoon salt ⅛ teaspoon pepper 2 cups cooked shrimp	Add onion, green pepper, sour cream, milk, salt, pepper and shrimp. Stir well; then smooth top. **Microwave at High 10 to 12 Minutes,** stirring after 6 minutes, until hot.
1 cup (4-oz.) shredded cheddar cheese	Sprinkle cheese over top. **Microwave at High 1 Minute,** until melted.

Makes 6 to 8 servings

Shrimp Gumbo

SHRIMP IN PARMESAN BUTTER

POWER LEVEL: High (10)
MICROWAVE TIME: 7¼ to 8¼ min., total

36 large raw shrimp, peeled and deveined	"Butterfly" shrimp by cutting each piece lengthwise halfway through and separating the 2 sides to form thin, flat piece of shrimp.
1 cup (½-lb.) butter 3 tablespoons capers, including liquid 2 cloves garlic, minced 2 tablespoons lemon juice	In 1-qt. measure place butter. **Microwave at High 1¼ Minutes,** until melted. Stir in capers, garlic and lemon juice. Pour ⅔ of butter in 12×8×2-in. dish. Arrange shrimp in sauce.
1 cup (4-oz.) grated Parmesan cheese	Top with cheese, then remaining butter. Cover with wax paper.

Microwave at High 6 to 7 Minutes, rotating dish ½ turn after 3 minutes, until shrimp is opaque and firm.

Makes 3 to 4 servings

SHERRIED SHRIMP ROCKEFELLER

This won $5,000 in a recent microwave recipe contest.

POWER LEVEL: Defrost and High (10)
MICROWAVE TIME: 30 to 33 min., total

2 pkgs. (10-oz. each) frozen chopped spinach	In 10-in. square casserole or 12x8x2-in. dish place unwrapped, frozen blocks of spinach. **Microwave at Defrost 10 Minutes.** Break up blocks. **Microwave at High 3 to 4 Minutes** more, until just completely thawed. Drain well, squeezing out as much juice as possible. Spread over bottom of casserole. Distribute shrimp evenly over spinach.
1 lb. medium to large raw shrimp, peeled, deveined	
1 can (10½-oz.) condensed cream of shrimp soup	In 1-qt. glass measure stir together undiluted soup, cheese and sherry. **Microwave at High 4 Minutes,** stirring after 2 minutes, until cheese is melted. Set aside while preparing crumb topping.
1 cup (4-oz.) shredded sharp cheddar cheese	
3 tablespoons cooking sherry	
2 medium slices fresh bread	Break bread in tiny bits or coarsely crumb in blender. Place in small glass bowl and add butter.
3 tablespoons butter	

Microwave at High 1 Minute, stirring after ½ minute, until butter is distributed among crumbs. Pour hot sauce over casserole and distribute crumbs over top. Sprinkle with paprika, if desired. Cover with wax paper.

Microwave at High 12 to 14 Minutes, rotating dish ½ turn after 5 minutes. Let stand, covered, 5 minutes before serving.

Makes 4 servings

SWEET AND SOUR SHRIMP

Garnish with chopped bacon and green onion slices.

POWER LEVEL: High (10)   **Cook Code: 60**
MICROWAVE TIME: 6 to 8 min., total

1 recipe Sweet and Sour Sauce, page 176	Stir together Sweet and Sour Sauce, shrimp and drained pineapple slices. **Microwave at High 6 to 8 Minutes,** stirring gently after 3 minutes.
1 lb. cleaned and cooked shrimp	
1 can (8-oz.) pineapple slices, drained	

Makes 4 to 5 servings

SHRIMP NEWBURG

POWER LEVEL: High (10) and Medium (5)
MICROWAVE TIME: 16 to 21 min., total

¼ cup butter	In 2-qt. casserole place butter, onion and mushrooms. **Microwave at High 2 to 3 Minutes,** until bubbly.
¼ cup chopped green onion	
1 jar (4-oz.) sliced mushrooms, drained	
2 tablespoons flour	Stir in flour and salt. **Microwave at High 1 Minute,** to blend.
½ teaspoon salt	
1¼ cups milk	Stir in milk. **Microwave at High 5 to 6 Minutes,** stirring after 3 minutes.
¼ cup sherry	Stir in sherry. Stir small amount of sauce into yolks. Add yolk mixture to sauce; stir well. **Microwave at Medium 2 to 3 Minutes,** stirring after 1 minute.
2 egg yolks	
12 oz. frozen cooked shrimp, defrosted	Stir in shrimp. **Microwave at Medium 6 to 8 Minutes,** stirring after 3 minutes, until heated through.

Makes about 4 servings

JAMBALAYA

POWER LEVEL: High (10)
MICROWAVE TIME: 14 to 17 min., total

2 cups diced cooked ham	In 2-qt. casserole place ham, green pepper, onion, garlic and butter. **Microwave at High 6 to 7 Minutes** or until vegetables are tender.
½ cup chopped green pepper	
½ cup chopped onion	
1 garlic clove, minced	
2 tablespoons butter	
1 can (10¾-oz.) condensed tomato soup	Stir in soup, water, shrimp, bay leaf, oregano, salt and pepper. **Microwave at High 4 Minutes.**
⅓ cup water	
½ cup shrimp, or 1 can (4½-oz.), drained	
1 medium bay leaf, crushed	
¼ teaspoon crushed oregano	
⅛ teaspoon salt	
Dash pepper	
1½ cups cooked rice	Stir in rice. **Microwave at High 4 to 6 Minutes** more, or until bubbly.

Makes 4 servings

SCALLOPED OYSTERS

POWER LEVEL: High (10)
MICROWAVE TIME: 13 to 15 min., total

3 cans (12-oz. each) frozen oysters, thawed (about 4 cups)	Reserving ¼ cup liquid, drain oysters.
¾ cup melted butter **2 cups fine soda cracker crumbs (about 40 small squares)** **1 teaspoon salt** **⅛ teaspoon pepper** **⅛ teaspoon nutmeg**	In small mixing bowl mix together butter and crumbs. In 10×6×2-in. dish layer ⅓ of crumb mixture, ½ of drained oysters, ½ of seasonings, then ⅓ of remaining crumbs, rest of oysters, seasonings and crumbs.
¼ cup milk	Mix milk with oyster liquid and pour evenly over top.

With knife, poke 3 to 4 holes through layers so liquid goes to bottom. **Microwave at High 7 Minutes.** Sprinkle with ¼ cup parsley. Rotate dish ½ turn. **Microwave 6 to 8 Minutes,** until oysters are firm when pierced with fork.

Makes about 6 servings

CRAB IMPERIAL

POWER LEVEL: High (10), Medium (5) and
Medium High (7)
MICROWAVE TIME: 12½ to 16 min., total

2 tablespoons butter **2 tablespoons unsifted all-purpose flour** **1 teaspoon salt** **¾ teaspoon pepper** **1 teaspoon dry mustard**	In 1½-qt. casserole place butter. **Microwave at High ½ Minute,** until melted. Stir in flour, salt, pepper and mustard until smooth. **Microwave at High 1 Minute.**
1 cup dairy half & half **1 teaspoon lemon juice** **2 teaspoons Worcestershire sauce** **2 tablespoons minced green pepper** **2 tablespoons minced pimiento**	Very slowly stir in half & half until mixture is smooth. Add lemon juice, Worcestershire sauce, green pepper and pimiento. **Microwave at High 4 to 4½ Minutes,** until thickened, stirring every minute.
1 egg, beaten	Stir a little of hot mixture into egg, then add egg to rest of sauce. **Microwave at Medium 1 to 2 Minutes.**
1 lb. lump crabmeat **½ cup fine dry bread crumbs** **¼ cup melted butter**	Drain crabmeat. Remove any shell or cartilage. Stir sauce into crab. Divide crab mixture into 6 to 8 shells or small ramekins. Combine crumbs and butter. Divide over top. **Microwave at Medium High 6 to 8 Minutes,** until heated.

Makes 6 to 8 servings

CLASSIC FRENCH CREAMED SCALLOPS

Commonly known as Coquilles St. Jacques. Large scallop shells are natural microwave utensils for this.

POWER LEVEL: High (10), Med. (5) and Med. High (7)
MICROWAVE TIME: 17 to 22 min., total

3 tablespoons butter **1 jar (4-oz.) sliced mushrooms** **2 green onions, sliced** **¼ cup chopped celery**	In 2-qt. casserole place butter, mushrooms, onions and celery. **Microwave at High 2 to 3 Minutes,** stirring after 1 minute.
2 tablespoons flour **½ teaspoon salt** **¼ teaspoon thyme** **1 tablespoon pimiento, chopped** **⅓ cup white wine** **1 lb. raw scallops**	Stir in flour, salt thyme and pimiento well, then wine and scallops, stirring again. **Microwave at High 5 to 6 Minutes,** stirring after 3 minutes, until thickened.
¼ cup dairy half & half **1 egg yolk, beaten**	Stir in half & half and egg yolk. **Microwave at Medium 3 to 4 Minutes,** stirring after 2 minutes.

Divide mixture among 4 scallop shells. Top with Crumb Mixture (below). Cover with wax paper. **Microwave at Medium High 7 to 9 Minutes,** rearranging after 4 minutes, until hot.

Makes 4 servings

Crumb Mixture: In small bowl, place 2 tablespoons butter. **Microwave at High ¼ to ½ Minute,** until melted. Stir in ¼ cup fine dry bread crumbs and 2 tablespoons Parmesan cheese.

Crab Imperial

Large Shellfish

MICROLESSON

Arrange large shellfish in the cooking dish so that the light colored underside is up during the first half of the cooking period. Because of its size, a whole lobster needs a small amount of water for added steam. Lobster tails and crab legs steam in their own natural moisture. When done, lobster and lobster tails should still be slightly translucent in the center. Cooking will be completed during standing time.

LARGE SHELLFISH CHART POWER LEVEL: High (10)

TYPE	TIME MIN.	COOK CODE	TYPE	TIME MIN.	COOK CODE
Crab Legs			**Lobster Tails**		
(8-10-oz.)	1-3 to 4	30	(8-10-oz.)	2-5½ to 6	60
(8-10-oz.)	2-5 to 6	50	(8-10-oz.)	4-9 to 11	90
(8-10-oz.)	4-9 to 11	90	(12-16-oz.)	1-5 to 6	50
Lobster Tails			**Whole Lobster**		
(8-10-oz.)	1-3 to 4	30	(1½-lb.)	9 to 11	90

HOW TO MICROWAVE LOBSTER TAILS AND CRAB LEGS

Arrange lobster tails in baking dish with underside up. (No water added.) Cover tightly with plastic wrap, turning back corner to vent. **Microwave at High** for half the time.

Remove tails from dish. Cut through back of shell and meat, leaving undershell intact.

Spread to expose meat. Loosen meat from shell with fingers.

Brush lobster meat with mixture of 1 tablespoon melted butter and 1 tablespoon lemon juice. Cover and **Microwave** second half of time. Meat should still be slightly translucent in the center. Let stand 5 minutes.

Arrange crab legs in baking dish with light colored side up. (No water added.) Cover tightly with plastic wrap, turning back corner to vent. **Microwave at High** for half the time.

Turn over, so dark side is up. Cover, **Microwave** until flesh at ends of legs is opaque. Let stand 5 minutes.

Microwaved Whole Lobster

HOW TO MICROWAVE A WHOLE LOBSTER   Cook Code: 90

Plunge the tip of a heavy knife into live lobster between the head and first segment to sever the spinal cord, which kills lobster. Lobster may show signs of movement for a few minutes.
Alternate Method: Place lobster in sinkful of warm water for 15 minutes.

Peg the tail to prevent curling by inserting a wooden skewer lengthwise through the meat. At this time, or after lobster is cooked, cut through the undershell of the body and remove the intestinal vein and small sack below the head.

Arrange lobster in baking dish with the back down and add ½ cup hot water. Cover tightly with plastic wrap, turning back one corner to vent. **Microwave at High** turning lobster over after 6 minutes.

MIXED SEAFOOD CASSEROLE

POWER LEVEL: High (10) and Medium High (7)
MICROWAVE TIME: 34 to 40 min., total

3 cups fresh bread cubes (3 medium slices bread)	In 8-in. square dish place bread cubes. **Microwave at High 3 to 4 Minutes,** stirring every 2 minutes, until crisp. Remove about half of cubes and save for top layer.
2 cups mixed seafood or 2 cans (7-oz.) tuna, shrimp or crab* 1 cup chopped onion 1 cup chopped celery ½ cup mayonnaise	In large mixing bowl mix together seafood, onion, celery and mayonnaise. Spread over bread cubes in dish. Cover seafood mixture with remaining half of bread cubes.
2 eggs 1 cup milk 1 can (10-oz.) condensed cream of mushroom soup	In small bowl beat eggs well and mix in milk and soup. Pour over casserole. **Microwave at Medium High 30 to 34 Minutes,** rotating dish ¼ turn every 10 minutes, until set but still slightly soft in center.
1 cup (4-oz.) shredded cheddar cheese Paprika	Sprinkle top with cheese, then paprika. **Microwave at Medium High 1 to 2 Minutes,** until cheese is melted. Let stand 5 to 10 minutes before serving.

Makes 6 to 8 servings

*Canned tuna can be undrained, but canned shrimp or crab should be drained.

FISH AND SHELLFISH CONVENIENCE CHART

POWER LEVEL: **High (10)**

ITEM	TIME MIN.	COOK CODE	COMMENTS
Alaska King Crab Newburg (6½-oz. pouch)	4—6	40	Puncture pouch with fork to vent.
Deviled Crabs (6-oz. pkg.)	3—4	30	Rotate dish ½ turn after 2 minutes. Will not be crisp.
Fish 'N' Chips (14-oz. pkg.)	7—9	70	Distribute evenly in large dish. Will not be crisp.
Fish Fillets With Crumb Coating (8-oz. pkg.)	4½—6	50	Distribute evenly in dish and rotate ½ turn after 3 minutes. Will not be crisp.

Make your own TV dinners by freezing prepared seafood entrees and other foods in reuseable TV trays. Reheat according to directions on page 29.

LOBSTER THERMIDOR

An enriched version of creamed lobster, often served in the shells of the lobster tails from which the meat was removed. See page 12 for tips on rearranging food portions.

POWER LEVEL: High (10) and Medium (5)
MICROWAVE TIME: 15 to 19 min., total

2 tablespoons butter 1 can (3-oz.) mushroom slices, drained 2 tablespoons chopped onion	In 1½-qt. casserole place butter, mushrooms and onions. **Microwave at High 3 Minutes,** stirring after 2 minutes.
2 tablespoons unsifted all-purpose flour ¼ teaspoon salt ⅛ teaspoon pepper ⅛ teaspoon paprika	Stir in flour, salt, pepper and paprika until smooth. **Microwave at High 1 Minute.**
¼ cup chicken broth ½ cup dairy half & half	Slowly stir in broth and half & half. **Microwave at High 3 to 4 Minutes,** stirring after 2 minutes, until thickened.
1 egg yolk, beaten 2 tablespoons sherry wine 2 cups cooked lobster	Stir part of hot mixture into egg yolk, then add egg to rest of hot mixture. Stir in sherry.

Microwave at Medium 3 to 4 Minutes, stirring after 2 minutes. Stir in lobster. Refill 4 tail shells of lobster with creamed mixture, or use 4 large scallop shells or au gratin dishes if desired. Cover with Crumb Mixture (below). Cover with wax paper. **Microwave at High 5 to 7 Minutes,** rearranging after 3 minutes, until heated through.

Makes 4 servings

Crumb Mixture: In small bowl, place 2 tablespoons butter. **Microwave at High ¼ to ½ Minute,** until melted. Stir in ¼ cup fine dry bread crumbs and 2 tablespoons Parmesan cheese.

All these frozen seafood entrees can be heated to serving temperature at High.

ITEM	TIME MIN.	COOK CODE	COMMENTS
Fish Sticks (9-oz. pkg.)	4½—6	50	Distribute evenly in dish and rotate ½ turn after 3 minutes. Will not be crisp.
Shrimp Croquettes (12-oz. pkg.)	4—6	40	Pierce sauce pouch with fork and place with food on plate. Cover with wax paper. Rotate dish ½ turn after 2 minutes.
Shrimp Newburg (6½-oz. pkg.)	4—6	40	Puncture top with fork to vent.
Tuna Noodle Casserole (11½-oz. pkg.)	7—9	70	Place in 1-qt. casserole with cover. Stir after 4 minutes and before serving.

Eggs & Cheese

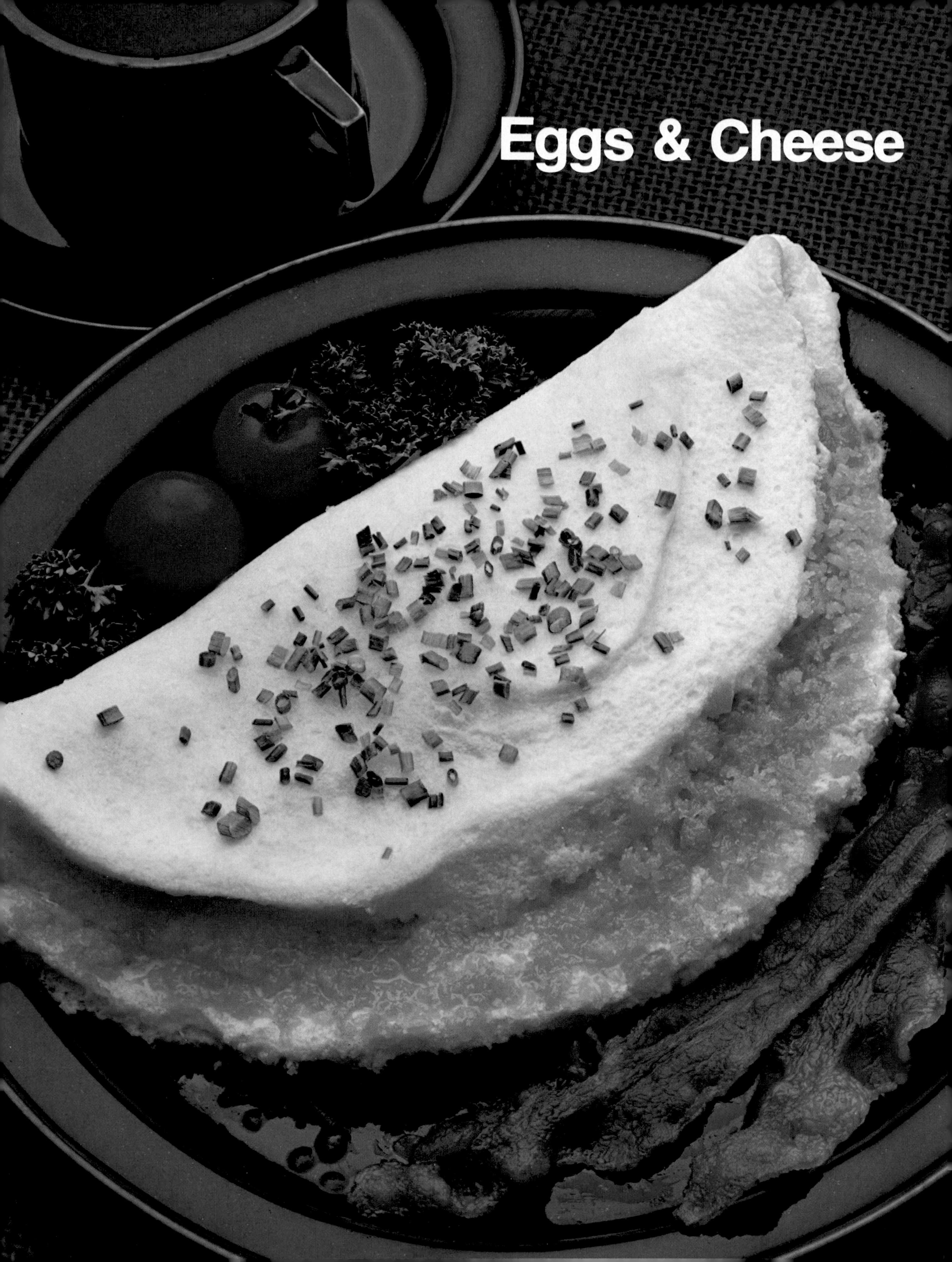

Eggs

Eggs are versatile; they can be prepared in a variety of ways, each with its own character. Although omelets and poached eggs are both eggs, they are completely different. Here we present the basic ways of cooking eggs. All but one microwave well. Do not try to hard boil eggs in the microwave oven. They expand during cooking and burst the shell.

HOW TO MICROWAVE SCRAMBLED EGGS

Place 1 teaspoon butter per egg in a glass measure or casserole. **Microwave at High** until melted.

Scramble eggs with the melted butter and 1 tablespoon milk per egg.

Place in oven. Estimate ¾ minute per egg and **Microwave at High** for ½ of total time.

HOW TO MICROWAVE BASIC EGGS

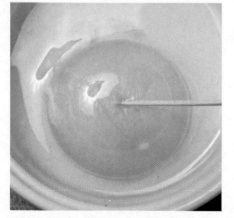

Puncture membrane of yolk to prevent bursting when microwaving shirred or poached eggs.

Microwave shirred eggs in buttered custard cups. Puncture membrane and cover. **Microwave ¾ to 1 Minute** per egg at **Medium**, rotating ½ turn after ½ minute.

Poach eggs by microwaving 2 cups hot tap water 5 to 6 minutes at **High,** until boiling. Break eggs onto plate; puncture membrane. Swirl boiling water with spoon and slip in eggs gently. Cover and **Microwave at Medium 1 Minute** per egg. Let stand in water a few minutes.

Eggs microwave rapidly, and since they are a delicate food, toughen when overcooked. The yolks, which have a higher fat content, cook faster than the whites. Poach eggs at Low Power to allow the whites time to set without toughening the edges or overcooking the yolks.

When yolks and whites are mixed together, eggs may be cooked at higher power settings. Omelets, which need time to set, are cooked at Medium, while scrambled eggs, which are stirred, are microwaved at High. Scrambled eggs are one of the foods which microwave better than they cook conventionally. Not only do they take less time and need less stirring, but they are fluffier and greater in volume. For easy clean up, scrambled eggs may be microwaved in a plastic-coated paper bowl.

Stir set portions from the outside to the center. Repeat 1 or 2 times during remaining cooking period.

When Done, eggs should be just past the runny stage.

After Standing 1 or 2 minutes, eggs will be set.

Fry eggs in the Brown 'N Sear Dish. Preheat dish at **High** 2 minutes for 1 or 2 eggs, plus 1 minute for each additional egg. Add ½ tablespoon butter per egg. Break eggs into dish, cover and **Microwave ¾ Minute** per egg, or to desired doneness.

Puffy Omelets are microwaved in a pie plate and folded over a filling. See recipes on page 181.

Never attempt to hard-cook eggs or reheat eggs in shells.

EGG SUBSTITUTE (EGG BEATERS)

HOW TO DEFROST: Microwave 1 package (equivalent to 4 eggs) at Defrost 1½ minutes. Turn carton over and Microwave at Defrost 1½ minutes more. Open carton and stir well. Microwave at Defrost 1 to 1½ minutes more, stirring every ¼ minute.

HOW TO MICROWAVE: Measure ¼ cup mixture per "egg" desired (package equals 4 eggs). Microwave in small glass bowl or microwave-proof container 1 minute per egg. Stirring after ½ total time.

POACHED EGGS WITH SPANISH SAUCE

These are known as Huevos Rancheros in the Southwestern United States.

POWER LEVEL: High (10) and Medium (5)
MICROWAVE TIME: 17 to 20 min., total

⅓ cup finely chopped onions ⅓ cup finely chopped green pepper 1 clove garlic, crushed 2 tablespoons cooking oil	In 1-qt. casserole stir together onion, green pepper, garlic and oil. **Microwave at High 3 to 4 Minutes,** until onion is tender.
1 can (16-oz.) tomatoes, drained 1 to 2 teaspoons chili powder ¼ teaspoon salt ⅛ teaspoon pepper ⅛ teaspoon oregano	Add tomatoes, chili powder, salt, pepper and oregano. **Microwave at High 5 to 7 Minutes,** stirring after 3 minutes, until thickened and hot.
4 poached eggs (page 178) ¼ to ½ cup shredded cheddar cheese	Place poached eggs on serving plates. Spoon sauce over eggs. Sprinkle with cheese.

Makes 2 to 4 servings

EGGS BENEDICT

POWER LEVEL: High (10) and Medium (5)
MICROWAVE TIME: 14 to 15 min., total

4 poached eggs (page 178)	Poach eggs and allow to stand as directed.
2 egg yolks 1 tablespoon lemon juice ½ teaspoon dry mustard ⅛ teaspoon salt ½ cup (¼-lb.) butter	While eggs are standing, make Hollandaise sauce. In container of electric blender measure egg yolks, lemon juice, mustard and salt. In 1-qt. glass measure place butter. **Microwave at High 1 Minute** until hot and bubbly. Turn electric blender to highest speed and gradually add butter, blending until creamy and thickened.
8 thin slices (¼-in. thick) Canadian bacon	Just before serving, microwave Canadian bacon which has been arranged in single layer on microwave ovenproof plate. Cover with wax paper. **Microwave at High 4 Minutes,** rotating dish ½ turn after 2 minutes.
4 English muffins, split and toasted	Assemble Eggs Benedict by arranging 2 slices of Canadian bacon, then a poached egg over each of 4 English muffin halves. Top eggs with Hollandaise Sauce. Butter remaining muffin halves and serve as accompaniment. Decorate with parsley if desired.

Makes 4 servings

MICROLESSON: HOW TO MICROWAVE A PUFFY CHEESE OMELET

Fold together yolk mixture and beaten whites gently. Carefully pour into buttered pie plate.

Microwave at Medium 6 to 8 Minutes, rotating the dish ½ turn after 3 minutes.

Check appearance for doneness. The omelet will be set but still glossy on top.

EGGS AND COTTAGE CHEESE SCRAMBLE

This brunch dish has a rich but delicate flavor. Add the cottage cheese at the last minute to melt it slightly.

POWER LEVEL: High (10)
MICROWAVE TIME: 8½ to 11 min., total

3 tablespoons butter **¼ cup finely chopped green onions**	.In 3-qt. casserole place butter and onions. **Microwave at High 2 Minutes.** Stir.
9 eggs **1½ cups diced, cooked ham or other firm pre-cooked meat such as salami or dried beef**	.Add eggs to casserole and beat well. Stir in meat. **Microwave at High 6 to 8 Minutes,** stirring every ½ minute.
½ cup creamed cottage cheese	.Stir in cottage cheese. **Microwave at High ½ to 1 Minute,** just until cottage cheese is slightly melted. Do not overmelt, or cheese becomes runny.

Makes 6 servings

FRENCH OMELET

French omelets need a hot pan surface to cook properly. This one, made in the Brown 'N Sear Dish, looks best when rolled to form a cylinder; it does not fold easily. This recipe serves 1 to 2 people. For more than 2 omelets we recommend the range top.

POWER LEVEL: High (10)
MICROWAVE TIME: 4 to 4½ min., total

1 tablespoon butter **3 eggs, well beaten** **Salt** **Pepper**	.Preheat empty, uncovered Brown 'N Sear Dish. **Microwave at High 2 Minutes.** Immediately add butter and tip dish to melt. Stir in eggs. **Microwave at High 2 to 2½ Minutes,** rotating dish ¼ turn every ½ minute, until almost set. Remove from oven. Immediately tip dish and roll up into cylindrical-shape omelet.

Makes 1 to 2 servings

PUFFY CHEESE OMELET

POWER LEVEL: High (10) and Medium (5)
MICROWAVE TIME: 7½ to 10 min., total

3 eggs, separated **⅓ cup mayonnaise** **2 tablespoons water**	.In largest mixer bowl beat egg whites at highest speed of mixer, until soft peaks form. Then in smaller bowl, using same beaters, beat yolks, mayonnaise and water. Gently pour yolk mixture over beaten whites. Fold together carefully.
2 tablespoons butter	.In 9-in. pie plate place butter. **Microwave at High 1 Minute,** swirl to coat dish. Carefully pour egg mixture into pie plate. **Microwave at Medium 6 to 8 Minutes,** rotating dish ½ turn after 3 minutes, until set but still glossy on top.
½ cup finely shredded cheddar cheese	.Sprinkle cheese over omelet.

Microwave at Medium ½ to 1 Minute, until cheese is slightly melted. Quickly run spatula or turner around sides and bottom of dish. Fold half of omelet over the other half. Gently slide onto serving plate. Sprinkle with chives, if desired.

Makes 1 to 2 servings

JELLY OMELET

POWER LEVEL: High (10) and Medium (5)
MICROWAVE TIME: 6 to 7 min., total

¼ to ⅓ cup strawberry or currant jelly	.In custard cup place jelly. **Microwave at High 1 Minute,** until jelly is soft and can be stirred smooth. Set aside.
3 eggs, separated **2 tablespoons water**	.In largest mixer bowl beat egg whites at highest speed of mixer, until soft peaks form. Then, in smaller bowl, using same beaters, beat yolks and water. Gently pour yolk mixture over beaten whites. Fold together carefully.
1 tablespoon butter	.In 9-in. pie plate place butter. **Microwave at High 1 Minute,** swirl to coat dish.

Carefully pour egg mixture into pie plate. **Microwave at Medium 4 to 5 Minutes,** rotating dish ¼ turn every minute, until set but still glossy on top. Spoon jelly over half of omelet. Quickly run spatula or turner around sides and bottom of dish. Fold plain half of omelet over jelly half. Gently slide onto serving plate. If desired, sprinkle cinnamon-sugar over omelet before serving.

Makes 1 to 2 servings

Quiche

Quiche is simple farm-style food which has earned a gourmet reputation because it tastes so good. A quiche is a pie shell filled with chopped cooked meat, cheese and a creamy custard. Substitute about ½ cup seafood for the bacon, and any firm cheese for the Swiss, if desired. In the province of Lorraine, French farmers use bacon, cheese and onions. Quiche is so versatile that wedges make a hearty supper, while small pieces provide a distinctive appetizer.

Microwaved quiche differs from conventionally baked because the milk or cream is heated before the custard is prepared. The warm filling microwaves more evenly, allowing the center to set without overcooking the edges. With microwaving, you have tender custard in about half the time.

HOW TO MICROWAVE QUICHE LORRAINE

Brush pastry with a mixture of 1 egg yolk and 1 teaspoon Worcestershire sauce. Prick pastry with fork. **Microwave at High,** rotating dish ½ turn after about ½ time.

Fill pastry with crumbled cooked bacon, grated cheese and green onions. Pour in hot custard mixture. **Microwave at Medium High,** rotating dish ¼ turn every 2 minutes.

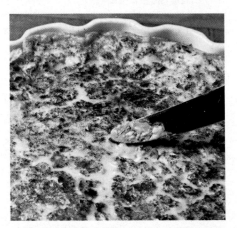

Metal Knife inserted in the center will come out coated with partially cooked custard when quiche is done. Center will set during the 5 minutes of standing time.

CLASSIC QUICHE LORRAINE

POWER LEVEL: Medium High (7)
MICROWAVE TIME: 14 to 18 min., total

6 strips crisp cooked bacon, crumbled **1 cup grated Swiss cheese** **3 green onions, chopped** **1 Quiche Pastry**	Reserve 2 tablespoons each of bacon and cheese and 1 tablespoon onion. Sprinkle remaining bacon, cheese and onion over bottom of microwaved Quiche Pastry (right).
2 tablespoons flour **1 teaspoon salt** **¼ teaspoon nutmeg** **Dash cayenne** **1 cup milk** **1 cup whipping cream**	In 1-qt. measure mix flour, salt, nutmeg and cayenne pepper. Gradually stir in milk and cream. **Microwave at Medium High 7 Minutes.** Stir every 2 minutes.
4 eggs	In 1-qt. casserole beat eggs well.

Gradually stir mixture into eggs. **Microwave at Medium High 1 to 3 Minutes,** stirring every ½ minute, until thick. Pour into pastry. Top with bacon, cheese and onion. **Microwave at Medium High 6 to 8 Minutes,** rotating dish ¼ turn every 2 minutes, until almost set. Let stand 5 minutes.

Makes 1 (9-in.) quiche, about 6 servings

QUICHE PASTRY

POWER LEVEL: High (10) **Cook Code:** 40
MICROWAVE TIME: 4 to 6 min., total

1 cup unsifted all-purpose flour **½ teaspoon salt** **3 tablespoons shortening** **3 tablespoons cold butter**	In small mixing bowl stir together flour and salt. With pastry blender, cut in shortening until it has the appearance of cornmeal. Cut in butter until particles form the size of peas.
2 tablespoons cold water	Sprinkle mixture with cold water. Blend lightly with fingers until dough holds together and can be formed into ball. Roll out to fit 9-in. quiche dish.
1 egg yolk **1 teaspoon Worcestershire sauce**	Brush pastry with mixture of egg yolk and Worcestershire sauce. Prick pastry with fork.

Microwave at High 4 to 6 Minutes, rotating dish ½ turn after 2½ minutes.

Makes 1 (9-in.) quiche pastry

GOLDEN ONION QUICHE

POWER LEVEL: High (10) and Medium High (7)
MICROWAVE TIME: 14 to 18 min., total

1 commercially frozen pie crust **Worcestershire sauce (about 2 teaspoons)**	Remove pastry from foil pan to glass 8-in. pie plate. **Microwave at High ½ to 1 Minute,** until softened. With fingers, press firmly in pie plate. Brush inside with Worcestershire sauce. Prick pastry. Place pie plate in the oven on trivet or inverted saucer. **Microwave at High 3 to 4 Minutes,** rotating plate ½ turn after 2 minutes.
1 cup (4-oz.) shredded Mozzarella or pizza cheese	Sprinkle cheese over bottom of pie shell.
3 eggs **½ cup whipping cream** **3 drops hot pepper sauce (tabasco)**	With fork, beat together eggs, cream and hot pepper sauce. Pour over cheese in pie shell.
1 can (3-oz.) French fried onions	With sharp knife, cut through onions in can to chop medium fine. Pour over top and lightly press down.
1 tablespoon dried or frozen chives	Sprinkle chives over top.

Microwave at Medium High 11 to 13 Minutes, rotating pie ½ turn after 6 minutes. Let stand about 5 minutes to firm slightly before serving.

Makes 1 (8-in.) pie, about 6 servings

Golden Onion Quiche and its variations have been favorites with our customers ever since Medium High Power was available. It is easy to make because it starts with convenience ingredients.

VARIATIONS:

BACON AND CHEESE QUICHE

Follow recipe for Golden Onion Quiche (left) except sprinkle 4 slices crisp-microwaved bacon, crumbled over cheese before adding custard mixture. Substitute shredded Swiss cheese for Mozzarella, if desired.

HAM AND CHEESE QUICHE

Follow recipe for Golden Onion Quiche (left) except substitute sharp cheddar cheese for Mozzarella. Before adding filling, spread 1 can (4-oz.) deviled ham over bottom of microwaved pastry crust. Then add cheese and rest of filling ingredients. **Microwave at Medium High 12 to 15 Minutes,** rotating pie ½ turn after 7 minutes.

GREEN CHILIES QUICHE

Especially appropriate cut in small wedges and served as an appetizer.

Follow recipe for Golden Onion Quiche (left) except sprinkle 2 tablespoons chopped green chilies over cheese before adding custard mixture.

SALMON OR TUNA QUICHE

Follow recipe for Golden Onion Quiche (left) except spoon 1 can (6½-oz.) drained flaked tuna or salmon over bottom of microwaved pie shell before adding cheese and other filling ingredients. **Microwave at Medium High 11 to 13 Minutes,** rotating pie ½ turn after 6 minutes.

Golden Onion Quiche

Souffles

Souffles must be specially formulated for microwaving, so you cannot adapt conventional recipes. Because it cooks so quickly, a microwaved souffle need to be stabilized. For this reason we use evaporated milk in making the cream sauce base.

A microwaved souffle rises very high because it does not form a crust. It requires a larger dish than conventionally baked. A 2½-qt. souffle dish is the minimum size for a 6-egg souffle. Souffles can be microwaved with a combination of Low and Medium Power and should be rotated frequently.

When done, the souffle will be dry on top with a creamy meringue in the center. Traditionally, this creamy center is served as a "sauce". See page 223 for Spinach Souffle, a vegetable variation of Cheese Souffle.

Selecting the right size souffle dish is important for success. If unsure of your dish's capacity, fill to the top with measured amount of water.

CHEESE SOUFFLE

POWER LEVEL: High (10), Low (3) and Medium (5)
MICROWAVE TIME: 23 to 30 min., total

¼ **cup unsifted** . . . . **all-purpose flour** ¾ **teaspoon salt** ½ **teaspoon dry mustard** ⅛ **teaspoon paprika** 1 **can (13-oz.)** **evaporated milk**	In 1½-qt. casserole blend together flour, salt, mustard and paprika. Stir in evaporated milk. **Microwave at High 4 to 6 Minutes,** stirring every 2 minutes, until thickened.
2 **cups (8-oz.) shredded** **sharp cheddar** **cheese**	Stir cheese into hot sauce. **Microwave at High 1 to 2 Minutes,** until smooth.
6 **eggs, separated** . . . . 1 **teaspoon cream of** **tartar**	In large mixer bowl beat egg whites with cream of tartar until stiff but not dry. Set aside and, using same beaters, beat yolks in medium mixer bowl until thick and lemon colored.

Slowly pour cheese mixture over beaten yolks, beating until well combined. Gently pour over beaten egg whites and fold together gently just until blended. Pour into ungreased 2½-qt. souffle dish. **Microwave at Low 10 Minutes,** rotating dish ¼ turn every 5 minutes, **Microwave at Medium 12 to 14 Minutes** more, rotating dish ¼ turn every 5 minutes, until puffed top edges are beginning to appear dry and souffle has "set" appearance. Serve immediately.

Makes 6 to 8 servings

PARMESAN AND CHEDDAR CHEESE SOUFFLE

This combination gives a distinctive sharp cheese flavor to the souffle.

Prepare Cheese Souffle (above) except substitute 1 cup grated Parmesan cheese for 1 cup of the sharp cheddar.

CHOCOLATE SOUFFLE

This tastes like fluffy chocolate pudding. A crack may appear on top, and is normal with this souffle.

POWER LEVEL: High (10), Low (3) and Medium (5)
MICROWAVE TIME: 22 to 26 min., total

¼ **cup cocoa** . . . . ¼ **cup unsifted** **all-purpose flour** ½ **cup sugar** 1 **teaspoon salt** 2 **cans (5-oz. each)** **evaporated milk**	In 1-qt. measure mix cocoa, flour, sugar and salt to blend. Add milk and stir smooth. **Microwave at High 6 Minutes,** stirring after 2 minutes, then after each additional minute, until thickened.
¼ **cup butter**	Stir butter into hot mixture.
6 **eggs, separated** . . . . ¾ **teaspoon cream of** **tartar** ½ **cup sugar**	In large mixer bowl beat egg whites with cream of tartar until foamy. Gradually add sugar, beating to a stiff, glossy meringue.

With same beaters, beat egg yolks in medium mixer bowl until thick and lemon colored. Add chocolate mixture and beat smooth. Gently pour chocolate mixture over meringue and fold together gently, just until blended. Pour into ungreased 3-qt. souffle dish. **Microwave at Low 10 Minutes,** rotating dish ¼ turn every 5 minutes, **Microwave at Medium 12 to 14 Minutes** more, rotating dish ¼ turn every 5 minutes, until puffed top edges are beginning to appear dry and souffle has "set" appearance. Serve immediately.

Makes 6 to 8 servings

CHOCOLATE CREAM CHEESE SOUFFLE

Prepare Chocolate Souffle (above), except add package (8-Oz.) softened cream cheese along with butter. Stir until smooth and continue as in recipe. Instead of time given in recipe above, **Microwave at Low 10 Minutes** and at **Medium 16 to 18 Minutes.** This souffle has a less airy, but firm and stable consistency.

TIPS FOR MICROWAVING A SOUFFLE

Beat egg whites until stiff but not dry. Set aside, and with the same beaters, beat egg yolks until thick and lemon colored. Mix yolks with prepared cheese sauce.

Fold egg-cheese mixture into whites, using a rubber spatula to cut down to bottom of dish, move across the bottom, and lift the egg whites up over top of sauce.

Pour into souffle dish. **Microwave at Low 10 Minutes,** then **Microwave at Medium 12 to 14 Minutes,** rotate dish ¼ turn every 5 minutes until top appears dry.

Cheese Souffle

Melted Cheese Sandwich

TIPS FOR MICROWAVING CHEESE

Cheese

Natural cheese reacts to microwaving much as it does to conventional cooking, but faster. Because of its high fat content it melts quickly and tends to become stringy when overcooked. Where cheese must be cooked for more than a few moments, layer it between other ingredients and use Medium Power, or use process cheese, which is less apt to become stringy. Many cheese dishes make good appetizers. Try our selection of cheese fondues next time you entertain.

MELTED CHEESE SANDWICH

POWER LEVEL: Medium High (7)
MICROWAVE TIME: 4 min., total

2 slices bread	In conventional toaster, toast bread. At the same time, preheat empty and uncovered Brown 'N Sear Dish at **Medium High 3 Minutes.**
Butter . . . . **2 slices processed cheese**	When toasted, assemble sandwich and butter outside surfaces. Place in Brown 'N Sear Dish. **Microwave at Medium High ½ Minute** per side.

Makes 1 sandwich

Cubed process cheese combines with cooked macaroni and evaporated milk for a quick and easy casserole. To use natural cheese, fold cooked macaroni into homemade cheese sauce.

Add cheese toppings to vegetables, casseroles and hamburgers after cooking. Heat from the food melts the cheese. Shredded cheese on pizza and nachos is microwaved a few seconds to melt it.

CHEESE FONDUE WITH NATURAL CHEESE

It is important to whisk or stir the fondue every minute after the cheese is added, and to cook only until melted. The kirsch, while a classic ingredient, is optional.

POWER LEVEL: High (10) and Medium (5)
MICROWAVE TIME: 7 to 8 min., total

1 cup dry white wine	In 2-qt. microwave oven-proof fondue pot or casserole place wine and kirsch. **Microwave at High 4 Minutes,** until very hot.
2 tablespoons kirsch	
2½ cups (10-oz.) .... **shredded natural Gruyere cheese** **2½ cups (10-oz.) shredded natural baby Swiss cheese** **2 tablespoons unsifted all-purpose flour** **⅛ teaspoon pepper Dash nutmeg (optional)**	Toss cheeses with flour, pepper and nutmeg, until cheese is well coated. When wine is very hot, whisk or stir in cheese quickly. Cover. **Microwave at Medium 3 to 4 Minutes,** stirring briskly every minute, until cheese is just melted. Serve immediately with cubes of crusty French bread for dipping.
	Makes about 4 servings

Cheese Fondue

CHEESE FONDUE WITH PROCESSED CHEESE

Processed cheese gives the fondue a very smooth, even texture.

Follow recipe above, except substitute processed Gruyere and Swiss cheeses for the natural cheeses. Or, as an alternate, use 5 cups (20-oz.) shredded Swiss cheese and omit Gruyere.

QUICK AND EASY FONDUE

This recipe can easily be doubled or tripled to use as a party dip for crackers or the traditional bread cubes. Increase time about 2 minutes.

POWER LEVEL: High (10)   **Cook Code:** 30
MICROWAVE TIME: 3 to 4 min., total

1 can (10-oz.) .... **condensed cream of shrimp soup** **1 roll (6-oz.) process garlic cheese, cubed**	In 1-qt. casserole stir together soup and cheese cubes. **Microwave at High 3 to 4 Minutes,** stirring after 2 minutes, until cheese is melted.
	Makes about 2 to 3 servings

CHEESE SANDWICH CASSEROLE

POWER LEVEL: Medium (5)   **Cook Code:** 95
MICROWAVE TIME: 9 to 11 min., total

4 slices bread .... **Butter** **2 cups (8-oz.) shredded cheddar cheese**	Spread each bread slice with butter. In 10x6x2-in. dish place 2 slices bread, butter side up. Top with 1 cup cheese. Repeat layers.
2 eggs .... **1 cup dairy half & half** **2 tablespoons butter, melted** **½ teaspoon salt** **½ teaspoon dry mustard** **¼ teaspoon paprika Dash cayenne pepper**	In mixing bowl beat eggs. Blend in half & half, butter, salt, mustard, paprika and cayenne pepper. Pour over sandwiches. Cover with wax paper. **Microwave at Medium 9 to 11 Minutes,** rotating dish ½ turn after 5 minutes. Let stand 5 minutes before serving.
	Makes 2 or 4 servings

Cheese Rarebit

CHEESE RAREBIT

Rarebit is a rich cheese sauce traditionally served over toast points or other types of toasted bread.

POWER LEVEL: High (10) and Medium (5)
MICROWAVE TIME: 5 to 7 min., total

8 oz. pasteurized . . . .
    processed cheese,
    diced
1 tablespoon butter
	In 1-qt. casserole, place cheese and butter. **Microwave at High 2 to 3 Minutes,** stirring every minute, until melted and cheese can be stirred smooth.

¼ teaspoon salt . . . .
¼ teaspoon dry mustard
½ teaspoon
    Worcestershire
    sauce
    Dash cayenne pepper
¼ cup dairy half & half
1 egg yolk, beaten
	Add salt, mustard, Worchestershire sauce and cayenne pepper. Quickly stir in half & half and egg yolk. **Microwave at Medium 3 to 4 Minutes,** stirring every minute, until hot.

Makes 3 to 4 servings

CHEESE ENCHILADAS

POWER LEVEL: High (10)
MICROWAVE TIME: 12½ to 15¾ min., total

1 lb. ricotta cheese . . . . . .
    (2 cups)
1 egg
1 cup chopped green
    onions
2 tablespoons chopped
    green chilies
1 teaspoon cumin
1 cup (4-oz.) shredded
    Jack cheese
	In mixing bowl stir together ricotta, egg, onions, chillies, cumin and Jack cheese.

8 fresh corn or flour . . . . .
    tortillas, (about 7-in.
    diameter) or, 10 to 12
    canned tortillas (5-in.
    diameter)
	Wrap tortillas in damp towel. **Microwave at High ½ to ¾ Minute,** until pliable. Divide filling among tortillas. Roll up each one tightly.

1 can (10-oz.) . . . . **enchilada sauce**	In lightly greased 12×8×2-in. dish place rolls, seam side down. Pour sauce over rolls. **Microwave at High 11 to 13 Minutes,** rotating dish ½ turn after 6 minutes, until filling begins to bubble.

2 cups (8-oz.) . . . .
    shredded cheddar
    cheese
	Cover with cheddar cheese. **Microwave at High 1 to 2 Minutes,** until cheese is almost melted.

Sour cream and . . . .
    chopped green
    onions
	Garnish with sour cream and green onions.

Makes 4 generous servings

Rotate and Stir cheese dishes frequently because of their delicate nature.

CHEESE PIE WITH HAMBURGER CRUST

POWER LEVEL: High (10) and Medium (5)
MICROWAVE TIME: 15 to 17 min., total

1 egg .... **½ cup milk** **2 cups fresh bread, cubed (3 slices)**	In large mixing bowl beat egg slightly. Add milk and bread. Toss lightly, then let stand few minutes, until most of liquid is absorbed.
½ lb. ground chuck **beef** **1 teaspoon Worcestershire sauce** **1 teaspoon salt** **¼ teaspoon thyme** **¼ teaspoon dried parsley** **1¼ cups sliced green onions, including tops, divided**	To bread mixture add beef, Worcestershire sauce, salt, thyme, parsley and ¼ cup onions. Mix lightly until combined. Spoon into 9-in. pie plate and spread to line bottom and sides of plate. Sprinkle remaining green onions over crust.
3 eggs .... **1 cup (4-oz.) shredded Swiss cheese** **3 to 4 drops liquid pepper seasoning (tabasco)** **½ teaspoon salt** **⅓ cup milk** **Paprika**	In same bowl beat eggs until foamy. Stir in cheese, liquid pepper seasoning, salt and milk. Pour over green onions in meat crust. Sprinkle lightly with paprika.

Microwave at High 5 Minutes, then rotate dish ¼ turn. **Microwave at Medium 10 to 12 Minutes,** rotating dish ¼ turn after 5 minutes. Center will be soft but set when done.

Makes 6 to 8 servings

MICROWAVE CHEESE TOPPINGS

The following toppings may be prepared to garnish favorite vegetables or casseroles.

Cheese Topping for Vegetables: In small mixing bowl place 1 jar or pkg. (8-oz.) processed cheddar cheese food. **Microwave at Medium High 2 to 3 Minutes,** stirring after 2 minutes, until cheese is melted and can be stirred smooth. For thinner topping, add 1 to 2 tablespoons milk, beer or tomato juice. Add chopped parsley and/or garlic salt for more color or flavor.

Cheese Topping for Casseroles: In small mixing bowl place ¼ cup butter. **Microwave at High ½ to 1 Minute,** until melted. Stir in ½ cup fine dry bread or cracker crumbs, ¼ cup Parmesan cheese and ¼ teaspoon paprika. **Microwave at Medium High 2 to 3 minutes,** stirring after 1 minute.

CHEESE PUDDING

This interesting casserole is a good substitute for potatoes, rice or pasta in a full course menu. Or serve it as a luncheon or supper dish, along with a salad.

POWER LEVEL: High (10), Med. (5) and Med. High (7)
MICROWAVE TIME: 20¼ to 25½ min., total

2 cups water .... **4 eggs**	Poach eggs hard; into 1½-qt. casserole pour water. **Microwave at High 5 to 6 Minutes,** until boiling. Meanwhile, break eggs into saucer and puncture membrane around yolk with toothpick. Slip eggs into boiling water. **Microwave at Medium 5 to 6 Minutes,** until yolks begin to harden. Let stand several minutes in water. Remove and grate or chop finely.
1 cup buttery cracker crumbs .... **2 cups (double recipe) thick White Sauce, page 191** **2 cups (8-oz.) shredded cheddar cheese** **2 jars (4-oz.) sliced pimiento, drained**	Into 8-in. square dish place ½ of cracker crumbs. Cover with ½ of white sauce, ½ of cheese, ½ of pimiento and ½ of eggs. Repeat layers. Cover with Buttered Crumbs (below). **Microwave at Medium High 9 to 11 Minutes,** rotating dish ½ turn after 5 minutes, until heated through.

Makes about 8 servings

Buttered Crumbs: In 1 cup measure place 2 tablespoons butter. **Microwave at High ¼ to ½ Minute,** until melted. Add ½ cup fine dry bread crumbs. **Microwave at Medium High 1 to 2 Minutes,** until browned.

EGGS & CHEESE CONVENIENCE CHART

ITEM	POWER LEVEL	TIME MINUTES	COMMENTS
Egg Substitute (egg beaters) (8-oz. carton)			See page 180.
Cheese Souffle (12-oz. pkg.)	Defrost	9 to 13	To Defrost: Place in 8-in. pie plate. Rotate ½ turn after 3 minutes. Stir.
	Medium High	9 to 11	To Cook: Divide between 3 or 4 buttered custard cups, 6 or 7-oz. Rearrange after 4 minutes. Souffles are done when center is set.
Welsh Rarebit (10-oz. pkg.)	High	5 to 6	Remove from foil container and place in suitable dish. Stir every 2 minutes.

Gravies & Main Dish Sauces

Gravies and sauces microwave easily because there is no scorching or lumping or constant stirring. They save time in cooking and clean-up, too. Make them right in the cup you use for measuring or in the microwave oven-proof sauce boat you use for serving.

POULTRY GIBLET GRAVY

POWER LEVEL: Medium (5) and High (10)
MICROWAVE TIME: 21 to 29 min., total

Giblets from a 3-lb. chicken **1 cup water**	In 1-qt. casserole place giblets. Prick each giblet several times with fork. Add water. Cover. **Microwave at Medium 16 to 20 Minutes,** stirring after 10 minutes, until tender. Chop medium fine.
¼ cup poultry drippings **¼ cup flour** **½ teaspoon salt** **¼ teaspoon celery salt** **Dash pepper**	In separate 1-qt. casserole place drippings. **Microwave at High 1 to 2 Minutes,** until hot. Stir in flour, salt, celery salt and pepper until smooth.
Broth from giblets plus water to make 1¼ cups	Gradually stir in broth until well blended. **Microwave at High 2 to 4 Minutes,** stirring every minute. Add chopped giblets. **Microwave at High 2 to 3 Minutes** more, stirring every minute, until thickened.

Makes about 1½ cups

Poultry Giblet Gravy

TIPS FOR MICROWAVING GRAVIES AND SAUCES

Use More flour or cornstarch to thicken microwaved gravies and sauces, they will not reduce by evaporation.

Combine flour, butter and salt in a glass measure when making White Sauce. Microwave until butter melts and bubbles. Stir and microwave 1 minute more to cook flour.

Stir often to bring the cooked portions from the outside of the cup to the center. Use a wire whisk or a table fork for a smooth sauce with minimum stirring.

MILK GRAVY

Be sure to use a 1-qt. utensil to prevent boilover. These proportions are for gravy which runs easily from spoon. For thicker gravy, which mounds from spoon, use ⅓ cup flour.

POWER LEVEL: High (10)
MICROWAVE TIME: 6 to 9 min., total

¼ cup chicken or beef drippings	In 1-qt. measuring cup, measure drippings. **Microwave at High 1 to 2 Minutes,** until hot. Add flour and salt. Stir well. Stir in milk slowly. **Microwave at High 5 to 7 Minutes,** stirring every minute.
¼ cup flour	
¼ teaspoon salt	
1¼ cups milk	

Makes about 1½ cups

VARIATIONS:

Cream Gravy: Prepare Milk Gravy as above, except, instead of 1¼ cups milk, use ⅔ cup milk and ⅔ cup whipping cream.

Brown Gravy: Prepare Milk Gravy or Cream Gravy as above, using beef or lamb drippings and adding ½ teaspoon brown bouquet sauce.

BASIC WHITE SAUCE

POWER LEVEL: High (10)
MICROWAVE TIME: 5 to 6 min., total

2 tablespoons butter	In 1-qt. glass measure place butter, flour and salt. **Microwave at High 2 Minutes** stirring after 1 minute.
2 tablespoons flour	
½ teaspoon salt	
1 cup milk	Gradually stir in milk. **Microwave at High 3 to 4 Minutes,** stirring every minute until thick and bubbly.

Makes 1 cup

VARIATIONS:

Cheese Sauce: To finished sauce, add 1 cup (4-oz.) shredded sharp cheese and a dash of cayenne pepper. **Microwave at High 1 to 2 Minutes,** to melt cheese.

Mornay Sauce: To finished sauce, add ½ cup shredded Swiss, Gruyere or Parmesan cheese, 1 teaspoon lemon juice and a dash of cayenne pepper.

Curry Sauce: Add 2 to 3 teaspoons curry powder along with flour. Microwave as above.

Dill Sauce: To finished sauce, add 2 teaspoons dill weed and 1 teaspoon lemon juice.

Horseradish Sauce: To finished sauce, add 1 to 2 teaspoons cream style horseradish.

Thick White Sauce: Use 3 tablespoons flour instead of 2 tablespoons.

Asparagus with White Sauce

HOLLANDAISE SAUCE FOR MICROWAVERS

We have tried many recipes for microwaving Hollandaise Sauce, even the "never-fail" ones, and our recommendation is to use the blender method. The microwave oven helps you by rapidly melting the butter.

You can reheat leftover Hollandaise Sauce successfully at Low Power for ¼ to ½ minute. Stir and let the sauce stand before continuing to reheat; it is so delicate that it can curdle easily even upon reheating if you set the timer for too long.

POWER LEVEL: High (10)   **Cook Code: 10**
MICROWAVE TIME: 1 to 2 min., total

2 egg yolks	Into container of electric blender measure yolks, juice, mustard and salt.
1 tablespoon lemon juice	
½ teaspoon dry mustard	
⅛ teaspoon salt	
½ cup (¼-lb.) butter	In glass measuring cup place butter. **Microwave at High 1 to 2 Minutes,** until hot and bubbly. Turn electric blender to highest speed and gradually add butter, mixing well until Hollandaise is creamy and thickened.

Makes about ½ cup

SWEET AND SOUR SAUCE

This piquant sauce is so versatile that it goes with just about every type of meat, poultry and seafood. It's very good with hamburgers, especially if you increase garlic to 1 clove. The 10 drops liquid pepper seasoning gives the sauce zip.

POWER LEVEL: High (10)   **Cook Code: 60**
MICROWAVE TIME: 6 to 8 min., total

½ cup sugar	In 1½-qt. casserole stir together sugar, cornstarch and water, until well blended.
2 tablespoons cornstarch	
¼ cup cold water	
1 can (8-oz.) crushed pineapple . . .	Stir in undrained pineapple, pepper, pimiento, garlic, vinegar, soy sauce and pepper seasoning. Cover. **Microwave at High 6 to 8 Minutes,** stirring every 2 minutes, until clear and thickened. Let sauce stand 5 to 10 minutes, to develop flavor, before serving.
½ cup chopped green pepper	
¼ cup (4-oz. can) chopped pimiento	
½ clove garlic, mashed	
½ cup cider vinegar	
2 tablespoons soy sauce	
10 drops liquid pepper seasoning (tabasco)	

Makes about 1¾ cups

BEARNAISE SAUCE

Serve this sauce over steaks, poached eggs on toast, or microwaved green vegetables.

POWER LEVEL: High (10)   **Cook Code: 10**
MICROWAVE TIME: 1 to 2 min., total

4 egg yolks	In blender container place yolks, onion, vinegar and wine.
1 teaspoon instant minced onion	
1 teaspoon tarragon vinegar	
1 teaspoon white wine	
½ cup (¼-lb.) butter	In glass measure place butter. **Microwave at High 1 to 2 Minutes,** until hot and bubbly. Turn electric blender to highest speed and gradually add butter, blending until sauce is creamy and thickened.

Makes about ½ cup

WHIPPED BUTTERS

Savory garnishes for sliced, roasted meats or plain vegetables.

POWER LEVEL: Low (3)
MICROWAVE TIME: ½ to ¾ min., total

1. In small glass mixer bowl place ½ cup (¾-lb.) butter. **Microwave at Low ½ to ¾ Minute,** until softened.
2. Add ingredients from one of the variations.
3. Whip with electric mixer, at high speed, until fluffy.

Makes ½ cup

VARIATIONS:

Herbed Butter: Add 2 teaspoons minced parsley, 2 teaspoons lemon juice, ¼ teaspoon thyme, ¼ teaspoon salt and ¼ teaspoon pepper.

Parsley Garlic Butter: Add ½ cup minced parsley, 2 cloves minced garlic, 2 teaspoons minced onion, 2 teaspoons lemon juice and 1 teaspoon dry mustard.

Dill Butter: Add 4 teaspoons dill weed, ½ teaspoon salt, ⅛ teaspoon pepper and 2 hard cooked egg yolks, sieved. To hard cook egg yolks: Place yolks in 6-oz. custard cup. Add 1 tablespoon water. Cover with plastic wrap. **Microwave at Medium 1 Minute.** Let stand a few minutes, then remove from water to cool.

ALMOND BUTTER SAUCE

POWER LEVEL: High (10)
MICROWAVE TIME: 6 to 7 min., total

¼ **cup slivered almonds** ½ **cup (¼-lb.) butter,** **divided**	In 9-in. pie plate place almonds and 1 teaspoon butter. **Microwave at High 5 to 6 Minutes,** stirring every 2 minutes, until toasted. Add remaining butter. **Microwave at High 1 Minute,** until melted.
½ **teaspoon seasoned** **salt**	Stir in seasoned salt. Serve warm.

Makes ½ cup

Toast nuts, such as for Almond Butter Sauce, stirring often, until golden brown to develop flavor and crunchiness. Butter and salt add flavor.

LEMON BUTTER SAUCE

A favorite sauce for fish and fish loaves, and for some vegetables, such as asparagus and broccoli.

POWER LEVEL: High (10)
MICROWAVE TIME: ¼ to ½ min., total

¼ **cup butter**	In 1-cup glass measure place butter. **Microwave at High ¼ to ½ Minute,** until melted.
1 tablespoon fresh **lemon juice** **1 tablespoon snipped** **parsley** **Dash pepper**	Stir lemon juice, parsley and pepper into melted butter. Keep warm.

Makes about ¼ cup

COLORFUL MARMALADE SAUCE

This bright sauce looks and tastes good over duck, chicken, turkey and ham. It serves as a glaze as well as a sauce. Use sweet, not bitter, orange marmalade.

POWER LEVEL: High (10)   **Cook Code:** 50
MICROWAVE TIME: 5 to 7 min., total

1 cup sweet orange **marmalade** **1 can (8-oz.) tomato** **sauce** **2 tablespoons** **chopped onion** **1½ teaspoons soy** **sauce** **1 teaspoon ground** **ginger** ½ **cup sliced almonds**	In 1½-qt. casserole combine marmalade, tomato sauce, onion, soy sauce, ginger and almonds. **Microwave at High 5 to 7 Minutes,** stirring every 2 minutes, until hot and well combined.

Makes about 2 cups

RAISIN SAUCE

Traditionally served with ham or pork.

POWER LEVEL: High (10)   **Cook Code:** 40
MICROWAVE TIME: 4 to 6 min., total

½ **cup brown sugar** **(packed)** **2 tablespoons** **cornstarch** **1½ teaspoons dry** **mustard** ⅛ **teaspoon ground** **cloves**	In 1-qt. measuring cup or casserole blend together brown sugar, cornstarch, mustard and cloves, until well combined.
1 cup water or **apple cider** **2 tablespoons lemon** **juice** ¼ **cup raisins** **2 tablespoons butter**	Stir in water and lemon juice until smooth. Add raisins and butter. **Microwave at High 4 to 6 Minutes,** stirring every 2 minutes, until clear and thickened.

Makes about 1¼ cups

Mushrooms should remain light in color when cooked. Darkening denotes overcooking.

MUSHROOM SAUCE

This is elegant for steaks or chops

POWER LEVEL: Medium High (7)
MICROWAVE TIME: 6 to 7 min., total

2 cups sliced fresh mushrooms **¼ cup butter**	In 1-qt. casserole place mushrooms and butter. Cover. **Microwave at Medium High 3 Minutes.**
¼ cup water **¼ cup sherry wine or additional water** **1 tablespoon cornstarch** **⅛ teaspoon salt**	Mix together water, sherry, cornstarch and salt. Gradually stir into mushrooms. Cover. **Microwave at Medium High 3 to 4 Minutes,** stirring after 2 minutes, until thickened.

Makes about 2 cups

BARBECUE SAUCE

The traditional sauce to use when cooking ribs and chicken. Or, slice leftover beef or pork into barbecue sauce and serve warm as an entree or sandwich filling.

POWER LEVEL: High (10) **Cook Code: 50**
MICROWAVE TIME: 5 to 7 min., total

1 cup chili sauce **½ cup water** **¼ cup lemon juice** **1 tablespoon cooking oil** **2 tablespoons brown sugar (packed)** **½ teaspoon salt** **¼ teaspoon paprika** **¼ teaspoon liquid pepper seasoning (tabasco)** **1 tablespoon Worcestershire sauce**	In 1-qt. casserole thoroughly combine chili sauce, water, lemon juice, cooking oil, brown sugar, salt, paprika, pepper seasoning and Worcestershire sauce. Cover. **Microwave at High 5 to 7 Minutes,** stirring after 3 minutes, until hot. Use as desired.

Makes 2 cups

CLASSIC ITALIAN SAUCE

Complements pasta, meatballs, meat slices and cooked chicken pieces.

POWER LEVEL: High (10)
MICROWAVE TIME: 15 to 18 min., total

1 large onion, chopped **3 tablespoons olive or cooking oil** **3 cloves garlic, minced**	In 3-qt. casserole place onion, oil and garlic. **Microwave at High 3 to 4 Minutes,** stirring after 2 minutes, until onion is limp.
2 cans (15-oz. each) tomato sauce **2 cans (6-oz. each) tomato paste** **⅔ cup burgundy wine, beef broth or tomato juice** **2 tablespoons brown sugar** **2 teaspoons Worcestershire sauce** **1 teaspoon oregano** **1 teaspoon basil** **1 teaspoon salt** **½ teaspoon pepper**	Add tomato sauce, tomato paste, wine, broth or juice, brown sugar, Worcestershire sauce, oregano, basil, salt and pepper. Mix together well. Cover. **Microwave at High 12 to 14 Minutes,** stirring after 6 minutes, until very hot.

Makes about 2 quarts

Italian Sauce With Meat: Add 2-lb. ground chuck beef, crumbled, seasoned and cooked.

Italian Sauce With Mushrooms: Add 2-lb. fresh mushrooms, sliced and sauteed.

CLAM SAUCE

This is a popular sauce for spaghetti or other pasta. If possible, buy a green (spinach) pasta to serve with this clear sauce.

POWER LEVEL: High (10)
MICROWAVE TIME: 8 to 10 min., total

2 tablespoons olive oil **3 cloves garlic, minced** **¼ teaspoon salt**	In 1-qt. casserole place oil, garlic and salt. **Microwave at High 3 Minutes,** until softened.
2 cans (6.5-oz. each) minced clams **¼ cup water** **1 tablespoon cornstarch** **¼ cup minced parsley**	Drain clams, reserving juice. Set aside. Stir together water and cornstarch. Add to garlic along with clam juice and parsley. **Microwave at High 4 Minutes,** stirring after 2 minutes, until thickened. Stir in clams. **Microwave at High 1 to 2 Minutes,** until hot.

Makes about 2 cups

Pasta, Rice & Cereal

Among microwave cooks and microwave cookbooks, pasta and rice are a controversial subject. They take about the same time to soften, whether you cook them by microwave or conventionally. Advocates of microwaved pasta insist that they have a better flavor and firm, "al dente" texture. Other people prefer to cook them conventionally because this leaves the microwave oven free to cook the sauce or main dish.

Both sides agree that microwaving is a perfect way to reheat pasta and rice. Reheated conventionally, pasta and rice will dry out unless you add more water, which overcooks them. Tightly covered with plastic wrap, pasta and rice reheat to "fresh cooked" flavor and texture. Undercook pasta and rice 3 to 5 minutes if you are using it in a casserole which requires further cooking.

Many of our recipes in the main dish sections call for quick-cooking rice, because regular rice will not be cooked in the short times needed for the other ingredients. Make this same substitution in adapting your own recipes.

For sauces try Italian Sauce and variations, page 194, with spaghetti; Clam Sauce, page 194, with linguine; Flavored Butters, page 193, with noodles or rice.

QUICK AND EASY MACARONI AND CHEESE

A family-type favorite. For added zip, stir in a few drops Worcestershire sauce.

POWER LEVEL: High (10)
MICROWAVE TIME: 16 to 18 min., total

1 pkg. (7-oz.) elbow macaroni	Cook macaroni (see chart at right), except **Microwave 10 Minutes.**
1 block pkg. (1-lb.) pasteurized process cheese spread **1 can (5⅓-oz.) evaporated milk**	Cut cheese into cubes. Into 3-qt. casserole place cheese with macaroni and milk. Toss together until cheese is distributed.

Microwave at High 6 to 8 Minutes, stirring after 3 minutes, until cheese is melted and mixture bubbles. Stir to blend.

Makes 6 to 8 servings

Rotate layered casseroles, which cannot be stirred, for even heat distribution.

CREAMY MACARONI AND CHEESE

POWER LEVEL: High (10) and Medium High (7)
MICROWAVE TIME: 23 to 27 min., total

1 pkg. (7-oz.) elbow macaroni	Cook macaroni (see chart at right), except **Microwave 10 Minutes.** Drain well and return to same casserole.
¼ cup butter	In 1-qt. measure place butter. **Microwave at High ½ to 1 Minute,** to melt.
6 tablespoons flour **1 teaspoon salt** **2 cups milk**	Blend in flour and salt. Stir in milk until smooth. **Microwave at High 5½ to 6 Minutes,** stirring with table fork every minute, until thickened.
2 cups (8-oz.) grated sharp cheddar cheese	Stir in cheese until completely melted.

Stir sauce into drained macaroni, mixing well. **Microwave at Medium High 7 to 10 Minutes,** stirring every 3 minutes. If desired sprinkle top with paprika or buttered crumbs before serving.

Makes 6 to 8 servings

SPAGHETTI-CHEESE CASSEROLE

As a garnish, save out a few olive slices from sauce to decorate top.

POWER LEVEL: High (10)
MICROWAVE TIME: 17 to 19 min., total

1 pkg. (7-oz.) spaghetti	Cook spaghetti (see chart at right), except **Microwave 9 Minutes.**
1 can (10½-oz.) condensed cream of mushroom soup **½ cup milk** **1 teaspoon instant minced onion** **⅛ teaspoon pepper** **½ cup sliced stuffed olives**	In small bowl mix soup, milk, onion, pepper and olives.
2 cups (8-oz.) cheddar cheese, cubed	In greased 1½-qt. casserole alternate layers of spaghetti, cheese and soup mixture. **Microwave at High 8 to 10 Minutes,** rotating dish ¼ turn after 4 minutes.

Makes 4 to 6 servings

NOTE: This casserole is a good meat accompaniment or makes a nice luncheon dish, served with sliced tomato salad.

HOW TO MICROWAVE PASTA & RICE

Combine pasta or rice with very hot tap water and salt in the recommended cooking dish. Add oil if needed.

Cover tightly with casserole cover or plastic wrap, turned back at one corner to vent. **Microwave at High.**

Stir or rearrange after ½ the time. Recover and continue microwaving. Drain immediately.

PASTA & RICE MICROWAVING CHART   POWER LEVEL: **High (10)**

FOOD TYPE	AMOUNT	UTENSIL	WATER SALT & OIL	TIME MIN.	COOK CODE	GENERAL DIRECTIONS
Macaroni	6 to 8-oz. pkg.	2-qt. casserole	3 cups water 2 teaspoons salt	15—18	150	Stir after 10 minutes.
Rotini	16-oz. pkg.	3-qt. casserole	6 cups water 1 teaspoon salt	13—16	130	Stir after 10 minutes. Check rotini after 10 minutes as this cooks faster than other types.
Spaghetti or Linguine	16-oz. pkg.	13×9×2-in. dish	6 to 7 cups water 1 tablespoon salt 1 tablespoon oil	16—19	160	Rearrange after 10 minutes.
Spaghetti or Linguine	7-oz. pkg.	13×9×2-in. dish	6 to 7 cups water ½ teaspoon salt 1 tablespoon oil	12—14	120	Rearrange after 8 minutes.
Egg Noodles, Narrow	3 cups or 6-oz.	3-qt. casserole	4 cups water 1 teaspoon salt	12—15	120	Time is the same for spinach or regular. Stir after 7 minutes.
Egg Noodles, Wide	8-oz.	3-qt. casserole	6 cups water 1 teaspoon salt 1 teaspoon oil	23—25	230	Stir after 10 minutes.
Lasagna	16-oz. pkg.	13×9×2-in. dish	Cover with water placing ½ teaspoon salt in bottom of dish 1 tablespoon oil	17—18	170	Rearrange after 7 minutes.
Lasagna	½ pkg.	13×9×2-in. dish	Cover with water placing ½ teaspoon salt in bottom of dish 1 tablespoon oil	11—13	110	Rearrange after 6 minutes.
Manicotti	10 to 12 pieces, about 5-oz. pkg.	12×8×2-in. dish	Brush with oil first then cover with water	22—25	220	Using fork turn over every 5 minutes to prevent sticking.
Long Grain Rice	1 cup	3-qt. casserole	2¼ cups water 1 teaspoon salt	18—21	180	Stir after 10 minutes.
Minute Rice	1½ cups	2-qt. casserole	1½ cups water ½ teaspoon salt	4—6	40	Stir after 2 minutes. Let stand 5 minutes before serving.
Rice-Vermicelli Mixes	8-oz. pkg.	2-qt. casserole	Follow package directions	18—22	180	Stir every 6 minutes. Let stand 5 minutes before serving.
Instant Pasta Lunch	1 serving	Mug or container provided	Follow package directions	3—4	30	Let stand 1 to 2 minutes.

Lasagna

LASAGNA

Lasagna may be made and refrigerated. Add about 4 to 6 minutes to total cooking time.

POWER LEVEL: High (10)
MICROWAVE TIME: 28 to 34 min., total

½ pkg. (½-lb.) . . . . lasagna noodles	Cook noodles (see chart, page 197), except **Microwave 8 Minutes.**
2 cans (8-oz. each) . . . . . . tomato sauce 1 can (6-oz.) tomato paste 1 tablespoon leaf oregano 2 teaspoons basil ½ teaspoon salt ¼ teaspoon garlic powder or 1 garlic clove, minced	In large bowl mix together tomato sauce, tomato paste, oregano, basil, salt and garlic. Spread ½ cup sauce over bottom of 12×8×2-in. dish.
1 lb. ground chuck . . . . . . beef cooked, drained	Mix beef with remaining sauce.
2 cups (1-pt.) small . . . . . . curd cottage cheese 1 egg 1 tablespoon dried parsley flakes ½ teaspoon salt 1 pkg. (6-oz.) sliced mozzarella cheese	In small bowl mix together cottage cheese, egg, parsley and salt. Layer 3 noodles, half of cottage cheese mixture, half of mozzarella cheese, half of tomato sauce in dish. Repeat layers.
½ cup grated . . . . Parmesan cheese	Sprinkle Parmesan cheese over top. Cover with wax paper.

Microwave at High 20 to 26 Minutes, rotating dish ½ turn every 8 minutes. Letting lasagna stand about 10 minutes helps it hold shape when cutting.

Makes 6 to 8 servings

CHEESE STUFFED MANICOTTI

Add cooked meatballs or sausages for an even heartier dish.

POWER LEVEL: High (10)
MICROWAVE TIME: 35 to 38 min., total

10 manicotti	Cook manicotti (see chart, page 197), except **Microwave 20 Minutes.**
1½ cups (6-oz.) . . . . shredded mozzarella cheese 2 cups (1-pt.) ricotta cheese ½ cup Romano cheese 1 can (7¾-oz.) spinach, drained ½ teaspoon garlic powder ½ teaspoon salt ¼ teaspoon pepper	Reserve about ⅓ cup cheese for topping. Combine rest of mozzarella with ricotta, Romano, spinach, garlic, salt and pepper. Stuff cooked manicotti with cheese filling. Rearrange in 12×8×2-in. dish.
1 can (15-oz.) . . . . tomato sauce Marjoram	Pour tomato sauce over top, covering all manicotti. Sprinkle with cheese and marjoram. Cover with wax paper.

Microwave at High 15 to 18 Minutes, rotating dish ½ turn after 8 minutes, until hot.

Makes 4 servings

NOODLES ROMANOFF

A traditional combination of noodles, cheese and sour cream.

POWER LEVEL: High (10)
MICROWAVE TIME: 19 to 21 min., total

1 pkg. (7 to 8-oz.) . . . . narrow noodles	Cook noodles (see chart, page 197), except **Microwave 9 Minutes.** Place cooked noodles in 3-qt. casserole.
1 cup cottage cheese . . . . . 1 cup (8-oz.) dairy sour cream ¼ cup chopped stuffed olives 1 teaspoon instant minced onion ½ teaspoon salt ½ teaspoon Worcestershire sauce Dash liquid pepper seasoning (tabasco)	Add cheese, sour cream, olives, onion, salt, Worcestershire sauce and liquid pepper. Mix well. Cover. **Microwave at High 8 Minutes,** stirring after 4 minutes, until hot.
1 cup (4-oz.) shredded . . . . . sharp cheese	Sprinkle cheese on top. **Microwave at High 2 to 4 Minutes,** more, uncovered.

Makes 6 servings

PASTA & RICE CONVENIENCE CHART

Canned or frozen pasta and rice should be removed from metal containers, placed in a casserole or dish of appropriate size and tightly covered. Check at minimum time.

POWER LEVEL: **High (10)**

ITEM	TIME MIN.	COOK CODE	COMMENTS
CANNED			
Or use temperature probe and dial 150°.			
Macaroni & Cheese, Ravioli, Spaghetti, Spanish Rice, (12 to 15-oz.)	2—4	20	Stir after ½ time and before serving.
Lasagna (40-oz.)	8—10	80	Stir after ½ time and before serving.
FROZEN			
Rice Dishes (10-oz. pouch)	6—8	60	Puncture pouch. Flex after ½ time.
Macaroni & Cheese, Macaroni & Beef, (8-oz. pkg.)	5—6	50	Stir after 3 minutes.
Macaroni & Cheese Stuffed Shells, Spaghetti & Meatballs (11 to 14-oz.)	6—8	60	Stir after ½ time and before serving.
Macaroni & Cheese (2-lb.)	15—22	150	Stir after ½ time and before serving.
Lasagna (3-lb. 8-oz.)	33—37	330	Rotate dish ½ turn every 10 minutes. Let stand 5 to 10 minutes before serving.

*NOTE: Mug type pasta or instant pasta lunch, see chart page 197.

JIFFY SPANISH RICE

POWER LEVEL: High (10)
MICROWAVE TIME: 13 to 17 min., total

1 lb. ground chuck beef 1 cup packaged precooked (minute) rice 1 can (1-lb. 12-oz.) tomatoes, undrained, cut up 1 tablespoon instant minced onion 1 to 2 tablespoons chili powder 2 teaspoons salt ⅛ teaspoon pepper	In 3-qt. casserole crumble beef. **Microwave at High 5 to 6 Minutes,** stirring after 3 minutes. Drain. Add rice, tomatoes, onion, chili powder, salt and pepper. Cover. **Microwave at High 8 to 11 Minutes,** stirring after 4 minutes. Stir well. Let stand, covered, about 5 to 10 minutes before serving.

Makes 4 to 6 servings

RIPE OLIVE RISOTTO

Risotto means rice casserole. This combination is colorful with olives and pimiento.

POWER LEVEL: High (10)
MICROWAVE TIME: 22 to 24 min., total

¼ cup butter or cooking oil 1 cup finely chopped onion ⅓ cup chopped celery 1 cup uncooked long grain rice 2 cups chicken bouillon 1 teaspoon salt ¼ teaspoon pepper	In 2-qt. casserole combine butter, onion, celery, rice, bouillon, salt and pepper. Cover. **Microwave at High 20 Minutes,** stirring after 10 minutes.
½ cup chopped ripe olives 1 can (4-oz.) mushroom stems and pieces, drained 1 jar (2-oz.) pimiento strips ¼ cup grated Parmesan cheese	Add olives, mushrooms, pimiento and cheese. Stir to mix well. **Microwave at High 2 to 4 Minutes.** Stir before serving.

Makes 6 to 8 servings

SAVORY TOMATO RICE

This casserole is very juicy immediately after microwaving. Stir and let stand uncovered a few minutes before serving. Very good with pork or chicken.

POWER LEVEL: High (10) **Cook Code:** 230
MICROWAVE TIME: 23 to 25 min., total

4 strips bacon, cooked and crumbled 1 can (1-lb.) tomatoes, undrained, cut up ½ cup uncooked long grain rice ½ cup chili sauce ¼ cup finely chopped green pepper 2 tablespoons instant minced onion 1 teaspoon brown sugar 1 teaspoon salt ⅛ teaspoon pepper ½ teaspoon Worcestershire sauce 2 cups hot tap water	In 2-qt. casserole place bacon, tomatoes, rice, chili sauce, green pepper, onion, brown sugar, salt, pepper, Worcestershire sauce and water. Mix well. Cover. **Microwave at High 23 to 25 Minutes,** stirring every 8 minutes, until hot and rice is done.

Makes 4 to 6 servings

Cereals microwave in a simple, 1-step process. You don't have to boil the water first or stir frequently during cooking. Microwaved cereals make clean up easy; the cereal does not stick to the cooking dish. Family members can microwave single servings of instant cereal in paper bowls. There'll be no dirty dishes in the sink after breakfast.

HOW TO MICROWAVE CEREALS

Mix cereal and hottest tap water in a bowl large enough to prevent boilover. Microwave at High, uncovered.

Stir half way through the cooking time. For softer cereal, let stand a few minutes after microwaving.

CEREAL MICROWAVING CHART   POWER LEVEL: **High (10)**

TYPE CEREAL	NO. OF SERVINGS	INGREDIENTS WATER	SALT	CEREAL	CONTAINER	TIME MIN.	COOK CODE
Oatmeal, Quick*	1	¾ cup	¼ teaspoon	⅓ cup	16-oz. cereal bowl	1—2	10
	2	1½ cups	½ teaspoon	⅔ cup	1½-qt. casserole	2—3	20
	4	3 cups	¾ teaspoon	1⅓ cups	2-qt. casserole	5—6	50
	6	4 cups	1 teaspoon	2 cups	3-qt. casserole	7—8	70
Oatmeal, Old-Fashioned	1	¾ cup	¼ teaspoon	⅓ cup	1-qt. casserole	3—5	30
	2	1½ cups	½ teaspoon	⅔ cup	2-qt. casserole	6—7	60
	4	3 cups	¾ teaspoon	1⅓ cups	3-qt. casserole	8—9	80
	6	4 cups	1 teaspoon	2 cups	3-qt. casserole	10—11	100
Cornmeal	1	⅔ cup	¼ teaspoon	3 tablespoons	16-oz. cereal bowl	2—2½	20
	2	1⅓ cups	½ teaspoon	⅓ cup	1½-qt. casserole	3—3½	30
	4	2⅔ cups	¾ teaspoon	⅔ cup	2-qt. casserole	4½—5	40
	6	4 cups	1 teaspoon	1 cup	2-qt. casserole	5½—6	50
Grits, Quick*	1	¾ cup	Dash	3 tablespoons	16-oz. cereal bowl	3—4	30
	2	1⅓ cups	¼ teaspoon	⅓ cup	1½-qt. casserole	6—7	60
	4	2⅔ cups	¾ teaspoon	⅔ cup	2-qt. casserole	8—9	80
	6	4 cups	1 teaspoon	1 cup	2-qt. casserole	10—11	100
Cream of Wheat	1	1 cup	⅛ teaspoon	2½ tablespoons	1-qt. casserole	3—4	30
	2	1¾ cups	¼ teaspoon	⅓ cup	2-qt. casserole	5—6	50
	4	3½ cups	½ teaspoon	⅔ cup	3-qt. casserole	7—8	70
	6	5 cups	1 teaspoon	1 cup	3-qt. casserole	9—10	90
Cream of Rice	1	¾ cup	Dash	3 tablespoons	16-oz. cereal bowl	1½—2	10
	2	1⅓ cups	¼ teaspoon	⅓ cup	1½-qt. casserole	2—3	20
	4	2⅔ cups	½ teaspoon	⅔ cup	2-qt. casserole	3½—4½	40
	6	4 cups	1 teaspoon	1 cup	2-qt. casserole	6—7	60

*Single servings of instant oatmeal or grits (about 1-oz. pkg.): Follow package directions for amount of water. **Microwave at High ½ to 1 Minute.**

Old-Fashioned Oatmeal

GRITS AND CHEESE CASSEROLE

POWER LEVEL: High (10)
MICROWAVE TIME: 28 to 33 min., total

4 cups hot tap water . . . . . **1 cup quick grits** **1 teaspoon salt**	In 3-qt. casserole place water, grits and salt. **Microwave at High 10 to 12 Minutes,** uncovered, stirring after 5 minutes.
6 tablespoons butter, sliced **8 oz. pasteurized processed cheese* cut into cubes**	Add butter and cheese to grits. Mix well. **Microwave at High 1 to 2 Minutes,** until melted, stirring well.
2 eggs, beaten . . . . **Milk** **½ teaspoon garlic powder** **Dash hot pepper sauce (tabasco)**	In 1-cup measure beat eggs and fill to 1 cup line with milk. Add garlic powder and pepper sauce. Quickly stir into grits. Pour into well greased 12×8× 2-in. dish.
1 cup coarsely crushed corn flakes **2 tablespoons butter Paprika**	Sprinkle corn flakes over top. Dot with butter. Sprinkle with paprika. **Microwave at High 17 to 19 Minutes,** rotating dish ½ turn after 9 minutes, until set. Serve in squares. Especially good with ham.

Makes 8 to 10 servings

*1 roll (5-oz.) garlic cheese may be substituted for processed cheese and garlic powder. Reduce final cooking time by about 2 minutes.

MOLASSES CORNMEAL PUDDING

Known as Indian Pudding in the New England states. Serve with vanilla ice cream, cream or hard sauce.

POWER LEVEL: High (10) and Medium High (7)
MICROWAVE TIME: 23 to 25 min., total

3 cups milk . . . . **⅔ cup dark molasses**	In 2-qt. casserole stir together milk and molasses. **Microwave at High 5 Minutes.**
⅔ cup yellow cornmeal . . . . **⅓ cup sugar** **1 teaspoon salt** **¾ teaspoon cinnamon** **¾ teaspoon nutmeg** **¼ cup butter**	In small bowl mix together cornmeal, sugar, salt, cinnamon and nutmeg. Gradually stir into hot milk mixture. Add butter. Cover. **Microwave at High 14 Minutes,** stirring every 2 to 3 minutes, until smooth and thickened. (If a softer consistency is preferred, add 1 cup milk at this time.)

Microwave at Medium High 4 to 6 Minutes more until consistency resembles that of cornmeal mush. Let stand about 10 minutes before serving.

Makes about 8 servings

Vegetables

Vegetables

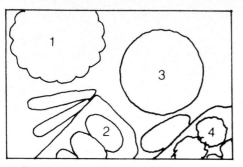

1. Fresh Broccoli, page 208
2. Twice Baked Potatoes, page 222
3. Squash Combo, page 223
4. Tomato Halves, page 224

With microwaving, vegetables are not only an essential part of the meal, they're one of the best parts. Fresh, frozen or canned, microwaved vegetables retain their attractive color, fresh taste and natural texture. Since you add only a small amount of water, you don't drain off flavor and nutrients before serving.

Vegetables with a high natural moisture content will taste more like themselves than you've ever experienced before. Until you taste microwaved corn on the cob, you'll never realize how much good corn taste you discarded with the cooking water.

Nutrition research indicates that many microwaved vegetables and fruits lose less water-soluble vitamin C than when cooked conventionally. This is due to shorter cooking time and to the fact that less cooking water is needed when microwaving fruits and vegetables.

Vegetables should be microwaved covered with vented plastic wrap or a casserole lid. Vegetables cooked in their skins, such as potatoes, are already so tightly covered that they should be pricked with a fork before cooking in order to release excess steam.

Salt vegetables after cooking, or put salt in the casserole with the water before adding vegetables. Salting the tops of vegetables before microwaving causes darkened, dried-out spots.

Vegetables continue to cook after they are removed from the microwave oven. Three to five minutes standing time is necessary to finish cooking and develop flavors. This is especially important where indicated in recipes or chart. Our recipes are timed for tender texture. If you prefer crisper vegetables, reduce cooking time a minute or two. For very soft texture, increase the time.

MICROLESSON: FACTORS AFFECTING EVEN COOKING OF VEGETABLES

SIZE OF VEGETABLE PIECES

Small Pieces cook faster than large ones. Cut vegetables, such as carrots, to uniform size. Unless otherwise directed, vegetables should be tightly covered.

TYPES OF VEGETABLES

Fresh vegetables microwave without added moisture or by adding just a small amount of water or butter to provide steam.

Large or Uneven Pieces should be arranged with thinner or more tender portions toward the center of the dish. Rotate dish ½ turn halfway through cooking time.

Whole or Chunky vegetables should be turned over half way through cooking time. Pierce vegetables cooked in skins, such as potatoes or squash, with fork.

Frozen Vegetables may be heated in pouch, package or freezer container. Puncture pouch before heating, and flex halfway through cooking to distribute heat.

Canned or Cooked vegetables reheat without flavor loss. With temperature probe, include small amount of liquid. Place probe tip in center of dish and heat to 150°.

MICROLESSON: SUCCESS TECHNIQUES FOR MICROWAVING VEGETABLES

Rearrange stacked vegetables like corn on the cob after ½ the cooking time. Move ears on the top, which receive more microwave energy, to the bottom layer.

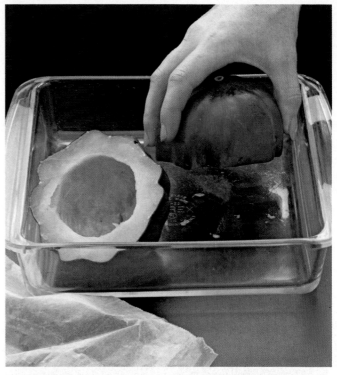

Reposition large vegetable pieces like squash after ½ the cooking time. Move squash halves from corner to corner, diagonally and turn them over.

Cover vegetables in a dish with a casserole lid or with vented plastic wrap. The peel or husks of some vegetables provide a natural covering, while others may simply be wrapped in plastic without using a dish.

Add water to create steam around vegetables microwaved in a covered casserole. Steam surrounding individual pieces contributes both speed and even heating. If you wish to salt vegetables before microwaving them, add it before the vegetables and water.

Potatoes

Potatoes have long been among those favorite foods at the top of the list for microwaving. However, there are a few special tips you should follow for best results.

Select medium size fresh potatoes, 6 to 8-oz. in size. Dry or old potatoes should be peeled, diced and cooked in a casserole with water; when cooked as whole potatoes those which are especially dried-out due to age can burst into flames in the recommended time for fresh potatoes.

Prick potatoes with a fork in several places so that steam can escape during microwaving, and follow the steps below. Microwave times will vary according to number of potatoes; see chart, page 210. Allow a brief standing time after microwaving so potato can continue to soften.

Butter and salt are traditional accompaniments for microwaved potatoes. So are sour cream and chives. But more elaborate toppings of cooked bacon crumbles and sauces such as cheese sauce are also convenient to make quickly in the microwave oven, as special last-minute finishes.

Microwaved Potato with Cheese Sauce, page 191

MICROLESSON: HOW TO MICROWAVE POTATOES

Place pricked potatoes on paper towel to abosorb moisture, if desired. Check microwave times on chart, page 210. Arrange about 1-in. apart in a ring.

Turn Over and Rearrange potatoes after ½ the time.

Touch potatoes at end of cooking time. They may feel somewhat firm but they will complete cooking in about 5 minutes standing time.

VEGETABLE MICROWAVING CHART   ■ FRESH   ■ FROZEN

VEGETABLE	AMOUNT	PROCEDURE	POWER LEVEL	TIME MINUTES	COMMENTS
Artichokes Fresh	4 medium	Prepare by discarding tough outer leaves. Snip tips with scissors and cut off stems. In 3-qt. casserole place 1 cup water and ½ teaspoon salt. Add artichokes. Cover. Rotate dish ½ turn after 7 minutes. Test for doneness: At minimum time, try to pull a leaf from whole artichoke. If it comes away freely, artichoke is done.	High **Cook Code:** 140	14 to 15	Drain artichokes upside down before serving. Curry mayonnaise is easy accompaniment; mix 1 cup mayonnaise with 1 to 2 teaspoons curry powder. Artichokes are eaten by pulling off leaves and, with teeth, scraping tender green inner leaf; cut heart into chunks and eat.
Asparagus Fresh Cuts	1 lb. (3 cups, cut into 1 to 2-in. pieces)	In 2-qt. casserole place ¼ cup water and ½ teaspoon salt; add asparagus. Cover. Stir asparagus every 3 minutes.	High **Cook Code:** 90	9 to 11	If pieces are longer than 4-in. lengths microwave at Medium following technique below.
Asparagus Fresh Spears	1 lb.	In 10×6×2-in. dish place ¼ cup water and ¼ teaspoon salt. Add asparagus, arranging thicker pieces to outside of dish with tender tops to center. Cover dish with plastic wrap turning back corner to vent. Rotate dish ½ turn after 5 min.	Medium High **Cook Code:** 117	11 to 13	Larger, more mature stem ends should be peeled.
Asparagus Frozen Spears	10-oz. pkg.	In 1-qt. casserole place ½ teaspoon salt and asparagus spears. Cover. Rearrange asparagus after 4 minutes.	High **Cook Code:** 80	8 to 10	No water is needed with this frozen vegetable. Let stand 5 minutes.
Beans Fresh Green & Wax	1 lb. cut in half	In 1½-qt. casserole place ½ cup water and ½ teaspoon salt. Add beans. Cover. Stir beans after 7 minutes.	High **Cook Code:** 160	16 to 18	Tenderness in beans varies. Test beans after 15 minutes to determine if more cooking is needed.
Beans Frozen French Cut Green & Wax	10-oz. pkg. (about 2 cups)	In 1-qt. casserole place 2 tablespoons water and ½ teaspoon salt. Add beans. Cover. Stir beans after 5 minutes.	High **Cook Code:** 90	9 to 11	For 2 packages or about 4 cups frozen beans microwave 15 to 18 minutes.
Beans Frozen Lima	10-oz. pkg. (about 2 cups)	In 1-qt. casserole place ¼ cup water and ½ teaspoon salt. Add limas. Cover. Stir beans after 4 minutes.	High **Cook Code:** 80	8 to 9	For 2 packages or about 4 cups frozen limas microwave 10 to 12 minutes.
Beets Fresh Whole	1 bunch (5 medium)	In 2-qt. casserole place ½ cup water and ½ teaspoon salt; add beets. Cover. Stir beets after 11 minutes.	High **Cook Code:** 220	22 to 25	After cooking, skins peel easily. Slice or dice and season.
Broccoli Fresh Cut	1 bunch (1¼ to 1½ lb.) cut into 1-in. pieces	In 2-qt. casserole place ¼ cup water and ½ teaspoon salt. Add broccoli. Cover. Stir broccoli after 6 minutes.	High **Cook Code:** 120	12 to 14	Broccoli cooks most evenly cut in 1-in. pieces.
Broccoli Fresh Spears	1 bunch (1¼ to 1½ lb.)	In 13×9×2-in. dish place ¼ cup water and ½ teaspoon salt. Arrange broccoli spears with stalks to outside of dish and flowerets in center. Cover with plastic wrap, turning back one corner to vent. Rotate dish ½ turn after 6 minutes.	Medium High **Cook Code:** 117	11 to 13	Larger, more mature stalks should be peeled. As an alternate arrangement place in circular dish, flowers to center, stalks to edges. Let stand 5 minutes.
Broccoli Frozen Chopped	10-oz. pkg. (about 2 cups)	In 1-qt. casserole place 2 tablespoons water and ½ teaspoon salt. Add broccoli. Cover. Break up and stir broccoli after 7 minutes.	High **Cook Code:** 90	9 to 11	For 2 packages or about 4 cups frozen broccoli microwave 12 to 15 minutes.

VEGETABLE	AMOUNT	PROCEDURE	POWER LEVEL	TIME MINUTES	COMMENTS
Broccoli Frozen Spears	10-oz. pkg.	In 1-qt. casserole place 3 table-spoons water and ½ teaspoon salt. Add broccoli. Cover. Rearrange broccoli after 4 minutes.	High **Cook Code:** 80	8 to 10	Broccoli should be rearranged carefully to avoid breaking tender flower tips. Let stand 5 minutes.
Brussels Sprouts Fresh	1 lb.	In 1½-qt. casserole, place ¼ cup water and ½ teaspoon salt. Add brussels sprouts. Cover. Stir brussels sprouts after 4 minutes.	High **Cook Code:** 70	7 to 9	Trim dry or old outer leaves and cut extra-large sprouts in half before cooking. Let stand 5 minutes.
Brussels Sprouts Frozen	10-oz. pkg. (1½ to 2 cups)	In 1-qt. casserole place 2 table-spoons water and ½ teaspoon salt. Add brussels sprouts. Cover. Stir brussels sprouts after 4 minutes.	High **Cook Code:** 80	8 to 10	For 2 packages or about 3 to 4 cups frozen brussels sprouts microwave 12 to 15 minutes.
Cabbage Fresh Chopped	1 medium head (about 2 lbs.)	In 1½ or 2-qt. casserole place ¼ cup water and ½ teaspoon salt. Add cabbage. Cover. Stir cabbage after 5 minutes.	High **Cook Code:** 90	9 to 11	Use large enough casserole so cabbage fits loosely. Let stand 5 minutes.
Cabbage Fresh Wedges	1 medium head (about 2 lbs.)	In 2 or 3-qt. casserole place ¼ cup water and ½ teaspoon salt. Add cabbage. Cover. Rearrange cabbage after 7 minutes.	High **Cook Code:** 130	13 to 15	Use large enough casserole so cabbage fits loosely. Let stand 5 minutes.
Carrots Fresh Whole	1 to 2 lb. (see time column)	In 1½-qt. casserole place ½ cup water and ¼ teaspoon salt; add carrots. Cover. Rearrange carrots after half of time.	High 1 lb.- **Cook Code:** 110 2 lb.- **Cook Code:** 180	11 to 13 18 to 20	Size of carrots affects cooking time; larger carrots take longer time.
Carrots Fresh Sliced	1 lb. (6 to 8 carrots)	In 1½-qt. casserole place ¼ cup water and ½ teaspoon salt; add slices. Cover. Stir carrots after 7 minutes.	High **Cook Code:** 90	9 to 12	Cut slices about ½-in. thick. Old carrots take longer to cook. Diagonally sliced carrots reduce cooking time by about 2 minutes.
Carrots Frozen Sliced	10-oz. pkg. (about 2 cups)	In 1-qt. casserole place 2 table-spoons water and ½ teaspoon salt. Add carrots. Cover. Stir carrots after 4 minutes.	High **Cook Code:** 80	8 to 10	
Carrots & Peas Frozen	10-oz. pkg. (about 2 cups)	In 1-qt. casserole place 2 table-spoons water and ½ teaspoon salt. Add vegetables. Cover. Stir carrots and peas after 3 minutes.	High **Cook Code:** 60	6 to 8	For 2 packages or about 4 cups microwave about 8 to 11 minutes. Let stand 5 minutes.
Cauliflower Fresh Whole	1 medium head (about 1½ lb.)	In 1½-qt. casserole place ½ cup water and ¼ teaspoon salt. Place cauliflower stem side down. Cover. Turn cauliflower over after 7 minutes.	Medium High **Cook Code:** 127	12 to 16	Let stand about 5 minutes before serving. If desired, surround on platter with French style green beans.
Cauliflower Fresh Flowerets	1 medium head (about 1½ lb.) cut into flowerets	In 1½-qt. casserole place ½ cup water and ¼ teaspoon salt; add flowerets. Cover. Stir cauliflower after 6 minutes.	High **Cook Code:** 120	12 to 14	Let stand 5 minutes.
Cauliflower Frozen Flowerets	10-oz. pkg. (about 1½ cups)	In 1-qt. casserole place 2 table-spoons water and ½ teaspoon salt. Add flowerets. Cover. Stir cauli-flower after 4 minutes.	High **Cook Code:** 80	8 to 9	For 2 packages or about 3 cups flowerets microwave 12 to 14 minutes.
Celery Fresh	4 cups ½-in. slices	In 2-qt. casserole place ¼ cup wa-ter and ¼ teaspoon salt; add cel-ery. Cover. Stir celery every 4 minutes.	High **Cook Code:** 110	11 to 13	Celery is crisp-tender when cooked.

VEGETABLE	AMOUNT	PROCEDURE	POWER LEVEL	TIME MINUTES	COMMENTS
Corn Frozen Kernel	10-oz. pkg. (about 2 cups)	In 1-qt. casserole place 2 table-spoons water and ½ teaspoon salt; add corn. Stir corn after 3 minutes.	High **Cook Code:** 50	5 to 7	For 2 packages or about 4 cups microwave 9 to 11 minutes.
Corn on the Cob Fresh	1 to 5 ears (see time column)	In 2 or 3-qt. casserole place corn. If corn is in husk, use no water; if corn has been husked, add ¼ cup water. Cover. If ears are stacked in casserole rearrange after half of time.	High	3 to 4 per ear	For convenience and freshest flavor, microwave corn in husk.
Corn on the Cob Frozen	1 to 6 ears (see time column)	In 2 or 3-qt. casserole place corn. (No additional water needed.) Cover tightly with lid or plastic wrap. Turn over after half of time. Let stand 5 minutes after microwaving.	High	1 ear 5 to 6 min., over 1 ear 3 to 4 min. per ear	Corn should lay flat in dish. Use oblong glass casserole if necessary.
Eggplant Fresh	1 medium (about 1 lb.) 4 cups cubed	In 2-qt. casserole place 2 table-spoons water and ¼ teaspoon salt; add peeled, diced eggplant. Cover. Stir eggplant after 3 minutes.	High **Cook Code:** 50	5 to 6	If peeled, cubed vegetable is prepared ahead of cooking, cover with salted water to retain color and flavor. Let stand 5 min.
Mushrooms Fresh Sliced	½ to 1 lb. (see time column)	In 1½-qt. casserole place 2 table-spoons butter or water for each ½ lb. mushrooms. Add mushrooms. Cover. Stir mushrooms after half of time.	High ½-lb.- 3 to 5 **Cook Code:** 30 1 lb.- 5 to 8 **Cook Code:** 50		Don't overcook. As soon as color begins to darken remove from oven and let stand a few minutes before serving. If mush-rooms are thinly sliced they will take minimum time.
Onions Fresh	4 to 8 medium quartered	In 1 or 2-qt. casserole place ½ cup water and ½ teaspoon salt; add onions. Cover. Stir onions after half of time.	High 4- 10 to 12 **Cook Code:** 100 8- 14 to 16 **Cook Code:** 140		Timing gives tender but not mushy onions.
Okra Frozen Whole	10-oz. pkg.	In 1-qt. casserole place 2 table-spoons water and ½ teaspoon salt; add okra. Cover. Rearrange every 3 minutes.	High **Cook Code:** 70	7 to 9	
Parsnips Fresh	1 lb. (2 to 3 cups cubed)	In 1½-qt. casserole place ¼ cup water and ¼ teaspoon salt; add peeled, cubed parsnips. Cover. Stir parsnips after 4 minutes.	High **Cook Code:** 80	8 to 10	Age of parsnips affects micro-waving time.
Peas Fresh Shelled	2 lb.	In 1-qt. casserole place ¼ cup water and ½ teaspoon salt; add peas. Cover. Stir peas after 6 minutes. After microwaving, add 1 table-spoon butter and let stand 5 min-utes.	High* **Cook Code:** 120	12 to 14	*Fresh young peas microwave best at High. Mature peas (yel-low color, some sprouts) should be microwaved at Low Power for longer time.
Peas Frozen Shelled	10-oz. pkg. (about 2 cups)	In 1-qt. casserole place 2 table-spoons water and ½ teaspoon salt; add peas. Cover. Stir peas after 3 minutes.	High **Cook Code:** 50	5 to 6	For 2 packages or about 4 cups microwave 8 to 10 minutes.
Peas & Onions Frozen	10-oz. pkg. (about 2 cups)	In 1-qt. casserole place 2 table-spoons water and ½ teaspoon salt; add peas and onions. Cover. Stir peas and onions after 3 minutes.	High **Cook Code:** 60	6 to 8	For 2 packages or about 4 cups microwave 9 to 12 minutes.
Potatoes Fresh Whole Sweet or White	6 to 8-oz. each (see time column)	Pierce with cooking fork. Place on paper towel on shelf of microwave oven, 1-in. apart. Turn potatoes over and rearrange after half of time.	High 1-4 to 6 **Cook Code:** 40 2-6 to 8 **Cook Code:** 60 3-8 to 12 **Cook Code:** 80 4-12 to 16 **Cook Code:** 120 5-16 to 20 **Cook Code:** 160		Potatoes may still feel firm when done; let stand to soften. Dry or old potatoes do not microwave well whole. Peel and dice them before microwaving.

See page 11 for step-by-step picture directions.

NOTE: When microwaving more than 2 potatoes, moisture can collect in oven. This does not harm food or oven and will evaporate (or may be wiped with cloth) when door is opened. Cook potatoes just until done. Excessive cooking dehy-drates them.

VEGETABLE	AMOUNT	PROCEDURE	POWER LEVEL	TIME MINUTES	COMMENTS
Potatoes Fresh Cubed White	4 potatoes (6 to 8-oz. each)	Peel potatoes and cut into small pieces (1-in. cubes). Place in 2-qt. casserole with ½ cup water. Cover. Stir potatoes after 6 minutes.	High **Cook Code:** 120	12 to 14	Drain potatoes and mash with electric mixer, adding 1 teaspoon salt, ¾ cup milk and 2 tablespoons butter.
Spinach Fresh	10 to 16-oz. washed	In 2-qt. casserole place ¼ teaspoon salt; add washed spinach (no extra water needed). Cover. Stir spinach after 4 minutes.	High **Cook Code:** 70	7 to 9	Water which clings to leaves is enough moisture to create steam for cooking.
Spinach Frozen Chopped & Leaf	10-oz. pkg.	In 1-qt. casserole place 3 tablespoons water and ½ teaspoon salt. Add spinach. Break up and stir well after 5 minutes.	High **Cook Code:** 70	7 to 8	
Squash Fresh Summer & Yellow	1 lb. sliced or cubed	In 1½-qt. casserole place ¼ cup water and ½ teaspoon salt; add squash. Cover. Stir squash after 5 minutes.	High **Cook Code:** 100	10 to 12	If desired, add 2 tablespoons butter to water before microwaving.
Squash Fresh Winter (Acorn or Butternut)	1 to 2 squash (about 1 lb. each)	Cut in half and remove fibrous membranes. In 8-in. square dish or 12×8×2-in. oblong dish, place squash cut side down. Cover with wax paper. Turn cut side up and brush with butter (sprinkle with brown sugar if desired) after 8 minutes.	High **Cook Code:** 90	9 to 14	Wax paper cover is best to hold right amount of steam. Let stand 5 minutes.
Squash Frozen Summer	10-oz. pkg. (about 1½ cups)	In 1-qt. casserole place ½ teaspoon salt and squash (no extra water needed). Cover. Stir squash after 3 minutes.	High **Cook Code:** 50	5 to 7	Ice crystals in frozen squash provide enough moisture for microwaving. For 2 packages or about 3 cups microwave 8 to 11 minutes.
Succotash Frozen	10-oz. pkg. (about 2 cups)	In 1-qt. casserole place 2 tablespoons water and ½ teaspoon salt; add succotash. Cover. Stir succotash after 4 minutes.	High **Cook Code:** 80	8 to 9	For 2 packages or 4 cups frozen succotash microwave 12 to 14 minutes.
Turnips Fresh	1 lb. cubed (2 to 3 medium)	In 1½-qt. casserole place 3 tablespoons water and ¼ teaspoon salt; add peeled cubed turnips. Cover. Stir turnips after 5 minutes.	High **Cook Code:** 100	10 to 12	If desired, turnips can be mashed with added butter after microwaving.
Vegetables, Mixed Frozen	10-oz. pkg. (about 2 cups)	In 1-qt. casserole place 3 tablespoons water and ½ teaspoon salt; add vegetables. Cover. Stir vegetables after 5 minutes.	High **Cook Code:** 90	9 to 10	Lima beans are last vegetable to cook; check them for tenderness. Stir and let stand 5 minutes before serving. For 2 packages or 4 cups frozen mixed vegetables microwave 14 to 16 minutes.
Zucchini Fresh	1 lb. sliced or cubed	In 1½-qt. casserole place ¼ cup water and ½ teaspoon salt; add zucchini. Cover. Stir zucchini after 5 minutes.	High **Cook Code:** 100	10 to 12	If desired, add 2 tablespoons butter to water before microwaving.

VEGETABLE SUMMARY: Always add salt to water before adding vegetable. Times here are for just-tender texture. Reduce time a minute or two for crisp-tender; increase time for very soft texture. Remember to allow standing time of 3 to 5 minutes after cooking, if possible. If you cook more, or less, vegetables than described in the chart, be sure to adjust the time accordingly.

CONVENIENCE VEGETABLES

MICROLESSON: MICROWAVING CONVENIENCE VEGETABLES

Starting Temperatures vary for different convenience vegetables and determine cooking times. A canned vegetable, for example, requires less time than its frozen counterpart. Check package labels and chart on page 213 for heating directions.

Vegetable Mixtures microwave best when all vegetables cook in the same time. Some vegetables like lima beans or large pieces require more time. Check large pieces to be sure they are done.

Whole Large Vegetables like stuffed potatoes should be arranged in a ring so that all sides receive equal amounts of microwave energy and cook evenly. Cover loosely with wax paper.

A Trivet, uncovered, is useful for microwaving frozen vegetables like breaded zucchini which need a crisp, dry exterior. Cook them conventionally if a very crisp texture is desired.

VEGETABLE CONVENIENCE FOODS

VEGETABLE	PROCEDURE	POWER LEVEL	TIME MIN.	COOK CODE
Breaded Vegetables 7-oz. pkg., Frozen	Arrange food in a ring shape on trivet or plate suitable for microwave oven. Microwave uncovered. Rotate dish ½ turn after 2 minutes. Breading will not be as crisp as when cooked conventionally.	High	3½—4½	30
Canned Vegetables	Place vegetables in serving dish suitable for microwave oven. Use about ½ cup liquid. Cover dish with plastic wrap. As a general rule, when heating more than 2 cups of vegetables, check at about half of cooking time. Stir or rearrange to shorten total cooking time. Or use temperature probe set to 150°.	High	8—9-oz.- 1½—2½ 15—17-oz.- 3½—4½ 28—32-oz. 5—7	20 40 50
Casserole, Vegetable 8 to 10-oz. pkg., Frozen	Place food in 1-qt. casserole. Cover. Stir after 4 minutes.	High	5—7	50
Casserole, Vegetable 11 to 12-oz. pkg., Frozen	Place food in 1-qt. casserole. Cover. Stir after 4 minutes.	High	7—9	70
Potatoes Baked, Stuffed, Frozen	Examine potatoes to see that mashed filling is encased in potato skin, NOT FOIL. Place potato(es) on plate suitable for microwave oven. Cover with wax paper. Rotate dish ½ turn after half of cooking time.	High	1 - 3—4 2 - 5—6 3 - 7—8 4 - 9—10	30 50 70 90
Potatoes Canned German Potato Salad 15½-oz. can	Place food in 1-qt. casserole. Cover. Stir after 2 minutes. Stir before serving. At minimum time food is warm; at maximum time, hot.	High	2—4	20
Potatoes Instant Mashed	Use utensil size amounts of water, milk, butter and salt on package. Cover. After heating, briskly stir in potatoes, adding extra 1 to 2 tablespoons dry mix.	High (Or heat liquid with temperature probe set to 200°.)	5	50
Potatoes Dried Mixes 5.5-oz. pkg.	Place food in 3-qt. casserole. Use package directions for amount of water, milk and butter. Cover. Microwave 15 to 20 minutes, stirring after half the time, or check package for microwave directions.	High	15—20	150
Souffle 11-oz. pkg., Frozen	To Defrost: Place food in 8-in. pie plate. Stir.	Low	9—11	93
	To Cook: Divide equally between 3 or 4 buttered custard cups (6 or 7-oz.) Rearrange after 3 minutes. Souffles are done when center is set. Invert on serving plate.	Medium High	9—11	97

Black-Eyed Peas and Rice

BLACK-EYED PEAS AND RICE

This is the well known "Hopping John". Eat it on New Year's Day for good luck.

POWER LEVEL: High (10)
MICROWAVE TIME: 12½ to 17 min., total

4 slices bacon, diced	In 2-qt casserole, place diced bacon. Cover with paper towel. **Microwave at High 2½ to 3 Minutes.**
1 medium onion, chopped	Add chopped onion to bacon. Stir well and **Microwave at High 2 to 4 Minutes** more, uncovered.
1 can (16-oz.) black-eyed peas **1 cup instant-type (minute) rice** **1 cup hot water** **1 teaspoon salt** **¼ teaspoon pepper**	Add peas, rice, water, salt and pepper. Cover with casserole lid or vented plastic wrap. **Microwave at High 8 to 10 Minutes.** Let stand covered 5 to 10 minutes.

Makes 4 to 6 servings

To Use Long Grain Rice: Substitute 2 cups cooked long grain rice and reduce water to ½ cup. Check after minimum time.

COOKING DRIED BEANS AND PEAS

POWER LEVEL: High (10) and Medium (5)
MICROWAVE TIME: See Recipe

1. Place specified amount of beans and water in casserole. Cover.
2. **Microwave at High** to bring to boil, then **Microwave at Medium** until tender. Cooking time depends on variety and amounts. See recommendations below.

GREAT NORTHERN BEANS

1 pkg. (12-oz.) rinsed beans (2 cups) **6½ cups water** **1 small onion, sliced** **½ carrot** **½ stalk celery** **4 strips cooked bacon, crumbled** **2 teaspoons salt** **¼ teaspoon pepper**	In 3-qt. casserole place beans and water. Add onion, carrot, celery, bacon, salt and pepper. Cover. **Microwave at High 20 Minutes.** Stir. Recover. **Microwave at Medium 1 Hour 40 Minutes to 1 Hour 50 Minutes** until tender, stirring every 35 minutes.

For Ranch Style Beans: Remove celery and carrot from above mixture. Add 2 tablespoons brown sugar, 1 tablespoon dark molasses and ½ teaspoon dry mustard. Stir well and cover. **Microwave at Medium High 20 to 30 Minutes,** stirring after 10 minutes.

Makes 8 to 10 servings

BARBECUE BAKED BEANS

POWER LEVEL: High (10) and Medium (5)
MICROWAVE TIME: 2 hr., 20 min. to 2 hr., 25 min., total

1 lb. dry navy beans **Water to cover**	Pick over and wash beans well. In 3-qt. casserole, soak beans in water to cover overnight.
6 cups water	Next day, drain off soaking water, leaving beans in 2-qt. casserole. Add the 6 cups water. Cover casserole and **Microwave at High 20 to 25 Minutes. Microwave at Medium 1 Hour,** until tender.
4 slices diced raw bacon (¼-lb.) **½ cup brown sugar (packed)** **½ cup ketchup** **½ cup chopped onion** **2 teaspoons salt** **1½ teaspoons prepared mustard** **½ teaspoon black pepper**	Stir beans well and add bacon, brown sugar, ketchup, onion, salt, mustard and black pepper. **Microwave at Medium 1 Hour** more.

Makes 6 to 8 servings

NOTE: There is plenty of savory juice. If drier consistency is desired, stir casserole and **Microwave at High 15 to 20 Minutes** uncovered, stirring after 10 minutes.

SPLIT PEAS

1 cup split peas	In 3-qt. casserole place peas
4 cups water	and water. Add ham hock,
1 ham hock	celery, onion and lemon
1 stalk celery, cut in half	juice. Cover. **Microwave at**
1 small onion, sliced	**High 15 Minutes.** Stir well.
1 tablespoon lemon	**Microwave at Medium 40**
juice	**to 50 Minutes** until tender,
	stirring well every 30
	minutes.

For Split Pea Soup: Remove celery. Slice and return to casserole. Remove ham hock. Cut meat into small pieces, return to casserole. Add 1 cup water and stir well. Cover. **Microwave at Medium 5 to 10 Minutes** more, until hot.

Makes 6 to 8 servings

PINTO BEANS

1 pkg. (1-lb.) beans, ...	In 3-qt. casserole place
rinsed	beans and water. Add ham
6½ cups water	hock and onion. Cover. **Mi-**
1 ham hock	**crowave at High 30 Min-**
1 small onion, sliced	**utes,** stirring after 15 minutes. **Microwave at Medium 1 Hour 45 Minutes to 2 Hours** until tender, stirring every 45 minutes.

For "Let's Eat" Bean Soup: Remove ham hock. Cut meat into small pieces, return to casserole. Add water to thin soup as desired. Cover.   Microwave to heat.

Makes 6 to 8 servings

POPULAR GREEN BEAN CASSEROLE

POWER LEVEL: Low (3) and High (10)   TEMP: 170°
APPROX. MICROWAVE TIME: 20 to 24 min.

3 pkgs. (10-oz. each)	Defrost beans by placing
frozen French-style	packages in single layer
green beans	in microwave oven. **Microwave at Low 10 to 12 Minutes,** turning over and rearranging packages every 2 to 3 minutes.
1 can (10-oz.) cream of . . .	Separate beans into 2-qt.
mushroom soup	casserole. Mix with
½ cup milk	canned soup, milk and pi-
1 jar (2-oz.) pimiento,	miento to blend well.
sliced and drained	
1 can (3-oz.) French	Arrange onions in a ring
fried onions	around edge of dish.

Insert temperature probe so tip rests on center bottom of dish. Cover with plastic wrap, arranging loosely around probe to vent. Attach cable end at receptacle. **Microwave at High. Set Temp, Set 170°.** When oven signals, let stand, covered, about 10 minutes before serving. Toss to mix, if desired.

Makes about 8 servings

Golden Stuffed Artichokes

GOLDEN STUFFED ARTICHOKES

POWER LEVEL: High (10)
MICROWAVE TIME: 27 to 31 min., total

4 medium artichokes	.Prepare artichokes by discarding the tough outer leaves. Snip tips off with scissors and cut off stems. In 3-qt. casserole place artichokes with salted water. Cover. **Microwave at High 14 to 15 Minutes,** rotating dish ½ turn after 7 minutes. Remove and place artichokes upside down to partially cool.
1 cup water	
½ teaspoon salt	
1 pkg. (6-oz.) chicken . . .	.In 1½-qt. casserole, combine vegetable seasoning packet from stuffing mix, water and butter. Cover. **Microwave at High 4 to 5 Minutes.** Stir crumbs into mixture just to moisten. Cover and let stand.
flavor top-of-range	
type stuffing mix	
with crumbs	
1½ cups water	
¼ cup butter	
2 small carrots, grated . . .	.In 1-qt. casserole combine carrots, onion and oil. Cover. **Microwave at High 5 Minutes,** until vegetables are soft. Add these vegetables to bread stuffing along with cashews.
1 small onion, diced	
1 tablespoon olive oil	
1 pkg. (3¼-oz.)	
cashews, salted	

Force the center of each artichoke open to form a well. Remove the center leaves and the choke (the choke is the fuzzy, purple-tinged area covering the heart, or base of the artichoke) with a spoon. Stuff artichokes with cashew-carrot stuffing. Rearrange in 3-qt. casserole. **Microwave at High 4 to 6 Minutes,** uncovered, until heated.

Makes 4 stuffed artichokes

Hot Bean Salad

HOT BEAN SALAD

This sweet-sour bean salad tastes even better when made in advance. Reheat before serving.

POWER LEVEL: High (10)
MICROWAVE TIME: 13 to 15 min., total

4 strips bacon . . . . .Using scissors, snip bacon strips into small pieces into 2-qt. casserole. **Microwave at High 3 to 4 Minutes,** stirring after 2 minutes. With slotted spoon, remove cooked bacon pieces to paper towels to drain.

½ cup sugar . . . . .To bacon drippings in casserole, add sugar and cornstarch, blending well. Stir in salt, pepper and vinegar. **Microwave at High 4 to 5 Minutes,** until thick.
1 tablespoon cornstarch
1 teaspoon salt
¼ teaspoon pepper
⅔ cup vinegar

1 can (1-lb.) cut green beans, drained . . . .Add drained beans and onion slices to sauce in casserole, stirring well. Cover. **Microwave at High 6 Minutes,** stirring after 3 minutes. Let compote stand 10 minutes before serving to blend flavors. Sprinkle cooked bacon pieces over top and serve.
1 can (1-lb.) cut wax beans, drained
1 can (15-oz.) red kidney beans, drained
1 onion, sliced

Makes 8 to 10 first course servings
or 4 to 5 servings as vegetable

CHEEZY BROCCOLI

6-oz. can water chestnuts, drained and sliced or slivered almonds can be added as option.

POWER LEVEL: High (10)
MICROWAVE TIME: 17 to 22 min., total

1 pkg. (10-oz.) frozen chopped broccoli . . . . .Place unopened package of broccoli on end in microwave oven. **Microwave at High 3 to 4 Minutes,** turning over after 2 minutes. Set aside.

1 cup packaged precooked (minute) rice . . . . .In 1½-qt. casserole combine rice, soup, milk, cheese, salt, pepper. **Microwave at High 2 to 4 Minutes,** until cheese melts and can be blended easily.
1 can (10¾-oz.) condensed cream of chicken soup
½ cup milk
1 jar (8-oz.) pasteurized processed cheese food
2 teaspoons salt
¼ teaspoon pepper

¼ cup chopped onion . . . . .To cheese mixture, add onion, celery and broccoli. Stir thoroughly. Pour in lightly greased 8-in. square dish. **Microwave at High 12 to 14 Minutes,** rotating dish ¼ turn after 5 minutes. Let stand 5 minutes before serving.
½ cup chopped celery

Makes 6 servings

SWEET-SOUR BEETS

POWER LEVEL: High (10)
MICROWAVE TIME: 21 to 25 min., total

1 medium bunch beets (about 1-lb.) **1 cup warm tap water**	Wash and remove tops from beets. Place in 1½-qt. casserole with water. Cover. **Microwave at High 11 to 13 Minutes,** until fork tender. Place beets in cold water. Peel and quarter.
2 tablespoons butter **2 tablespoons cider vinegar** **2 tablespoons sugar**	Return beets to casserole. Add butter, vinegar and sugar. Cover. **Microwave at High 10 to 12 Minutes,** stirring after 5 minutes.

Makes 3 to 4 servings

CABBAGE PATCH CASSEROLE

If you prefer, you may substitute 2 cups homemade Cheese Sauce, page 191, for the diluted cheese soup in this recipe.

POWER LEVEL: High (10)
MICROWAVE TIME: 22 to 26 min., total

1 medium head cabbage **2 tablespoons water** **½ teaspoon salt**	Chop cabbage into small pieces. Place in 2-qt. casserole along with water and salt. Cover. **Microwave at High 12 to 14 Minutes,** rearranging cabbage after 5 minutes. Drain off liquid.
4 strips bacon	Separate and place strips of bacon on a double thickness of paper towels which have been placed on a paper or pottery plate. Cover with single layer of paper towel. **Microwave at High 4 Minutes.** Crumble.
1 can (10¾-oz.) condensed cheddar cheese soup **½ cup milk**	Mix together crumbled bacon, soup and milk until well blended. Pour over cooked cabbage and mix thoroughly. Cover. **Microwave at High 5 to 6 Minutes.** Stir.
1 can (3-oz.) French fried onions	Sprinkle onions over top of casserole. **Microwave at High 1 to 2 Minutes** more, uncovered, until lightly bubbling around edges.

Makes 6 servings

HARVARD BEETS

POWER LEVEL: High (10)
MICROWAVE TIME: 20 to 26 min., total

1 medium bunch beets (about 1-lb.) **1 cup warm tap water**	Wash and remove tops from beets. Place beets and water in 1½-qt. casserole. Cover. **Microwave at High 11 to 13 Minutes,** until fork tender. Remove beets from oven and place in cool water. Peel and slice or cube as desired.
1 tablespoon cornstarch **1 tablespoon sugar** **¾ teaspoon salt** **Dash pepper** **⅔ cup water** **¼ cup vinegar**	In same 1½-qt. casserole stir together cornstarch, sugar, salt, pepper, water and vinegar. **Microwave at High 4 to 5 Minutes,** until thickened, stirring after 2 minutes. Add beets and **Microwave at High 5 to 8 Minutes,** until hot, or, if desired, serve cold.

Makes 4 servings

COLORFUL CARROT RING

POWER LEVEL: High (10) and Medium High (7)
MICROWAVE TIME: 26 to 30 min., total

½ cup water* **½ teaspoon salt** **2 lbs. carrots, peeled**	In 3-qt. casserole place water, salt and carrots. Cover. **Microwave at High 18 to 20 Minutes,** rearranging after 9 minutes, until tender. Drain. Press carrots through coarse sieve with back of wooden spoon, or for more coarse texture run through meat grinder.
¼ cup softened butter **2 egg yolks** **2 tablespoons brown sugar (packed)** **1 teaspoon salt** **½ teaspoon pepper**	To the sieved carrots add butter, egg yolks, brown sugar, salt and pepper. Generously butter 1-qt. casserole. Place small drinking glass (3-in. or less diameter, 4 to 5-in. high) in center of dish. Pack carrot mixture evenly around glass. Cover with plastic wrap, turning one edge back 2-in. to vent.

Microwave at Medium High 8 to 10 Minutes, until hot. Let stand 5 minutes to set. Twist glass to remove, then invert on serving plate. Garnish with chopped parsley and cooked, crumbled bacon if desired.

*NOTE: ½ teaspoon chicken bouillon granules may be added for additional flavor.

Makes 4 to 6 servings

SUNDAY GLAZED CARROTS

POWER LEVEL: High (10)
MICROWAVE TIME: 11 to 15 min., total

1 lb., about 6 to 8 .... **medium carrots** **2 tablespoons butter** **¼ cup brown sugar** **(packed)**	Wash and cut carrots into ½-in. diagonal slices. Place in 1-qt. casserole with butter and brown sugar. Cover. **Microwave at High 9 to 11 Minutes,** stirring after 5 minutes.
2 tablespoons cold .... **water** **1½ teaspoons** **cornstarch** **¼ cup pecans,** **coarsely chopped** **(optional)**	Mix water and cornstarch until smooth. Stir into carrot mixture. Add pecans. Cover. **Microwave at High 2 to 4 Minutes,** until thickened. Stir before serving.

Makes 3 to 4 servings

TO DOUBLE THIS RECIPE: Use 2-qt. casserole and double the ingredients. Microwave the carrots 15 minutes, stirring after 7 minutes. Add thickening and microwave 4 to 6 minutes more.

Sunday Glazed Carrots

CREAMY CAULIFLOWER

POWER LEVEL: High (10)
MICROWAVE TIME: 23 to 26 min., total

½ teaspoon salt .... **2 tablespoons water** **2 pkgs. (10-oz. each)** **frozen cauliflower**	In 2-qt. casserole place salt and water. Add cauliflower. **Microwave at High 12 to 14 Minutes,** rearranging after 6 minutes, until just done. Place in strainer or colander to drain.
1 tablespoon butter, ... **softened** **1 tablespoon flour** **½ cup milk** **1 cup small curd** **cottage cheese** **½ cup shredded** **cheddar cheese** **1 tablespoon chopped** **pimiento** **½ teaspoon salt** **⅛ teaspoon pepper**	In same 2-qt. casserole, stir to mix butter and flour. Stir in milk, cheeses, pimiento and seasonings. **Microwave at High 6 Minutes,** stirring after 3 minutes, until cheese melts and mixture thickens.
½ cup crushed corn ...... **flakes** **½ teaspoon paprika** **½ teaspoon dill weed**	Mix cauliflower gently into sauce and sprinkle top with corn flakes mixed with paprika and dill weed. **Microwave at High 5 to 6 Minutes,** until hot.

Makes 6 servings

CAULIFLOWER AU GRATIN

For convenience, this recipe uses herb-seasoned stuffing mix, but you may substitute coarse bread crumbs dried in the microwave oven.

POWER LEVEL: High (10)
MICROWAVE TIME: 9 to 11 min., total

1 pkg. (10-oz.) frozen .... **cauliflower** **2 tablespoons water** **½ teaspoon salt**	In 1½-qt. casserole place cauliflower in water and salt. **Microwave at High 8 to 9 Minutes,** stirring after 4 minutes. Drain off liquid from dish.
¼ cup herb-seasoned .... **stuffing mix** **½ cup shredded mild** **cheese**	Sprinkle stuffing mix then cheese over cauliflower. **Microwave at High 1 to 2 Minutes,** uncovered, until cheese melts.

Makes 2 to 3 servings

Dry Bread Crumb Topping for Vegetables: Instead of using prepared stuffing mix, croutons or bread crumbs, you can make your own vegetable topping. Dry fresh bread in the microwave and combine crumbs with butter or margarine and your favorite seasonings. Follow directions for croutons on page 67 except make bread pieces smaller.

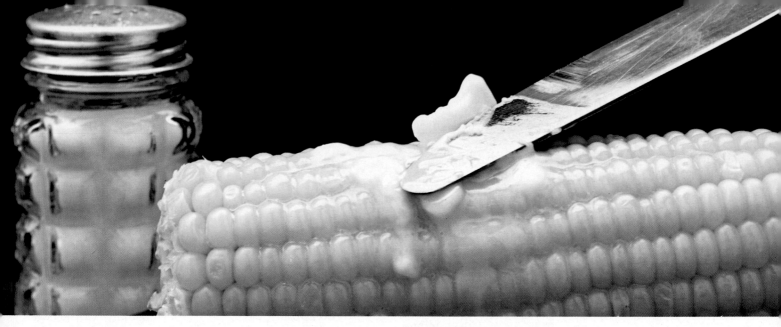

Corn on the cob is a microwave specialty, see page 210.

CELERY AND PEAS, BRAISED

POWER LEVEL: High (10)
MICROWAVE TIME: 12 to 14 min., total

2 cups celery slices, ¼-in. thick **⅓ cup chopped onion** **2 tablespoons butter** **2 tablespoons water** **½ teaspoon salt**	In 2-qt. casserole combine vegetables, butter, water and salt. Cover. **Microwave at High 6 Minutes.** Stir.
1 pkg. (10-oz.) frozen peas	Add peas. Cover. **Microwave at High 6 to 8 Minutes,** stirring after 4 minutes.

Makes 6 servings

CORN PUDDING

POWER LEVEL: Medium High (7)
MICROWAVE TIME: 11 to 13 min., total

1 egg **½ cup milk** **1 tablespoon sugar** **1 can (16-oz.) cream-style corn** **¾ cup crushed crackers** **2 tablespoons butter, cut in pieces**	Place egg in 1½-qt. casserole and beat well with fork. Stir in milk, sugar, corn, crackers and butter. **Microwave at Medium High 5 Minutes** and stir well.
Paprika	Sprinkle with paprika. **Microwave at Medium High 6 to 8 Minutes.** When done, center will be just barely set.

Makes 4 servings

SOUTHERN STUFFED EGGPLANT

POWER LEVEL: High (10)
MICROWAVE TIME: 13 to 18 min., total

1 medium eggplant **2 tablespoons water**	Cut eggplant in half. Scoop out insides leaving outer shell intact. Dice the scooped-out eggplant into 2-qt. casserole. Add water. Cover. **Microwave at High 5 to 6 Minutes,** stirring after 3 minutes.
¼ cup chopped onion **2 tablespoons butter** **2 teaspoons chopped parsley** **1 can (10½-oz.) condensed cream of mushroom soup** **¼ teaspoon salt** **⅛ teaspoon pepper** **1 teaspoon Worcestershire sauce** **½ cup butter-cracker crumbs** **½ cup coarsely chopped salted peanuts, if desired**	In 1½-qt. casserole, place onion, butter and parsley. **Microwave at High 2 to 3 Minutes,** until onion is softened. Add to eggplant with soup, salt, pepper, Worcestershire sauce, crumbs and peanuts; blend well. Evenly divide filling between the 2 shells. Place in 12×8×2-in dish.
½ cup water	Add water to dish. Cover with plastic wrap, turning back one corner to vent. **Microwave at High 5 to 7 Minutes,** rotating dish ½ turn after 3 minutes, until hot.
¼ cup butter-cracker crumbs **Paprika**	Sprinkle crumbs and paprika over top. **Microwave at High 1 to 2 Minutes,** until bubbly.

Makes 4 servings

EGGPLANT ITALIANO

This hearty vegetable casserole goes well with plain meats such as roasts, lamb, ham or chicken.

POWER LEVEL: High (10)
MICROWAVE TIME: 15 to 18 min., total

1 medium eggplant ..... .Pare eggplant; slice ⅛-in. thick.

2 cans (8-oz. each) tomato sauce
1 to 2 teaspoons oregano
½ cup shredded sharp cheese, optional
......Spread 2 tablespoons tomato sauce in bottom of 2-qt. casserole. Layer half of eggplant, 1 can tomato sauce, half of oregano and half of sharp cheese. Repeat layers. Cover. **Microwave at High 14 to 16 Minutes,** rotating dish ¼ turn after 8 minutes.

1 pkg. (6-oz.) mozzarella cheese, sliced
...........Add mozzarella cheese. **Microwave at High 1 to 2 Minutes,** until cheese has melted.

Makes 4 to 6 servings

WILTED LETTUCE SALAD

POWER LEVEL: High (10)
MICROWAVE TIME: 5 to 6 min., total

3 strips bacon ....With scissors, snip bacon into 1-in. pieces into 3-qt. casserole. **Microwave at High 3 Minutes,** until crisp. With slotted spoon, remove bacon to paper towels to drain.

¼ cup vinegar ....To drippings in casserole
2 teaspoons sugar
¼ teaspoon salt
⅛ teaspoon pepper
⅛ teaspoon crushed dried tarragon
¼ cup chopped celery
1 tablespoon sliced green onion
add vinegar, sugar, salt, pepper and tarragon. **Microwave at High 2 to 3 Minutes** to boil. Stir in celery and onion.

1 medium head of lettuce, torn (about 8 cups total)
2 medium oranges, sectioned, each section seeded and cut in half*
.....Gradually add lettuce to hot dressing, tossing to coat each piece, just until slightly wilted. Add orange segments and crisp bacon pieces and toss again lightly. Serve immediately.

Makes 8 to 10 servings

*Or substitute 1 can (11-oz.) Mandarin oranges, drained.

LIMA BEAN SPECIAL

POWER LEVEL: High (10)
MICROWAVE TIME: 14 to 15 min., total

4 strips bacon ....With scissors, snip bacon into 1-in. pieces into 2-qt. casserole. **Microwave at High 4 Minutes,** until crisp. With slotted spoon, remove bacon to paper towels to drain.

1 pkg. (10-oz.) frozen lima beans
½ cup chopped unpared red apple
¼ cup green pepper
½ cup water
¼ teaspoon salt
¼ teaspoon crushed rosemary
.In same 2-qt. casserole, combine beans, apple, green pepper, water, salt and rosemary. Cover. **Microwave at High 10 to 11 Minutes,** stirring after 5 minutes. Stir in reserved bacon before serving.

Makes 4 servings

ZESTY SEASONED ONIONS

Using this recipe as a guide, try garnishing onions with different herb and cheese combinations, bacon crumbles, crushed crackers or potato chips.

POWER LEVEL: High (10)
MICROWAVE TIME: See Recipe

Large whole onions ..... .Wash and halve onions. Arrange in dish suggested below, depending on number of onions.

For each onion ....Sprinkle seasonings over
1 tablespoon steak sauce
1 tablespoon Worcestershire sauce
1 to 2 drops tobasco sauce
1 tablespoon butter
¼ teaspoon garlic salt
1 teaspoon Parmesan cheese
onion halves. **Microwave at High** according to chart below.

AMOUNT	DISH	TIME MIN.	COOK CODE
1 (2 halves)	1-qt. casserole (covered)	4—5	40
2 (4 halves)	1½-qt. casserole (covered)	8—9	80
3 (6 halves)	2-qt. casserole (covered)	11—13	110

NOTE: A good side dish with roasted or broiled meats.

HOT GERMAN POTATO SALAD

POWER LEVEL: High (10)
MICROWAVE TIME: 24 to 27 min., total

4 medium potatoes . . . . .Wash and pierce potatoes through with fork. Place on paper towel in microwave oven. **Microwave at High 12 to 14 Minutes,** turning over and rearranging after 6 minutes, or until tender. Remove from oven, cool slightly, peel potatoes and cut in ⅛-in. slices to make about 4 cups.

6 strips bacon . . . . .In 2-qt. casserole cut bacon in small pieces. Cover with paper towel. **Microwave at High about 6 Minutes,** stirring after 3 minutes, until crisp. With slotted spoon remove bacon to paper towels to drain. Set aside.

2 tablespoons flour . . . . .Stir flour, sugar and sea-
¼ cup sugar sonings into bacon fat un-
1½ teaspoons salt til smooth. **Microwave at**
½ teaspoon celery **High 1 to 2 Minutes,** until
seed bubbly, stirring after 1 min-
⅛ teaspoon pepper ute.

1 cup water . . . . .Add water and vinegar to
½ cup vinegar flour mixture. **Microwave at High 5 Minutes,** until mixture boils and thickens, stirring after 1 minute. Remove from oven and stir smooth. Add potatoes and bacon; stir gently so potatoes hold their shape. Cover casserole and let stand until ready to serve.

Makes 4 to 6 servings

Potato Ideas: Slice microwaved whole potatoes and top with crisp crumbled bacon, cooked crumbled sausage, chopped hard-cooked eggs, soft processed cheese spread or with melted butter and your favorite herbs or seasoned salt.

Use these same toppings when you cook dry or old potatoes which must be peeled and diced for microwaving.

Give whole baked potatoes a more conventionally-cooked appearance by brushing skin with melted butter, meat drippings, soy or steak sauce after microwaving.

Hot German Potato Salad

GREEN AND GOLD POTATO CASSEROLE

POWER LEVEL: High (10)
MICROWAVE TIME: 18½ to 22 min., total

3 or 4 large potatoes . . . . .Peel potatoes and onions.
2 large onions Slice in ¼-in. slices. Layer in 2-qt. casserole.

3 tablespoons butter . . . .Dot butter over top. Then
1½ cups hot tap water pour over the hot water
2 teaspoons instant mixed with the chicken
chicken bouillon bouillon. Cover. **Micro-**
seasoning or 2 **wave at High 18 to 21**
chicken bouillon **Minutes,** until potatoes are
cubes tender, stirring after 10 minutes.

¼ cup shredded sharp . . .Uncover casserole and
cheese sprinkle with cheese and
1 teaspoon minced parsley. **Microwave at**
parsley **High ½ to 1 Minute,** uncovered, or until cheese melts.

Makes 6 to 8 servings

SCALLOPED POTATOES

If desired, sprinkle top with paprika and/or ½ cup shredded sharp cheese after cooking. Cheese melts as casserole stands.

POWER LEVEL: High (10)
MICROWAVE TIME: 25½ to 29½ min., total

3 tablespoons butter	In 1-qt. glass measure, place butter. **Microwave at High ½ Minute,** or until melted. Blend in flour and seasonings. Gradually stir in milk. **Microwave at High 8 to 10 Minutes,** stirring every 3 minutes.
2 tablespoons flour	
1 teaspoon salt	
¼ teaspoon pepper	
3 cups milk	
3½ to 4 cups thinly	Layer half of potatoes, onion and sauce in greased 3-qt. casserole. Repeat layers. Cover.
sliced white potatoes (about 3 medium)	
2 tablespoons minced onion	

Microwave at High 17 to 19 Minutes, stirring after 10 minutes. Remove from oven and let stand 5 minutes before serving.

Makes 4 to 6 servings

TWICE BAKED POTATOES

POWER LEVEL: High (10)
MICROWAVE TIME: See Recipe

Potatoes	Microwave desired number of potatoes according to chart, page 194. Slice the top from each potato. With teaspoon, remove center of potatoes to mixing bowl, leaving shells intact.
For each potato	To mixing bowl add butter, sour cream, salt and pepper. Mix with electric mixer until smooth. Divide potato mixture evenly among shells, mounding, if necessary. Sprinkle with chives if desired. Place potatoes on plate suitable for microwave oven. Potatoes may be refrigerated at this point if desired.
2 tablespoons butter	
2 tablespoons sour cream	
¼ teaspoon salt	
Dash pepper	

If potatoes are microwaved immediately **Microwave at High 1 Minute** per potato. If more than 2 potatoes are microwaved at one time, arrange in a circle and rotate dish ½ turn after half of time.

If potatoes are microwaved from refrigerator temperature, increase time for each potato by ½ minute.

POTATO-CHEESE HURRY UP

POWER LEVEL: High (10)   **Cook Code: 90**
MICROWAVE TIME: 9 to 11 min., total

1 can (10½-oz.)	Mix together soup, onions, cheese, dill weed, salt and pepper in 1½-qt. casserole.
condensed cream of celery soup	
½ cup chopped onions	
½ cup shredded cheddar cheese	
¼ teaspoon dill weed	
1 teaspoon salt	
¼ teaspoon pepper	
2 cans (1-lb. each)	Add potatoes and mix thoroughly. **Microwave at High 9 to 11 Minutes,** stirring after 5 minutes.
sliced white potatoes, drained	
2 tablespoons grated	Stir and sprinkle cheese on top before serving.
Parmesan cheese	

Makes 4 to 6 servings

EGGPLANT-VEGETABLE CASSEROLE

This casserole, known as Ratatouille in Southern France, combines eggplant, green pepper, onion, zucchini and tomato in the classic seasonings of Provence.

POWER LEVEL: High (10) and Medium (5)
MICROWAVE TIME: 19 to 23 min., total

1 medium eggplant, ...	In 3-qt. casserole, mix together eggplant, green pepper, onion, oil and garlic. Cover. **Microwave at High 6 to 7 Minutes,** or until onions are transparent.
peeled and cut into ½-in. cubes	
1 large green pepper, cut into strips	
1 large onion, thickly sliced	
3 tablespoons olive or cooking oil	
1 clove garlic, finely chopped	
2 medium zucchini, ...	Stir in zucchini and cover. **Microwave at High 5 to 6 Minutes.**
sliced ¼-in. thick	
2 to 3 large tomatoes, ...	Gently stir in tomatoes, parsley, basil, salt, pepper and bay leaf. **Microwave at Medium 8 to 10 Minutes,** or until vegetables are barely tender.
peeled (if desired) and cut in wedges or 1 can (16-oz.) tomato wedges, drained	
2 teaspoons minced parsley	
1 teaspoon basil	
1 teaspoon salt	
⅛ teaspoon pepper	
1 bay leaf	

Makes 6 to 8 servings

SPINACH-CHEESE SOUFFLE

Souffles designed for conventional baking cannot be adapted to microwaving without changing the recipe. One of the "success ingredients" in this recipe is the evaporated milk.

POWER LEVEL: Defrost, High (10) and Medium (5)
MICROWAVE TIME: 31 to 40 min., total

1 pkg. (10-oz.) frozen . . . . . Microwave spinach in
chopped spinach package. **Microwave at Defrost 8 to 10 Minutes,** turning over after 2 minutes, until no ice remains. Remove spinach from package. With hands, squeeze out all juice and set aside.

¼ cup unsifted . . . . In 1½-qt. casserole, blend
  all-purpose flour together flour, salt, mustard and paprika. Gradually stir in evaporated milk. **Microwave at High 4 to 6 Minutes,** until thickened, stirring every 2 minutes.
¾ teaspoon salt
½ teaspoon dry mustard
⅛ teaspoon paprika
1 can (13-oz.) evaporated milk (1⅔ cups)

1 cup (4-oz.) sharp . . . . Stir cheese and
  cheddar cheese squeezed-out spinach into hot sauce. **Microwave at High 1 to 2 Minutes,** until cheese melts.

6 eggs, separated . . . . Beat egg whites with
1 teaspoon cream of cream of tartar until stiff
  tartar but not dry. Set aside and, using same beater beat yolks until thick and lemon colored. Slowly pour spinach-cheese mixture over beaten egg yolks beating constantly until well combined. Gently pour over beaten egg whites and fold together gently just until blended. Pour into ungreased 2½-qt. souffle dish. **Microwave at Medium 18 to 22 Minutes,** rotating dish ¼ turn every 5 minutes, until puffed top edges are beginning to appear dry and souffle has "set" appearance.

Makes 4 to 6 servings

NOTE: Center of souffle will remain creamy.

SQUASH COMBO

POWER LEVEL: High (10)   TEMP: 200°
MICROWAVE TIME: 12 to 15 min. **Cook Code:** 120

1 lb. zucchini squash . . . . .Wash squash and cut into
  (4 medium) chunks, alternating yellow
1 lb. yellow squash and zucchini into 2-qt.
  (4 medium) casserole. Arrange undrained pimiento strips over top. Add water and dot with butter.
1 jar (2-oz.) pimiento
2 tablespoons water
2 tablespoons butter

Insert temperature probe so tip rests on center bottom of dish. Cover with plastic wrap, arranging loosely around probe to vent. Attach cable end at receptacle. **Microwave at High. Set Temp, Set 200°.** When oven signals, let squash stand, covered, about 10 minutes before serving. Toss to mix, if desired.

Makes 6 to 8 servings

PECAN CRISP SQUASH

Squash is easy to cut into halves if microwaved 1 to 2 minutes at High. Let stand a few minutes before cutting.

POWER LEVEL: High (10)
MICROWAVE TIME: 12 to 14 min., total

2 acorn squash . . . . .Cut squash in half length-
  (about 1 lb. each) wise. Remove seeds and fibrous membranes. Place cut side down in 12×8×2-in. dish. Cover with plastic wrap turning back one corner to vent. **Microwave at High 6 Minutes,** rotating dish ½ turn after 3 minutes.

⅔ cup butter-cracker . . . . .While squash is cooking,
  crumbs toss together crumbs, pe-
⅓ cup coarsely cans, butter, brown sugar,
  chopped pecans salt and nutmeg.
⅓ cup butter, melted
3 tablespoons brown sugar (packed)
½ teaspoon salt
¼ teaspoon nutmeg

After squash have cooked 6 minutes, turn cut-side-up and divide filling among the 4 halves. Recover with plastic wrap and **Microwave at High 6 to 8 Minutes,** until squash is tender. Remove plastic wrap and let stand 5 minutes until serving.

Makes 4 servings

NOTE: Recipe may be doubled for a party. Microwave squash in 13×9×2-in. dish, cut-side-down, about 10 minutes; turn over and fill. Recover. Finish microwaving 9 to 12 minutes more.

Rotate Tomato Halves ½ turn after half of cooking time.

TOMATO HALVES

For a simple version of this recipe, sprinkle tomato halves with Butter Crumb Topping (below) and microwave as directed.

POWER LEVEL: High (10)
MICROWAVE TIME: See Recipe

Tomatoes	Wash and halve tomatoes. Arrange in dish suggested below.
For each tomato half: . . . . **½ teaspoon instant minced onion** **½ teaspoon sugar** **½ teaspoon sweet basil** **¼ teaspon salt** **Dash pepper** **1 tablespoon crushed potato or corn chips**	Sprinkle each tomato half with seasonings. **Microwave at High** according to times below. Time may vary due to size and variety of tomato. Rotate dish ½ turn after ½ of cooking time.

NUMBER OF TOMATOES	DISH	TIME MIN.	COOK CODE
2 halves	Place on microwave oven proof plate of suitable size.	2—2½	20
4 halves*		3—4	30
6 to 8 halves*		5—6	50

*Arrange in ring shape.

Butter Crumb Topping: In small mixing bowl combine ¼ cup melted butter, 1 cup fine dry bread crumbs and ¼ to ½ teaspoon dill weed (or other desired seasoning). **Microwave at Medium High 2 to 3 Minutes,** stirring after 1 minute. Good with tomatoes, cauliflower, broccoli and asparagus. Makes 1 cup. **Cook Code:** 20

TOMATO PEPPER QUICKIE

POWER LEVEL: High (10)
MICROWAVE TIME: 7½ to 8½ min., total

2 medium green peppers, cut into chunks **1 medium onion** **½ teaspoon basil** **1 teaspoon salt** **2 tablespoons water**	In 1-qt. casserole place green pepper. Cut onion into ¼-in. slices, separate into rings and lay on top of green pepper. Sprinkle on seasonings. Add water. Cover. **Microwave at High 6 Minutes,** stirring after 3 minutes.
2 medium ripe tomatoes or 1 can (1-lb.) tomato wedges, drained	Cut tomatoes into ¾-in. wedges and arrange over casserole. Cover. **Microwave at High 1½ to 2½ Minutes** more, until tomatoes are justed heated.

Makes 4 servings

ZIPPY ZUCCHINI

POWER LEVEL: High (10) and Medium High (7)
MICROWAVE TIME: 16 to 18 min., total

4 cups zucchini, cut into chunks (2 medium) **½ medium onion, thinly sliced**	Place zucchini and onion in 2-qt. casserole. Cover with plastic wrap turning one edge back slightly to vent, or casserole lid. **Microwave at High 7 Minutes,** stirring after 3 minutes. Drain.
4 eggs, beaten **1½ cups (6-oz.) shredded cheddar cheese** **1 jar (2-oz.) pimiento, drained** **½ teaspoon salt** **⅛ teaspoon pepper**	In large bowl mix together eggs, cheese, pimiento, salt and pepper. Add zucchini and onions, stirring well. Grease dish in which vegetables were cooked. Pour mixture into dish and cover with paper towel.

Microwave at Medium High 5 Minutes. Stir and re-cover with paper towel. **Microwave at Medium High 4 to 6 Minutes** more, giving dish ½ turn after 3 minutes.

Makes 4 servings

TOSSED VEGETABLE DRESSING

This unusual tossed vegetable dressing combines crunchy, quick cooked vegetables tossed with savory croutons. As a bonus, each serving is only about 87 calories. Toss just before serving.

POWER LEVEL: High (10)
MICROWAVE TIME: 9 to 11 min., total

2 chicken bouillon cubes	In 3-qt. casserole, place bouillon cubes and water.
1 tablespoon water	**Microwave at High ½ Minute.** Stir to blend.
2 tablespoons butter	Add butter, salt and pepper. **Microwave at High ½ Minute** more to melt and blend.
1 teaspoon salt	
¼ teaspoon pepper	
2 eggs, well beaten	Quickly whisk eggs into hot mixture. Then toss in vegetables to mix well. Cover. **Microwave at High 8 to 10 Minutes** stirring mixture after 4 minutes. Vegetables should be just crisp-tender.
1½ cups finely grated carrots	
1 cup finely chopped onions	
2½ cups (8-oz.) sliced fresh mushrooms	
¾ cup finely chopped parsley, slightly packed down in cup	
1 pkg. (6-oz.)	Remove vegetables from oven and toss in croutons. To retain best crispy texture of dressing, serve immediately.
seasoned croutons	

Makes 12 (½-cup) servings
about 87 calories each

COUNTRY GREEN BEANS

POWER LEVEL: High (10)
MICROWAVE TIME: 14 to 16 min., total

4 strips bacon, cut into ½-in. pieces	In 1½-qt. casserole place bacon. **Microwave at High 4 Minutes,** or until crisp.
1 can (16-oz.) cut green beans	Reserving ½ cup juice, drain beans. To bacon, add beans, reserved juice, potato, onion and salt. Cover. **Microwave at High 10 to 12 Minutes,** stirring after 5 minutes, until potato is tender. Let stand 5 minutes before serving.
1 medium potato, peeled and diced in ½-in. cubes	
1 small onion, cut into eighths	
½ teaspoon salt	

Makes 4 servings

YELLOW SQUASHEROLE

POWER LEVEL: High (10) and Medium (5)
MICROWAVE TIME: 16½ to 21 min., total

2 tablespoons butter	In 1-qt. casserole place butter. **Microwave at High ½ to 1 Minute** until melted. Add crumbs and pecans. **Microwave at High 2 Minutes** stirring after 1 minute. Pour crumbs onto wax paper and set aside.
¼ cup buttery flavored cracker crumbs	
¼ cup chopped pecans	
¼ cup water	In same casserole, place water, salt and squash. Cover. **Microwave at High 8 to 10 Minutes** stirring after 4 minutes until tender. Drain.
½ teaspoon salt	
1 lb. yellow squash, sliced	
¼ cup mayonnaise	Mix together mayonnaise, egg, cheese, butter, sugar and onion. Pour over squash, mixing well. **Microwave at Medium 4 Minutes.** Stir, then add crumb topping. **Microwave at Medium 2 to 4 Minutes** more until center is set. Let stand 5 minutes before serving.
1 egg, beaten	
½ cup shredded cheddar cheese	
2 tablespoons butter, melted	
1½ teaspoons sugar	
¼ to ½ teaspoon instant minced onion	

Makes about 4 servings

YAMS HAWAIIAN STYLE

POWER LEVEL: High (10)
MICROWAVE TIME: 6 to 8 min., total

2 cans (1-lb. 2-oz. each) yams or sweet potatoes, drained	Slice yams into ½-in. thick pieces. Combine with pineapple, butter, sugar and cinnamon in 2-qt. casserole. **Microwave at High 4 Minutes.** Stir.
1 can (8½-oz.) crushed pineapple	
½ cup melted butter	
¼ cup granulated sugar	
1 teaspoon cinnamon	
½ cup coarsely chopped pecans	Sprinkle top with pecans and brown sugar. **Microwave at High 2 to 4 Minutes.** If dish is not hot and topping melted after 2 minutes, rotate dish ¼ turn before continuing to microwave.
¼ cup light brown sugar (packed)	

Makes 6 to 8 servings

NOTE: If desired, yams may be mashed with the first 4 ingredients, then cooked. Finish with brown sugar nut topping and continue to microwave as above.

Blanching Vegetables

For those who like to freeze fresh vegetables while they are in season, highest in quality and lowest in price, the microwave oven is a great help. It's especially useful to home gardeners, since vegetable crops do not ripen uniformly.   You can pick vegetables as they reach the peak of flavor, even if you have only a few servings. Minutes after the vegetables are picked, you'll have them blanched and ready-to-freeze, without spending all day in a steamy kitchen, handling heavy pots of boiling water.

HOW TO BLANCH AND FREEZE VEGETABLES

Prepare vegetables (wash, peel, slice or dice) as you would for regular cooking. Measure 1 quart or 1 pound of vegetables into the recommended casserole. Add water, as given in the chart. DO NOT ADD SALT. Cover.

Set Power at High. Microwave for ½ the minimum time and stir. Recover the casserole and microwave for second ½ of minimum time. Stir again.

Check for Doneness. Vegetables should have an evenly bright color throughout. If all the vegetables are not evenly bright, recover the casserole and microwave for maximum time. Drain vegetables.

POWER LEVEL: **High (10)**

VEGETABLE	AMOUNT	CASSEROLE SIZE	WATER	TIME MIN.	COOK CODE
Asparagus	1-lb. cut into 1 to 2-in. pieces	2-qt.	¼ cup	3—4	30
Beans, Green or Wax	1-lb.	1½-qt.	½ cup	4—6	40
Broccoli (1-in. cuts)	1 bunch 1¼ to 1½ lb.	2-qt.	½ cup	4—5½	40
Carrots	1-lb. sliced	1½-qt.	¼ cup	4—6	40
Cauliflower	1 head, cut into flowerets	2-qt.	½ cup	4—5½	40
Corn on the Cob*					

*Special Directions for Corn On The Cob

For most even blanching, cut corn off the cob before blanching. Blanch corn cut from 4 ears at a time. Place cut corn in 1-qt. casserole. Add ¼ cup water. Cover. **Microwave 4 to 5 Minutes,** stirring after 2 minutes. Cool by setting casserole in ice water, stirring occasionally until cool.

Microwaving Frozen Blanched Vegetables

A 1-pint container holds about the same amount of vegetables as a 10-ounce package of commercially frozen vegetables. To microwave this amount, follow directions on the Vegetable Microwaving Chart, page 208. If you package vegetables in smaller or larger amounts, adjust the casserole size, amount of water and microwaving time proportionately.

DO NOT OVER-COOK. Home-frozen vegetables taste best when cooked to crisp-tender. Microwave for a minimum time, then let stand, covered, an additional 5 to 10 minutes to finish softening and develop flavor.

Plunge vegetables into ice water immediately, to prevent further cooking. Spread them on paper towels and blot with additional towels to absorb excess moisture.

Package in freezing containers or boil-in-bag pouches. Label packages with type of vegetable, amount and date. Freeze.

To loose-pack vegetables in larger containers or bags, spread individual pieces on cookie sheet. Place in freezer until vegetables are frozen, then place loose pieces in containers. Seal, label and freeze.

POWER LEVEL: **High (10)**

VEGETABLE	AMOUNT	CASSEROLE SIZE	WATER	TIME MIN.	COOK CODE
Onions	4 medium quartered	1-qt.	½ cup	3—4½	30
Parsnips	1-lb. cubed	1½-qt.	¼ cup	2½—4	30
Peas	2-lb. shelled	1-qt.	¼ cup	3½—5	40
Spinach	1-lb. washed	2-qt.	None	2½—3½	30
Squash, Summer, Yellow	1-lb. sliced or cubed	1½-qt.	¼ cup	3—4½	30
Turnips	1-lb. cubed	1½-qt.	¼ cup	3—4½	30
Zucchini	1-lb. sliced or cubed	1½-qt.	¼ cup	3—4½	30

For vegetables not given on the chart, refer to the Vegetable Microwaving Chart, page 208. Follow directions for fresh vegetables, but DO NOT ADD SALT. Blanching time will be ¼ to ⅓ the regular cooking time. Stir, test and cool as directed in blanching steps.

Breads

Quick breads really are quick with microwaving. Whether you start from scratch or use a mix, you'll have fresh, hot muffins, breads or coffee cakes in minutes. Microwaved quick breads have an even texture and greater volume than conventionally baked, but they do not brown. Use batters with color, such as corn, bran or spice bread, or a topping. For "up-side-down" breads, butter the baking dish and coat the bottom and sides with topping. Savory or sweet toppings add appetite as well as eye appeal.

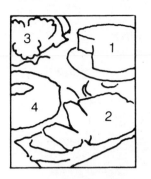

1. Cornbread Ring, page 232
2. Savory Cheese Bread, page 236
3. Bran Nut Muffins, page 231
4. Stacked Maple Nut Rings, page 234

Savory Toppings on microwaved quick breads are shown below in comparison with conventional and microwaved breads without toppings. See Quick Bread Toppings, next page.

Conventional   Microwaved   Crushed French   Crumbled Bacon   Sauteed Onions   Taco Seasoning
                              Fried Onions   & Shredded   & Green Pepper   Mix
                                                Cheddar Cheese   With Paprika

Sweet Toppings on microwaved quick breads are shown below in comparison with conventional and microwaved breads without toppings. See Quick Bread Toppings, next page.

Conventional   Microwaved   Nut-Crunch   Microwaved   Cinnamon &   Chopped Nuts
                              Topping   Toasted Coconut   Sugar

HOW TO MICROWAVE MUFFINS

Cupcaker, assures good shape and even cooking for muffins and cupcakes. Fill paper liners uniformly, half full.

Paper Hot Drink Cups substitute for cupcaker. Cut tops off cups, leaving 1-in. sides. Place paper liner in each and fill half full. Arrange in a ring on flat plate.

Rotate cupcaker ¼ turn, or rearrange homemade muffin cups, after half the time.

Test after minimum time. A wooden pick inserted in center comes out clean. Muffins will appear barely set; there may be moist spots on the surface.

FLUFFY MUFFINS

Select a topping (at right) to add color to top of muffins. This versatile quick bread batter is also used for Simple Coffee Cake, page 233.

POWER LEVEL: Medium High (7)
MICROWAVE TIME: See Recipe

2 cups unsifted . . . . **all-purpose flour** **½ cup sugar** **3 teaspoons baking powder** **½ teaspoon salt**	.In mixing bowl stir together flour, sugar, baking powder and salt. Make a well in center of dry mixture.
2 eggs, beaten . . . . **½ cup cooking oil** **½ cup milk**	.Combine eggs, oil and milk. Add all at once to dry ingredients and stir just to moisten. Fill paper lined microwave containers, see comments, ½ full. Microwave according to chart below. Muffins are done when toothpick stuck in center comes out clean.

MUFFINS	TIME MIN.	COOK CODE	COMMENTS
1	½—1		For best shape use microwave cupcaker or make reusable "homemade muffin cups" by cutting down paper hot drink cups. Check for doneness at minimum time. Redistribute after ½ of cooking time. If using cupcaker, rotate ¼ turn. Rich, thick batters may take longest time.
2	1¼—1½	17	
3	1¾—2	17	
4	2¼—2½	27	
5	3—4	37	
6	3½—4½	47	

Makes about 14 muffins

FLUFFY MUFFINS VARIATIONS

Fold ½ cup raisins or rinsed, drained blueberries into batter (top with cinnamon sugar); or add ½ cup shredded cheese (top with bacon-cheese topping); or add ½ cup chopped nuts (top with toasted coconut).

SAVORY OR SWEET TOPPING FOR MICROWAVED MUFFINS & BREADS

Before microwaving, sprinkle suggested toppings over 12 muffins or a bread ring made with muffin or cornbread batter. Microwave as for Cornbread (page 232) or Muffins (left).

SAVORY TOPPINGS:

Onion: Crush ½ can (3-oz.) French fried onions.

Bacon-Cheese: Microwave 3 slices bacon until very crisp, finely crumble. Mix with ⅓ cup grated sharp cheddar cheese.

Onion-Green Pepper: Saute ¼ cup each of chopped vegetables in 1 teaspoon butter 3 to 4 minutes at High. Sprinkle with paprika.

Taco Seasoning Mix: Use ½ pkg. (1¼-oz.).

SWEET TOPPINGS:

Nut Crunch: Cut together with pastry blender: ¼ cup flour, 2 tablespoons brown sugar (packed), 2 tablespoons butter and ¼ cup chopped nuts.

Microwaved Coconut: Spread 1 pkg. (4-oz.) shredded coconut in 9-in. pie plate. Microwave at High 5 to 6 Minutes, stirring after 2 minutes and then every minute, until evenly toasted.

Cinnamon, Sugar or Chopped Nuts: Use about ⅓ cup.

APPLESAUCE GINGER GEMS

POWER LEVEL: Medium High (7)
MICROWAVE TIME: See Recipe

1 pkg. (about 14-oz.) . . . . . **gingerbread mix** **Applesauce** **Egg, if package directs**	In mixing bowl prepare gingerbread batter as package directs, except substitute applesauce for amount of water called for on package. Add egg if package directs.

Microwave at Medium High, using same directions as Fluffy Muffins. If desired, sprinkle tops of muffins with cinnamon and drizzle with Simple Glaze (below) before serving.

Makes about 2 dozen

PUMPKIN GEMS

Gems is an old-fashioned word for small muffins or cupcakes. These muffins keep very well if tightly covered.

POWER LEVEL: Medium High (7)
MICROWAVE TIME: See Recipe

1⅓ cups sugar . . . . **⅓ cup shortening** **2 eggs** **1 cup mashed pumpkin**	In large mixing bowl beat together sugar, shortening and eggs. Stir in pumpkin.
1⅓ cups unsifted . . . . **all-purpose flour** **1 teaspoon baking soda** **¼ teaspoon baking powder** **¾ teaspoon salt** **½ teaspoon cinnamon** **½ teaspoon nutmeg**	Stir together flour, soda, baking powder, salt, cinnamon and nutmeg. Add to pumpkin mixture, stirring well.
½ teaspoon vanilla . . . . . **⅓ cup water** **½ cup chopped nuts**	Mix in vanilla, water and nuts.

Microwave at Medium High using same directions as Fluffy Muffins. If desired, sprinkle tops of muffins with cinnamon and drizzle with Simple Glaze before serving.

Makes about 25 gems

Simple Glaze: Stir together ½ cup sifted confectioners sugar, 1 to 2 tablespoons milk or hot water, ¼ teaspoon vanilla extract and ⅛ teaspoon salt.

Blueberry Fluffy Muffins

BRAN NUT MUFFINS

POWER LEVEL: Medium High (7)
MICROWAVE TIME: See Recipe

2 cups unsifted . . . . **all-purpose flour** **1 cup sugar** **5 teaspoons baking powder** **1½ teaspoons salt** **2 cups whole bran cereal** **1 cup chopped nuts (or raisins)**	In large mixing bowl stir together flour, sugar, baking powder, salt, bran and nuts or raisins.
2 eggs . . . . **1½ cups milk** **½ cup cooking oil**	Combine eggs, milk and oil. Stir into dry mixture just until all flour is dampened. Fill paper lined muffin cups ½ full.
¼ cup crushed bran cereal or chopped nuts	Sprinkle muffins with cereal or nuts. **Microwave at Medium High** using same directions as Fluffy Muffins.

Makes about 24 muffins

Ring Molds are best for even cooking. Many varieties can be purchased or you can improvise with utensils you already own.

BASIC NUT RING

To vary this recipe, add 1 cup chopped dates or cranberries.

POWER LEVEL: Medium High (7)   **Cook Code:** 97
MICROWAVE TIME: 9 to 12 min., total

1¾ cups unsifted all-purpose flour	In large mixing bowl stir together flour, sugar, baking powder and salt.
⅔ cup brown sugar	
2 teaspoons baking powder	
1 teaspoon salt	
1 cup milk	Measure milk into 1-pt. glass measure. Add egg and oil. Beat well. Add to flour mxture along with ¾ cup nuts. Stir until flour is moistened.
1 egg	
3 tablespoons cooking oil	
1 cup finely chopped nuts, divided	

Grease 2-qt. or 9-in. microwave plastic ring mold and sprinkle with remaining ¼ cup nuts. **Microwave at Medium High 9 to 12 Minutes,** rotating ¼ turn every 4 minutes, until dry and firm on top and toothpick stuck in center comes out clean. Let stand 5 minutes before inverting onto serving plate. Serve warm or cool.

Makes 1 (9-in.) ring

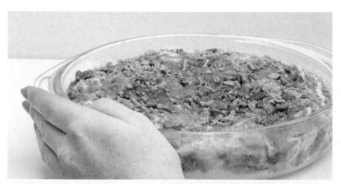

Rotate quick breads and coffee cakes for even cooking. Follow recipe directions for frequency of rotating.

CORNBREAD RING

POWER LEVEL: High (10) and Medium (5)
MICROWAVE TIME: 9 to 11 min., total

1 cup yellow cornmeal	In large mixing bowl, stir together cornmeal, flour, sugar, baking powder and salt.
1 cup unsifted all-purpose flour	
2 tablespoons sugar	
4 teaspoons baking powder	
½ teaspoon salt	
1 egg	Add egg, milk and cooking oil. Beat until smooth, about 1 minute.
1 cup milk	
½ cup cooking oil	
½ cup finely crushed French fried onions (about ½ of 3-oz. can)	Place onions and cheese in well-greased 8-in. round dish. Tilt to coat all sides, reserving excess crumbs. Place a small drinking glass (3-in. or less diameter, 4 to 5-in. high) in center of dish. Pour batter around glass and sprinkle with reserved crumbs.
1 tablespoon Parmesan cheese	

Microwave at Medium 6 Minutes, rotating dish ½ turn after 3 minutes. **Microwave at High 3 to 5 Minutes** more, rotating dish ½ turn after 2 minutes, until toothpick stuck in center comes out clean. Turn out on cooling rack or serving plate. Serve warm.

Makes 1 (8-in.) ring

TRADITIONAL STEAMED BROWN BREAD

POWER LEVEL: Medium (5)   **Cook Code:** 185
MICROWAVE TIME: 18 to 22 min., total

¾ cup cornmeal	Stir together cornmeal, whole wheat flour, rye flour, baking soda and salt.
¾ cup whole wheat flour	
¾ cup rye flour	
1½ teaspoons baking soda	
½ teaspoon salt	
½ cup dark molasses	Stir in molasses, buttermilk and raisins thoroughly.
1¼ cups buttermilk	
¾ cup raisins	

Pour into greased 2-qt. or 9-in. ring mold. Cover dish tightly with plastic wrap so bread steams as it cooks. **Microwave at Medium 18 to 22 Minutes,** rotating dish ¼ turn every 6 minutes. Unmold and let ring stand 10 minutes before slicing.

Makes 1 (9-in.) ring

Coffee Cakes

Coffee cakes may be microwaved in a round dish, rather than a ring. The richer, sweeter batter cooks evenly, so there will be no depression in the center. Like other quick breads, coffee cakes do not brown, and need a colorful topping or simple icing to give them a finished appearance.

EVERYDAY COFFEE CAKE

Biscuit mix recipe.

POWER LEVEL: High (10)   **Cook Code:** 50
MICROWAVE TIME: 5 to 7 min., total

1½ cups buttermilk biscuit mix **¼ cup sugar**	In mixing bowl stir together biscuit mix and sugar.
½ cup milk **1 egg** **2 tablespoons cooking oil**	Add milk, egg and oil. Beat by hand, mixing well. Pour into greased 8-in. round dish.
⅓ cup buttermilk biscuit mix **⅓ cup brown sugar (packed)** **2 tablespoons butter** **1 teaspoon cinnamon** **¼ cup chopped nuts**	Blend biscuit mix, brown sugar, butter and cinnamon until crumbly. Sprinkle over batter and sprinkle with nuts. **Microwave at High 5 to 7 Minutes,** rotating dish ¼ turn every 2 minutes. Cool 15 minutes; drizzle with Fine Glaze. Serve warm.

Fine Glaze: Stir together ¾ cup confectioners sugar and 1 tablespoon milk. From tip of spoon, drizzle glaze over cake in spoke fashion.

Makes 1 (8-in. round) cake

Coffee Cakes microwave very quickly, and should be checked for doneness after the minimum cooking time. The cake is done when a wooden pick inserted in the center comes out clean. There may be some doughiness on the outside, which will disappear on standing. Drizzle icing or glaze over the cake to finish.

Stacked Maple Nut Rings, page 234

SIMPLE COFFEE CAKE

Scratch recipe.

POWER LEVEL: High (10)   **Cook Code:** 50
MICROWAVE TIME: 5 to 7 min., total

2 cups unsifted all-purpose flour **½ cup sugar** **3 teaspoons baking powder** **½ teaspoon salt**	In mixing bowl stir flour with sugar, baking powder and salt. Make a well in center of dry mixture.
2 eggs, beaten **½ cup cooking oil** **½ cup milk**	Combine eggs, oil and milk. Add all at once to dry ingredients and stir just to moisten.

Pour into greased 8-in. round dish and sprinkle with Topping (below). **Microwave at High 5 to 7 Minutes,** rotating dish ¼ turn every 2 minutes. Cool 15 minutes; if desired, drizzle with Fine Glaze (left).

Topping: Blend 2 tablespoons flour, 1 tablespoon cinnamon, 1 tablespoon cocoa, ⅓ cup sugar and ¼ cup cold butter until crumbly.

Makes 1 (8-in. round) coffee cake

MAPLE-NUT RING

POWER LEVEL: Medium High (7)   **Cook Code:** 77
MICROWAVE TIME: 7 to 9 min., total

⅓ cup finely chopped walnuts **2 tablespoons brown sugar (packed)** **2 tablespoons sugar** **1 teaspoon cinnamon**	Invert 6-oz. custard cup in center of lightly greased 8-in. round dish. In small bowl, mix together walnuts, brown sugar, sugar and cinnamon.
¼ cup maple syrup **1 roll (10-oz.) refrigerated buttermilk biscuits**	Place maple syrup in small bowl. Coat each biscuit with syrup, then sugar-nut mixture. Arrange in circle in prepared dish, overlapping edges.

Microwave at Medium High 7 to 9 Minutes, rotating dish ¼ turn every 2 minutes. Let cool 5 minutes. Remove custard cup and invert onto serving plate. Sprinkle with any remaining sugar-nut mixture. Serve warm.

Makes 1 (8-in.) ring

STACKED MAPLE-NUT RINGS

Make two rings, inverting one on top of the other. Drizzle with confectioners sugar glaze made by mixing 1 cup confectioners sugar and 1 to 2 tablespoons milk.

CHERRY CARAMEL RING

POWER LEVEL: High (10) and Medium High (7)
MICROWAVE TIME: 7½ to 9½ min., total

¼ cup butter	Place butter in 8-in. round dish. **Microwave at High ½ to ¾ Minute,** until melted.
½ cup brown sugar (packed) **2 tablespoons light corn syrup** **½ cup pecan halves** **¼ cup maraschino cherries, quartered**	Sprinkle sugar over butter and add corn syrup. Stir well with fork. Place drinking glass in center of dish. Sprinkle with pecans and cherries.
1 roll (10-oz.) refrigerated buttermilk biscuits	Arrange biscuits over mixture in dish in petal shape, squeezing to fit, if necessary. **Microwave at Medium High 7 to 9 Minutes,** rotating dish ¼ turn every 2 minutes. Let cool 5 minutes. Remove glass and invert onto serving plate. Let dish stand over rolls a few minutes so remaining syrup in dish may drizzle over rolls. Serve warm.

Makes 1 (8-in.) ring

HOW TO MICROWAVE A CARAMEL BISCUIT RING

Prepare topping in bottom of an improvised tube pan made by placing a drinking glass about 4-in. high or inverted 6-oz. custard cup, in an 8-in. dish or use a microwave tube pan.

Arrange biscuits on topping. Check at minimum cooking time; ring will seem moist and hardly set. Let stand 5 minutes and invert onto plate. Syrup gives ring a golden caramel color.

Inverted onto a serving plate, the ring has a rich caramel-colored syrup over the top and sides, although the bottoms of the biscuits are not brown.

CONVENIENCE BREADS

One of the best uses for the microwave oven is defrosting frozen convenience breads and warming bakery products. The Defrost setting provides rapid defrosting and warming, yet keeps breads tender.

Coffee cakes packaged in foil should be removed from the container. If the cardboard cover is not foil-lined it may be used as a plate under cake. Other breads may be placed on pottery or paper plates before heating. Individual breads arranged in circle heat most evenly.

Metal Twist Ties must be removed before package of rolls or bread is placed in oven. Under some conditions, metal twist ties can cause package to catch fire.

CONVENIENCE BREADS DEFROSTING AND WARMING CHART

POWER LEVEL: **Defrost**

ITEM	TIME MINUTES	COMMENTS
DEFROSTING		
Bread or Buns (1-lb. pkg.)	2 to 3	Turn over after 1 minute.
Heat & Serve Rolls (7-oz. pkg.)	2 to 3	Rotate ¼ turn after 1 minute.
Coffee Cake (11 to 13-oz. pkg.)	4 to 6	Rotate ¼ turn after 2 minutes.
Coffee Cake (6½-oz. pkg.)	2 to 3	No turn needed.
Coffee Ring (10-oz. pkg.)	2 to 2½	Rotate ½ turn after 1 minute.
Sweet Rolls, Crumb Cakes, Pull-aparts (8¾ to 12-oz. pkg.)	2 to 3	Rotate ½ turn after 1 minute.

ITEM	TIME MINUTES	COMMENTS
Doughnuts (1 to 3)	½ to 1	No turn needed.
Doughnuts (4 to 6)	1 to 1¼	No turn needed.
Doughnuts (1 box of 12 glazed)	1½ to 2	Rotate ½ turn after ½ minute.
French Toast (2 slices)	3½ to 4	Rotate ½ turn after 2 minutes.
French Toast (4 slices)	5½ to 6	Rotate ½ turn after 3 minutes.
WARMING (room temperature)		
Dinner Rolls (1 to 3)	½ to ¾	No turn needed.
Dinner Rolls (4 to 6)	¾ to 1¼	No turn needed.
Doughnuts	½ to 1	Rotate more than 6.

Cherry Caramel Ring

Breads/Yeast

The microwave oven can be used to defrost frozen yeast bread dough. Step-by-step instructions are given on page 237.

Bread recipes need to be specially formulated for microwaving, such as those given below. Breads cooked in a microwave oven do not brown or develop a crust as they do conventionally because there is no hot air in the oven to dry out the surface. You will probably prefer to cook your favorite bread recipes conventionally for this reason. When finished, microwaved breads appear dry and set on top but not brown or crusty. When touched, the surface springs back. Toppings can provide a colorful finished appearance.

Savory Cheese Bread, created especially for microwaving contains butter and cheese for richness. A topping adds color and flavor. Low shape provides maximum exposure to microwave energy for even cooking.

APPLE CIRCLE COFFEE CAKES

POWER LEVEL: Medium High (7) **Cook Code:** 107
MICROWAVE TIME: 10 to 13 min., total

½ cup (¼-lb.) butter, melted 2 teaspoons cinnamon 1 cup chopped pecans ⅔ cup dark brown sugar	Divide butter, cinnamon, nuts and sugar equally between two 8-in. round dishes. Mix well.
1 can (1-lb., 4-oz.) apple slices, drained	Place apple slices on top of sugar mixture, set aside.
2¾ cups unsifted all-purpose flour 2 tablespoons sugar 1 teaspoon grated lemon rind ½ teaspoon salt ½ cup (¼-lb.) butter,	In large mixing bowl place flour, sugar, lemon rind, salt and butter. Cut through mixture with pastry blender until mixture resembles coarse meal.
1 pkg. (¼-oz.) active dry yeast ¼ cup warm water ½ cup milk 1 egg, beaten	Dissolve yeast in warm water. Add to crumbly mixture along with milk and egg. Beat with spoon until well blended. Divide dough and spread evenly over apples.

Let cakes rise in warm place, 1 hour, until dough is puffy. Microwave one cake at a time. **Microwave at Medium High 10 to 13 Minutes,** rotating dish ¼ turn every 3 minutes.

SAVORY CHEESE BREAD

POWER LEVEL: Medium (5) **Cook Code:** 125
MICROWAVE TIME: 12 to 14 min., per loaf

2¾ cups unsifted all-purpose flour 2 tablespoons sugar ½ teaspoon salt ½ cup (¼-lb.) butter	In large mixing bowl place flour, sugar, salt and butter. Cut through mixture with pastry blender until mixture resembles coarse meal.
1 pkg. (¼-oz.) active dry yeast ¼ cup warm water 1 cup milk 1 egg, beaten	Dissolve yeast in warm water. Add to crumbly mixture along with milk and egg. Beat with spoon until well blended.
1 pkg. (½ of 2¾-oz. box) dry onion soup mix 1 cup (4-oz.) shredded cheddar cheese	Mix together 2 tablespoons onion soup mix and ¼ cup shredded cheese. Set aside. Add remaining soup mix and cheese to batter. Stir well.

Divide batter evenly between 2 well greased 8x4x3-in. dishes. Sprinkle loaves with reserved cheese mixture. Cover lightly and let rise in warm place 1½ to 2 hours, just until dough is slightly puffy.

Microwave one loaf at a time. **Microwave at Medium 12 to 14 Minutes,** rotating dish ¼ turn every 3 minutes. Let stand in dish 5 minutes.

Carefully remove breads to cooling rack. Serve warm or cool.

Makes 2 (8x4x3-in.) loaves

MICROLESSON: HOW TO MICROWAVE FROZEN CONVENIENCE BREADS

Place frozen coffee cake on its own cardboard lid to defrost and warm.

Arrange frozen baked muffins and rolls in a circle on a dinner plate to defrost and heat.

Place doughnuts and sweet rolls in a circle on paper towel or napkin.

Use trivet when microwaving rolls with moist or sweet fillings. The fillings heat faster than the breads; let stand a few minutes to equalize heat.

Overlap waffles or French toast on serving plate. Microwave pancakes are available in all-paper package.

Slice canned or deli brown bread, fruit cakes or nut breads and arrange in circle on plate. Cover with wax paper to microwave.

MICROLESSON: HOW TO DEFROST FROZEN BREAD

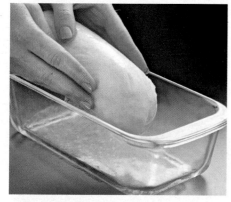

Place 1 tablespoon butter in 8×4×3-in. dish. **Microwave at High ½ Minute** to melt. Place 1-lb. loaf frozen dough in dish, turning over to coat all sides with butter.

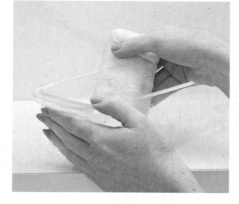

Defrost for a total time of 5 minutes, turning loaf over and rotating dish ¼ turn every ½ minute. Let rise 2 hours in a warm place until double. Top of loaf should be about 1-in. below top of dish.

Bake conventionally as package directs. Most packages recommend 375° for 30 to 40 minutes.

Desserts

Your microwave oven can help you prepare almost any dessert, both those you have baked in your conventional oven and those you have cooked on the range top. Candies, custards, puddings, fruits and frosting are usually easier to microwave than they are to cook on your range top. Microwave energy is absorbed from all surfaces, the top and sides as well as the bottom, so less stirring is needed to heat them evenly.

Baked desserts are likely to appear different when microwaved. Brownies, bars and dark batters such as gingerbread or chocolate cake are the exceptions.

Pastries and cakes do not brown, but because they are served with fillings or toppings, the difference will not be apparent when they are served. What will impress you is the time saved by microwaving them.

1. Pecan Sponge Roll, page 279
2. Layered Fudge, page 241
3. Rainbow Pretzels, page 244
4. Floating Islands, page 252
5. White Chocolate Nut Bark, page 243
6. Black Forest Trifle, page 254

HOW TO MICROWAVE PEANUT BRITTLE

Stir well to combine sugar and corn syrup. Stirring this mixture helps it to microwave evenly. Add peanuts, stirring well. Stir again when adding butter and vanilla.

Stir in baking soda until mixture is light and foamy. Spread out quickly on greased cookie sheet. When cool, flex sheet to remove.

Munching Peanut Brittle

Candies

Candies demonstrate many of the advantages of microwaving. Chocolate and caramelized mixtures which require careful attention and constant stirring by old-fashioned methods, microwave with occasional stirring.

Syrups and candies are very hot. Use care in stirring and when transfering mixtures from the microwave oven to your work counter.

MUNCHING PEANUT BRITTLE

This is the same old-fashioned recipe which required constant stirring in a black iron skillet. Stir only 4 times when microwaving.

POWER LEVEL: High (10)
MICROWAVE TIME: 8 to 11 min., total

1 cup sugar **½ cup white corn syrup**	In 1½-qt. casserole stir together sugar and syrup. **Microwave at High 4 Minutes.**
1 cup roasted, salted peanuts	Stir in peanuts. **Microwave at High 3 to 5 Minutes,** until light brown.
1 teaspoon butter **1 teaspoon vanilla extract**	Add butter and vanilla to syrup, blending well. **Microwave at High 1 to 2 Minutes** more. Peanuts will be lightly browned and syrup, very hot.
1 teaspoon baking soda	Add baking soda and gently stir until light and foamy.

Quickly pour mixture onto lightly greased cookie sheet, or unbuttered non-stick coated cookie sheet. Let cool ½ to 1 hour. When cool, break into small pieces and store in airtight container.

Makes about 1 pound

NOTE: If raw peanuts are used, add before microwaving, to the sugar-syrup mixture, along with ⅛ teaspoon salt.

ALMOND BRITTLE

Substitute 1 jar (7-oz.) dry roasted almonds for peanuts and 1 teaspoon almond extract for vanilla. Omit butter and add 1 cup (4-oz.) shredded coconut with 1 teaspoon almond extract.

PECAN OR CASHEW BRITTLE

Omit peanuts and add 1 cup pecan halves or 1 jar (7-oz.) dry-roasted cashews.

REAL CHOCOLATE FUDGE

POWER LEVEL: High (10) and Medium High (7)
MICROWAVE TIME: 16 to 20 min., total

2 cups sugar . . . .
⅛ teaspoon salt
¾ cup milk
**2 squares (2-oz.)
   unsweetened
   chocolate**
¼ cup butter
	In 3-qt. casserole stir to-gether sugar, salt and milk, mixing well. Add chocolate and butter. Cover. **Microwave at High 6 Minutes,** until hot and bubbly. Stir very well. **Microwave at Medium High 10 to 14 Minutes,** uncovered. Stir well every 5 minutes. When suf-ficiently cooked, a few drops of mixture will form a soft ball in cup of cold water. (Candy thermome-ter reads 235°.)

2 teaspoons vanilla	Let candy stand without stirring, at room tempera-ture, until lukewarm.* Add vanilla, beat with spoon or mixer until it begins to thicken and loses its gloss.
½ cup chopped nuts (optional)	Quickly stir in nuts and pour into 8×4×3-in. loaf dish which has been lined with wax paper (or use but-tered plate.) Cut when set.
	Makes about 1 pound

*Or place bowl in a pan of cool water or place in refriger-ator until lukewarm.

REAL PEANUT BUTTER FUDGE

Make Real Chocolate Fudge as above except substitute ⅓ cup crunchy peanut butter for chocolate and butter. If desired, use coarsely chopped salted peanuts for nuts in recipe, or omit nuts altogether.

LAYERED FUDGE

Prepare 2 (8-in.) loaf dishes by lining with wax paper. Prepare Real Chocolate Fudge and divide between the 2 dishes. Let set in refrigerator while preparing Real Pea-nut Butter Fudge. Divide evenly over chocolate fudge. Refrigerate until firm. Cut into squares. (Wiping knife with damp cloth between cuts best shows layered effect.)

For Shapely Square Pieces line loaf dish with wax pa-per. Use a 14×12-in. strip of wax paper (wax paper is 12-in. wide so cut 14-in. off roll); fold in half. Fit the 7-in. side on longest sides and bottom of loaf dish, leaving about 1-in. "handles" at each edge. When fudge is hard-ened, loosen fudge at narrow edges of loaf dish and lift out fudge in one piece using wax paper "handles". Pull off wax paper and, with sharp knife, cut into squares.

HOW TO MICROWAVE FUDGE

Combine first 5 ingredients in large bowl to prevent over-boiling. Stir very well when mixture is hot and chocolate melted. Then stir every 5 minutes.

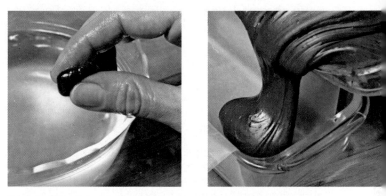

Soft ball will form from a small amount of mixture drop-ped into very cold water when fudge is sufficiently cook-ed. Line dish with 14×12-in. folded strip of wax paper. Use long ends to lift out fudge when set.

Real Chocolate Fudge

2-MINUTE FUDGE

POWER LEVEL: High (10)   **Cook Code:** 20
MICROWAVE TIME: 2 min., total

1 box (1-lb.) ....
    confectioners sugar
½ cup cocoa
¼ teaspoon salt
¼ cup milk
1 tablespoon vanilla
    extract
½ cup (¼-lb.) butter
	In 1½-qt. casserole stir sugar, cocoa, salt, milk and vanilla together until partially blended (mixture is too stiff to thoroughly blend in all of dry ingredients). Put butter over top in center of dish. **Microwave at High 2 Minutes,** or until milk feels warm on bottom of dish. Stir vigorously until smooth. If all butter has not melted in cooking, it will as mixture is stirred.

1 cup chopped nuts	Blend in nuts. Pour into wax paper lined (see page 241) 8×4×3-in. dish. Chill 1 hour in refrigerator or 20 to 30 minutes in freezer. Cut into squares.

Makes about 36 squares

COFFEE FONDANT

Prepare 2-Minute Fudge as above, except, omit cocoa and substitute 1 tablespoon instant coffee granules dissolved in 2 tablespoons milk. Before fondant sets, press "chocolate shot" decors into top.

TOFFEE HEATH SQUARES

POWER LEVEL: High (10)   **Cook Code:** 50
MICROWAVE TIME: 5 to 6 min., total

1 cup chopped nuts	Sprinkle nuts over bottom of buttered 8-in. square dish.
1 cup brown sugar ...... **(packed)** **⅓ cup butter** **3 tablespoons water**	In 1½-qt. casserole place brown sugar, butter and water. **Microwave at High 5 to 6 Minutes,** stirring after 2 minutes, until thick. Stir well, quickly spread over chopped nuts.
½ cup semi-sweet .... **chocolate pieces**	Sprinkle chocolate pieces over toffee. Cover dish so heat melts chocolate. Let stand 5 minutes. Spread chocolate evenly over top. Refrigerate to set. Turn out of dish and break into pieces to serve.

Makes about 1 pound

BROWN SUGAR FUDGE

Its old-fashioned name is Penuche. When done just right, it is soft and creamy. Overcooked, it can be dry and crumbly. It has same soft ball test as fudge, page 241.

POWER LEVEL: High (10)   **Cook Code:** 170
MICROWAVE TIME: 17 to 19 min., total

2 cups light brown .... **sugar (packed)** **1 cup whipping cream** **1 cup pure maple syrup***	In 3-qt. casserole stir together brown sugar, cream and syrup. **Microwave at High 17 to 19 Minutes,** stirring well after 7 minutes. When cooked, a few drops of the syrup will form a soft ball when dropped into a cup of cold water.
2 cups chopped walnuts	Let stand until lukewarm, then beat with electric mixer 10 to 12 minutes, until mixture becomes creamy. Add nuts and stir well. Pour into buttered 8-in. square dish. Refrigerate until set.

Makes about 36 squares

*Creamy fudge-like consistency occurs only if pure maple syrup is used. For candy with vanilla caramel-like consistency, substitute maple flavored pancake syrup.

MARSHMALLOW CRISP

POWER LEVEL: High (10)
MICROWAVE TIME: 4 to 5 min., total

¼ cup butter ....
1 pkg. (10-oz.) large
    marshmallows*
    (about 40)
5 cups crispy rice
    cereal
	In 3-qt. casserole place butter. **Microwave at High 1 Minute** to melt. Add marshmallows. Cover. **Microwave at High 3 to 4 Minutes.** Remove from oven and stir until butter is melted and marshmallows are well blended. Add cereal. Stir until well coated.

Press warm mixture evenly and firmly into lightly buttered 12×8×2-in. dish. Use wax paper or buttered spatula to press firmly into an even layer. Cool; cut into squares.

Makes 24 (2-in.) squares

*Or use 4 cups miniature marshmallows or 1 jar (9-oz.) marshmallow cream (about 2 cups).

VARIATIONS:

Peanut: Add 1 cup whole or chopped peanuts; or stir ¼ cup peanut butter into marshmallow mixture just before adding cereal.

Chocolate Dot: After cereal has been stirred into marshmallow mixture, quickly stir in 1 pkg. (6-oz.) semi-sweet chocolate pieces.

HOW TO MELT CHOCOLATE

Chocolate Bits may be melted in a paper bowl. Cover with plastic wrap and **Microwave at Medium or Low.** For 6-oz. pkg. (1 cup) **Microwave 3 to 4 Minutes,** until bits are glossy but hold their shape. They smooth out when stirred. Chocolate burns easily, so check at minimum time.

Chocolate Squares can be melted in paper wrappers, seam side up. Microwave up to 3 squares at **Medium or Low** about 1 to 2 minutes per square (1-oz.). For 4 to 6 squares, allow ½ to 1 minute per square. Melt until square feels soft. Beyond this point, chocolate will scorch or burn.

CHOCOLATE NUT BARK

POWER LEVEL: Medium (5) or Low (3)
MICROWAVE TIME: 4 to 6 min., total
Cook Code: 45 or 43

1 pkg. (12-oz.) semi-sweet or milk chocolate, broken or in squares	In 1-qt. casserole place chocolate. Cover. **Microwave at Medium or Low 4 to 6 Minutes.** Stir well.
1 cup whole toasted almonds or coarsely chopped Brazil nuts	Stir nuts into chocolate. Place a piece of wax paper on small cookie sheet. Spread chocolate mixture in a thin layer over wax paper. Refrigerate until firm, about 1 hour. Break into pieces.

Makes about 1 pound

VARIATIONS:

1. Use 16-oz. white chocolate and melt in 1½-qt. casserole 5 to 6 minutes. Good with whole almonds.

2. Any number of variations of chocolate and other ingredients are good: Cashews and semi-sweet chocolate, raisins and milk chocolate, even other dried fruits such as apricots and white chocolate. Candied cherries with white or milk chocolate are colorful for Christmas. Milk chocolate and peanuts is an all-time favorite combination.

ROCKY ROAD CANDY

POWER LEVEL: High (10)   **Cook Code:** 40
MICROWAVE TIME: 4 to 6 min., total

2 pkgs. (8-oz. each) semi-sweet chocolate squares ..... **1 can (15-oz.) sweetened condensed milk**	In 2-qt. casserole place unwrapped chocolate squares and milk. **Microwave at High 4 to 6 Minutes,** until mixture can be stirred smooth.
1 pkg. (10-oz.) miniature marshmallows .... **½ cup chopped nuts**	Quickly stir in marshmallows and nuts, blending well. Spread mixture in greased 12x8x2 in. square dish or pan. Refrigerate until firm. Cut into pieces.

CHOCOLATE RAISIN NUT CLUSTERS

POWER LEVEL: Low (3)   **Cook Code:** 43
MICROWAVE TIME: 4 to 5 min., total

1 pkg. (6-oz.) semi-sweet chocolate bits ...... **1 cup salted jumbo peanuts** **1 cup seedless raisins**	In 1½-qt. casserole place chocolate, peanuts and raisins. Cover. **Microwave at Low 4 to 5 Minutes,** or until chocolate is melted.

Stir mixture until chocolate covers peanuts and raisins. Drop by teaspoonfuls onto wax paper. Chill until firm.

Makes about 24 pieces

S'MORES

POWER LEVEL: High (10)
MICROWAVE TIME: ¼ min., per S'More

2 graham cracker squares **½ plain chocolate bar (1.05-oz.)** **1 large marshmallow**	On paper napkin place 1 graham cracker square. Top with chocolate and marshmallow. **Microwave at High ¼ Minute,** or until marshmallow puffs. Place remaining cracker over top and eat like a sandwich.

Makes 1 S'More

RAINBOW PRETZELS

POWER LEVEL: Medium (5)   **Cook Code:** 35
MICROWAVE TIME: 3 to 4 min., total

½ lb. white chocolate **2 tablespoons white corn syrup** **2 tablespoons butter** **1 tablespoon water**	In 1-qt. casserole place chocolate, syrup, butter and water. Cover. **Microwave at Medium 3 to 4 Minutes,** until melted. Stir well, until smooth.
Food coloring	Prepare up to 2 colors of Rainbow Pretzels per batch. Tint with food coloring as desired.
Miniature pretzel twists	Dip "mini-size" pretzels into mixture, removing excess. Place on cooling rack over wax paper to dry.

Makes about 1 cup, or enough to cover about 50 to 60 miniature pretzels

NOTE: If mixture becomes firm, **Microwave at Medium ½ to 1 Minute,** stirring smooth and adding a few drops of water if necessary.

CHOCOLATE CHOW MEIN "HAYSTACKS"

POWER LEVEL: Medium (5) or Low (3)
MICROWAVE TIME: 4 to 5½ min., total
Cook Code: 45 or 43

1 pkg. (6-oz.) semi-sweet chocolate pieces	In 3-qt. casserole or large bowl place chocolate pieces. Cover with lid or plastic wrap. **Microwave at Medium or Low 4 to 5½ Minutes,** until melted.
1 can (3-oz.) chow mein noodles	Stir chocolate smooth. Add noodles and, using 2 forks, toss to coat well. On strips of foil or wax paper form into 1½-in. clusters. Cool to set.

Makes about 24 (1½-in.) "Haystacks"

CHOCOLATE COVERED RUM BALLS

Some people call these "rumbles". Stale, unfrosted cake, finely crumbled, is even better than wafer crumbs.

POWER LEVEL: Low (3)   **Cook Code:** 53
MICROWAVE TIME: 5 to 6 min., total

2 cups fine vanilla wafer crumbs **1 cup finely chopped nuts** **¼ cup butter, melted** **¼ cup rum**	In mixing bowl place crumbs, nuts, butter and rum. Stir together well. Shape mixture into 1-in. balls. Refrigerate while melting chocolate.
6 squares semi-sweet chocolate	In 1-qt. casserole place chocolate. Cover. **Microwave at Low 5 to 6 Minutes,** until melted. Stir.

Dip balls into chocolate, coating well but removing excess chocolate. Excess chocolate can be removed by holding dipped ball on a fork and tapping on side of dish so excess chocolate drops into dish. Place on wax paper lined cookie sheet and refrigerate until set.

Makes about 36 rum balls

CHOCOLATE FONDUE

POWER LEVEL: Medium (5)
MICROWAVE TIME: 8 to 10 min., total

4 squares (1-oz. each) unsweetened or semi-sweet chocolate (see note) **1 cup dairy half & half**	In 1-qt. casserole place chocolate and half & half. **Microwave at Medium 5 to 6 Minutes,** or until chocolate melts. Stir well.
1 cup sugar **½ teaspoon vanilla extract**	Add sugar and vanilla. **Microwave at Medium 3 to 4 Minutes,** or until sugar is dissolved.

Serve immediately or transfer mixture to fondue pot. Serve with marshmallows, apple, pear, banana or pineapple chunks, strawberries, cherries, ladyfingers, cubes of firm pound cake or angel food cake, or cookies.

Makes 2 cups of fondue

NOTE: If you plan to use sweet dippers such as marshmallows or cookies, use unsweetened chocolate in fondue. If you plan to use fruits, use semi-sweet chocolate in fondue. To eat, spear the "dipper" on a fork and dip into fondue. Let excess drip off into pot, then eat. Kids will enjoy dipping firm cookies into fondue with their fingers.

Fruit Desserts

Pound Cake

Fruits microwave tender but still crisp, retain their fresh flavor, texture, color and shape. One reason for the flavor retention of microwaved fruit is the shorter cooking time. Another is that fruit is microwaved with little or no water, which intensifies the flavor of both fruit and juice as well as preserving water-soluble nutrients such as vitamin C.

DEFROSTING CHART

Properly defrosted fruit should be cold, firm and slightly icy for best flavor and texture. Remove any metal or foil from package and, if necessary, place fruit in a casserole. Be sure to check at minimum time and break up with a fork. Flex package to speed defrosting of fruit frozen in plastic pouches.

TYPE	POWER LEVEL	TIME MIN.	COOK CODE
Fruit (10 to 16-oz. pkg.)	Defrost	5—10	53
Fruit, plastic pouch (1 to 2 10-oz. pkgs.)	Defrost	5—10	53
Escalloped Apples (12-oz. pkg.)	High	6—8, covered	60

Defrosted fruit will be cold, firm and slightly icy. Pouch will be flexible and juices liquid.

QUICK STRAWBERRIES AND POUND CAKE DESSERT

Three separate defrostings make one good and easy assembled dessert.

POWER LEVEL: Defrost
MICROWAVE TIME: 9 to 12 min., total

1 frozen, baked, pound cake (about 12-oz.), unfrosted . . . Place cake on microwave ovenproof plate or board. **Microwave at Defrost 2 Minutes.** Let stand while defrosting berries.

2 pkg. (10-oz. each) frozen strawberries in plastic pouch . . . . . . Place unopened packages on microwave oven shelf. **Microwave at Defrost 5 to 8 Minutes,** removing from boxes, rotating and flexing packages after 1½ minutes.

1 pkg. (9-oz.) commercially frozen whipped topping . . . . Place topping container on microwave oven shelf. **Microwave at Defrost 2 Minutes,** turning over after 1 minute.

To serve, slice cake and serve slices topped with strawberries and whipped topping.

Makes 6 to 8 servings

Baked Apple

BAKED APPLES OR PEARS

The chart below is a good guide to time, but because fruit varies, time may vary too. Small, juicy apples and pears cook faster than larger, drier ones.

POWER LEVEL: High (10)
MICROWAVE TIME: See Recipe

Large whole apples or pears*	Core apples or pears. Slit through skin around center of each fruit to prevent bursting. Arrange in casserole, see chart below.

For each fruit: **2 tablespoons brown sugar** **⅛ teaspoon cinnamon** **1 teaspoon butter** **2 tablespoons water**	Fill each fruit core with brown sugar, cinnamon and butter. Pour total amount of water around fruit. Cover casserole. **Microwave at High** according to chart below.

*Peel pears before microwaving.

NO. OF FRUIT	CASSEROLE SIZE	TIME MIN.	COOK CODE
1	1-qt.	2—4	20
2	1½-qt.	4—5½	40
3	2-qt.	6—8	60
4	2-qt.	9—10	90

NOTE: When microwaving more than 1 apple, rotate dish ½ turn after ½ of time.

APPLESAUCE

POWER LEVEL: High (10)　　　　　　　**Cook Code:** 90
MICROWAVE TIME: 9 to 10 min., total

6 apples, pared, cored and quartered **¼ cup water**	In 2-qt. casserole place apples with water. Cover. **Microwave at High 9 to 10 Minutes,** stirring after 5 minutes, until fork-tender.
⅓ cup sugar **⅛ teaspoon salt** **⅛ teaspoon cinnamon, nutmeg or cloves (optional)**	Into blender container, place apple mixture, sugar, salt and spices, if desired. Blend until smooth.

Makes 3 to 4 cups

If blender is unavailable, mash with potato masher or put apples through ricer.

STREUSELED APPLES

Known conventionally as Apple Crisp. Vary this recipe by substituting other fresh or canned fruits for apples.

POWER LEVEL: High (10)　　　　　　　**Cook Code:** 90
MICROWAVE TIME: 9 to 12 min., total

6 cups sliced, peeled apples **¾ cup brown sugar (packed)**	In 8-in. square dish place apples and sugar.
½ cup unsifted all-purpose flour **⅓ cup brown sugar (packed)** **⅓ cup quick-cooking oats** **¼ cup butter** **½ teaspoon cinnamon**	With pastry blender mix flour, sugar, oats, butter and cinnamon until crumbly. Sprinkle over top of apples.

Microwave at High 9 to 12 Minutes, rotating dish ¼ turn after 5 minutes. Let stand few minutes before serving.

Makes 6 to 8 servings

Rotate dish ½ turn after ½ of time. One apple can be microwaved without rotating.

CARAMEL APPLES

POWER LEVEL: High (10) **Cook Code:** 20
MICROWAVE TIME: 1½ to 2½ min., total

½ of 14-oz. pkg. . . . . **caramels (about 25)** **1 tablespoon water**	In 1-pt. glass measure place unwrapped caramels and water. **Microwave at High 1½ to 2½ Minutes,** until mixture can be stirred smooth.
4 apples . . . . **4 wooden sticks** **(usually come with** **caramels)**	Insert sticks into stem ends of apples. Dip one apple at a time into caramel, coating evenly. Repeat. Place apples on buttered wax paper, stick side up, to set.

Makes 4 apples

BUTTERSCOTCH BANANAS

POWER LEVEL: High (10)
MICROWAVE TIME: 5 to 7 min., total

½ cup brown sugar . . . . **(packed)** **¼ cup rum** **¼ cup butter**	In 1½-qt. casserole stir together brown sugar and rum. Add butter. Cover. **Microwave at High 4 to 5 Minutes,** stirring after 2 minutes, until sugar is dissolved.
2 large ripe, firm . . . . **bananas**	Cut bananas lengthwise, then crosswise so there are 8 pieces. Add to syrup, stirring to coat each piece. **Microwave at High 1 to 2 Minutes,** until hot. Serve over ice cream.

Makes 4 servings

CHERRIES JUBILEE

POWER LEVEL: High (10)
MICROWAVE TIME: 5½ to 7½ min., total

2 cans (16-oz.) dark . . . . . . **sweet cherries** **3 tablespoons** **cornstarch** **1 tablespoon lemon** **juice** **1 teaspoon grated** **lemon rind** **¾ cup sugar**	Into 2-qt. casserole drain cherry syrup. Stir in cornstarch, lemon juice, rind and sugar. **Microwave at High 5 to 7 Minutes,** stirring after 3 minutes, until starting to thicken. Add cherries.
½ cup brandy	Measure brandy into glass measure. **Microwave at High ½ Minute.**

Pour 1 tablespoon heated brandy into metal tablespoon and remaining brandy over top of cherries. Ignite brandy in the tablespoon and pour over cherries. When flame has subsided, serve over ice cream.

Makes 8 to 10 servings

EASY FRUIT PUDDING

POWER LEVEL: High (10)
MICROWAVE TIME: 15 to 17 min., total

1 can (20 to 22-oz.) . . . . . . **cherry, blueberry,** **apple or other** **prepared fruit pie** **filling**	Spread pie filling in 8-in. square dish. **Microwave at High 4 Minutes,** stirring after 2 minutes, until heated through.
1 box (about 9-oz.) . . . . . . **1-layer cake mix** **(white, yellow or** **spice)** **¼ cup cold butter,** **thinly sliced**	Sprinkle dry cake mix evenly over fruit. Distribute butter slices over top.
2 tablespoons sugar . . . . . **mixed with 1** **teaspoon cinnamon,** **or ¼ cup finely** **chopped nuts**	Sprinkle cinnamon sugar or chopped nuts evenly over top.

Microwave at High 11 to 13 Minutes, rotating dish ¼ turn after 6 minutes. Serve warm with ice cream, if desired.

Makes 6 servings

ALL SEASONS FRUIT COMPOTE

This is a tangy, rather than sweet, fruit compote. It may also be served as a meat accompaniment.

POWER LEVEL: High (10) TEMP: 160°
APPROX. MICROWAVE TIME: 13 to 15 min.
Cook Code: 130

1 pkg. (12-oz.) dried . . . . . . **apricots** **1 can (1-lb.) sliced** **peaches, drained** **1 can (16-oz.) pitted** **bing cherries,** **undrained** **¾ cup brown sugar** **(packed)** **½ cup orange juice** **1 tablespoon grated** **orange peel** **¼ cup lemon juice** **1 tablespoon grated** **lemon rind**	In 2-qt. casserole place apricots and peaches. Drain cherry juice into small bowl. Add cherries to other fruit. To cherry juice add brown sugar, orange juice and peel, lemon juice and rind. Stir well. Pour over fruit. Insert temperature probe so tip is in center of food. Cover with plastic wrap, arranging loosely around probe to vent.

Attach cable end at receptacle. **Microwave at High. Set Temp, Set 160°.**

When oven signals, remove from oven and stir. Recover compote and chill overnight. Serve with garnish of sour cream, or omit garnish and serve with meat.

Makes 8 to 10 servings

STEWED DRIED FRUIT

POWER LEVEL: High (10)   **Cook Code:** 80
MICROWAVE TIME: 8 to 11 min., total

1 pkg. (12 to 16-oz.) ..... **dried apricots or prunes** **¼ cup sugar (optional)** **2 cups water**	.In 1½-qt. casserole place fruit, sugar (if desired), and water. Cover. **Microwave at High 8 to 11 Minutes,** until tender. Serve warm or cold.

Makes about 6 to 8 servings

FLAMING PEACHES

POWER LEVEL: High (10)
MICROWAVE TIME: 4¼ to 5¾ min., total

4 large fresh peaches, ... **or 1 can (29-oz.) peach halves**	.Peel and halve peaches and remove pits. In 10× 6×2-in. dish place peaches cut side up. For canned fruit, drain syrup, reserving 1 tablespoon.
¼ cup apricot jam .... **3 tablespoons sugar** **1 tablespoon peach syrup or water** **2 teaspoons lemon juice**	.In 1-cup glass measure place jam, sugar, syrup and juice. **Microwave at High 1 to 1½ Minutes,** or until sugar dissolves. Mix well. Pour over peaches.
8 teaspoons currant ..... **jelly** **8 tablespoons macaroon crumbs**	.Place 1 teaspoon currant jelly and 1 tablespoon macaroon crumbs on each peach half. **Microwave at High 3 to 4 Minutes,** rotating dish ½ turn after 2 minutes.
¼ cup brandy	.Measure brandy into 1-cup glass measuring cup and **Microwave at High ¼ Minute.** Remove 1 metal tablespoonful. Pour rest of brandy over peaches. Ignite brandy in spoon and pour over peaches to flame. Serve peaches hot with ice cream if desired.

Makes 8 servings

COLD LIME SOUFFLE

To prepare limes, first grate the rind then squeeze out the juice. This souffle mixture also makes an excellent chiffon pie filling and the lime version here is often known as Key Lime Pie when piled into a 9-in. shell.

POWER LEVEL: Medium High (7)   **Cook Code:** 47
MICROWAVE TIME: 4 to 6 min., total

1½ tablespoons gelatin ... **½ cup sugar** **4 egg yolks** **½ cup fresh lime juice (5 limes)**	In 1-qt. measuring cup stir together gelatin and sugar. Beat in egg yolks and lime juice. **Microwave at Medium High 4 to 6 Minutes,** until hot and well blended, stirring every 2 minutes.
2 tablespoons grated .... **lime peel** **5 drops green food coloring**	.To hot mixture, add lime peel and food coloring. Stir well. Cool mixture. While mixture is cooling, prepare souffle dish (see below).
6 egg whites .... **½ cup sugar** **1¼ cups whipping cream**	.When mixture is cool, beat egg whites, adding sugar gradually, to make soft meringue. Also beat whipping cream to soft peaks.

Fold cool lime mixture gently into soft meringue. Then lightly fold in whipped cream. Pile mixture into prepared souffle dish and chill until set, at least 3 hours. Remove wax paper collar. Garnish sides with chopped pistachio nuts (¼ to ½ cup needed).

Makes about 8 servings

To prepare souffle dish: Place a strip of double thick (folded) wax paper around edge of 1-qt. souffle dish so wax paper collar rises about 3-in. above edge of dish. Secure wax paper with tape. This technique allows mixture to be piled into dish above the rim. When souffle is set, paper collar is easily removed and souffle appears to have "risen" above edge of dish.

Fold wax paper to double thickness and wrap around edge of 1-qt. souffle dish to extend 3-in. above dish top. Secure with tape.

Fruit-Filled Pineapple

FRUIT-FILLED PINEAPPLE

POWER LEVEL: High (10) TEMP: 120°
APPROX. MICROWAVE TIME: 10 to 12 min.
Cook Code: 100

1 medium fresh pineapple	Cut pineapple, including leafy crown, in half lengthwise. Cut out fruit, leaving outside shell intact. Remove woody core; cut remaining fruit in chunks.
1 cup (3 to 4-oz.) shredded coconut **½ cup toasted sliced almonds** **1 can (11-oz.) mandarin orange sections, drained** **½ cup maraschino cherries without stems, drained** **½ cup sweet orange marmalade**	Toss pineapple chunks with coconut, almonds, oranges, cherries and marmalade. Place pineapple shells in 13×9×2-in. dish or on serving plate suitable for microwave oven. Fill shells with fruit mixture. Insert temperature probe so tip is in center of one of pineapple halves. Cover with wax paper. Attach cable end at receptacle. **Microwave at High. Set Temp, Set 120°.**
¼ cup light rum	Measure rum into glass measure. **Microwave at High ¼ Minute.** Remove 1 metal tablespoonful. Pour rest of rum over pineapple. Ignite rum in spoon and pour over pineapple to flame.

Makes 6 servings

The Temperature Probe, dialed to 120°, will signal when the pineapple is warm enough to develop flavor and be flamed.

Custards & Puddings

Custards and puddings are a microwave specialty. Conventionally baked custard must be set in a pan of water, which provides moisture to prevent drying and browning. On the range top you must stir custard or pudding constantly to keep it free from lumps. Delicate custard microwaves smooth and creamy with a minimum of stirring and the microwave oven does not dry or brown it. The variety of custards and puddings extends from simple desserts to dramatic looking presentations.

1. Caramel Flan, right
2. Bavarian Cream, page 253
3. Cup Custard, below
4. English Trifle, page 254

BASIC CASSEROLE CUSTARD

POWER LEVEL: High (10) and Low (3)
MICROWAVE TIME: 13 to 16 min., total

3 eggs	In 1-qt. casserole beat
¼ cup sugar	eggs, sugar, vanilla and
1 teaspoon vanilla	salt with table fork, until
⅛ teaspoon salt	very well blended and sugar is dissolved.
1½ cups milk	Scald milk in glass measure. **Microwave at High 3 to 4 Minutes.** Gradually add to egg mixture, stirring well.

Cover with casserole lid. **Microwave at Low 10 to 12 Minutes,** rotating dish ¼ turn every 2 minutes. Sprinkle top with nutmeg before serving, if desired.

Makes 6 to 8 servings

Cup Custards: Prepare custard mixture as above except pour into 4 (6-oz.) custard cups. Place in circle on shelf in microwave oven. **Microwave at Low 10 to 12 Minutes,** rearranging after 3 minutes. If some custards are done before others, remove those and continue cooking until all custards are cooked.

Custard Pie Filling: Prepare custard mixture as above except pour into 10-in. pie plate. Microwave as above. When cool, loosen with thin knife from edges of pie plate and shake to completely loosen. "Slip slide" from pie plate into 9 or 10-in. baked pastry or crumb crust.

CARAMEL FLAN

POWER LEVEL: High (10) and Low (3)
MICROWAVE TIME: 20 to 24 min., total

½ cup water	In 1-pt. glass measure place
½ cup sugar	water and sugar, stirring well. **Microwave at High 10 to 12 Minutes,** until light but rich brown. (Do not let syrup get too dark before taking from oven; it continues to cook after it has been microwaved.) Pour ¾ of caramel syrup into 1-qt. casserole and quickly rotate casserole to coat bottom and about half way up sides with caramel. Let cool to harden before adding custard. Drizzle remaining ¼ of syrup in fine ribbons onto ungreased cookie sheet to harden.
1 recipe Basic	Prepare custard in small
Casserole Custard	mixing bowl. Pour or strain mixture into caramel lined casserole. Cover with casserole lid.

Microwave at Low 10 to 12 Minutes, rotating dish ¼ turn every 2 minutes, until set. Chill thoroughly. Unmold onto serving plate which has shallow rim. Crush the syrup which has hardened into a brittle and sprinkle in a wreath shape over top of flan.

NOTE: Covering with casserole lid is important for success.

Makes 4 to 6 servings

Dramatic Caramel Flan is Basic Custard strained into a caramel-lined casserole. After microwaving, garnish it with crushed caramel brittle, on the right.

FLOATING ISLANDS

POWER LEVEL: High (10), Med. High (7) and Med. (5)
MICROWAVE TIME: 12 to 17 min., total

⅓ cup sugar . . . . 3 tablespoons cornstarch ¼ teaspoon salt 2¾ cups milk 2 drops yellow food coloring (optional)	In 2-qt. casserole blend together sugar, cornstarch and salt until well mixed. Add milk and food coloring, stirring until well blended. **Microwave at High 8 to 10 Minutes,** stirring every 3 minutes until smooth and slightly thickened.
2 egg yolks, well beaten	Stir a small amount of hot pudding quickly into yolks. Return egg mixture to hot pudding, mixing well. **Microwave at Medium High 2 to 4 Minutes,** stirring after 1 minute, until slightly thickened.
2 egg whites . . . . ¼ cup sugar	Beat egg whites until foamy, on high speed of mixer.

Gradually add sugar, beating to a stiff glossy meringue. Drop immediately in 8 to 10 mounds over hot pudding. **Microwave at Medium 2 to 3 Minutes** to set meringues slightly. Chill before serving.

Makes 6 to 8 servings

WAYS TO MICROWAVE INDIVIDUAL MERINGUES

On Pudding: The traditional way to serve Floating Islands is to drop mounds of meringue over hot pudding. **Microwave at Medium 2 to 3 Minutes.** Serve with small, crisp cookies, if desired.

VANILLA PUDDING

POWER LEVEL: High (10) and Medium High (7)
MICROWAVE TIME: 6 to 10 min., total

¾ cup sugar . . . . 2 tablespoons cornstarch ¼ teaspoon salt 2 cups milk	In 1½-qt. casserole blend together sugar, cornstarch and salt. Gradually stir in milk, mixing well. **Microwave at High 5 to 7 Minutes,** stirring every 3 minutes until mixture is smooth, thickened and clear.
2 egg yolks, slightly beaten, or 1 egg, well beaten	Stir a small amount of hot pudding quickly into egg yolks. Return egg mixture to hot pudding, mixing well. **Microwave at Medium High 1 to 3 Minutes,** stirring after 1 minute, until smooth and thickened.
2 tablespoons butter . . . . 1 teaspoon vanilla extract	Add butter and vanilla. Stir until butter is melted. Pour into serving dishes.

Makes 4 servings

CHOCOLATE PUDDING

Increase sugar to 1 cup. Add 2 squares (1-oz. each) unsweetened chocolate along with milk.

BUTTERSCOTCH PUDDING

Use brown sugar and increase butter to 3 tablespoons.

CREAMY RICE PUDDING

Prepare Vanilla Pudding except increase milk to 2½ cups. Into warm pudding, stir 2 cups cooked rice.

On Brown Paper: For best shape cook pudding for maximum time and microwave meringues separately. Place sheet of brown wrapping paper on a flat cookie sheet and drop 6 to 8 mounds of meringue in a circle on paper. Slide paper from cookie sheet into oven. **Microwave at Medium 2 to 3 Minutes.** Slide back onto cookie sheet and remove from oven to cool.

BASIC BREAD PUDDING

POWER LEVEL: High (10) and Medium High (7)
MICROWAVE TIME: 13 to 16 min., total

4 cups bread cubes lightly packed into cup (4 to 5 slices) **½ cup brown sugar (packed)** **¼ teaspoon salt** **½ cup raisins (optional)**	Spread bread cubes evenly in 8-in. round dish. Sprinkle evenly with brown sugar, salt, then raisins.
2 cups milk **¼ cup butter** **2 eggs**	Measure milk into 1-qt. measuring cup. Add butter. **Microwave at High 4 Minutes,** until butter is melted and milk is warm. Rapidly stir in eggs with a fork and mix well. Pour over bread cubes in dish.

Microwave at Medium High 9 to 12 Minutes, rotating dish ¼ turn after 6 minutes. When cooked, center may still be slightly soft but it will set up as pudding cools. Serve warm or chilled.

Makes about 6 servings

Bread Pudding when fully cooked may still be moist and slightly soft in the center. It will firm up as it cools.

BAVARIAN CREAM

This is basic custard sauce to which gelatin is added so it can be molded. It is lightened with meringue and whipped cream.

POWER LEVEL: High (10) and Medium High (7)
MICROWAVE TIME: 10 to 14 min., total

⅓ cup sugar **3 tablespoons cornstarch** **2 tablespoons unflavored gelatin** **¼ teaspoon salt** **2¾ cups milk**	In 2-qt. casserole blend together sugar, cornstarch, gelatin and salt, until well mixed. Gradually add milk, stirring until well blended. **Microwave at High 8 to 10 Minutes,** stirring every 3 minutes, until smooth and slightly thickened.
2 egg yolks, well beaten **1 teaspoon vanilla extract**	Stir a small amount of hot pudding quickly into egg yolks. Return egg mixture to hot pudding, mixing well. **Microwave at Medium High 2 to 4 Minutes,** stirring after 1 minute. Cool in refrigerator until mixture mounds slightly, about 1½ hours. Stir in vanilla.
2 egg whites **¼ cup sugar** **1 cup whipping cream, whipped**	When gelatin mixture has cooled, beat egg whites until foamy.

Gradually add sugar, beating to a soft meringue. Fold cooled gelatin mixture into meringue; fold in whipped cream. Pile mixture into 4½ to 5-cup mold. Chill until set. Unmold and serve with fruit garnish.

Makes 6 to 8 servings

NESSELRODE BAVARIAN

Definitely a holiday dessert.

1 recipe Bavarian Cream (above) **1 jar (10-oz.) nesselrode fruit mixture**	Into 2-qt. fluted mold, distribute about ¼ of Bavarian cream, ⅓ of nesselrode, ¼ of cream, ⅓ of nesselrode, ¼ of cream, last of nesselrode and last ¼ of cream on top.

(Layering technique best distributes fruit and cream.) Chill until set. Unmold onto plate which has a fairly high rim (about 1-in.). Some of nesselrode syrup will separate from bavarian upon unmolding and high rim is needed to contain syrup. Spoon syrup over Nesselrode Bavarian as it is served.

Makes about 8 servings

A 1-qt. glass measure is an easy mixing bowl for microwaving puddings and other foods you boil. Handle stays cool during short microwaving time.

PUDDING TRIFLE

POWER LEVEL: High (10) and Medium High (7)
MICROWAVE TIME: 9 to 13 min., total

1 pkg. (3¾-oz.) vanilla pudding mix, not instant **2½ cups milk**	In 1½-qt. casserole place pudding. Gradually add milk, stirring to blend well. **Microwave at High 6 to 8 Minutes,** stirring every 3 minutes, until thickened.
2 egg yolks, beaten	Gradually stir half of pudding into beaten yolks. Return egg mixture to casserole, stirring well. **Microwave at Medium High 3 to 5 Minutes** more, stirring after 2 minutes, until thickened. Cool.
1 (8-in.) microwaved yellow or white cake layer **½ cup cherry preserves** **¼ to ½ cup sherry, rum or pineapple juice**	Split cake layer and fill with preserves. Cut into pieces and arrange half in 2-qt. casserole. Sprinkle with half of sherry and cover with half of cooled pudding. Repeat.
1 cup whipping cream **3 tablespoons confectioners sugar**	Whip cream with confectioners sugar until soft peaks form. Spread over pudding. Chill 4 hours or more before serving.

Makes 8 to 12 servings

BLACK FOREST TRIFLE

Make Pudding Trifle, above, except substitute chocolate pudding mix for vanilla and chocolate cake layer for yellow or white. Instead of cherry preserves, fill the split cake layer with 1 can (22-oz.) cherry pie filling.

Arrange filled cake in 12×8×2-in. dish and sprinkle with ½ cup rum or brandy. Pour cooled chocolate pudding over all. Top with sweetened whipped cream as in above recipe and garnish with maraschino cherries, if desired.

COOKING COMMERCIAL DRY PUDDING MIX

Since there is less evaporation in microwaving, microwaved pudding is often creamier in texture, lighter in color and greater in volume than it is conventionally.

POWER LEVEL: High (10)   **Cook Code:** 60
MICROWAVE TIME: 6 to 8 min., total

1 pkg. (3¾-oz.) pudding or pie filling mix **½ cup milk**	Empty pudding mix into 1-qt. glass measure. Add ½ cup milk and stir until all mix is moistened and blended.
1½ cups milk	Add 1½ cups more milk and blend well.

Microwave at High 6 to 8 Minutes, stirring thoroughly every 3 minutes. Pour into 4 or 5 serving dishes. Cover top of pudding with wax paper or plastic wrap to prevent "skin" from forming on top, if desired. Serve cool.

Makes 4 to 5 servings

ENGLISH TRIFLE

POWER LEVEL: High (10) and Medium High (7)
MICROWAVE TIME: 11 to 12 min., total

½ cup sugar **½ teaspoon salt** **2 tablespoons cornstarch** **2½ cups milk**	In 1½-qt. casserole mix together sugar, salt and cornstarch. Gradually stir in milk. **Microwave at High 7 Minutes,** stirring every 3 minutes, until slightly thickened.
4 egg yolks, beaten **2 teaspoons vanilla extract**	Stir in a little over half thickened mixture into beaten egg yolks. Return mixture to casserole blending well. **Microwave at Medium High 4 to 5 Minutes** more, stirring after 2 minutes. Cool; then stir in vanilla.
1 (8-in.) microwaved yellow or white cake layer **½ cup raspberry preserves** **¼ to ½ cup sherry**	Split cake and fill with preserves. Cut preserve-filled cake into 12 pieces and place half in 2 to 3-qt. serving dish. Sprinkle with half of sherry and cover with half of custard. Repeat.
1 cup whipping cream **3 tablespoons confectioners sugar** **¼ cup toasted, sliced almonds**	Whip cream with confectioners sugar until peaks form. Spread over custard. Sprinkle with almonds. Chill 4 hours or more before serving.

Makes 9 to 12 servings

Pies

Because microwaved pie shells set and cook rapidly, plain pastry does not brown. Flavored pastry and toppings brushed on before baking have appealing color.

Trivet or inverted plate or glass dish, placed under pie shell helps it microwave evenly.

Check For Doneness on the bottom of the crust, which is critical. It should look opaque and dry. Top will be dry and blistered. A clear glass utensil is best because you can see the bottom.

BASIC PASTRY SHELL

POWER LEVEL: High (10)   **Cook Code:** 50
MICROWAVE TIME: 5 to 6 min., total

1 cup unsifted . . . . **all-purpose flour** **1 teaspoon salt** **6 tablespoons** **shortening***	In small bowl place flour and salt. With pastry blender cut in shortening, until mixture resembles the size of small peas.
2 tablespoons ice water . . .	Sprinkle water over flour-shortening mixture. Stir with fork to form ball.

Roll out on floured pastry cloth with rolling pin to ⅛-in. thickness. Let stand a few minutes before shaping. Use to line 9-in. pie plate shaping pastry to the edge of pie plate. Prick pastry with fork. Place on microwave trivet or on inverted plate or glass dish. **Microwave at High 5 to 6 Minutes,** rotating dish ½ turn after 3 minutes. Pastry is done when it looks dry and blistered and is not doughy.

Makes 1 (9-in.) pastry shell

*If desired, 3 tablespoons cold butter and 3 tablespoons shortening may be used for color and more flavor.

CHOCOLATE PASTRY SHELL

To flour add only ½ teaspoon salt along with 2 tablespoons cocoa and ⅓ cup sugar.

Plain microwaved pastry looks different from conventionally baked. From top to bottom: Conventional, Microwaved, Molasses, Maple Syrup, Chocolate Pastry, Dark Corn Syrup, Vanilla, Egg Yolk Toppings.

Crumb Crusts are perfect pie partners. Their crunchy texture complements light and airy or smooth and creamy fillings. They are also faster to make than pastry crusts. Reserve 2 tablespoons crumbs to garnish top of pie, if desired. For easy removal, set pie plate on towel dampened with hot water for a few minutes. Vary the character of pies by using different crumbs. To make 1¼ cups of fine crumbs, use 15 to 18 squares of graham crackers, 18 to 22 medium gingersnaps, 18 to 20 chocolate (not cream filled) wafers, 30 to 36 vanilla wafers. When using pecan sandies 1½ to 1¾ cups crumbs are needed, about 18 to 20 cookies.

TOASTED COCONUT PIE SHELL

This shell is good for ice cream pies. Make 8-in. pie shell. Fill with 1-qt. favorite ice cream. Freeze. Drizzle top with sundae sauce, garnish with coconut, nuts or fruit.

POWER LEVEL: High (10)
MICROWAVE TIME: 6½ to 7½ min., total

3 tablespoons butter	In 8 or 9-in. pie plate place
1 can (3½-oz.) flaked coconut	butter. **Microwave at High ½ Minute,** until melted. Add coconut.

Microwave at High 6 to 7 Minutes, stir every 2 minutes, then every minute after 4 minutes, until coconut is evenly browned. Spread in pie plate. Cool before filling.

Makes 1 (8 or 9-in.) pie shell

NUT CRUNCH PASTRY SHELL

POWER LEVEL: High (10)
MICROWAVE TIME: 6 to 8 min., total

1 cup flour	In small mixing bowl place
½ cup light brown sugar (packed)	flour and brown sugar. With pastry blender, cut in
½ cup butter	butter until mixture is crumbly. Mix in nuts.
1 cup finely chopped pecans or walnuts	

Place mixture loosely in 9-in. pie plate. **Microwave at High 4 to 5 Minutes,** stirring every 1 or 2 minutes. Stir after cooking; if desired, reserve 2 tablespoons mixture to garnish top. Press remainder of hot crumbs into pie plate. **Microwave at High 2 to 3 Minutes,** until set, rotating dish ¼ turn every minute. Cool before filling.

Makes 1 (9-in.) shell

Remove crumb crust easily from pie plate by placing the plate on a warm, damp towel for a few minutes.

CRUMB PIE SHELL

A pretty scalloped pie shell, such as the one used in the Grasshopper Pie, page 260, can easily be made by lining the bottom of a pie plate with ½ of this recipe, then standing small whole cookies around the sides of plate.

POWER LEVEL: High (10)
MICROWAVE TIME: 2½ to 3 min., total

¼ cup butter . . . . .In 9-in. pie plate place butter. **Microwave at High ½**
1¼ cups fine cookie **Minute,** until melted. Blend
crumbs (vanilla in crumbs and sugar. If de-
wafer, graham sired, reserve 2 table-
cracker, chocolate spoons crumb mixture for
wafer, gingersnaps, garnish. Press firmly and
etc.) evenly into 9-in. pie plate.
2 tablespoons sugar **Microwave at High 2 to**
2½ Minutes, rotating dish
½ turn after 1 minute.

Makes 1 (9-in.) crumb shell

FROZEN CHOCOLATE ALMOND PIE

This pie cuts well straight from the freezer. No thawing is necessary. Use a wet knife for sharpest cut.

POWER LEVEL: High (10)   **Cook Code:** 30
MICROWAVE TIME: 3 to 4 min., total

1 Crumb Pie Shell . . . . . . .Microwave pie shell. Cool.
made with vanilla
wafers, above
or Chocolate Pastry
Crust, page 255

4 milk chocolate candy . . . .In 2-qt. casserole place
bars with almonds candy, marshmallows and
(1.15-oz. each) milk. **Microwave at High 3**
½ of 10-oz. pkg. large **to 4 Minutes,** stirring after
marshmallows 2 minutes, until mixture
(about 20) can be stirred smooth.
½ cup milk Chill in refrigerator about
30 to 40 minutes, or in pan
of ice water until thickened,
stirring occasionally.

1 cup whipping cream, ...Fold whipped cream into
whipped cooled chocolate mixture.
Pile into pie shell and
freeze until firm.

To serve, garnish pie wedges with whipped cream, chocolate curls and/or additional almonds, if desired.

Makes 1 (9-in.) pie

ROCKY ROAD CHOCOLATE ALMOND PIE

Microwave chocolate and milk, then stir in 2 cups miniature marshmallows. Stir well, but do not melt marshmallows.

Rocky Road Chocolate Almond Pie

FRUIT PARFAIT PIE

See suggestions below for a variety of flavors.

POWER LEVEL: High (10)
MICROWAVE TIME: 4 to 6 min.

1 Crumb Pie Shell, ...Drain syrup from fruit into
above, cooled 1-qt. measuring cup; add
1 can (1-lb., 4-oz.) water to make 1½ cups
crushed or small total liquid. Cover measur-
pieces of fruit ing cup with wax paper.
Microwave at High 4 to 6
Minutes, until boiling.

1 pkg. (3-oz.) fruit . . . . .To boiling liquid, add gela-
flavored gelatin tin. Stir until dissolved. Stir
1 pt. vanilla ice cream in ice cream by spoonfuls.

Chill 20 to 30 minutes, until thickened but not set. Fold in the reserved fruit and pour into crust. Chill at least 1 hour.

Makes 1 (9-in.) pie

Suggested Flavor Combinations: Crushed pineapple, pineapple or lime gelatin in Nut Crunch Pastry Shell, page 256; peach slices, peach or raspberry gelatin in Graham Cracker Crumb Shell, above; mandarin orange sections, orange or lemon gelatin in Toasted Coconut Shell, page 256; fruit cocktail, cherry or lemon gelatin in Gingersnap Crumb Shell, above.

Pecan Pie

PECAN PIE

Traditional pecan pie microwaves in about a third of the time required to cook it conventionally. Ingredients give pie a rich, golden-brown color.

POWER LEVEL: High (10) and Medium High (7)
MICROWAVE TIME: 13½ to 19 min., total

1 Basic Pastry Shell, ... **page 255** **1 egg yolk** **1 tablespoon dark corn syrup**	Roll out pastry and fit into 9-in. pie plate. Brush inside of shell with mixture of egg yolk and corn syrup. Prick pastry. **Microwave at High 5 to 6 Minutes,** rotating dish ½ turn after 3 minutes.
¼ cup butter	In large glass mixing bowl place butter. **Microwave at High ½ to 1 Minute,** until melted.
3 whole eggs, plus . . . . . . **extra egg white** **1 cup dark corn syrup** **⅓ cup brown sugar (packed)** **1 tablespoon flour** **1 teaspoon vanilla** **1½ cups pecan halves**	Add eggs to melted butter. Beat with fork to mix eggs well. Blend in syrup, sugar, flour and vanilla. Then, mix in pecan halves. Pour into crust. **Microwave at Medium High 8 to 12 Minutes,** rotating ¼ turn every 3 minutes. When done, top surface is dry and puffed and filling is set.

Makes 1 (9-in.) pie

Maple Nut Pie: Use pure maple syrup in place of dark corn syrup and walnuts instead of pecans.

MICROLESSON: HOW TO MICROWAVE PECAN PIE

Brush pie shell with egg yolk-corn syrup mixture. Prick pastry.

Microwave at High 5 to 6 minutes before filling pie shell. Rotate ½ turn after 3 minutes.

Fill shell and **Microwave at Medium High 8 to 12 Minutes,** rotating ¼ turn every 3 minutes.

BASIC VANILLA CREAM PIE

For a richer filling, increase sugar to ¾ cup and butter to 2 tablespoons. Substitute half and half (half milk half cream) for milk.

POWER LEVEL: High (10)
MICROWAVE TIME: 9 to 11 min.

⅔ cup sugar **3 tablespoons cornstarch** **¼ teaspoon salt** **2 cups milk**	In large glass mixing bowl or 1½-qt. casserole, stir together sugar, cornstarch and salt to blend well. Add small amount of milk to make smooth thin paste, then gradually add rest of milk and stir smooth. **Microwave at High 8 to 9 Minutes,** stirring every 2 minutes, until smooth and thickened.
3 egg yolks, slightly beaten	Stir half of hot milk mixture into egg yolks, then add yolk mixture back to milk in dish. **Microwave at High 1 to 2 Minutes,** until mixture is thick and glossy.
1 tablespoon butter **1 teaspoon vanilla** **1 microwaved pastry shell, page 255**	Stir in butter and vanilla. Pour mixture into cooled pastry shell. Finish with Meringue (see Lemon Meringue Pie recipe below), or, if desired, chill pie and top with whipped cream.

Coconut Cream Pie: Before making basic filling, place 1 cup flaked coconut in 9-in. glass pie plate. **Microwave at High 5 to 7 Minutes,** stirring every ¾ to 1 minute, until lightly toasted. Reserve about 2 tablespoons toasted coconut for decorating top of pie, add remainder to basic filling at the same time butter is added.

Makes 1 (9-in.) pie

TIPS FOR MAKING MERINGUE

Meringue will set in a microwave oven but top will not brown. Meringue sets best when spread over hot filling. Beat meringue during the last few minutes while the filling cooks.

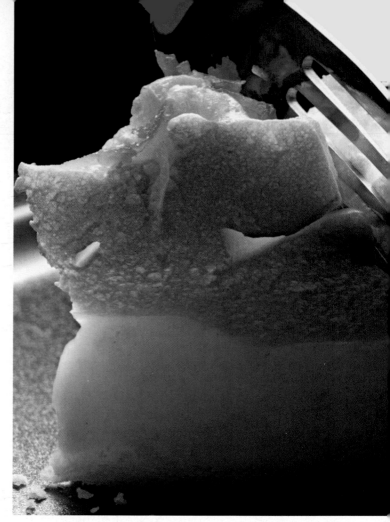

Lemon Meringue Pie

LEMON MERINGUE PIE

POWER LEVEL: High (10), Med. High (7) and Med. (5)
MICROWAVE TIME: 13 to 18 min., total

1 cup sugar **⅓ cup cornstarch** **⅛ teaspoon salt** **2 cups cold water** **1 to 2 drops yellow food color**	In 2-qt. casserole mix together sugar, cornstarch and salt. Blend in water and food color; stir smooth. **Microwave at High 6 to 8 Minutes,** stirring after 3 minutes, until slightly thickened.
3 egg yolks	In medium bowl beat yolks well. Add hot sauce; mix well. **Microwave at Medium High 4 to 6 Minutes,** stirring after 2 minutes, until thick.
3 tablespoons butter **¼ cup fresh lemon juice** **2 teaspoons grated lemon rind** **1 microwaved pastry shell, page 255**	Stir butter, juice and rind into mixture. Pour into pastry. Finish with meringue or, if desired, cool and decorate pie with whipped cream.

Meringue: Beat 3 egg whites with ½ teaspoon cream of tartar until stiff peaks form. Gradually beat in 6 tablespoons sugar to make glossy meringue. Spread over pie. **Microwave at Medium 3 to 4 Minutes,** until meringue is set (top won't brown).

Makes 1 (9-in.) pie

HOW TO MICROWAVE MARSHMALLOW PIE FILLING

Combine milk or other liquid with marshmallows. **Microwave at High 2 to 3 minutes.**

Air heats and expands inside marshmallows, causing them to puff up before they melt.

Stir mixture until smooth. Chill until cool and thickened before adding flavoring and whipped cream.

FLUFFY MARSHMALLOW PIES

POWER LEVEL: High (10)   **Cook Code:** 20
MICROWAVE TIME: 2 to 4 min., total

Crumb Pie Shell, ... **page 257**	Microwave Crumb Pie Shell using the flavor of cookie that best complements filling. Cool.
1 pkg. (10-oz.) large . . . . . **marshmallows** **½ cup milk**	In 3-qt. casserole place marshmallows and milk. Cover. **Microwave at High 2 to 4 Minutes,** until mixture can be stirred smooth. Chill in refrigerator (about 30 to 40 minutes) or in pan of ice water, until thickened, stirring occasionally.
1 cup whipping cream, . . . **whipped** **Special pie ingredient (see right)**	Fold in whipped cream and special pie ingredient. Pour into crust and decorate with reserved crumbs or additional whipped cream, if desired. Refrigerate several hours or overnight.

Makes 1 (9-in.) pie

FRUIT PIE VARIATIONS:

PEACH OR BERRY PIE

Fold in 1¾ to 2 cups peeled and sliced fresh peaches, sliced fresh strawberries or fresh whole raspberries.

LIQUEUR PIE VARIATIONS:

These pies are soft and creamy when served from refrigerator; for firm pieces which hold sharp cut, serve frozen. Frozen pie releases easily from bottom of pie plate if set a few minutes on towel dampened with hot water.

GRASSHOPPER PIE

Into cooled marshmallow mixture, stir ¼ cup green creme de menthe and 2 tablespoons white creme de cocoa. Garnish with mounds of additional whipped cream and chocolate curls.

BRANDY ALEXANDER PIE

Into cooled marshmallow mixture, stir ¼ cup dark creme de cocoa and 2 tablespoons brandy.

KAHLUA PIE

Add 1 teaspoon instant coffee powder to marshmallows and milk. Into cooled marshmallow mixture, stir ½ cup kahlua liqueur.

Grasshopper Pie

AMBROSIA PIE

POWER LEVEL: High (10)
MICROWAVE TIME: 4½ to 5 min., total

1 envelope (1-oz.) **unflavored gelatin** **⅔ cup sugar** **⅛ teaspoon salt** **½ cup water**	.In 2-qt. casserole, stir together gelatin, sugar, salt and water. **Microwave at High 2½ to 3 Minutes,** until gelatin is melted and sugar is dissolved.
1 can (6-oz.) frozen **orange juice** **concentrate**	.Into hot mixture, stir frozen concentrate until melted and blended in. Chill until cool and thickened but not set.
1 pkg. (9-oz.) **commercially frozen** **whipped topping** **1 Toasted Coconut Pie** **Shell, page 256** **microwaved in 9-in.** **pie plate**	.Place topping container on microwave oven shelf. **Microwave at Defrost 2 Minutes,** turning over after 1 minute. Fold defrosted whipped topping into cooled orange mixture. Pile lightly into Coconut Pie Shell. Chill until firm.

If desired, decorate with fresh strawberry slices.

Makes 1 (9-in.) pie

APPLE GRAHAM PIE

POWER LEVEL: High (10)   TEMP: 200°
APPROX. MICROWAVE TIME: 8 to 10 min.

½ cup (¼-lb.) butter **¼ cup sugar** **2 cups graham cracker** **crumbs**	.In large glass mixing bowl place butter. **Microwave at High 1 Minute,** until melted. Add sugar and crumbs. Mix well. Press half of mixture firmly and evenly into 9-in. pie plate.
5 cups thinly sliced **apples (4 to 6** **medium)** **½ cup sugar** **1 teaspoon cinnamon**	.In large mixing bowl place apple slices; they should be ⅛ to ¼-in. thick. Add sugar and cinnamon, mixing well. Mound and press down into crumb crust.

Cover apples with remaining crumbs to make top crust. Press crumbs down firmly, especially at edges, to prevent boilover.

Insert temperature probe so tip is in center of pie. Cover with wax paper. Attach cable end at receptacle. **Microwave at High. Set Temp, Set 200°.** When oven signals, remove pie and let stand 10 minutes covered with wax paper. Remove wax paper so crumb topping is allowed to dry and crisp. Serve warm or cold.

Makes 1 (9-in.) pie

BRANDIED CRANBERRY PIE

POWER LEVEL: High (10)   **Cook Code:** 140
MICROWAVE TIME: 14 to 16 min., total

2 cups prepared . . . . **graham cracker crumbs** **¼ cup sugar** **½ cup butter, melted**	.In small bowl mix together crumbs, sugar and butter. Pat half of mixture firmly into 9-in. pie plate.
1 can (16-oz.) whole . . . . **cranberry sauce** **1¼ cups prepared mincemeat** **1 cup coarsely chopped pecans** **2 tablespoons sugar** **2 tablespoons butter, melted** **¼ cup brandy** **2 tablespoons cornstarch**	.In mixing bowl stir together cranberry sauce, mincemeat, pecans, sugar, butter, brandy and cornstarch. Spread mixture over crust. Pat remaining crumbs firmly in wreath around outside edge of pie forming a firm unbroken crust about 2-in. wide. (Center of pie remains open for attractive finished appearance.)

Cover with wax paper. **Microwave at High 14 to 16 Minutes,** rotating dish ¼ turn after 7 minutes. Remove pie and let stand 10 minutes, covered with wax paper. Then remove wax paper so crumb topping is allowed to dry and crisp. Serve warm or cold.

TO FLAME PIE: Measure ¼ cup brandy into glass measuring cup. **Microwave at High ¼ Minute.** Remove 1 metal tablespoonful and pour the rest over the pie. Using lighter or long match, warm and ignite brandy in tablespoon. Pour over pie to ignite brandy on top of pie.

DEFROSTING FROZEN PRE-BAKED PIES

Remove whole pie from foil pan to an 8 or 9-in. glass pie plate. Or cut in wedges and place on serving plates.

POWER LEVEL: **Defrost**

TYPE	TIME MINUTES	COMMENTS
Fruit or Nut Pie whole (8-in.)	7 to 9	Rotate ½ turn after 4 minutes. Let stand a few minutes before serving.
Fruit or Nut Pie wedge (1 or 2 slices)	1 to 3	
Cream or Custard Pie whole (14-oz.)	3 to 4	Rotate ½ turn after 1½ minutes.
Cream or Custard Pie whole (26-oz.)	4 to 5	Rotate ½ turn after 4 minutes. Let stand a few minutes before serving.
Cream or Custard Pie wedge (1 to 3 slices)	½ to 1	

PUMPKIN PIE

POWER LEVEL: High (10) and Medium High (7)
MICROWAVE TIME: 23 to 27 min., total

½ cup (¼-lb.) butter	.In 10-in. pie plate place butter. **Microwave at High 1 Minute,** until melted.
2 cups vanilla wafer crumbs **2 tablespoons sugar**	.Add crumbs and sugar; mix well. Firmly press on bottom and up sides of dish. **Microwave at High 2 Minutes,** rotating dish ½ turn after 1 minute.
1 can (16-oz.) mashed . . . . **pumpkin** **1 cup brown sugar (packed)** **1 tablespoon pumpkin pie spice** **1 tablespoon flour** **½ teaspoon salt** **1 can (13-oz.) evaporated milk** **2 eggs, beaten**	.In 2-qt. casserole blend together pumpkin, brown sugar, pumpkin pie spice, flour, salt, evaporated milk and eggs. **Microwave at Medium High 12 to 14 Minutes,** stirring every 5 minutes, until hot and thickened.

Pour hot pumpkin custard filling into prepared pie shell. **Microwave at Medium High 8 to 10 Minutes,** rotating dish ½ turn after 4 minutes. The pie is done when the edges are set and the center is still slightly soft (very much like a conventionally baked pie). Let stand at room temperature about 15 to 20 minutes to set and cool before serving.

Makes 1 (10-in.) pie

2 PUMPKIN PIES: Prepare crust in 2 (8-in.) pie plates. Divide hot filling between pie shells. Microwave 1 pie at a time. **Microwave at Medium High 6 to 8 Minutes,** rotating dish ½ turn after 3 minutes.

HEATING FRUIT AND NUT PIES FROM THE REFRIGERATOR

Defrosted fruit and nut pies may be heated with the temperature probe set at 120°. For a single slice, set High Power. For a whole pie (in glass pie plate), set Medium High Power.

Time per slice is about ½ to 1 minute. For whole pie, allow about 2 minutes. Let stand a few minutes before serving.

Soften hard ice cream by microwaving at Medium or Low about ¼ minute. It's easier to scoop into servings or over pie.

Chocolate Chip Bars

Cookies

Brownies and bar cookies exemplify the best of micro-waved baking. Their taste, texture and appearance compare favorably with conventional baking and they can be ready to serve in 6 to 10 minutes. We don't recommend drop cookies for microwaving because the oven will not accommodate large batches. Instead, we've adapted some popular bar cookies for microwaving.

Small cookie has brown spots inside because cooking begins below the surface. Large cookie microwaves more evenly. Cookies are done when they are just set.

CHOCOLATE CHIP BARS

POWER LEVEL: High (10)	**Cook Code:** 50
MICROWAVE TIME: 5 to 7 min., total	

½ **cup butter, softened** . . .In small mixer bowl cream
¾ **cup brown sugar** together butter and sugar,
   (packed) until fluffy. Add egg, milk
 1 egg and vanilla. Mix well.
 1 tablespoon milk
 1 teaspoon vanilla
   extract

1¼ **cups unsifted** . . . . .Stir together flour, baking
   all-purpose flour powder and salt. Add to
½ **teaspoon baking** creamed mixture. Blend
   powder well. Stir in ½ cup choco-
⅛ **teaspoon salt** late pieces and nuts.
 1 cup (6-oz.) Spread in paper towel-
   semi-sweet lined 8-in. square dish.
   chocolate pieces, Sprinkle with remaining ½
   divided cup chocolate pieces. **Mi-**
½ **cup chopped nuts** **crowave at High 5 to 7**
   (optional) **Minutes,** rotating dish ¼
turn every 2 minutes, until
done. Cool and cut into
bars.

Makes about 24 bars

See MICROLESSON for Chocolate Chip Bars on the following pages.

MICROLESSON: HOW TO MICROWAVE CHOCOLATE CHIP BARS

Line 8-in. square baking dish with paper towel, if desired. Bars will be easier to remove from pan.

Drop dough in four equal mounds in dish. Spread evenly. Top with remaining chocolate pieces.

Microwave at High 5 to 7 Minutes, rotating dish ¼ turn every 2 minutes.

TOASTED OAT SHORTBREAD

The microwave-toasted oats and coconut provide both brown color and tasty flavor.

POWER LEVEL: High (10)
MICROWAVE TIME: 10 to 12 min., total

½ cup flaked coconut **1 cup uncooked quick-cooking oats**	In 9-in. glass pie plate, place coconut. **Microwave at High 4 Minutes,** stirring after each minute. Add oats and **Microwave at High 2 Minutes** more, stirring every ½ minute.*
½ cup butter, softened **¼ cup dark brown sugar** **¼ teaspoon salt** **1 egg** **¼ cup chopped nuts**	In large mixing bowl, cream together butter and sugar. Add salt, egg, nuts and toasted coconut and oats mixture. Beat until well blended.
½ teaspoon baking powder **1½ teaspoons vanilla extract** **1 cup unsifted all-purpose flour**	To beaten mixture add baking powder, vanilla and flour. Blend until smooth. With hands pat mixture into greased 8-in. square dish.

Before microwaving, cut dough into 1½-in. squares. **Microwave at High 4 to 6 Minutes,** rotating dish ¼ turn every minute. Remove from oven and cut warm cookies into squares, following original cutting lines.

Makes about 16 cookies

*NOTE: Frequent stirring is important for even toasting.

RASPBERRY TART SQUARES

POWER LEVEL: High (10)
MICROWAVE TIME: 8 to 10½ min., total

¾ cup butter **1 cup brown sugar** **1½ cups unsifted all-purpose flour** **1 teaspoon baking powder** **½ teaspoon salt** **1½ cups quick-cooking oatmeal** **1 cup finely chopped pecans**	In 8-in. square dish, place butter. **Microwave at High 1 to 1½ Minutes,** until melted. Stir in brown sugar, flour, baking powder, salt, oatmeal and pecans; blend well. Remove half of crumb mixture to bowl or wax paper. Pat remaining crumbs evenly over bottom of dish.
1 jar (12-oz.) raspberry jam	Cover patted-out crumbs with raspberry jam and sprinkle with remaining crumbs over top.

Microwave at High 7 to 9 Minutes, rotating dish ¼ turn after 4 minutes.

Makes about 30 squares

HOW TO MICROWAVE COOKIE MIXES

Select 12-oz. to 16-oz. packets of cookie mix. Prepare mix as directed on package except be sure liquid totals 2 tablespoons. (You may have to increase water measurement called for on the package.) Spread batter in lightly greased 8-in. square dish. **Microwave at High 7 to 9 Minutes,** rotating dish ¼ turn every 2 minutes. Do not overcook; when done, top surface will appear somewhat dry. Cool 5 to 10 minutes before cutting.

Makes about 16 squares

Place baking dish directly on counter top to cool.

Invert dish onto cutting board to remove bars.

Peel off paper towel and cut in bars or squares.

DATE-NUT BARS

A tasty variation is to stir about ½ cup cut-up orange slice candies or candied cherries into the date mixture before cooking.

POWER LEVEL: HIGH (10)
MICROWAVE TIME: 10½ to 13 min.

½ lb. (8-oz.) pitted dates, cut up **¼ cup sugar** **½ cup water**	.In 1-qt. glass measuring cup or mixing bowl, place dates, sugar and water. **Microwave at High 2 to 3 minutes,** until well blended and thick.
½ cup butter **1 cup brown sugar (packed)** **2 eggs** **1¾ cups unsifted all-purpose flour** **1 teaspoon baking soda** **¼ teaspoon salt** **1 teaspoon vanilla** **1 cup chopped pecans**	.In large glass mixing bowl, place butter. **Microwave at High ½ to 1 minute,** just until softened. Beat in sugar and eggs well, then add flour, soda, salt and vanilla. Mix well, then stir in nuts.

In 8-in. square dish, spread half of brown sugar batter. Cover evenly with date mixture then drop remaining batter over date layer in mounds. Carefully spread to smooth top. **Microwave at High 8 to 9 minutes,** rotating ¼ turn every 2 minutes until firm, and center will spring back when lightly pressed. Place directly on heat-proof counter or board to cool 15 to 20 minutes before cutting.

Makes about 20 bars

MOLASSES SPICE BARS

Sprinkle top with powdered sugar for an attractive finish.

POWER LEVEL: High (10)
MICROWAVE TIME: 8 to 10 min., total

2 eggs **1 cup sugar** **½ teaspoon salt** **1 teaspoon vanilla**	.In small bowl at medium speed on mixer, beat together eggs, sugar, salt and vanilla, about 1 minute until light.
½ cup (¼-lb.) butter, melted **¼ cup dark molasses**	.Add butter and molasses. Continue beating until thoroughly blended.
1¼ cups flour **1 teaspoon cinnamon** **½ teaspoon allspice** **1 tablespoon cocoa**	.Mix in flour, cocoa and spices at low speed.
1 cup chopped nuts	.Stir in ½ cup nuts. Spread evenly in greased 8-in. square dish. Sprinkle remaining nuts on top.

Microwave at High 8 to 10 Minutes, rotating dish ¼ turn every 2 minutes.

Makes about 20 bars

VARIATION:

Honey Spice Bars: Substitute honey for molasses. Increase cinnamon to 2 teaspoons if desired.

BASIC BROWNIES

POWER LEVEL: High (10)   **Cook Code:** 60
MICROWAVE TIME: 6 to 8 min., total

2 eggs . . . . **1 cup sugar** **½ teaspoon salt** **1 teaspoon vanilla extract**	In small bowl at medium speed on mixer, beat together eggs, sugar, salt and vanilla, about 1 minute until light.
½ cup (¼-lb.) butter, ... **melted**	Add melted butter. Continue beating until thoroughly blended.
¾ cup unsifted . . . . **all-purpose flour** **½ cup cocoa**	Mix in flour and cocoa at low speed.
1 cup chopped nuts	Stir in nuts. Spread evenly in greased 8-in. square dish.

Microwave at High 6 to 8 Minutes, rotating dish ¼ turn every 2 minutes. When done, top looks dry and will spring back when lightly touched. Cut when cold.

Makes about 20 brownies

NOTE: 1 pkg. (6-oz.) semi-sweet chocolate pieces, or 1 cup flaked or shredded coconut may be substituted for nuts.

Basic Brownies

THREE-LAYER BROWNIES

POWER LEVEL: High (10)
MICROWAVE TIME: 7½ to 9 min., total

2 squares . . . . **unsweetened chocolate** **⅓ cup butter**	In small glass mixing bowl place chocolate and butter. **Microwave at High 2½ to 3 Minutes,** until melted.
1 cup sugar . . . . **2 eggs** **1 teaspoon vanilla extract**	Add sugar, eggs and vanilla. Beat 2 minutes.
⅔ cup unsifted . . . . **all-purpose flour** **½ teaspoon salt** **½ cup chopped nuts (optional)**	Stir in flour and salt just until well blended. Pour into paper towel lined 8-in. square dish.* Sprinkle nuts over batter.

Microwave at High 5 to 6 Minutes, rotating dish ¼ turn every minute. Remove from oven and cool while making icing and glaze.

*See Microlesson, page 264.

BROWNED BUTTER ICING   **Cook Code:** 50

In 1-qt. glass measure or medium mixing bowl place ¼ cup butter. Cover with wax paper. **Microwave at High 5 to 6 Minutes,** until butter is golden brown. Remove from oven and blend in 2 cups sifted confectioners sugar, 2 tablespoons milk and ½ teaspoon vanilla extract. Spread over top of brownies in dish.

CHOCOLATE GLAZE   **Cook Code:** 20

In 1-cup glass measure place 1 square (1-oz.) semi-sweet or unsweetened chocolate and 1 tablespoon butter. **Microwave at High 2 to 2½ Minutes,** or until melted. Cool slightly and drizzle over icing on brownies. Refrigerate until cool and icing and glaze are set up.

Makes about 20 brownies or
8 to 9 dessert size portions

BROWNIES FROM A MIX

POWER LEVEL: High (10)   **Cook Code:** 60
MICROWAVE TIME: 6 to 8 min., total

1 pkg. (about 1-lb.) . . . . **brownie mix** **Water** **Eggs** **Chopped Nuts (optional)**	Prepare cookie dough as package directs. Spread evenly in lightly greased 8-in. round or square dish. **Microwave at High 6 to 8 minutes,** rotating dish ¼ turn every 2 minutes.

When done, top feels firm when lightly pressed. To prevent dryness, do not overcook. Let stand directly on heat-proof counter or wooden board to cool.

Makes about 20 brownies

Family Size Brownies: Prepare cookie dough as package directs and divide between 2 (8-in.) round dishes. Microwave one dish at a time as directed above, except check for doneness after 5 minutes.

FRESH APPLE BARS

For a less rich dessert, omit pastry bottom, and pour apple batter directly into lightly greased 8-in. square dish.

POWER LEVEL: High (10)
MICROWAVE TIME: 8 to 10 min., total

½ **cup flour** . . . . .In small mixing bowl,
½ **cup brown sugar** blend flour, brown sugar,
¼ **cup butter,** butter and nuts with fork
   softened or pastry blender. Press
¼ **cup chopped nuts** mixture into ungreased
8-in. square dish. **Microwave at High 1 Minute.** Set aside.

 1 egg . . . . .In the same bowl, com-
¾ **cup brown sugar** bine egg, brown sugar,
⅓ **cup butter, melted** butter and vanilla. Blend
½ **teaspoon vanilla** well. Stir in dry ingredi-
¾ **cup flour** ents until moistened.
½ **teaspoon salt** Fold in apples and nuts.
½ **teaspoon baking soda** Spread evenly over
½ **teaspoon cinnamon** base. **Microwave at**
 1 cup pared fresh **High 7 to 9 Minutes,**
   apples, finely rotating dish ¼ turn every
   chopped (about 2 minutes.
   2 small apples)
½ **cup chopped nuts**

   Confectioners . . . . .When cooled, sprinkle
   sugar top with sugar.

Makes about 16 bars

CHOCOLATE TOFFEE BARS

POWER LEVEL: High (10)
MICROWAVE TIME: 4 to 4½ min., total

11 graham cracker . . . . . .In 12×8×2-in. dish ar-
   squares range graham cracker
squares to cover bottom.

½ **cup (¼-lb.) butter** . . . . .In 1-qt. casserole place
½ **cup brown sugar** butter and brown sugar.
   (packed) **Microwave at High 2 Minutes.** Stir well.

½ **cup confectioners** . . . . .Blend in confectioners
   sugar sugar, cornstarch, salt,
 1 tablespoon coconut and nuts. Spread
   cornstarch evenly over graham crack-
¼ **teaspoon salt** ers.
 1 cup coconut
½ **cup chopped nuts**

 1 cup (6-oz.) . . . . .Sprinkle chocolate pieces
   semi-sweet over top. **Microwave at**
   chocolate pieces **High 2 to 2½ Minutes.** Let stand a few minutes, then spread chocolate over bars. Cool before cutting.

Makes 24 bars

SWEET-TART LEMON SQUARES

POWER LEVEL: High (10)   **Cook Code:** 80
MICROWAVE TIME: 8 to 10 min., total

 1 can (14-oz.) . . . . .In small mixing bowl stir to-
   sweetened gether milk, lemon juice
   condensed milk and rind, until thick and
½ **cup lemon juice** smooth. Set aside.
 1 teaspoon grated
   lemon rind
   (optional)

1½ **cups graham** . . . . .Mix together crumbs, sug-
   cracker crumbs ar and butter. Place about
⅓ **cup brown sugar** ⅔ of mixture in 8-in. square
   (packed) dish and press firmly into
⅓ **cup butter, melted** bottom of dish. Add milk mixture and spread even-ly. Sprinkle remaining crumb mixture over top and pat down gently.

Microwave at High 8 to 10 Minutes, rotating dish ¼ turn after 4 minutes. Cut in small squares as cookies or in larger pieces as dessert.

Makes 16 to 24 cookies
or 9 desserts

CHOCOLATE-FILLED WAFER BARS

POWER LEVEL: Medium High (7) and High (10)
MICROWAVE TIME: 7½ to 11 min.

 1 pkg. (6-oz.) semi- . . . . . .In small glass mixing bowl
   sweet chocolate or 1-pt. glass measuring
   pieces cup place chocolate
 1 can (14-oz.) pieces and milk. **Micro-**
   sweetened **wave at Medium High 3**
   condensed milk **to 4 Minutes,** until mix-ture can be stirred smooth.

¼ **cup butter** . . . . .In 8-in. square dish place
¼ **cup peanut butter** butter and peanut butter.
1½ **cups vanilla wafer** **Microwave at High ½ to**
   crumbs or **1 Minute,** until softened
   graham cracker enough to stir smooth.
   crumbs Mix in crumbs and brown
⅓ **cup brown sugar** sugar well to make crum-
   (packed) bly mixture.

Remove half of mixture to separate bowl or piece of wax paper. Press remaining half of crumbs evenly over bottom of 8-in. dish. Spread with chocolate mixture, then evenly distribute remaining crumbs over top. Pat down lightly. **Microwave at High 4 to 6 Minutes,** rotating dish ¼ turn after 3 minutes, until top appears set. Center will be soft but will set up when cool. Cut into bars when cool.

Makes 20 to 25 bars

Substitute peanut butter chips or butterscotch morsels for semi-sweet chocolate pieces.

Cakes

MICROLESSON

The growing popularity of microwaved cakes is indicated by the many new utensils being developed for cooking them. Microwave instructions are available from major cake mix manufacturers. Expect microwaved cakes to look different; they will not brown and the tops will be somewhat uneven, since they do not develop a dry crust to contain expansion. For this reason they are moist, airy, fluffy and have greater volume. Since most cakes are frosted or served with a topping you won't notice the difference in appearance but you will appreciate the time saved in baking.

Volume and Browning. The microwaved cake does not brown or develop a crust but has greater volume than the conventionally baked cake. A fluted tube dish allows heat to penetrate all sides.

Cake Mix Batters. Moist and fluffy types are best for microwaving. Extra ingredients like oil and eggs add richness which helps in microwaving.

Chocolate Cake From A Mix

Homemade Cake Batters. Those rich in sugar, fat and sometimes eggs microwave best. Cakes made with oil microwave especially well.

Not Recommended. Cakes like chiffon and angel food needing dry heat do not microwave well. White cakes often lack the richness of egg yolks and butter, important in microwaving.

MICROLESSON: HOW TO MICROWAVE A RING MOLD CAKE

Select a dish to accommodate the high rising characteristic of micro-waved cakes. A 16-cup capacity is large enough for most recipes.

Grease dish lightly and line with some streusel or finely chopped nuts, if desired. This eliminates the need to frost the finished cake.

Prepare batter according to recipe and pour evenly into dish. Cut through batter with spatula to remove air bubbles.

MICROLESSON: ROUND OR SQUARE LAYER CAKES

Line an 8-in. round or square dish with paper towel or wax paper. Or grease bottom and sides lightly. It will hold about 2 cups batter.

Microwave and Rotate according to recipe directions. Rotating helps dis-tribute heat for even cooking.

Let Stand 5 to 10 minutes on counter top. Loosen edges carefully with spatula. Turn cake out of dish on wire rack or platter.

YELLOW CAKE MIX FLAVOR VARIATIONS:
ORANGE-COCONUT CAKE

The type of cake you could call "Sunshine Cake".

Before preparing batter, toast ½ cup shredded coconut by placing in glass 9-in. pie plate. **Microwave at High 2 Minutes,** stirring every ½ minute. Grate the peel of 1 orange and squeeze out juice. Measure juice and add water to equal total amount of water called for on cake mix box. Prepare batter from 2-layer yellow cake mix, except substitute the orange juice liquid for water. Fold grated orange peel and toasted coconut into finished batter. Microwave as for fluted tube cake or in layers, see chart, page 272.

CHERRY-NUT CAKE

This is best as a fluted tube cake because of its cherry topping.

Before preparing batter, measure ¼ cup maraschino cherry juice (from bottled maraschino cherries) into measuring cup. Add water to equal total amount of water called for on cake mix box. Prepare batter from 2-layer yellow cake mix, except substitute the maraschino cherry liquid for water. Into greased 16-cup fluted plastic microwave ring mold, pour about ½ cup batter. Arrange 8 chopped maraschino cherries over batter and sprinkle with ¼ cup finely chopped nuts. Fold an additional ¼ cup finely chopped nuts into batter and carefully pour into mold. Microwave as on chart, page 272.

Microwave and Rotate the dish as the recipe directs.

Test for doneness. Cake touched lightly should spring back, and toothpick inserted should come out clean. Also, cake will begin to pull away from pan sides.

Let Stand on counter about 5 minutes, then invert onto serving plate.

Remove paper towel or wax paper and allow to cool.

Refrigerate 10 to 15 minutes if cake does not seem firm enough to frost.

Do Not Use rectangular shapes such as a 12×8×2-in. dish. Round or square layers are preferred for microwaving cakes.

OTHER CAKE MIX FLAVOR VARIATIONS:

CREOLE CHOCOLATE CAKE

Prepare batter from 2-layer chocolate or devils food cake mix, adding the following ingredients before beating: ¼ cup instant coffee granules, ½ teaspoon cinnamon, ¼ teaspoon allspice and ¼ teaspoon nutmeg. Microwave as for fluted tube cake or in layers, see chart, page 272.

PUMPKIN-SPICE CAKE

In large mixing bowl, combine 2-layer spice cake mix, 1 (16 oz.) can pumpkin pie filling (spiced), ½ cup water and 3 eggs. Beat at highest speed for 2 minutes. Microwave as for fluted tub cake or in layers, see chart, page 272.

Glaze: 1 cup confectioners sugar, ¼ teaspoon pumpkin pie spice and 1 to 2 tablespoons milk.

Microwaved Cake (second from left) looks different from conventional cake (above), until it is frosted or topped (at right).

Whipped Topping with Drizzled Chocolate

Peach Upside Down Cake, page 278

MICROWAVING CAKES FROM COMMERCIAL MIXES

While some microwave experts recommend a reduction of the water called for on the package directions, we have found that the full amount of water results in a moist, eating quality cake and we recommend that cake batter be made following package directions exactly.

Amount of batter for 2-layer cake is often too much for 2 round 8-in. cake layers because batter rises higher when microwaved than it does conventionally. Fill cake dishes only half full and use any leftover batter for cupcakes. You will get about ½ dozen extra cupcakes when using some mixes.

New microwave cake utensils made of plastic are designed to accommodate the greater expansion of cake batter. The round layer cake utensils hold half of batter from a 2-layer cake mix and the fluted and straight-sided molds hold all of batter from a 2-layer package. They are very convenient if you microwave cakes often.

Top appearance of microwave cakes is uneven. Best shape may be obtained when Medium power is used.

Immediately following this chart are recipes for some of the most popular cake mix variations. They may be microwaved according to the chart below.

DISH SIZE*	AMOUNT OF BATTER	MICROWAVE AT **Medium High**	ROTATE DISH ¼ TURN EVERY
8-in. round (glass)	about 2 cups	8 to 9 Minutes	3 Minutes
9-in. round (microwave plastic or ceramic)	about 3 cups	8 to 9 Minutes	3 Minutes
8-in. square (glass)	about 2½ cups	9 to 10 Minutes	2 Minutes
Tube Cake	about 2½ cups	8 to 9 Minutes	3 Minutes
16-cup Fluted or Straight-sided ring mold (microwave plastic or ceramic)	all of batter for 2-layer cake	For this cake **Microwave at High 11 to 14 Minutes**, rotating dish ¼ turn every 3 minutes. Let stand 5 to 10 minutes before inverting to cool. **Cook Code**: 110	

*NOTE: Dishes should be lightly greased or lined with paper towel or wax paper for easy removal.

Powdered Sugar   Coconut Microwave   Cherry Pie Filling   Brown Sugar and Pecans
                        Topping, page 281

HOW TO COOK CAKE MIX VARIATIONS

Batters which start with packaged cake mix microwave best in a 16-cup microwave plastic or ceramic ring mold. Cake layers may also be done. Refer to chart, page 272, for microwave times. Let stand directly on heat-proof surface to cool.

"MIX EASY" PUDDING POUND CAKE

1 pkg. (2-layer) yellow cake mix	. . . .In large mixer bowl place cake mix, pudding mix, eggs, water and oil. Blend on low speed of mixer until just moistened, then beat 4 minutes at medium speed. If desired, top cooled cake with Chocolate Glaze.
1 pkg. (3¾-oz.) instant lemon or vanilla pudding mix	
4 eggs	
1 cup water	
¼ cup cooking oil	

"MIX EASY" SOUR CREAM CAKE

1 pkg. (2-layer) yellow cake mix	. . . . .In large mixer bowl place cake mix, eggs, sour cream, oil and sugar. Blend on low speed of mixer, just until moistened, then beat 4 minutes at medium speed. If desired, top batter with Easy Streusel before microwaving.
4 eggs	
1 cup (8-oz.) sour cream	
¾ cup cooking oil	
½ cup sugar	

TOPPINGS FOR "MIX EASY" CAKES

Quick Glaze: Stir together 1 cup sifted confectioners sugar, 1 to 2 tablespoons milk or hot water, ¼ teaspoon vanilla extract and ⅛ teaspoon salt.

Chocolate Glaze: In 1½-qt. casserole place 2 squares (2-oz.) unsweetened chocolate and 1 tablespoon butter. **Microwave at Low 3 to 4 Minutes,** until melted. Stir. Add 2½ cups sifted confectioners sugar, ¼ cup boiling water and ⅛ teaspoon salt. Stir smooth.

Easy Streusel: Stir together ½ cup finely chopped nuts, ¼ cup sugar and 1 teaspoon cinnamon.

NOTE: If you are microwaving "MIX EASY" Sour Cream Cake in fluted tube pan, coat greased pan with some of streusel. Add half of batter and sprinkle on rest of streusel. Cover with rest of batter and microwave.

EASY CHOCOLATE CAKE

POWER LEVEL: High (10)   **Cook Code:** 70
MICROWAVE TIME: 7 to 9 min., total

½ pkg. (2-layer size) fudge cake mix (about 2 cups dry mix)	. . . . .In bottom of ungreased 8-in. square dish place dry cake mix. Add egg, vanilla, oil and water. Stir with fork until smooth and creamy.
1 egg	
½ teaspoon vanilla extract	
⅓ cup cooking oil	
¾ cup water	
½ cup semi-sweet chocolate pieces	. . . . . . .Sprinkle chocolate pieces over top.

Microwave at High 7 to 9 Minutes (½ turn after 4 minutes). Serve warm or cool with ice cream or whipped topping.

Makes 1 (8-in. square) cake

MICROLESSON: HOW TO MICROWAVE FRUIT-TOPPED LAYER CAKE

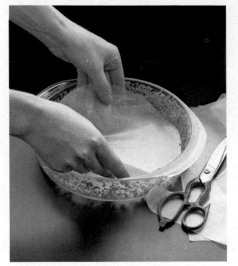  

Grease sides only of two 8-in. round dishes. Add nuts and rotate dishes so that nuts coat sides. Line bottoms with wax paper.

Spoon half of fruit filling in each dish, be careful not to disturb nut coating.

Measure 2 cups cake batter for each dish. Pour carefully over fruit.

FRUIT-TOPPED LAYER CAKE

Some good flavor combinations to try with this technique are: yellow cake mix with peach pie filling, spice cake mix with apple pie filling and chocolate or yellow cake mix with cherry pie filling.

POWER LEVEL: High (10)   **Cook Code:** 80
MICROWAVE TIME: 8 to 10 min., per cake

¼ cup finely ground nuts . . . . . . Grease only sides of 2 (8-in.) round dishes. Sprinkle with nuts and rotate dishes until nuts coat sides. Line each dish with wax paper cut in circle to fit bottom.

1 can (20 to 22-oz.) pie filling . . . . . . Divide pie filling between wax paper lined dishes, using care not to disturb nut-coated sides. Pour 2 cups of prepared cake batter into each dish.
1 pkg. (2-layer) cake mix, prepared as package directs

Microwave one cake at a time. **Microwave at High 8 to 10 Minutes,** rotating dish ¼ turn every 2 minutes, until toothpick inserted in center comes out clean. Let cake stand 10 minutes directly on heat-proof counter or wooden board.

If tops of cakes are not even, slice small amount from tops so they may be stacked. Invert 1 layer on serving plate. Invert and stack second layer on top. If desired, frost sides of cake with whipped cream or whipped dessert topping.

Makes 1 (8-in.) layer cake

HOW TO MICROWAVE SPECIAL CAKE MIXES

Chart below lists types of cakes in this category.

1. Prepare batter according to package directions.
2. Pour batter into greased 8-in. round dish.
3. Microwave at High and rotate dish as described in chart below.
4. Cake is done when toothpick stuck in center comes out clean.
5. Let cake stand directly on heat-proof counter or wooden board to cool.

POWER LEVEL: **High (10)**

CAKE	TIME MIN.	COOK CODE	COMMENTS
Boston Cream Pie	5 to 7 ¼ turn every 1½ minutes	50	Prepare custard filling and frosting as package directs. Remove ¼ cup batter.
Pineapple Upside Down Cake	9 to 12 ¼ turn every 2 minutes	90	To prevent spillover, remove ¼ cup batter to make 2 cupcakes.
Snackin' Cake	8 to 10 ¼ turn every 2 minutes	80	If ring shape is desired, place drinking glass (2-in. diameter), open side up in center of dish. Reduce time by 3 minutes.

Cook layers separately. **Microwave at High 8 to 10 Minutes,** rotating dish ¼ turn every 2 minutes.

Insert toothpick in cake (not into fruit); it should come out clean. Let stand 10 minutes on heat-proof counter. Turn out by inverting onto cooling racks or serving dish. Even up cake tops if necessary.

Peel Back wax paper carefully from top of cake. Cool until firm enough to stack if desired. Serve with whipped cream or ice cream.

HOW TO MICROWAVE CUPCAKES

Select a recipe from this section, or use your favorite homemade recipe (except do not use angel food or chiffon batters). For best shape, spoon into paper lined microwave cupcaker or "paper forms" described for muffins, page 230. Fill paper liners only ½ full.

You may also microwave cupcakes in double or triple thickness of paper liners only (without cupcaker or "paper forms"), but shape may be uneven. Cupcakes microwave very quickly; check for doneness at minimum time.

See pages 230 and 231 for muffin topping ideas and cooking tips which can be adapted to cupcake recipes.

CUPCAKE COOKING CHART

POWER LEVEL: **High (10)**

CUPCAKES	TIME MINUTES	COMMENTS
1	¼ to ½	If cooking more than 2, arrange in circle on shelf and rotate after ½ of time. With microwave cupcaker utensil, rotate ¼ turn after ½ time. Some cupcakes may be done before others; remove cooked cupcakes and continue microwaving the rest a few seconds more.
2	¾ to 1	
3	1 to 1¼	
4	1¼ to 1½	
5	1¾ to 2	
6	2½ to 3	

CHOCOLATE CHIP FILLED CUPCAKES

Batter from 2-layer chocolate cake mix
Chocolate Chip Filling (below)

.......Prepare cupcake liners, if desired (left). To make each cupcake, measure about 2 tablespoons batter into liner. Cover with 2 to 3 teaspoons filling.

Microwave cupcakes as shown on chart (left). As cupcakes cook, filling forms in center.

Makes 30 cupcakes

Chocolate Chip Filling: Stir together 1 pkg. (8-oz.) softened cream cheese, ⅓ cup sugar, 1 egg, ⅛ teaspoon salt, until well mixed. Blend in 1 pkg. (6-oz.) chocolate chips.

ICE CREAM 'N' CAKE CONES

1. Spoon 2 to 3 tablespoons of chocolate or fudge cake batter from mix into flat bottomed ice cream cones. Press a cherry, nut half, caramel or a few chocolate chips into batter.

2. Bake according to Cupcake Chart, left.

½ batter recipe makes 25 to 30 cones

Fluted Tubes and straight-sided ring molds make attractive shapes for microwaved cakes.

FLUTED TUBE CAKES

Cakes on these pages and fruit cakes on page 279 are especially good for the fluted tube shape. This shape is not only attractive but ideal for microwaving because it promotes the most even heat distribution.

POPULAR CARROT CAKE

POWER LEVEL: High (10) **Cook Code:** 120
MICROWAVE TIME: 12 to 15 min., total

1½ **cups sugar** . . . . 1 **cup cooking oil** 1 **teaspoon vanilla** **extract** 3 **eggs**	In large mixing bowl blend sugar, oil and vanilla. Add eggs and beat well.
1½ **cups unsifted** . . . . **all-purpose flour** ¾ **teaspoon salt** 1¼ **teaspoons baking** **soda** 2½ **teaspoons cinnamon**	In small bowl, stir together flour, salt, soda and cinnamon. Add to sugar-egg mixture and mix in.
2¼ **cups raw grated** . . . . . . **carrots** ½ **cup chopped** **walnuts**	Fold in carrots and walnuts. Pour batter into 16-cup plastic microwave fluted or straight-sided ring mold.

Microwave at High 12 to 15 Minutes, rotating dish ¼ turn every 4 minutes. Let stand directly on heat-proof counter or wooden board 10 minutes before inverting. Glaze with Cream Cheese Glaze, page 281, if desired.

Makes 1 (10-in.) tube cake

SPICY APPLESAUCE CAKE

POWER LEVEL: High (10) **Cook Code:** 90
MICROWAVE TIME: 9 to 12 min., total

1⅓ **cups unsifted** . . . . **all-purpose flour** 1 **cup sugar** 1 **teaspoon baking** **soda** ½ **teaspoon salt** ½ **teaspoon cinnamon** ½ **teaspoon nutmeg** ¼ **teaspoon allspice** 1½ **tablespoons cocoa** ⅓ **cup cooking oil** 1 **egg** 1 **cup applesauce** ½ **cup chopped dates** ½ **cup raisins** ½ **cup chopped nuts**	In large mixer bowl place flour, sugar, soda, salt, spices, cocoa, oil, egg and applesauce. Beat 2 minutes at lowest speed of mixer. Stir in fruits and nuts until blended. Pour into greased 16-cup plastic microwave fluted or straight-sided ring mold. **Microwave at High 9 to 12 Minutes,** rotating dish ¼ turn every 3 minutes. Let cake stand 5 minutes before inverting.

Makes 1 (10-in.) tube cake

OLD-FASHIONED BUTTERMILK CAKE

POWER LEVEL: High (10)   **Cook Code:** 100
MICROWAVE TIME: 10 to 12 min., total

2½ cups unsifted . . . . **all-purpose flour** **¾ cup sugar** **1 cup brown sugar (packed)** **1 teaspoon nutmeg** **1 teaspoon salt** **¾ cup cooking oil**	In large mixing bowl blend together with pastry blender, flour, sugar, brown sugar, nutmeg, salt and oil until crumbly. Reserve 1 cup of this mixture.
2 eggs, beaten . . . . **1 teaspoon baking powder** **1 cup buttermilk** **1 teaspoon baking soda**	To rest of crumbly mixture, add eggs, baking powder and buttermilk mixed with soda. Stir until smooth.
½ cup chopped . . . . **walnuts** **3 teaspoons cinnamon**	Mix reserved crumbs with nuts and cinnamon.

Coat bottom and sides of greased 16-cup plastic microwave fluted or straight-sided ring mold with ¼ cup of crumb mixture. Into coated mold, distribute ⅔ of batter. Sprinkle with remaining crumb mixture. Carefully distribute remaining ⅓ of batter over crumbs. **Microwave at High 10 to 12 Minutes,** rotating dish ¼ turn every 4 minutes. Let cake stand 5 minutes before inverting. Glaze when cool with Butter Glaze (below).

Makes 1 (10-in.) tube cake

Butter Glaze: Stir together ¼ cup soft butter, 1 teaspoon vanilla extract, 1 cup confectioner's sugar and 1 tablespoon strong coffee until smooth.

FLUTED PINEAPPLE-COCONUT RING

POWER LEVEL: High (10)
MICROWAVE TIME: 17 to 21 min., total

1 pkg. (4-oz.) . . . . **shredded coconut** **1 pkg. (2-layer size) yellow cake mix** **1 pkg. (3¾-oz.) instant vanilla pudding mix** **1 can (8¼-oz.) crushed pineapple, undrained** **1 cup (8-oz.) sour cream** **2 eggs**	In 9-in. pie plate, spread coconut. **Microwave at High 5 to 7 Minutes,** stirring every ¾ to 1 minute, until golden brown. Cool. Generously grease 16-cup plastic microwave fluted ring mold. Coat mold well with toasted coconut.

In large mixing bowl, place cake mix, pudding mix, undrained pineapple, sour cream and eggs. Blend batter with low speed of mixer to moisten; beat 2 minutes at medium speed. Pour into coated mold. **Microwave at High 12 to 14 Minutes,** rotating dish ¼ turn every 3 minutes. Let stand 15 minutes before inverting.

Makes 1 (10-in.) tube cake

SOUTHERN BANANA-PINEAPPLE CAKE

POWER LEVEL: High (10)
MICROWAVE TIME: 9 to 12 min.

1½ cups unsifted . . . . **all-purpose flour** **1 cup sugar** **½ teaspoon salt** **½ teaspoon baking soda** **½ teaspoon cinnamon** **2 eggs** **½ cup cooking oil**	In large mixing bowl stir together flour, sugar, salt, baking soda and cinnamon. In small mixing bowl, beat eggs and oil well with mixer. Pour egg-oil mixture over dry ingredients and using spoon (not mixer) stir until moistened.
¾ teaspoon vanilla . . . . . **extract** **1 can (6-oz.) crushed pineapple** **½ cup chopped pecans** **1 cup chopped banana (2 medium)**	Stir in vanilla, pineapple and nuts, then bananas. Spoon into greased 16-cup plastic microwave fluted or straight-sided ring mold. **Microwave at High 9 to 12 Minutes,** rotating cake ¼ turn every 3 minutes.

Let cake stand 5 minutes before inverting. Frost cake with Cream Cheese Glaze, page 281, if desired.

Makes 1 (10-in.) tube cake

CRANBERRY-ORANGE SPICE CAKE

POWER LEVEL: High (10)
MICROWAVE TIME: 11 to 13 min.

½ cup butter, softened . . . **1 cup sugar** **1 egg**	In large mixing bowl place butter, sugar and egg. Beat well with medium speed of mixer until fluffy.
1½ cups unsifted . . . . **all-purpose flour** **¼ teaspoon salt** **1 teaspoon baking soda** **1 teaspoon ground cinnamon** **½ teaspoon ground cloves**	Add flour, salt, baking soda, cinnamon and cloves. Blend, using low speed, until moistened.
1 jar (14-oz.) . . . . **cranberry-orange relish** **1 cup raisins** **½ cup coarsely chopped walnuts**	Add relish, raisins and nuts. Mix until blended.

Pour batter into greased 16-cup plastic microwave fluted or straight-sided ring mold. **Microwave at High 11 to 13 Minutes,** rotating dish ¼ turn every 4 minutes. When done, top areas around center tube appear dry and set, but edges of cake appear moist and foamy. Let cake stand 10 minutes before inverting.

Makes 1 (10-in.) tube cake

Pineapple Upside Down Cake

PINEAPPLE UPSIDE DOWN CAKE

For variety substitute peaches for pineapple and almond extract for vanilla.

POWER LEVEL: High (10)
MICROWAVE TIME: 9¾ to 13 min., total

¼ cup butter	.In 8-in. round dish place butter. **Microwave at High ¾ to 1 Minute,** to melt. Sprinkle sugar over butter. Drain pineapple (save liquid) on paper towels and arrange in dish. Decorate with cherries.
⅓ cup brown sugar (packed)	
1 can (8¼-oz.) pineapple slices	
4 maraschino or candied cherries, cut in half	
1¼ cups unsifted all-purpose flour	.In small mixer bowl place flour, sugar, baking powder, salt, shortening, egg, liquid and vanilla. Beat 3 minutes on lowest mixer speed, scraping bowl constantly first ½ minute. Carefully spread batter over fruit in dish.
¾ cup sugar	
2 teaspoons baking powder	
½ teaspoon salt	
⅓ cup soft shortening	
1 egg	
Liquid from pineapple plus milk to total ½ cup	
1 teaspoon vanilla extract	

Microwave at High 9 to 12 Minutes, rotating dish ¼ turn every 3 minutes. Some batter may run onto edges of dish, but will not spill. When done, toothpick stuck in cake comes out clean. Invert cake onto plate, let dish stand over cake a few minutes. Serve hot or warm.

Makes 1 (8-in.) round cake

CHOCOLATE BEAUTY CAKE

Coconut-Nut Microwave Topping, page 281, is especially good with this cake.

POWER LEVEL: High (10)   **Cook Code:** 80
MICROWAVE TIME: 8 to 10 min., total

1½ cups unsifted all-purpose flour	.In mixing bowl stir together flour, sugar, cocoa, soda and salt. Add water and stir to a stiff shiny batter, about 100 strokes.
1 cup brown sugar (packed)	
¼ cup cocoa	
1 teaspoon baking soda	
½ teaspoon salt	
½ cup water	
½ cup water	.Add additional ½ cup water, oil, vinegar and vanilla. Stir until smooth and well blended. 150 strokes.
⅓ cup cooking oil	
1 tablespoon vinegar	
1½ teaspoons vanilla extract	

Place drinking glass in center of greased 1½-qt. casserole. Pour batter into casserole. **Microwave at High 8 to 10 Minutes,** rotating dish ¼ turn every 2 minutes. Let stand on heat-proof counter 5 to 10 minutes to cool. Remove glass, invert onto serving plate. Finish with favorite frosting.

Makes 1 (8-in. ring) cake

HONEY DRIZZLE CAKE

This recipe won $5,000 in a microwave recipe contest.

POWER LEVEL: High (10)   **Cook Code:** 160
MICROWAVE TIME: 16 to 18 min., total

5 eggs	.Separate eggs. In large mixer bowl beat egg whites until foamy. Gradually beat in ¼ cup sugar and salt until fluffy.
¼ cup sugar	
⅛ teaspoon salt	
½ cup sugar	.In small bowl beat egg yolks, ½ cup sugar and vanilla until thick and pale.
1 teaspoon vanilla extract	
1½ cups chopped pecans	.Fold yolk mixture into egg whites thoroughly. Blend pecans, wafer crumbs, baking powder and cinnamon; sprinkle over top. Fold all ingredients together well.
1½ cups fine vanilla wafer crumbs	
1½ teaspoons baking powder	
½ teaspoon cinnamon	

Pour into greased 8-in. square dish. **Microwave at High 8 to 10 Minutes,** rotating dish ¼ turn every 2 minutes. Remove cake and cook Honey Syrup (below). Carefully pour syrup over cake. Serve in small pieces, warm or cold, with unsweetened whipped cream.

Honey Syrup: In 2-qt. casserole stir together 1 cup water, 1 cup sugar and ½ cup honey. **Microwave at High 8 Minutes,** stirring after 4 minutes. **Cook Code:** 80

Makes 1 (8-in. square) cake

PECAN SPONGE ROLL

Fill Pecan Sponge Roll with vanilla ice cream instead of cream filling for a good make-ahead frozen dessert. Serve in slices with chocolate sauce.

POWER LEVEL: High (10)   **Cook Code:** 60
MICROWAVE TIME: 6 to 8 min., total

Prepare paper on which to microwave Pecan Sponge Roll. Cut a sheet of wax paper into a piece 28-in. long by 10-in. wide. Fold in half, making a double thickness of paper 14×10-in. in size. Cut a piece of brown paper (from grocery bag, if desired) same size and place under wax paper for added support. Generously butter top of wax paper.

4 eggs, separated	.In small mixer bowl, beat egg whites, until stiff. In
½ cup sifted confectioners sugar	large mixer bowl, beat egg yolks and sugar until thick and pale in color. Add va-
2 teaspoons vanilla extract	nilla. Mix pecans with bak-
1½ cups ground pecans or pecan meal*	ing powder and fold into egg yolk mixture. Fold in
¾ teaspoon baking powder	stiffly beaten egg whites.

Spread batter evenly on buttered wax paper to within 1-in. of edges. Handling carefully, place cake in microwave oven.** **Microwave at High 6 to 8 Minutes,** rotating cake ½ turn after 3 minutes, until toothpick stuck in cake comes out clean. Let cake stand in microwave oven 1 minute, then carefully transfer to cooling rack. Cover with dish towel wrung out with cold water. Let cool.

When cool, remove towel and spread Vanilla Filling over cake. Roll up as for jelly roll starting at short side and peeling off wax paper as cake is rolled. Sprinkle with powdered sugar just before serving, or if desired, top with vanilla glaze.

Makes 12 (1-in.) slices

*Ground pecans are found packaged at grocery stores, especially at holiday time. Or, if desired, whir pecans in blender until finely ground.

Vanilla Filling: In small mixer bowl, place 2 cups well-chilled whipping cream and 1 pkg. (3¾-oz.) instant vanilla pudding mix. Beat at high speed of mixer until thick and fluffy.

Vanilla Glaze: In small bowl stir together 1 cup confectioners sugar, 1 tablespoon corn syrup and 1 tablespoon water. **Microwave at Low ½ to 1 Minute,** just until luke-warm. Stir well and pour over Pecan Roll to glaze.

**NOTE: To easily transfer batter and paper to oven, place a cookie sheet under the paper. Slide batter-topped paper from cookie sheet into oven. Same cookie sheet can be used to transfer baked cake from oven.

TRADITIONAL BRANDY FRUIT CAKE

POWER LEVEL: High (10)
MICROWAVE TIME: 13 to 17 min.

½ cup (¼-lb.) butter, softened	. . . . .In large mixing bowl cream together butter and sugar,
1 cup light brown sugar	until fluffy. Add eggs, mix-ing well.
2 eggs	
1½ cups unsifted all-purpose flour	. . . . . . .Stir together flour, baking powder, salt, and cinna-
½ teaspoon baking powder	mon. Add to creamed mix-ture along with brandy
½ teaspoon salt	Blend well.
½ teaspoon cinnamon	
¼ cup brandy	
1 pkg. (8-oz.) chopped dates	. . . . .In large bowl, mix together fruits and nuts. Fold into
½ lb. mixed candied fruit	batter. Pour into lightly greased 16-cup plastic
¼ lb. whole candied cherries	microwave fluted or straight-sided ring mold.
¼ lb. pecan halves (about 1 cup)	

Microwave at High 13 to 17 Minutes, rotating dish ¼ turn every 2 minutes, until cake tester stuck in center comes out clean. Let stand 20 minutes directly on heat-proof counter before turning out onto serving plate. Brush with white corn syrup if glazed top is desired. When cold, sprinkle with brandy and wrap in foil or plastic. Age in cool place 4 to 6 weeks.

Makes 1 (10-in.) fruitcake

ORANGE-GLAZED FRUIT CAKE

POWER LEVEL: High (10)   **Cook Code:** 170
MICROWAVE TIME: 17 to 21 min., total

1 cup (3-oz.) coconut	. . . .In mixing bowl stir together coconut, flour, sugar and
1 cup unsifted all-purpose flour	baking powder.
1½ cups confectioners sugar	
2 teaspoons baking powder	
¾ cup butter, melted	. . . . .Add butter, eggs and milk. Mix well.
3 eggs, beaten	
½ cup milk	
2 cups chopped candied fruit	. . . . . . .Stir in fruit and nuts. Pour batter into greased 16-cup
1½ cups chopped pecans	plastic microwave fluted or straight-sided ring mold.

Microwave at High 14 to 16 Minutes, rotating dish ¼ turn every 4 minutes. Spoon glaze over hot cake.

Orange Glaze: In 1-qt. casserole stir together ½ cup sugar and ½ cup orange juice. Cover. **Microwave at High 3 to 5 Minutes,** until boiling.

Makes 1 (10-in.) tube cake

EARLY AMERICAN GINGERBREAD

Serve warm, topped with Citrus Sauce, page 283, or whipped cream, if desired.

POWER LEVEL: High (10)   **Cook Code:** 90
MICROWAVE TIME: 9 to 11 min., total

1½ cups unsifted . . . . **all-purpose flour** **½ cup sugar** **¾ teaspoon baking soda** **½ teaspoon ginger** **½ teaspoon cinnamon** **½ teaspoon salt**	.In mixing bowl stir together flour, sugar, baking soda, ginger, cinnamon and salt.
½ cup soft shortening . . . **1 egg** **½ cup light molasses** **½ cup hottest tap water**	.Add shortening, egg, molasses and water. Beat 2 minutes on medium speed of mixer until well blended.

Pour batter into greased 8-in. square dish. **Microwave at High 9 to 11 Minutes,** rotating dish ¼ turn every 2 minutes. When cake is done let stand directly on heat-proof counter or wooden board to cool.

Makes 8 servings

CONVENIENCE CAKE DEFROSTING CHART

Cakes packaged in foil should be removed from the foil and placed on a plate, or on an all cardboard lid. Frosted layer cakes can be defrosted on the styrofoam base.

Watch icing and frosting closely as they melt easily. Defrosted cakes should be cool and easy to cut. Let cakes stand 2 to 5 minutes before serving.

POWER LEVEL: **Defrost**

ITEM	TIME MINUTES	COMMENTS
2 to 3-layer, frosted (17-oz.)	2	Rotate ½ turn after 1 minute.
1 piece, frosted	½	
1-layer, frosted, filled or topped (12½ to 16-oz.)	2 to 3	Rotate ½ turn after 1 minute.
Pound Cake (11¼-oz.)	2	Rotate ½ turn after 1 minute.
1 piece Pound Cake	½	
Cheesecake, plain or fruit topped (17 to 19-oz.)	4 to 5	Rotate ¼ turn every 2 minutes. Let stand 5 minutes to complete defrosting.
Crunch Cakes and Cupcakes (1 or 2)	½ to 1	
Crunch Cakes and Cupcakes (3 or 4)	1 to 2	Arrange in circle on plate. Rotate ½ turn after ½ minute.
Crunch Cakes and Cupcakes (5 to 8)	2 to 3	Arrange in circle on plate. Rotate ½ turn after ¾ minute.

BASIC CHEESECAKE

POWER LEVEL: High (10) and Medium (5)
MICROWAVE TIME: 19¾ to 22½ min., total

4 tablespoons butter . . . . **1 cup fine crumbs (graham cracker or chocolate cookie)** **2 tablespoons sugar**	.In 8-in. round dish place butter. **Microwave at High ¼ to ½ Minute,** to melt. Stir in crumbs and sugar. Press mixture on bottom and sides of dish. **Microwave at High 1½ to 2 Minutes,** rotating dish ½ turn after 1 minute, until set.
4 eggs . . . . **1 cup sugar** **2 pkgs. (8-oz. each) cream cheese, softened** **2 teaspoons vanilla extract** **¼ teaspoon salt**	.In blender place eggs, sugar, cream cheese, vanilla and salt. Blend on high 1 minute until smooth. (If mixed with electric mixer, use large mixer bowl and mix at high 3 minutes.) pour over back of spoon into crust, to prevent breaking of crust.

Microwave at Medium 18 to 20 Minutes, rotating dish ¼ turn every 6 minutes until center is almost set. Refrigerate at least 3 hours before serving.

Makes 1 (8-in.) cheesecake

STEAMED PUDDING

POWER LEVEL: High (10) and Medium High (7)
MICROWAVE TIME: 17 to 19½ min., total

1 cup water . . . . **1 cup seedless raisins or cranberries**	.Measure water into glass measure. **Microwave at High 2 to 2½ Minutes,** until at rolling boil. Pour over fruit and let stand.
2 tablespoons . . . . **softened butter** **½ cup sugar** **½ cup molasses** **1 egg**	.Beat together butter, sugar, molasses and egg.
1½ cups unsifted . . . . **all-purpose flour** **1 teaspoon baking soda** **1 teaspoon salt**	.Stir together flour, baking soda and salt. Add flour mixture and fruit with water to creamed mixture.

Lightly grease a 2-qt. casserole, then place a 2-in. diameter drinking glass (open side up) in center. Pour batter around glass. Cover dish well with plastic wrap, **Microwave at Medium High 15 to 17 Minutes,** rotating dish ¼ turn every 2 minutes, until pudding appears set, but glossy. Remove from oven with pot holders.

Let stand 10 to 20 minutes, twist glass to remove. Unmold onto cooling rack. When cold, wrap well and allow pudding to age about a week before slicing. Serve with Hard Sauce or Citrus Sauce, page 283.

Makes about 10 to 12 servings

EASY FUDGE FROSTING

POWER LEVEL: High (10)   **Cook Code:** 30
MICROWAVE TIME: 3 to 4 min., total

1 cup sugar . . . . In 1½-qt. casserole com-
¼ cup butter   bine sugar, butter and
¼ cup evaporated milk   evaporated milk. **Micro-**
                             wave at High 3 to 4 Min-
                             utes, uncovered, stirring
                             after 2 minutes, until
                             bubbly.

1 cup (6-oz.) . . . . Add chocolate pieces,
   semi-sweet   marshmallow creme and
   chocolate pieces   vanilla to hot mixture. Stir
1 cup marshmallow   until well blended. Excel-
   creme   lent on brownies or plain
1 teaspoon vanilla   cake layers.
   extract

Makes about 2 cups frosting

BASIC CONFECTIONERS SUGAR FROSTING

POWER LEVEL: High (10)   **Cook Code:** 10
MICROWAVE TIME: 1 to 2 min., total

1 pkg. (1-lb.) . . . . In 1½-qt. casserole place
   confectioners sugar   sugar, milk, salt and vanilla
¼ cup milk   and stir just to blend slight-
¼ teaspoon salt   ly (mixture is too stiff to mix
1 teaspoon vanilla   thoroughly). Add butter on
   extract   top.
¼ cup butter

Microwave at High 1 to 2 Minutes, until mixture can be
beaten smooth.

NOTE: Add additional 1 to 2 teaspoons milk if mixture is
too stiff.

Makes enough frosting for
2 (8-in.) round or square layers

BUTTERCREAM FROSTING

Using above recipe, decrease milk to 2 tablespoons and
increase butter to ½ cup. Microwave as above. If mixture
gets too hot, it will be runny and may run off of cake. Let
frosting stand in bowl a few minutes, stirring occasionally, before icing cake. As it cools, it thickens.

COCONUT-NUT FROSTING FROM A MIX

POWER LEVEL: High (10)   **Cook Code:** 10
MICROWAVE TIME: 1 to 1½ min., total

1 pkg. (9.9-oz.) coconut . .In 1-qt. casserole place
   nut frosting mix   frosting mix, milk and but-
   Milk   ter (use amounts on pack-
   Butter   age). **Microwave at High**
                             1 to 1½ Minutes, until mix-
                             ture can be stirred smooth.

Easy Fudge Frosting

COCONUT MICROWAVE TOPPING

POWER LEVEL: High (10)   **Cook Code:** 20
MICROWAVE TIME: 2 min., total

1 cup brown sugar . . . . . .In 1-qt. casserole blend to-
   (packed)   gether brown sugar, corn-
1 tablespoon   starch and milk. Add but-
   cornstarch   ter. **Microwave at High 2**
2 tablespoons milk   **Minutes,** stirring after 1
2 tablespoons butter   minute.

½ cup flaked coconut . . . . .Stir mixture well, then stir in
                             coconut. Pour over cooled
                             cake.

Makes enough frosting for
2 (8-in.) round or square layers

Coconut-Nut Microwave Topping: Add ¼ to ½ cup
chopped nuts (walnuts, pecans or peanuts) along with
coconut.

CREAM CHEESE GLAZE

POWER LEVEL: High (10)
MICROWAVE TIME: ¼ to ½ min., total

1 (3-oz.) pkg. . . . . .In small glass mixing bowl
   cream cheese   place cheese. **Microwave**
½ cup confectioners   **at High ¼ to ½ Minute,**
   sugar   just to soften. Add sugar,
3 tablespoons butter   butter, milk and vanilla.
1½ tablespoons milk   Beat with mixer until
1 teaspoon vanilla   smooth.
   extract

Sauces

Delicious, smooth and creamy dessert sauces micro-wave with exceptional ease and speed. With conventional cooking, they require care in melting chocolate or dissolving sugar mixtures, and constant stirring to prevent scorching and lumps. With microwave cooking, stirring is minimal and sauces are ready in 2 to 7 minutes.

QUICKIE CHOCOLATE SAUCE

POWER LEVEL: High (10)   **Cook Code:** 10
MICROWAVE TIME: 1½ to 2½ min., total

½ cup light corn syrup **1 pkg. (6-oz.)** **semi-sweet** **chocolate pieces** **1 tablespoon butter**	In 1-pt. glass measure, measure syrup. Stir in chocolate and butter. **Microwave at High 1½ to 2½ Minutes.** Stir until completely smooth.
¼ cup dairy half & half **or milk** **¼ teaspoon vanilla or** **rum extract**	Blend in half & half and vanilla. Serve warm or cold.

Makes about 1½ cups

SCRUMPTIOUS BUTTERSCOTCH SAUCE

POWER LEVEL: High (10)   **Cook Code:** 30
MICROWAVE TIME: 3½ to 4½ min., total

1 tablespoon **cornstarch** **1¼ cups light brown** **sugar (packed)** **½ cup dairy half & half** **2 tablespoons light** **corn syrup** **⅛ teaspoon salt** **¼ cup butter**	In 1½-qt. casserole stir together cornstarch and brown sugar. Stir in half & half, corn syrup and salt. Add butter. Cover. **Microwave at High 3½ to 4½ Minutes,** stirring after 2 minutes, until thickened and sugar is dissolved.
1 teaspoon vanilla **extract**	Add vanilla and stir until smooth and well blended. Serve warm or cold.

Makes 1½ cups

WONDERFUL MAPLE NUT SAUCE

Prepare recipe above, substituting 1 teaspoon maple flavoring for vanilla. Add ⅓ cup chopped nuts if desired.

Scrumptious Butterscotch Sauce

CRUNCHY CHOCOLATE SAUCE

POWER LEVEL: High (10)   **Cook Code:** 20
MICROWAVE TIME: 2½ to 4 min., total

¼ cup milk	In 1-pt. glass measure, measure milk. Drop in chocolate. **Microwave at High 1½ to 2 Minutes.** Blend well.
1 square (1-oz.) unsweetened chocolate	
¾ cup light brown sugar (packed)	Add sugar; stir to blend. **Microwave at High 1 to 2 Minutes,** until mixture boils.
¼ cup crunchy peanut butter	Add peanut butter and vanilla and stir until well blended. Serve warm or cool.
¼ teaspoon vanilla extract	

Makes 1 cup

FUDGE SAUCE

POWER LEVEL: High (10)   **Cook Code:** 40
MICROWAVE TIME: 4 to 5 min., total

1 cup sugar	In 3-qt. casserole stir together sugar, salt and milk, until blended. **Microwave at High 4 to 5 Minutes,** until boiling hard.
¼ teaspoon salt	
1 can (5.3-oz.) evaporated milk	
2 squares (2-oz.) unsweetened chocolate	Into boiling mixture stir chocolate until completely melted. Stir in butter and vanilla.
2 tablespoons butter	
1 teaspoon vanilla	

Makes about 1½ cups

FESTIVE RICH BUTTER SAUCE

POWER LEVEL: High (10)   **Cook Code:** 20
MICROWAVE TIME: 2½ to 3½ min., total

1 cup sugar	In 1-qt. casserole stir together sugar and half & half. Add butter. Cover. **Microwave at High 2½ to 3½ Minutes,** until sugar dissolves. Stir vigorously to combine. This rich sauce may separate slightly on standing. If so, stir again.
½ cup dairy half & half	
½ cup (¼-lb.) butter	

Makes 1½ cups

NOTE: If desired, ½ teaspoon rum extract or 1 tablespoon brandy, rum, sherry or fruit flavored brandy may be stirred into sauce after cooking.

CINNAMON SUGAR SAUCE

POWER LEVEL: High (10)   **Cook Code:** 30
MICROWAVE TIME: 3 to 4 min., total

½ cup sugar	In 1-qt. casserole stir together sugar, cornstarch, cinnamon and water, until completely smooth. Cover. **Microwave at High 3 to 4 Minutes,** stirring sauce after 1½ minutes.
1½ tablespoons cornstarch	
1 teaspoon cinnamon	
1 cup hot tap water	
2 tablespoons butter	Stir in butter until well blended. Serve warm.

Makes 1⅓ cups

CITRUS SAUCE

Prepare recipe above, omitting cinnamon. Stir 1 tablespoon lemon or orange juice and 1 to 2 teaspoons finely grated lemon or orange rind into sugar mixture.

HARD SAUCE

POWER LEVEL: High (10)   **Cook Code:** 10
MICROWAVE TIME: 1½ to 2 min., total

1 pkg. (1-lb.) confectioners sugar	In small glass mixer bowl or 1½-qt. casserole place sugar, salt and rum. Place butter on top. **Microwave at High 1½ to 2 Minutes.**
¼ teaspoon salt	
¼ cup rum or brandy*	
½ cup (¼-lb.) butter	

Beat on highest speed of mixer until smooth. Sauce will be soft and creamy after beating. If a true hard sauce is desired, refrigerate until hardened. Serve over plum pudding or other baked fruit puddings, or with fruit cake, gingerbread, applesauce cake, etc. Or use as "frosting" for fruit cake.

*Or use ¼ cup milk with 1 to 2 teaspoons vanilla, rum or brandy flavoring (or use orange or lemon extract).

Makes 2 cups

TOASTED ALMOND SAUCE

POWER LEVEL: High (10)
MICROWAVE TIME: 7 to 9 min., total

½ cup (¼-lb.) butter	In 1½-qt. casserole place butter. **Microwave at High 2 Minutes.**
3 pkgs. (2⅞-oz. each) sliced almonds	Add nuts and stir until well coated. **Microwave at High 5 to 7 Minutes,** stirring well after 3 minutes, until bubbly and golden brown.
1 jar (1-lb.) honey	Stir in honey until evenly mixed. Sprinkle generously with nutmeg. Serve hot.
Nutmeg	

Makes about 3 cups

TRUE BLUEBERRY SAUCE

POWER LEVEL: High (10)   **Cook Code:** 50
MICROWAVE TIME: 5 to 7 min., total

1 tablespoon lemon ...... In 1-qt. casserole stir to-
juice gether lemon juice and
2 tablespoons cornstarch. Add sugar and
cornstarch salt. Stir in undrained blue-
¼ cup sugar berries. **Microwave at**
⅛ teaspoon salt **High 5 to 7 Minutes,** stir-
1 can (16-oz.) ring every 2 minutes, until
blueberries sauce is thickened and
clear. Serve over ice
cream, pancakes or un-
frosted cake such as
pound cake.

Makes about 1½ cups

TO USE FROZEN BLUEBERRIES: Place 1 (10-oz.) punch package of blueberries in microwave oven. **Microwave at Defrost 4 to 6 Minutes,** just until berries can be separated. Substitute for canned blueberries. Add ½ to ¾ cup water for liquid, increasing cooking time, if necessary.

Mint on Mint Sundaes

CINNAMON GLAZED PINEAPPLE SAUCE

POWER LEVEL: High (10)   **Cook Code:** 60
MICROWAVE TIME: 6 to 7 min., total

1 can (13½-oz.) .... In 1-qt. casserole place
pineapple tidbits undrained pineapple. In
2 tablespoons sugar small cup mix together sug-
1 tablespoon ar, cornstarch and cinna-
cornstarch mon. Add to pineapple,
¼ teaspoon cinnamon stirring well. Cut butter in
2 tablespoons butter 2 pieces and place over
top. Cover.

Microwave at High 6 to 7 Minutes, stirring well after 3 minutes. Serve hot.

Makes 1⅔ cups sauce

MINT-ON-MINT SUNDAES

Chocolate mint sauce is also delicious on plain choco-late or chocolate ripple ice cream.

POWER LEVEL: Medium (5)   TEMP: 140°
APPROX. MICROWAVE TIME: 1 to 2 min.
Cook Code: 15

1 pkg. (6½-oz.) .... In 1-pt. glass measure
chocolate covered place unwrapped mint
mint patties** patties. Add cream.
¼ cup whipping cream

Insert temperature probe so tip rests on center bottom of cup. Cover with plastic wrap arranging loosely around probe to vent. Attach cable end at receptacle. **Microwave at Medium. Set Temp, Set 140°.**

When oven signals, stir sauce smooth. Serve warm chocolate mint sauce over mint ice cream.

**6½-oz. package contains about 24 patties, about 1¼-in. diameter each.

Makes about 1 cup sauce

HOW TO WARM COMMERCIAL SUNDAE SAUCES

Commercial sundae sauces and syrups seem special when warm. Pour sauce or syrup into microwave oven-proof pitcher or measure. Avoid heating in original glass containers which might not be heat tempered.

To soften a 12-oz. jar of cold sauce topping from the re-frigerator, **Microwave at High ½ Minute.** For hot fudge or butterscotch, heat about 1 minute more.

Try canned pie fillings as sundae toppings. Cherry or blueberry pie fillings are great favorites.

Jellies, Jams & Relishes

Like all fruits and vegetables cooked by microwave, jellies, jams and relishes retain their sparkling fresh flavor. Because microwave energy heats from all sides, not just the bottom, sugar mixtures do not scorch and need very little stirring. As with range top cooking, they boil up high, so be sure to use a large casserole. Since fruit juices do not evaporate in microwaving, we recommend using fruit pectin to thicken jellies, jams and preserves. You will also obtain a greater yield for the same amount of fruit.

GENERAL RECOMMENDATIONS FOR JELLY AND JAM MAKING

1. Use High Power on all recipes.

2. Whenever pectin is added — add gradually, stirring very well.

3. Use pot holders as sugar mixtures get very hot.

4. Avoid steam burns by lifting lid away from you when removing.

5. Pour jelly into hot sterilized jars or glasses; wipe off rim well, then seal with hot sterilized lids or paraffin. Sterilizing should be done in pot of boiling water on surface unit. Paraffin manufacturers recommend melting paraffin in a double boiler.

6. The United States Department of Agriculture recommends that you water-bath process the filled and sealed jars of chunky preserves and jams for about 5 minutes. This is especially necessary in warm or humid weather.

APPLE JELLY

POWER LEVEL: High (10)
MICROWAVE TIME: 13 to 17 min., total

2 cups bottled unsweetened apple juice	In 3-qt. casserole stir together apple juice and sugar. Cover. **Microwave at High 10 to 12 Minutes,** stirring after 6 minutes, until boiling.
3½ cups sugar	
½ bottle (6-oz.) liquid fruit pectin	Stir in pectin, mixing thoroughly. Cover. **Microwave at High 3 to 5 Minutes** more, until mixture returns to boil. Then, time for 1 minute of boiling. Stir and skim off foam if necessary. Ladle into prepared glasses. Seal.

Makes about 3 cups

Fresh Peach Jam

FRESH PEACH JAM

This recipe may also be prepared with defrosted frozen, unsweetened peaches.

POWER LEVEL: High (10)
MICROWAVE TIME: 15 to 19 min., total

4 cups peeled, pitted and finely chopped peaches	In 3-qt. casserole place peaches, lemon juice and pectin. Stir well. Cover. **Microwave at High 8 to 10 Minutes,** or until mixture is at a full rolling boil. Stir.
2 tablespoons lemon juice	
1 box (1¾-oz.) powdered fruit pectin	
5½ cups sugar	Add sugar to boiling mixture, stirring well.

Microwave at High 7 to 9 Minutes, uncovered, stirring after 4 minutes, until mixture reaches a full rolling boil. Then, time for 1 more minute of boiling. Skim off foam and stir jam about 5 minutes before ladling into prepared glasses. Seal.

Makes about 7 cups

SPARKLING CHAMPAGNE JELLY

Other wines such as red, rose, burgundy, port and white may be used in this recipe.

POWER LEVEL: High (10)
MICROWAVE TIME: 7 to 9 min., total

1¾ cups champagne . . . . .In 3-qt. casserole, stir to-
wine   gether champagne and
3 cups sugar   sugar. Cover. **Microwave
              at High 7 to 9 Minutes,**
              stirring after 4 minutes, un-
              til mixture begins to boil.
              Then, time for 1 minute
              more of boiling. Stir.

½ bottle liquid fruit . . . . . .Gradually stir pectin into
pectin   hot mixture, mixing well.
              Ladle into prepared glass-
              es.* Seal.

Makes about 4 cups

*For gift giving, place a washed bunch of fresh grapes in each glass before adding jelly. Especially pretty when sealed in custard cups with paraffin and unmolded on plate for serving. Use immediately; grapes show age after about 1 month.

FRESH STRAWBERRY JAM

POWER LEVEL: High (10)
MICROWAVE TIME: 17 to 21 min., total

4½ cups crushed fresh . . . .In 3-qt. casserole place
strawberries (wash   berries and pectin. Stir
and stem before   well. Cover. **Microwave at
crushing)**   High 8 to 10 Minutes,** until
1 box (1¾-oz.)   mixture is at a full rolling
powdered fruit   boil.
pectin

7 cups sugar . . . . .Add sugar to boiling mix-
              ture and stir well.

Microwave at High 9 to 11 Minutes, uncovered, stirring after 5 minutes, until mixture reaches a full rolling boil. Then, time for 1 minute of boiling. Skim off foam with metal spoon, stirring jam about 5 minutes before ladling into prepared glasses. Seal.

Makes about 8 cups

Jam and Jelly Mixtures will be hot, handle carefully.

STRAWBERRY JAM FROM FROZEN BERRIES

This spread can be made year round.

POWER LEVEL: High (10)
MICROWAVE TIME: 20 to 26 min., total

---

3 pkgs. (10-oz. each) . . . . .Place unopened pack-
strawberries in   ages in microwave oven.
plastic pouch   **Microwave at High 4 to 6
              Minutes,** checking at mini-
              mum time and rearranging
              fruit if continued defrosting
              is necessary.

2 tablespoons water . . . .Remove fruit from pouches
½ box (2½ tablespoons)   and place in 3-qt. casse-
powdered fruit   role. Crush the fruit. Add
pectin   water and pectin, stirring
              well. Cover. **Microwave at
              High 8 to 10 Minutes,** or
              until mixture is at a full roll-
              ing boil. Stir.

3 cups sugar . . . . .Add sugar to boiling mix-
              ture and stir well.

Microwave at High 8 to 10 Minutes, uncovered, stirring after 5 minutes, until mixture reaches a full rolling boil. Then, time for 1 minute of boiling. Skim off foam and stir jam about 5 minutes before ladling into prepared glasses. Seal.

Makes about 4½ cups

APPLESAUCE BUTTER

Start with about 1-qt. of applesauce to make this recipe. It is very good made with microwaved applesauce, page 230.

POWER LEVEL: High (10)
MICROWAVE TIME: 16 to 20 min., total

---

1 qt. (4 cups) . . . . .In 3-qt. casserole stir to-
applesauce (or 2   gether applesauce, pec-
cans, 16-oz. each)   tin, pumpkin pie spice and
1 pkg. (1¾-oz.)   cinnamon. Cover. **Micro-
powdered fruit**   wave at High 8 to 10 Min-
pectin**   utes,** stirring after 5 min-
1 tablespoon pumpkin   utes, until mixture boils.
pie spice
1 teaspoon cinnamon

4½ cups sugar . . . . .Add sugar to hot mixture,
              stirring well. Cover. **Micro-
              wave at High 8 to 10 Min-
              utes,** stirring every 4 min-
              utes, until mixture reaches
              a full boil. Then, time for 1
              minute of boiling. Stir well.
              Ladle into prepared glass-
              es. Seal.

Makes about 6 cups

GRAPE JELLY FROM FROZEN JUICE

POWER LEVEL: High (10)
MICROWAVE TIME: 13 to 16 min., total

1 can (6-oz.) frozen . . . . . .In 3-qt. casserole, blend
grape juice together grape juice and
concentrate, pectin. Stir in water. Cover.
defrosted **Microwave at High 7 to 8**
1 pkg. (1¾-oz.) **Minutes,** stirring well after
powdered fruit 4 minutes, until bubbles
pectin form around edge of dish.
2 cups hot tap water

3¾ cups sugar . . . . .Add sugar, mixing well.
Cover. **Microwave at High
6 to 8 Minutes,** stirring well
after 4 minutes, until mixture boils. Then, time for 1
minute of boiling. Stir and
skim off foam with metal
spoon. Ladle into prepar-
ed glasses. Seal.

Makes about 4 cups

PEACH CONSERVE

POWER LEVEL: High (10)
MICROWAVE TIME: 16 to 18 min., total

3½ cups peeled, pitted . . . . .In 3-qt. casserole place
finely chopped peaches, raisins, lemon
peaches peel, lemon juice, cinna-
½ cup dark seedless mon and pectin. Mix to-
raisins gether well. Cover. **Micro-**
¼ teaspoon grated **wave at High 10 Minutes,**
lemon peel stirring after 5 minutes.
2 tablespoons lemon
juice
¼ teaspoon cinnamon
1 box (1¾-oz.)
powdered fruit
pectin

5 cups sugar . . . . .Add sugar to hot mixture
mixing thoroughly. Cover.
**Microwave at High 6 to 8
Minutes** more, stirring after 4 minutes, until mixture
reaches a full boil. Stir,
then time for 1 more minute
of boiling.

½ cup brandy . . . . .Immediately stir in brandy
1 cup sliced, and nuts. With metal spoon
unblanched skim off foam if necessary.
almonds Ladle into prepared glasses. Seal.

Makes about 8 cups

SWEET CITRUS MARMALADE

*Be sure to remove most of white interior portion of orange
rind so sweetest, most natural orange flavor can be obtained.*

POWER LEVEL: High (10)
MICROWAVE TIME: 30 to 32 min., total

3 medium oranges . . . . . .Prepare rind portion from
2 medium lemons oranges and lemons first;
peel rind from fruit in quart-
ers. Laying rind white-side
up, scrape about half of
white layer from rind and
discard scraped material.
With sharp knife or scis-
sors, slice remaining rind
crosswise very thin.

1½ cups water . . . . .In 2-qt. casserole place
⅛ teaspoon baking rind with water and baking
soda soda. Cover. **Microwave
at High 12 Minutes,** stirring after 6 minutes. While
rind is cooking, section
fruit, removing and dis-
carding white membrane
and seeds. Chop. Add this
pulp and juice to the un-
drained cooked rind. Cov-
er. **Microwave at High 6
Minutes.**

5 cups sugar . . . . .In 3-qt. casserole measure
3 cups fruit mixture. Add
sugar, blending well. Cover. **Microwave at High 12
to 14 Minutes,** stirring after 6 minutes, until mixture
comes to a full boil. Then
time for 1 more minute of
boiling.

½ bottle (6-oz.) . . . . .Stir in pectin, mixing thor-
liquid fruit oughly. With metal spoon,
pectin skim off foam and stir 5
minutes to cool slightly.
Ladle into prepared jars.
Seal. If sealed with metal
lids and band, turn upside
down to prevent floating
fruit.

Makes about 5½ cups

PORT WINE CONSERVE

POWER LEVEL: High (10)   **Cook Code:** 80
MICROWAVE TIME: 8 to 10 min., total

1½ cups port wine **1 cup chopped raisins** **3 cups sugar**	In 3-qt. casserole stir together wine, raisins and sugar.
3 large cinnamon sticks **1 tablespoon grated orange peel** **¼ teaspoon whole cloves** **½ teaspoon cardamom, ground**	Prepare spice bag by placing cinnamon sticks, orange peel, cloves and cardamom on a square of cheesecloth. Fold cloth around contents and tie securely with string. Add bag to wine, stir and let stand 5 minutes. **Microwave 8 to 10 Minutes,** stirring well after 5 minutes, just until bubbles appear around edge; do not boil.
½ bottle liquid fruit pectin	Remove spice bag. Immediately stir pectin into hot mixture. Ladle into prepared glasses. Seal.

Makes about 3½ cups

CUCUMBER SANDWICH PICKLES

POWER LEVEL: High (10)
MICROWAVE TIME: 27 to 29 min., total

2 qts. ¼-in. slices small to medium cucumbers **½ cup salt** **2 qts. water**	In large mixing bowl place prepared cucumber slices Sprinkle with salt. Add water and let stand 2 to 3 hours. Drain and rinse.
1 cup vinegar **1 cup water**	In 2-qt. casserole place cucumbers, vinegar and water. Cover. **Microwave at High 10 Minutes,** stirring after 5 minutes, until tender. Drain.
2 cups vinegar **1 cup hot tap water** **1 cup sugar** **1 cup light brown sugar (packed)** **½ teaspoon mustard seed** **½ teaspoon celery seed** **½ teaspoon turmeric**	In 3-qt. casserole mix together vinegar, water, sugar, brown sugar, mustard seed, celery seed and turmeric. Cover. **Microwave at High 6 Minutes.** Stir well.

Add cucumbers. **Microwave at High 11 to 13 Minutes,** stirring after 6 minutes, until mixture reaches full boil. Immediately pack into sterilized jars, leaving ⅛-in. headspace. Seal. Let stand at least 24 hours before serving.

Makes about 3 pints

SHORTCUT WATERMELON PICKLES

You will need about ¾ of a medium, round-shaped watermelon to produce 3 quarts prepared pieces for recipe below. This new recipe cuts hours of soaking time.

POWER LEVEL: High (10)
MICROWAVE TIME: 85 min., total

3 qts. chunks white portion of watermelon (see below) **2 cups water**	In 3-qt. casserole place watermelon. Add water. Cover. **Microwave at High 30 Minutes,** stirring every 10 minutes. Let stand, covered, while cooking syrup.
1 tablespoon mixed pickling spice **2 cinnamon sticks, broken** **1 lemon, sliced thin** **3 cups sugar** **1½ cups white vinegar** **1 cup water**	Prepare spice bag by placing pickling spice, cinnamon sticks and lemon on a square of cheesecloth. Fold cloth around contents and tie securely with string. Place bag with sugar, vinegar and water in 2-qt. casserole. Stir and cover. **Microwave at High 20 Minutes,** stirring very well and uncovering after 10 minutes.

Just before syrup has finished cooking, drain off water from watermelon. Pour syrup, including spice bag, over watermelon in 3-qt. casserole. Cover. **Microwave at High 35 Minutes,** stirring every 10 minutes. Chunks should be tender and somewhat transparent; they will become more transparent after standing. Immediately ladle hot watermelon pickles into hot sterilized jars and seal with sterilized vacuum lids.

Makes about 5 cups

TO PREPARE WHITE PORTION OF WATERMELON: Work with ¼ of watermelon at a time. Scoop almost all of red portion from watermelon, but leave ⅛-in. of red for color. Cut rind into 1-in. strips. Cut green peel from strips, leaving white portion. Cube into about ½-in. pieces.

WHY HOME CANNING IS NOT RECOMMENDED FOR MICROWAVING

Canning should still be done on the range top and is not recommended for either the conventional or the microwave oven.

Special range top canning utensils rapidly bring the water and jars to a boil, and maintain consistent heat to each jar during the canning process. When pressure canners are used, temperatures above boiling are developed to preserve low acid or non-acid foods.

While it is an excellent appliance to use for cooking jelly and preserve mixtures, the microwave oven is not efficient in processing the canning jars.

COLORFUL CORN RELISH

POWER LEVEL: High (10)
MICROWAVE TIME: 16 to 18 min., total

1 cup sugar . . . . .In 3-qt. casserole stir to-
2 tablespoons gether sugar, cornstarch,
cornstarch minced onion, mustard
1 tablespoon instant seed, celery seed and tur-
minced onion meric. Gradually add vine-
1 tablespoon mustard gar and water, blending
seed well. Cover. **Microwave at**
1 teaspoon celery seed **High 5 Minutes.** Stir well.
¼ teaspoon turmeric
1 cup vinegar
¾ cup hot tap water

3 cans (12-oz. each) . . . . .Add corn to sauce. Cover.
whole kernel corn **Microwave at High 11 to**
with chopped **13 Minutes,** stirring well
peppers, drained after 6 minutes, until mix-
(about 5 cups)* ture boils. Stir well. Ladle
into prepared glasses.
Seal.

Makes about 5½ cups

*Sold as Mexicorn or Corn 'n' Peppers.

YEAR ROUND FRESH TOMATO RELISH

Delicious on hamburgers.

POWER LEVEL: High (10)
MICROWAVE TIME: 3 min., total

1 tablespoon prepared . . . .In 1½-qt. casserole stir to-
mustard gether mustard, brown
1 tablespoon brown sugar, vinegar and salt.
sugar (packed) **Microwave at High 1 Min-**
2 teaspoons white **ute.**
vinegar
½ teaspoon seasoned
salt

2 cups finely chopped . . . . .Add tomato, celery, green
tomato pepper and onion. **Micro-**
½ cup finely chopped **wave at High 2 Minutes,**
celery uncovered. Stir well and
½ cup finely chopped refrigerate at least 1 hour
green pepper before serving, to blend
¼ cup finely chopped flavors. Store leftovers in
green onion refrigerator.

Makes about 3 cups

SPICY COLESLAW RELISH

Serve hot over hot dogs, Polish sausage or bratwurst.

POWER LEVEL: High (10)
MICROWAVE TIME: 7½ to 9½ min., total

2 tablespoons butter . . . . .In 2-qt. casserole place
2 cups finely shredded butter. **Microwave at High**
cabbage **½ Minute,** until melted. To
1 chopped green pepper butter add cabbage,
1 small onion, chopped green pepper, onion, to-
2 medium tomatoes, matoes, vinegar, mustard,
chopped Worcestershire sauce,
2 tablespoons vinegar salt, pepper sauce and
2 teaspoons prepared pepper. Mix together well.
mustard Cover. **Microwave at High**
1 teaspoon **7 to 9 Minutes,** stirring af-
Worcestershire ter 4 minutes. Refrigerate
sauce leftovers.
½ teaspoon salt
¼ teaspoon hot pepper
sauce (tabasco)
⅛ teaspoon pepper

Makes about 4 cups

SEALING AND STORING RELISHES AND PICKLES FOR FUTURE USE

Proper procedures should be taken in sealing jars of relishes and pickles to assure their wholesomeness after storage. If relishes and pickles are to be stored on the shelf at room temperature, they must be vacuum sealed in glass jars with 2-piece metal lids available for that purpose.

Sterilize the jars and lids on top of your conventional range in a kettle of boiling water and keep in hot water until just before filling. Ladling the boiling hot relish or pickle mixture into hot jars and sealing with hot lids is the best way to assure a good vacuum seal. Be sure rim of jar is clean before adding lid; wipe with damp cloth just before sealing. To completely assure proper seal, the U.S. Department of Agriculture recommends proc-essing all relishes and pickles in water bath canner 10 to 15 minutes.

If you do not use the type of jars which may be vacuum sealed, store relishes and pickles in the refrigerator after they have cooled. Glass jars saved from purchased foodstuffs may be used as refrigerator storage jars, but do not use them for on-the-shelf storage at room temper-ature. Or, for gift giving, ladle relishes or pickles into attractive re-usable serving containers or glasses such as brandy snifters, unusual serving bowls, champagne glasses, etc. Cover with plastic wrap and store in refrig-erator until giving.

Beverages

Heating beverages is one of the most popular uses of the microwave oven. Whether brewed or instant, it takes only 1¼ to 1½ minutes to heat a cup of coffee or tea. These water-based beverages can be heated at High.

When heating more than 4 cups, arrange them in a circle for even heating. Use a 3 to 4-qt. casserole for large quantities.

Do Not attempt to defrost or heat beverages in narrow necked bottles. Pressure builds up in the lower part of the bottle, causing it to shatter.

CALIFORNIA COCOA

POWER LEVEL: High (10)　　　　**Cook Code:** 50
MICROWAVE TIME: 5 to 6 min., total

¼ **cup cocoa**	In 1-qt. glass measure combine cocoa and sugar. Add about ½ cup milk to make a smooth paste, then stir in remaining milk, orange rind and almond extract, blending thoroughly.
¼ **cup sugar**	
3 cups milk	
2 teaspoons grated fresh orange rind	
¼ **teaspoon almond extract**	
Cinnamon sticks	**Microwave at High 5 to 6 Minutes.** Pour into mugs and add cinnamon sticks for flavor and for stirring.

Makes 4 servings

WASSAIL

The traditional English holiday drink.

POWER LEVEL: High (10)　　　　**Cook Code:** 150
MICROWAVE TIME: 15 to 18 min., total

1 qt. apple cider	In 3-qt. casserole place cider, allspice, cloves, nutmeg, cinnamon sticks, orange juice, lemon juice, sugar and apples. **Microwave at High 15 to 18 Minutes,** until hot. Strain and serve.
1 teaspoon ground allspice	
½ **teaspoon ground cloves**	
¼ **teaspoon ground nutmeg**	
2 cinnamon sticks	
½ **cup orange juice**	
2 tablespoons lemon juice	
½ **cup sugar**	
2 tart medium apples, unpeeled and thinly sliced	

Makes 8 to 9 (½ cup) servings

Use the temperature probe, set at Medium and 140°, when heating cocoa and other milk-based beverages which boil over easily. Add marshmallow ¼ minute before cocoa is done. To heat by time, allow about 1½ to 2 minutes per cup. Time is longer than for reheating coffee because starting temperature of refrigerated milk is probably lower. Use cocoa mix or heat chocolate-flavored milk for fast cocoa.

TWIN BERRY SHRUB

Shrubs are old-fashioned sparkling punches made with berry juice and carbonated beverage.

POWER LEVEL: High (10)
MICROWAVE TIME: 13 to 16 min., total

2 pkg. (10-oz. each) frozen strawberries in pouch	Place all 4 packages of berries on oven shelf. **Microwave at High 12 to 14 Minutes,** turning packages over and rearranging after 6 minutes. When berries have completely thawed, sieve to remove all seeds.
2 pkg. (10-oz. each) frozen raspberries in pouch	
1 can (6-oz.) frozen lemonade concentrate	In small glass bowl place lemonade. **Microwave at High 1 to 2 Minutes.** Add to the sieved berry syrup. Chill.
2 qt. club soda, well chilled	Just before serving, blend berry juice mixture with club soda in festive glasses or in punch bowl. Decorate with lemon slices if desired.

Makes 3 quarts

IRISH COFFEE

POWER LEVEL: High (10)   **Cook Code:** 10
MICROWAVE TIME: 1½ to 2 min., total

3 tablespoons (1½-oz.) Irish whiskey	In 8-oz. stemmed glass, mug or coffee cup, place whiskey. Add sugar and coffee. Add water until container is about ¾ full. Mix well. **Microwave at High 1½ to 2 Minutes.** Mixture should be very hot but not boiling. Stir to dissolve all sugar.
1 to 2 teaspoons sugar	
1 tablespoon freeze dried or instant coffee	
Water	
Whipping cream	Whip cream until almost stiff. It should be stiff enough to pour from the bowl over a spoon, onto the surface of the coffee without blending.

Fill glass to brim with cream. Do not stir. Coffee should be sipped through the layer of cream.

Makes 1 serving

Irish Mist Coffee: Use Irish Mist Liqueur instead of Irish whiskey. This variation makes a very smooth, sippable drink.

HOT BUTTERED RUM

POWER LEVEL: High (10)   **Cook Code:** 10
MICROWAVE TIME: 1½ to 2 min., total

1 to 2 teaspoons granulated or brown sugar (packed)	In tall mug or cup place sugar and rum. Add water to ⅔ full. **Microwave at High 1½ to 2 Minutes,** until mixture is very hot but not boiling.
¼ cup (2-oz.) light or dark rum	
Water	
Butter	Add about ¼-in. thick slice butter. Sprinkle with nutmeg and serve with cinnamon stick for stirring.
Nutmeg	
Cinnamon stick	

Makes 1 serving

Old Boston Buttered Rum: Substitute apple cider for water and use lower amount of sugar.

KENTUCKY MINT JULEP

This is a tradition every year during the Kentucky Derby.

To make each drink: Pour 1 tablespoon Mint Syrup (below) into tall glass filled with very finely crushed ice. Slowly add 2-oz. Kentucky bourbon whiskey. Garnish with sprig of mint and add straw.

Mint Syrup: In 1-pt. measure mix together 1 cup sugar and ½ cup water. **Microwave at High 4 to 4½ Minutes,** until hot and sugar is dissolved. Stir well. Add 1 bunch (18 stalks) mint. Stir well. Strain into small glass jar. Cover tightly and refrigerate.

SOURS

Vary the liquor to change the character of the drink.

POWER LEVEL: High (10)   **Cook Code:** 10
MICROWAVE TIME: 1½ min., total

1 can (6-oz.) frozen lemonade concentrate	Remove concentrate from can to glass, microwave ovenproof pottery or stoneware pitcher. **Microwave at High 1½ Minutes,** until melted enough to stir. Add water and liquor and, if desired, ice cubes.
Water	
Liquor (see below)	

Makes about 4 drinks

Liquor: Use rum for daiquiris; bourbon for whiskey sours; or Scotch, orange slices and cherries for Scotch old-fashioneds.

Index

Defrosting Guide

POWER LEVEL: **Defrost**

MEAT	AMOUNT	FIRST HALF TIME/MINUTES	SECOND HALF TIME/MINUTES	COMMENTS
Bacon	1 package	2 to 3 per lb.	2 to 3 per lb.	Place unopened package in microwave oven. Turn over after first ½ of time. Microwave just until strips can be separated.
Franks	1 pound	3 to 5	none	Place unopened package in microwave oven. Microwave just until franks can be separated.
	½ pound	1½ to 2½	none	
Ground, Beef & Pork	1 pound	3	3	Scrape off softened meat after second ½ of time. Set aside. Break up remaining block, microwave 2 to 3 minutes more.
	2 pounds	6	5½ to 6	Scrape off softened meat after second ½ of time. Set aside. Break up remaining block, microwave 5 to 6 minutes more.
	5 pounds	11 to 12	11 to 12	Scrape off softened meat after second ½ of time. Set aside. Break up remaining block, microwave 11 to 14 minutes more. Second scraping may be needed.
Roast; Beef Chuck, Lamb & Veal Note: See cookbook for other types of beef roast.	Up to 6 lb.	2½ to 3 per lb.	2½ to 3 per lb.	Place wrapped roast in microwave oven. Rotate ½ turn after first timing. After second timing, unwrap and turn over onto trivet set over cooking dish. Shield any warm areas with foil. Repeat 1st and 2nd timings.
Roast, Pork	1 roast	5 to 6 per lb.	5 to 6 per lb.	Place wrapped roast in microwave oven. After first ½ of time, shield warm areas with foil. Turn over and place in roasting dish. Defrost for second ½ of time. Let stand 15 to 30 minutes.
Spareribs, Pork	1 package	2 to 4 per lb.	2 to 4 per lb.	Place wrapped package in microwave oven. Turn over after first ½ of time. After second ½ of time, separate pieces with table knife. Let stand to complete defrosting.
Steaks, Chops & Cutlets; Beef, Lamb, Pork & Veal	1 package	2 to 4 per lb.	2 to 4 per lb.	Place wrapped package in microwave oven. Turn over after first ½ of time. After second ½ of time, separate pieces with table knife, let stand to complete defrosting.
Sausage, Bulk	1-lb. tray	3	3	Scrape off softened meat after second ½ of time. Set aside. Break up remaining block, microwave 2 to 3 minutes more.
	1-lb. roll	2	2 to 3	Turn over after first ½ of time.
Sausage, Link	1 pound	2	1 to 2	Turn over after first ½ of time.
	8-oz.	2	1 to 2	Turn over after first ½ of time.
Sausage, Patties	12-oz. pkg.	1	1 to 2	Turn over after first ½ of time.

POULTRY	AMOUNT	FIRST HALF TIME/MINUTES	SECOND HALF TIME/MINUTES	COMMENTS
Chicken, Broiler-fryer, cut up	2½ to 3½-lb.	7 to 8	7 to 8	Place wrapped chicken in microwave oven. After ½ of time, unwrap and turn over. After second ½ of time, separate pieces and place in cooking dish. Microwave 2 to 4 minutes more, if necessary.
Whole	2½ to 3½-lb.	9 to 11	9 to 11	Place wrapped chicken in microwave oven. After ½ of time shield warm areas with foil.
Cornish Hens	1	3 to 4 per lb.	3 to 4 per lb.	Place wrapped package in microwave oven. Turn package over after first ½ of time. After second ½ of time, unwrap and shield ends of legs with foil. Microwave 3 to 4 minutes more.
Duckling	1	2 to 3 per lb.	2 to 3 per lb.	Place wrapped duckling in microwave oven. After first ½ of time, unwrap and turn over into cooking dish. Shield warm areas with foil.
Turkey	1	2½ to 3 per lb.	2½ to 3 per lb.	Place wrapped turkey breast side down in microwave oven. Rotate ½ turn after first timing. Let stand 10 minutes. After second timing, unwrap and shield warm areas with foil. Let stand 10 minutes. Turn turkey breast side up and repeat timings.